PERGAMON INTERNATIONAL LIBRARY
of Science, Technology, Engineering and Social Studies

*The 1000-volume original paperback library in aid of education,
industrial training and the enjoyment of leisure*

Publisher: Robert Maxwell, M.C.

The Sorcerer's Apprentice

An Anthropology of Public Policy

───── **Publisher's Notice to Educators** ─────

THE PERGAMON TEXTBOOK
INSPECTION COPY SERVICE

An inspection copy of any book published in the Pergamon International Library will gladly
be sent without obligation for consideration for course adoption or recommendation. Copies
may be retained for a period of 60 days from receipt and returned if not suitable. When a
particular title is adopted or recommended for adoption for class use and the
recommendation results in a sale of 12 or more copies, the inspection copy may be retained
with our compliments. If after examination the lecturer decides that the book is not suitable
for adoption but would like to retain it for his personal library, then our Educators' Discount
of 10% is allowed on the invoiced price. The Publishers will be pleased to receive suggestions
for revised editions and new titles to be published in this important International Library.

PERGAMON FRONTIERS OF THE ANTHROPOLOGY SERIES

Editor: CYRIL S. BELSHAW, *University of British Columbia, Canada*

Other Titles in the Series

BURRIDGE, K. O. L. *Encountering Aborigines*
McFEAT, T. *Small-Group Cultures*

Other Books of Interest

BARANSON, J. *Technology for Underdeveloped Areas*
EISENSTADT, S. N. *Readings in Social Evolution and Development*
HALPERN, F. *Survival: Black/White*
HARRIS, C. C. *Readings in Kinship in Urban Society*
JANSEN, C. J. *Readings in the Sociology of Migration*
KRUPINSKI, J. and STOLLER, A. *The Family in Australia*
MERHAV, M. *Technological Dependence, Monopoly and Growth*
RICHMOND, A. H. *Readings in Race and Ethnic Relations*
RIVKIN, S. *Technology Unbound*
STACEY, M. *Methods of Social Research*
SUTHERLAND, E. *Elements of Human and Social Geography—Some Anthropological Perspectives*
TEELING-SMITH, G. *Science, Industry and the State*

The Sorcerer's Apprentice
An Anthropology of Public Policy

CYRIL S. BELSHAW

PERGAMON PRESS INC.

New York · Toronto · Oxford
Sydney · Paris · Braunschweig

U.K.	Pergamon Press Ltd., Headington Hill Hall, Oxford OX3 0BW, England
U.S.A.	Pergamon Press Inc., Maxwell House, Fairview Park, Elmsford, New York 10523, U.S.A.
CANADA	Pergamon of Canada, Ltd., 207 Queen's Quay West, Toronto 1, Canada
AUSTRALIA	Pergamon Press (Aust.) Pty. Ltd., 19a Boundary Street, Rushcutters Bay, N.S.W. 2011, Australia
FRANCE	Pergamon Press SARL, 24 rue des Ecoles, 75240 Paris, Cedex 05, France
WEST GERMANY	Pergamon Press GmbH, D-3300 Braunschweig, Postfach 2923, Burgplatz 1, West Germany

Copyright © 1976 Cyril Belshaw

First edition 1976

Library of Congress Cataloging in Publication Data

Belshaw, Cyril S
The sorcerer's apprentice.

(Pergamon frontiers of anthropology; 4)
1. Applied anthropology. 2. Social policy.
I. Title.
GN320.B46 1975   309.1   74-22325
ISBN 0-08-018313-1
ISBN 0-08-018312-3 pbk.

Printed in Great Britain by A. Wheaton & Co., Exeter

To Betty

Contents

Part IV
Styles of Action

Part V
Values and Options

The Author

Cyril S. Belshaw (Ph.D., London School of Economics) is Editor, *Current Anthropology*, and Professor of Anthropology, University of British Columbia. Dr. Belshaw's field studies over the past several years have taken him to New Guinea, Fiji, Solomon Islands, New Hebrides, New Caledonia, and British Columbia. He was a member of the United Nations Economic and Social Council team to evaluate the effects of technical assistance to Thailand in 1965 and on various occasions has acted as a consultant for the Bureau of Social Affairs of the United Nations, and for UNESCO. He is on the Executive Committee of the International Social Science Council and the International Union of Anthropological and Ethnological Sciences and is Chairman of the Pacific Science Council's Committee for the Social Sciences and Humanities, and the IUAES Commission on Ethnocide. His previous books are in the fields of economic anthropology, applied anthropology, and university affairs. Dr. Belshaw is also the author of several social and cultural anthropology books.

The Sorcerer's Apprentice reflects his interest in examining the role of anthropology, and its relevance to world society.

Acknowledgments

THE preparation of this book was made possible by the award of a Canada Council Leave Fellowship, and a leave of absence from the University of British Columbia in 1972–3.

The theme has, however, been gestating ever since my entry into anthropology in the late 1940s, and perhaps even before. It has obviously been influenced by personal experience, as a colonial civil servant concerned with administration and development during World War II, as a student and young man influenced by my father's economics and by his international career with the Institute of Pacific Relations and with FAO, as a scholar drawn into some of the activities of the United Nations family, as a fieldworker talking with people caught up in the impact of world events upon village life, and as an administrator of a university department, discussing the profession of anthropology with colleagues in North America, Europe, Asia, and Latin America. Friends in all these contexts have influenced my thought and reading and, even more, have opened opportunities to see events at first hand and to obtain a variety of experiences that would otherwise have been denied me. It is to these friends, in many walks of life, from humblest villager concerned with his family's uncertain future to international civil servant on a dizzying pinnacle of world responsibility, that I owe my perspective. I know that those of them who will read the book will recognize their influence, and will understand that my statements do not intend to supplant their deeper knowledge, but are intended to lead to further conversation.

In all that has gone before, my family has played a special role. It is symbolic that my children have celebrated birthdays in five countries, in thatch huts and Swiss villas—a situation not uncommon for anthropologists. My wife has not only shared the long-term fieldwork, contributing her knowledge and understanding, but has helped live through the production of the earlier studies which, in various ways, have paved the way for this one. And for all of them, including this, her steadfast editorial sense has saved me many an embarrassment.

I wish to thank the following publishers for permission to make extensive quotations: Messrs. Weidenfeld and Nicolson for the passage from P. T. Bauer, *Dissent on Development*, quoted on pp. 184–5; the Society for Applied Anthropology for the passage written by Nancy Oestreich Lurie quoted on p. 229; Random House, Inc., for the passage from Charles A. Reich, *The Greening of America*, quoted on p. 312; the *Daily Californian* for the quotation from the letter by R. W. Rader on p. 318; and *The Times* of London for the passage from the article by Jeffrey Gray quoted on p. 319.

Les Mischabels, Montana, Valais, 1973   CYRIL S. BELSHAW
Vancouver, 1973–4

Perspectives

WHEN I made my decision to study anthropology, in the 1940s, my choice was affected by concerns that remain with me today. Even though anthropology was then a far less voluminous body of writing than it is now, with fewer well-developed subfields, it nevertheless seemed to offer perspectives which could add subtly to our understanding of man's condition. The comparison of social and cultural systems, and the analysis of function and conflict, were but two of the many important themes that carried lessons largely ignored by policy makers and by scholars in other disciplines. Anthropology needed not only to hone its tools but to offer the fruits of its labors to others.

Thirty years of work by innumerable scholars in many countries have increased data and knowledge. But we are still only partially applying ourselves to the real issues. Books on applied anthropology tend to deal with "exotic" culture. The time has come to make the link between our knowledge of other parts of the world and the issues that face industrialized society. Some anthropologists have indeed made the connection— Margaret Mead and Jules Henry, to name two. These beginnings must be strengthened. We should not be content with philosophizing comment drawn from subjective experience. Our research approaches social exchange, the function of myth, religious experience, and a host of other topics in special small-scale settings. We can follow through such topics with important results if we apply the same methods to studies of our own society, and we shall alter our view of our own world if we do so. Too few of us try.

The result is, in part, that the general public, and particularly the policy makers, regard anthropology as a curious discipline, containing many unreadable books, and a few which delight because of the quaint unreal worlds they seem to describe. This is to misrepresent the force and idea of anthropology. But it is the fault of the profession for not thinking out the wider implications of its work and for being unadventurous in speculating beyond the customary bounds. This book attempts to make part of the link. In doing so, it will infuriate some, because it deliberately ranges widely. I stray beyond my proper discipline and will therefore make mistakes. But it is important to me to run that risk. Mistakes can always be corrected. But I am trying to create an overall perspective which will suggest disagreement, provoke research in fields new to anthropology's tradition, and awaken scholars and some interested members of the public to a few of the issues, the dangers, and the promises of an anthropology of public policy.

We are often regarded as people who study other humans who live in villages in other countries. There is truth in this stereotype. In this book, however, I am going to devote very little space to the village world as such. Marshall McCluhan's concept of "the global village" is ear-catching, and somewhat suspect as an intellectual gimmick. We certainly do not have to be committed to the superficialities of that approach to recognize the more complex and deeper reality. The population of the world lives within *one* social system.

It is a simple, banal idea. But like so many other simple truths, it is difficult to put to work. The world social system is so complex that it cannot be grasped at one time in its totality. We must think about it in different ways, and often bit by bit. I try in this book to use a few of the ideas developed by anthropologists in their treatment of the village world, and to extend and amend them into the more complex analysis of a world social system.

This differs from the traditional anthropological approach, which is to see a community in "ecological" perspective—that is, to treat it as a system in symbiotic interaction with an immediate environment. Such an approach is a necessary part of the scene, but I want to go further and at least to raise questions (but seldom provide answers) about the global system in which we all live. And in taking this step, building upon abstract notions of social transactions, cultural systems, and the like, I find that we are inhibited, in analysis and in applied practice, by the ambiguous but powerful notion of nationalism. Time and again I have found myself faced with the necessity of accounting for it, clarifying it, and drawing implications about its effects. As I moved from the village to the wider world, the anthropological significance of nationalism became inescapable.

One of my long-standing complaints about anthropology has been that although its business is to look at the empirical reality of what might be termed alternative cultures, it does not speculate about what might be. As good objective scientists we note what is. But society is creative. It consists of men and women who are striving. David McClelland makes the untenable assumption that some people want to achieve and others don't. My perspective is that we *all* achieve. In an ultimate sense, society is itself policy making.

If we accept this simple premise, the way is open to us as anthropologists to ask some of the kinds of questions that are asked with less inhibition in other social sciences, more particularly economics and political science. We can ask, what do particular societies achieve? I have worked out the theoretical implications of this question, around the idea of comparative social performance, elsewhere. In this book, I want to bring the theory down to earth, but in minimizing jargon I hope I have not lost sight of some of the logical problems contained in the question.

And we can go on. What could societies achieve, if they did things somewhat differently? How much do we still need to find out in order to comment sensibly on alternatives? What are the logical traps in setting them out?

To invade such territory is to expose our intellectual troops to the possibility of glittering booty. Sensibly, many colleagues have been suspicious of such an enterprise. The power of influencing decisions can be heady, the rewards can look more real than they are, and we are tempted to convey our subjective values as objective or dogmatic truth. The advice of social science, and especially of anthropology, can be wrong-headed, falsely founded, and improperly motivated. It is of the greatest importance that anthropologists address themselves to world issues. It is also of the greatest importance that both the public and scholars themselves be reasonably aware of the possibilities and limitations of an anthropology of public policy. There have been too many false claims to success and wisdom. They have been counterproductive, inhibiting the evolution of innovative creativity. The theme runs through the whole of this book and is treated at length when I talk of the modes of action and advising. When I write for scholars, I hope some members of the public will be alerted. When I write in more general terms, I hope that specialist scholars will relate their interests and experience to the public need.

And, above all, I desperately hope that students, looking to their future, whether or not they are to be professional anthropologists, will take up some of the challenges that I am deliberately laying down.

Purists will accuse me of mixing my reading public. I make no excuses. The issues I raise are at what our scientific colleagues call the "interface" of the concerns and interests of scholars and the public. I believe that scholars must see, outside the confines of ideological rhetoric, the public implications of what they do, and that the public must be in a position to watch them doing it, with understanding. This book is an attempt to move in that direction.

PART I

Policy and Anthropology

CHAPTER 1

The Challenge of Policy

THE social sciences, including anthropology, are in a period of major upheaval. Their objectives, their methods, the ways in which the public recognizes and makes use of them, and the ways in which they organize to obtain results are all in dispute. It is quite possible that the social science of the 1980s will be unrecognizable to most of us working today.

The ordinary intelligent person looking at the problems of the world is asking questions of the social sciences in pointed ways. The questions imply a host of criticisms to which the social sciences must respond for reasons both of politics and of intellectual integrity. Although the public is more frequently than not misinformed or mistaken about the social sciences, this does not prevent the questions from being sharp, valid, and challenging.

The engineer is inclined to say, since my calculations indicate an appropriate solution to physical problems, why can't social scientists get people to accept the solution? Or, what is all the argument about, why can't social scientists summarize the social view for me and avoid the political bargaining? Or, will you predict values for me so that I can quantify their trends and run them through the computer to provide a systems model of social issues?

The politician has more serious arguments still. Why, he can say, when I employ social scientists to give me answers to a question, do the predictions turn out to be false? Why do I get radical emotive tracts instead of technical and definitive policy answers—how can I trust you? Quite apart from the innate methodological problems involved in answering policy questions, which many social scientists involved in consultation choose to ignore, the politician's problem is often based on his misuse of social science. By thinking of the social sciences as technical disciplines (in this, economists lead him by the nose), he expects quick answers to inappropriate questions, and finds enough scholars willing to play that game to bring about second-rate and disappointing results. At the same time, the serious social scientist is working away, producing results which are often scholastic or piecemeal (and hence insufficient for applied problems).

The citizen then joins with the politician to say, if it is true that I often ask the wrong questions, and am ignorant of what you have really achieved, why are you so secretive? Why do you hide behind your professional jargon—why don't you communicate? And, if it is true that providing answers to the world's great questions is complicated, why don't you put some of your resources into concentrated collaborative work instead of directing so much of your effort into meaningless refinements?

And then there are the accusations of the radical student. You people have sold out to the society which pays your bread. You build in to your applied models the values of those who buy you, and thus you avoid critical postures. You do not develop alternatives. You find it too dangerous to deal with problems and find it much more satisfying to handle the esoterica of kinship analysis, mathematical logic, or the collective consciousness. Youth has the problems and answers—go and find the facts to fit them.

In addressing such issues from the point of view of an anthropologist, I do not pretend to offer anything other than a very personal approach. But, for what that is worth, it is based upon almost a lifetime of involvement with anthropological research, with the strategy of the social sciences, and with considering answers to specific policy questions in a fairly wide variety of contexts.

Although it is personal, it is not, I hope, idiosyncratic or merely anecdotal. There are value perspectives that I have changed over the years but that I know are shared by many colleagues. It will I hope be apparent that I regard skepticism and a humility in advocating action as essential ingredients in the stance of a policy-oriented social scientist. I do so not because I regard social scientists as less competent than other advisers, but because of particular views about the limits of certainty and the choice of goals. In part the perspective rests upon a liberal philosophy. But it also rests upon an earlier, more formal, examination of the criteria of certainty in comparative social science,* the results of which will be reflected in much of the following discussion.

* See C. S. Belshaw, *The Conditions of Social Performance*, London: Routledge and Kegan Paul, 1970.

I have exercised the option of choosing my ground. Anthropology has much to say about race relations, comparative education, adolescence, sexual comportment, the nature and use of language, the meaning of art. I shall not deal systematically with these topics because they have not been central to my thought or experience, and because I do not believe that I know the issues sufficiently well. By the same token, the problems and knowledge of the American urban ghetto will not be followed, although other and more general questions of urban life and the internal division of societies will be. It should be possible for those who know of these things to modify and challenge my argument at appropriate places.

The concern with policy has never been absent from anthropology. Perhaps no other discipline, even in the social sciences, reflects so much of a preoccupation with values, both of the cultures observed and of the anthropologist himself. Until World War II had finished its grisly course, the number of anthropologists (particularly social and cultural anthropologists) throughout the world was miniscule. Except in the United States and the more developed countries, it is still small. Yet even in the early days of anthropology, when most anthropologists could expect to know one another, its interests and methods were diverse, reflecting a variety of intellectual antecedents from biology to sociology, and expressing a diversity of national and personal assumptions and concerns.

The discipline was deeply divided on the emphasis to be given to applied and policy interests. It would be interesting, if perhaps difficult, to explore the juxtaposition of scientific and welfare preoccupations among those who wrote about and observed the life of other peoples before anthropology became an academic subject. The romanticism of Rousseau and the measuring eye of Darwin reflect two themes, infinitely more complex now, with which every anthropologist must come to terms.

The lineal descendants of Rousseau ask, what is the nature of our identification with the values and interests of the people with whom we are working? Are our emotions dominated by the concern for the preservation of a valued way of life? Do we become their defenders and spokesmen? Or do we follow Darwin to see peoples at stages in evolutionary history, their state to be examined and analyzed? Our applied job is then to understand the inevitable movement and to soften the blows, even when they lead to the disappearance of the weakest. These dilemmas were present in the 19th century (when anthropology was born) and indeed in all previous centuries when commentators, administrators, and thinkers involved themselves in power relations across cultural boundaries.

Perhaps the first formal manifestation was in the parallel growth of ideas grouped around the notions of cultural and social change, the study of culture contact, and the process of applied anthropology. Some modern commentators have made much of the fact that these intellectual ideas grew in a context of imperialism and colonialism, and, both consciously and unconsciously, reflected a subservience to metropolitan power interest.

Such a view is far too simplistic. It does not give sufficient weight to the tremendous speed of historical developments, to the dearth of knowledge, or to the variety of perspectives already present in the infant discipline. When Sir James Frazer wrote *The Golden Bough* at the turn of the century, fieldwork in anthropology was yet to be invented and adopted. It was still considered proper to send questionnaires to Europeans in the field—missionaries, government servants; such eminent scholars as W. R. Rivers and C. G. Seligmann contacted their informants on board cruising ships or at mission stations. A parallel social separation was retained in some American anthropology, in which informants have been employed and paid to give information. Despite this kind of limitation and the inevitable value distortions which came from it, a great deal of such work was scientific rather than applied, and some of it was of inestimable worth. R. H. Codrington was a missionary, yet to him we owe the idea of *mana*; his work on Melanesian society is detached and faultless. The ideas of *tabu*, in both popular and scientific meaning, of totem, and of potlatch all came from observers working in such conditions. As each was incorporated into the perspective of administrators, it had immense consequences for the fate of particular peoples.

For a very large part of the world—most of Africa, Oceania, the Americas, and Asia—the imperial 19th century was one that indeed brought a clash of culture, of power, and the destruction and theft of resources. I live and work in a Canadian city of a million people. Although anthropology itself is, strictly speaking, hardly a hundred years old, when the subject was being founded the city in which I live did not exist. It was another fifty years before G. H. L. Pitt-Rivers used an anthropological perspective to debate the fate of peoples in *The Clash of Culture and the Contact of Races* and another five to ten years before the famous British, American, and German–Austrian schools of applied anthropology began to argue.

They were brought to argument by the field observation that all was far from well in the colonial world. Some, like Pitt-Rivers, were deeply pessimistic. Evolution was at work, and only the modernized would survive, but the process of modernization would itself kill off the weak. Others saw more strength as well as value in indigenous cultures, and, particularly in Britain, they rejected the idea of unidirectional evolution, replacing it with the more microcosmic and open-ended examination of social and cultural change. Missionaries produced surprisingly full and detached analyses of societies. From India to Fiji, colonial administrators produced a tradition of social and resource surveys (not merely for tax purposes) of great value to the present nation-states, and the French, British, and Dutch codified and studied customary law.

It is true that the interplay of ethnocentric ideas, academic philosophy, and an imperial interest in stability often produced wrong interpretations and biases of fact.* Such intellectual forces were, however, not all biased in the interest of the ruling power. The processes that generated them led to inadequate theoretical perspectives, sometimes picked up by government, by the indigenous establishment, and by indigenous revolutionaries. As anthropology changed, so did the theoretical models and the consequences for applied policy.

We hope that changes in the theory and the models lead to better applications. But it is important for our humility to recognize that present social science theory is also subject to change and movement, and what appears appropriate for application now will almost certainly be considered inappropriate ten years from now.

There was recognition of this problem in academic circles the moment scholars began debating papers dealing with policy and applications. In the 1930s numerous anthropologists turned away from application, because of the moral dilemmas involved, and because it was felt that human anthropologists simply did not know enough to be more than human commentators. Anthropology, according to many, did not have laws which could be applied to provide answers to practical problems.

Experiments took place, particularly in British territories, to determine whether anthropologists employed by governments could provide data or ideas for policy use. While anthropology was by no means the only influence at work, it helped in the process of linking the complex law required by modern nation-states to bases of customary law, allowing for pluralities of approach within single systems. While most land-tenure systems are distortions of (and not necessarily improvements on) traditional concepts, the influence of anthropology had little effect, in conflict

---

* For one example, see C. S. Belshaw, "The Effects of Limited Anthropological Theory on Problems of Fijian Administration," in Roland W. Force, ed., *Induced Political Change in the Pacific*, Honolulu: Bishop Museum Press, 1965, pp. 63–74.

with some imperial interests, in lessening and preventing land rape and chaos. Anthropologists themselves were blind to the potentiality of indigenous family systems to provide an entrepreneurial base and a launching pad for more modern business operations, but at least in some countries they had some effect in stopping destructive attacks on family and religious values.

Much of this was indeed conservative, for in those days almost everybody except the anthropologist was hell-bent on revolutionary destruction; only the anthropologist could give some voice to what he felt were the cries of the people to be left alone. But they were now in the wider world, for better or worse, and the anthropologist called for time—so that greater knowledge could make things better—and for understanding—so that policies could grapple with indigenous aspirations. Sometimes the pleas for understanding were used by revolutionaries, such as Jomo Kenyatta and the more sophisticated leaders of the Mau-Mau. More often, the plea for time and understanding, and the anthropologist's irritating habit of requiring long-term fieldwork before he would pronounce, put him in the light of the enemy of change, which was very seldom actually the case.

He was, however, the apostle of the right of people to have a minority culture, one of the first spokesmen for multiculturalism (though these phrases were not used). The anthropologist (even the government anthropologist) of the 1930s would in many respects have been the spiritual and political ally of those present-day colleagues—radical and otherwise—who are actively engaged in protest about the destruction of cultural minorities in Brazil, Asia, and Africa. In the world of the 1970s, these persecutions are occurring in independent nation-states, often in the name of nationhood. In the 1930s the stance of anthropology sometimes brought it in conflict with the indigenous political leaders who thought of nationality as one and indivisible, or who had been influenced by Western (particularly Marxist) sociopolitical ideas to consider indigenous social organization as archaic and unworthy of constructive change.

The kind of problem that practical anthropology was interested in and competent to deal with consisted in the interpretation of short-term change. It was to prophesy and forecast the effects of governmental or other interventions when interpretation was taking place across cultural boundaries. Apart from law and a little economics, anthropology was the *only* social science systematically concerned with cross-cultural interpretation.

This loneliness changed drastically after World War II. Scholars and potential scholars caught up in the armed forces were exposed in great numbers to a superficial cross-cultural experience which in some instances served to stimulate curiosity and to influence the direction of later careers. The creation of new States and the preparation of others for independence aroused the interest of economists and political scientists. The disciplines of economic development and comparative sociology were, if not born, established. But it was not until the mid-1950s that there was a substantial corps of social scientists, including those of the new nation-states, whose main interest was in policy questions in the developing world.

In the meantime, a concern with fast, practical results led governments and scholars alike into a series of traps. World War II had shown that almost anything was possible by way of social mobilization if the will, the power, and the skill were there. The spirit of the times was revolutionary, in the sense that people everywhere looked for and expected a new order in which sacred assumptions could, if necessary, be discarded and replaced. The welfare state and international order were two main foci of this spirit. Full-fledged independence in the colonial world was another.

The few anthropologists who dabbled in applied matters at this time nearly all had had some experience of human governance, but they felt they had to hurry. Some, like myself, left colonial administration because it did not seem to know enough, and was making consequential mistakes which delayed or complicated the construction of the bases of independence. We saw in the social sciences a chance to improve our understanding, and thus to ease the human pain that accompanied many adjustments, and to accelerate the achievement of goals. Some of us at the same time cautioned that the Western (even the indigenous elitist) definition of goals was not always that of the people. By pointing to conflict and trouble and suggesting ways of avoiding it, we were sometimes thought of as trouble-mongers; by asking for time to discover the truth so that action, when taken, could be sure rather than destructive, we were often branded as obscurantists. But time usually proved us nearly right.

Such activity was labeled "applied anthropology"; the applications of anthropology began to take place in industrial settings in Western European and American countries. Here the significance of the anthropological approach was mainly to add dimensions of value analysis and of intimate observational fieldwork to the perspectives of other disciplines. *Human Organization*, the journal of the Society for Applied Anthropology in the United States, reflects these preoccupations. But the pull of the esoteric was still strong in the oncoming generation, so that the momentum to use anthropological knowledge to examine our own society remained comparatively weak.

Unfortunately, the combination of these trends, coinciding with the competitive challenge of economics (which felt that it *could* provide technical answers), occasionally led anthropologists to try to be quick and technical. Usually, to do them credit, they spurned terms such as "social engineering" (which I myself have used), because this implies that the social engineer, or his master, sets the goals and devises the machinery that will best get people to follow them. Put bluntly in that way, the intervention of the social sciences, had they been effective, could have been Orwellian. Their own weakness saved them. At the same time, we have to remember that great world goals had been set, or were in formation, and were backed in the powerful nations with a secular missionary fervor. Rapid growth in the GNP was the cry; worldwide removal of malaria, eradication of illiteracy, cooperative self-help among those who could not afford to buy skills, eradication of malnutrition—these are only a few of the goals that the world community championed. Who can argue against them?

If they cannot be argued against, then government is justified in pursuing them, and social scientists are justified in suggesting measures that will make the goals and their consequences acceptable and achievable by the ordinary village community light years away from the seat of world government.

Again, who is the master of the "social engineer"? Could it not be the village people themselves? Could it not be a community in India, Oregon, or Saskatchewan? Sometimes indeed it was, and "social engineering" became "community development," with applied social scientists assisting local people to define their goals and find their means.

Perhaps there is more to the concept of social engineering than appeared during the peak of criticism. Perhaps all reformers are social engineers *manqués*. But the criticisms remain, and we will follow them in greater depth. In the meantime, it seems we may be in for a revival of social engineering, as political mission-bearers demand social science technology.

The world community has entered another of its great missionary periods. This time it is concentrated on the preservation of the environment and possibly on the removal of inequity and the preservation of minority culture. The first of these goals is now grist to the mill of the scientists and engineers who seek a social conscience and can turn away for a moment or two from the troubles of armaments and nuclear bombs.

They are forcing a much needed rigor and defense of social science operations, but at the same time are calling for technocratic answers to human questions. Some social scientists and futurologists have already responded; social engineering, whether we like it or not, is with us again, and we had better understand it and control it.

But the years of the 1950s were a long way from computerized models and systems analysis. The policy concept that first took hold was that of social welfare—the common good. It is interesting to note that in Britain even the academic concern with "social" matters was largely administrative. In all national and international government circles the idea that welfare could in some measure be administered led to a restrictive and mechanical emphasis in the interpretation of "social welfare." The emphasis persists and is almost totally in opposition to the way in which the social sciences view their world. The concentration of attention on standards of living somehow buried the concern with what is now called the quality of life. This was despite the success of a United Nations committee, chaired by an anthropologist, in gaining universal recognition for a distinction between "level of living" and "standard of living" and subsequent work to develop indices of a "welfare level of living."

The economists thought of world policy largely in growth terms; when they considered inequalities between nations, they linked growth and development. For a long time, the two ideas were fused and interchangeable, each writer adopting his own usage. In fact, the two ideas were mixed, and if we are to try to speculate about policies and causes, it is necessary to unravel them.

Growth is a term now more properly reserved for the expansion of defined entities—usually, but not necessarily, the Gross National Product. One has to talk of the growth *of something* that is *a part of* "the economy." It can just as easily be per capita real income, or the value of resources in use, or the volume of trade, or the level of living. Or it can be some combination of these in order to represent a holistic model of the movement of "the economy."

It may be argued that substantial long-term growth involves adjustments and innovations in the way in which people do things and organize to do them. Such adjustments and innovations are embodied in *development*, which (like growth) can be plus, minus, or zero. Plus development may be defined as an increase in the sophistication and complexity (when weighted for effectiveness) of the institutions and ideas of a socioeconomic system. Although development and growth are linked, the linkage is not a simplistic one-to-one arrangement. Further, substantial differences in policy hinge upon which of the two concepts is given priority—indeed, which parts of them. For, clearly, you can aim at developmental changes that will increase, for a given period, per capita real income at the expense of the level of living, if your definitions of real income and of level of living are based on different sets of indicators. Similarly, you may increase the GNP and reduce the level of living because of the proportion of the GNP allocated to armaments or capital investment. Similarly, in theory (though cases may be rare in practice), you can develop, as defined, and use up your effectiveness in doing present things better without increasing their volume; result: plus development, zero growth. Or, more commonly, you can use the increased effectiveness for increased investment in knowledge, yielding zero or plus growth depending on your growth definition and index, and on the time span of observation. You can also have development leading to rapid growth, which uses up the resources the system is designed to exploit, with the consequence of collapse (famine).

A good deal of the literature, particularly in the sociological perspective, that examines present social dynamics makes use of two terms representing variants of development—namely, industrialization and modernization. There is so little technical agreement about the precise definition of these terms that they are best left as common-sense words with common-sense emphases. Industrialization normally refers to a process in which organizations become more specialized for production and distribution purposes. This can seldom happen without increased division of labor, an improved use of monetary devices, and more sophisticated machine technology—three characteristics which are sometimes incorporated or implied in the definition. It is possible that they are independent, though necessary, variables. If the terms are to be used in a technical rather than a common-sense way, they should be separated so that we can see how they move and interact.

Modernization, once in vogue, is now somewhat in disfavor as an analytic idea, but unjustly so. The reason for the disfavor is simple, and it is a warning. Modernization implies changes in ways of doing things that bring those ways closer to those of the "modern" world. Most analysts implied, consciously or otherwise, that this meant copying the methods of the Western (capitalist or communist) world. It has taken a long time for the following anthropological observation to be accepted (even by development anthropologists): the sophisticated use of modern technology can take place in ways that do not mirror those of the Western world, and can in fact improve upon them for numerous relevant purposes.

Japan, a highly modern industrial State, has been selective and original in its use of modernity. Change is by no means according to unidirectional evolutionary rules. If an author uses "modernization" in an ethnocentric sense, the normal skepticism should be increased. But perhaps the idea can be kept more in accord with our knowledge of the realities if we do not attempt to use it in ways that permit comparative measurement. Instead we may think of it as loosely describing a state of affairs in which people are increasingly striving to be technically up to date, to borrow and adapt technical and organizational knowledge where it is needed, and to innovate to meet their own requirements. In this sense, modernization is hardly possible without original innovation and systematic enquiry—mere borrowing is not enough.

Growth, development, improved levels of living, industrialization, modernization—do these improve the quality of life? Perhaps, perhaps not.

Thus, we have yet another set of possibilities for the direction of major policy—namely, the improvement in the quality of life—which need not be compatible with certain forms of growth or development. But what is an improvement in the quality of life? Each one of us has different ideas perhaps. Are we not back to square one of welfare economics, the balancing of individual welfares and illfares to reach an impossible global conclusion? In practice, does this not put us into the political game in which the only valid analysis is the choice made by democratic voters as they cast their ballots? Is not the term "quality of life" simply a rather more woolly and emotionally satisfying, but somewhat meaningless, replacement of the more accurate statement "level of living"—extended and corrected to account for nonmaterial objectives, such as religion, aesthetics, and environmental quality?

My own belief is that we need a framework into which the various policy forms can be fitted. But it needs to be more rigorous in its treatment of the relations between actual human achievement and the goals of human endeavor. Yet it should not involve ethnocentric judgments about the value of this or that goal—of religion against nutrition, of laughter against a ten-hour working day. So I talk of *social performance*. To arrive at an idea of the way in which a social system is delivering the goods, so to speak, in the form of satisfactions (that is, how well it is performing in the eyes of its own people), it is necessary to carry through a number of steps.

The first is to construct a behavioral profile of culture for a given period of time. The profile should in fact be a quantitative listing (but not summation) of all the things that people do and achieve at that period. This is not summed, because the essence of the exercise is to work with differences in societal value judgments. The items that enter the profile are rather like those contained in a full field ethnography; games, sleep, leisure, work, consumption, exchange, and religious exercises should all be there.

The second step is to construct one or more potential profiles of culture, each relating to a specific future time period, say one year hence. The potential profile consists of expressions of hope, of desire, of valued expectation, so that if the population had its wishes (tied to a reasonable link with the possibility of resource use), in a year's time its profile would be different.

Basically (but with modifications which will appear later), the performance, achievement, or success of a society is described by the degree to which the two profiles match—or, if you like, by the distance between them. One can take a new measure of the behavioral profile in a year's time and observe the movements to or away from items in the potential profile. One could construct "idealized" standard profiles to represent some abstract or utopian view of society with which to compare both behavioral and potential profiles.

All of the above are simplistic statements which require substantial theoretical elaboration, and which cannot be converted into research operations without considerable trained manpower and technical skill. But they are basic criteria for successful "scientific" applied work.* To the extent that the criteria cannot be met in anthropology (or any other social science) applied advice will be defective and uncertain. We must, therefore, be led to the position that there will always be something relevant that we do *not* know. Our advice must be imperfect. The first requisite of a policy adviser is to recognize the inevitability of imperfection, without permitting that realization to destroy his initiative or sense of service.

We may have our utopias, we may try our hand at forecasting, we may indulge in futurology. But when we gaze in the crystal ball, we are involved in a kind of sorcery, a task for which the anthropologist is an apprentice, playing with forces that require much more work to be understood.

---

* For a theoretical approach to the elaboration of criteria for the rigorous understanding of performance, see my book *The Conditions of Social Performance, op. cit.*

CHAPTER 2

Anthropology as Social Science

IT IS not common for those who are engaged in the ordinary business of government to think of involving anthropologists in consultation, advice, or research, except in rather sharply defined areas involving minority cultures. My implicit argument is that the under-use of anthropology results in part from misconceptions about its nature as an academic discipline, and a lack of skill in linking it to the contributions of other social sciences. To do this, anthropology also must address itself to questions beyond its narrow confines, but legitimate to its methods. To build toward that goal, one must start with the present. Hence I shall briefly explore the characteristics and methods of anthropology, insofar as they may be relevant to policy analysis. What do anthropologists do?

The American Anthropologist (the journal of the American Anthropological Association), *Man* (the journal of the Royal Anthropological Institute), and *Current Anthropology* (a journal of international think-pieces) from time to time contain articles dealing with such subjects as archaeology, comparative and theoretical linguistics, the anatomy of primate ancestors, African religions, the distribution of pottery styles, the shape of stone tools, the kinship structure. In United States universities, while departments of anthropology usually organize their work around a core area of cultural and/or social anthropology, most (but by no means all) add archaeology, physical anthropology, and linguistics as subfields. Cultural anthropology tends to deal with all forms of cultural expression, the meaning and interpretation of that expression, its distribution, its history, and the factors that are responsible for its existence. Social anthropology tends to deal with human relations—describing, analyzing, and accounting for the various forms of social organization and structure that exist in human societies.

In Britain, most chairs and departments are centered on social anthropology, but some of the concerns of cultural anthropology are dealt with under this rubric. Archaeology and physical anthropology tend to be separated, and much of the American-style cultural anthropology goes on in museums rather than in university departments. In Europe, anthropology tends to be directed to non-European research, and the study of European phenomena until recently has been largely restricted to archaeology, folklore, folk customs, and rural artifacts. However, younger scholars are now hard at work dealing with the history and functioning of contemporary European communities.

The International Union of Anthropological and Ethnological Sciences, which holds World Congresses of Anthropology under UNESCO auspices and represents the international community of anthropological scholars, has a hard time reconciling these trends and deciding where it should be in the spectrum of intellectual activities. Because of the importance of biology in its history and in some of its present concerns, the IUAES is affiliated with the International Council of Scientific Unions, though not as a key member. Because it is possible to use history, to consider art, music, and folklore as subjects of study, to be concerned with architecture and archaeology, and to deal with the logical, philosophical, and religious systems of numerous cultures, it is not surprising that the Union is a central member of the International Council for Philosophical and Humanistic Studies. By the same token, it has representation as a social science discipline in the International Social Science Council. No other subject has quite this breadth, although geography and psychology also cross some such boundaries. To add to the confusion, the Union defines "Anthropology" to include archaeology and physical anthropology, and "Ethnology" to include social and cultural anthropology.

The strongest drive to retain the eclectic range of anthropological interest is in the United States, with echoes in some parts of Europe. The breadth of training of young students can become heavy, fact-filled, and ponderously encyclopedic, but the student does in the end have the possibility of choosing a specialty on the basis of direct experience with some subject matter; he also has the possibility of seeing connections between different types of subject matter, and thus of creating new and unexpected syntheses.

But there is another characteristic of anthropology which makes all this very difficult. To understand physical anthropology, it is much more important to have a first-hand knowledge of genetics and comparative anatomy, and to study the culture of movement, than it is to know about Manus religion or Azande witchcraft or Tallensi social organization. Anthropology can lay claim to producing influences that revolutionized the study of linguistics and that still have important effects, but an anthropological linguist who read only anthropology would not be doing his job. Archaeologists must know about carbon-dating, paleontology, geology, and a host of related topics that other anthropologists do not have to bother with; and, if they deal with certain times and places, they must be historians as well.

Different kinds of anthropologists need to make serious contact with different ranges of related disciplines, and to incorporate those disciplines into their methods and ways of thought. Unfortunately, the organization of anthropology as an eclectic subject tends to obscure this need, more particularly in social and cultural anthropology. There are eth-nomusicologists who know neither musical theory nor ethnography. There has been a fashionable upsurge in the study of human ecology in social anthropology, which for the most part has been carried out by individuals without any training in or knowledge of geography's vast experience with the concept, particularly over the past forty years. The recent use of formal and mathematical techniques in geography for the study of innovation, diffusion, and social systems has been largely ignored by anthropologists specializing in these very problems. When commenting on the nature of economic relations, anthropologists still write of such issues as "scarcity" and "economic surplus" as if they were common-sense words without the specialized meaning given to them in the argument of economics.

There is thus a very grave danger that anthropologists immersed in the ethnography of the real world approach it with an analytic superficiality which fails to make use of the intellectual achievements of sister disciplines. This is not quite a fair picture. The anthropologist who insists on knowing all of anthropology will indeed have very little time, unless he is a most unusual genius, to know all the related disciplines as well and to draw from them the ideas he may need for creative work. On the other hand, by definition, he has drawn his interdiscipline links in another way, and he will without doubt be immersed in factual subject matter, so that the resulting syntheses will be quite different from those based upon more restricted connections.

This creates the holistic bias of anthropology, which all anthropologists (even those who reject holism as a philosophical or methodological goal) share to a much greater extent than members of other disciplines. Anthropology is still thought of as "the study of man"—period. Anything goes. But more, even if man must be dissected to be analyzed, the object is to see the pieces together. An impossible task? But one which must on occasion be attempted if only to counterbalance, criticize, and correct the segmentation of other disciplines.

Most anthropologists find a place in this spectrum which does not move the lens over the whole range, but selects from it and then extends to different intellectual systems. There is thus an opportunity, piecemeal and unorganized though it may be, to influence political science, economics, and the history of art, and to draw ideas from them into anthropology. Thus, many anthropologists are social scientists rather than biologists, archaeologists, or humanists in the restricted sense. In this role, it is inevitable that their special methods and experiences lead them to question, revise, and sometimes muddle with the well-knit models, theories, and concepts of related subjects. This can be infuriating to our colleagues, particularly when the anthropological criticism is not based upon the language of the related discipline or cannot be fitted into the already worked-out paradigm.

It is thus natural that the discussion of issues of concern to anthropology opens up not only anthropology itself, but the contribution of all other social sciences; it is impossible to "think anthropology" in isolation from them. In this, anthropology differs fundamentally from, let us say, economics or psychology in principle, if not always in practice. On the whole, an anthropologist who thinks anthropology in isolation from at least a range of other related disciplines is a poor anthropologist.

This is true enough in the realm of pure scholarship, in the construction of abstract models and theories, and in the attempt to reach full understanding unfettered by applied or practical considerations. But it becomes inescapable the moment the goal is to provide answers to practical human problems, even, one might argue, if the goal is to provide a *full* understanding of any historic human event.

The necessary division of the social sciences into disciplines, and the widespread adoption of the concept "economic man," now fashionably followed in some quarters by "political man" and "hierarchical man," have served to obscure this truth. Yet it was learned (and for many years subsequently ignored) in economics, when theoretical and mathematical economists decided that their theories and techniques could *not* account for events in the real world of economic history, and that economic historians were low-level operators dealing with people, not with theory.

This is not as relevant now, since economists—with data better suited to their operations—have made much stronger empirical links, and historians of all kinds have begun to use concepts and models derived from other social science disciplines, and to make their own contribution to the development of such ideas. But the underlying issue remains. If I wish to understand or explain the activities of a household reacting to a social and physical environment as its members move through their life cycles, only anthropology among the social science disciplines comes near to claiming that it provides a holistic framework, taking all factors— internal and external—into account. If such an explanation is based only upon the anthropologist's training and the ideas of colleagues in anthropology, the conceptual tools are likely to be weak at certain points. For, in fact, many of the issues impinging on the life of the household can and should be thought of in terms of the structure of social relations (sociology and anthropology), the formation of values (anthropology and education), small group analysis (social psychology), power interactions (political science), choice of ends and means (economics), prior influences (history), jural status (sociology and law), the influence and relevance of space in social relations (geography), and the application of mathematical models—such as systems analysis, linear programming, and the like— scattered through all the disciplines.

The social science that is most frequently used by government and industry alike is clearly economics, followed to some extent by psychology and geography. This is not the place to provide a full account of the reasons for the predominance, but one or two points stand out. Economics has been successful in providing a highly logical, theoretical apparatus which was stimulated out of a concern for practical policy issues. Even the 19th-century analysis of fundamentals, the creation of "Robinson Crusoe" and economic man, the ideas of scarcity, diminishing returns, elasticity of demand or the rate of circulation of money, and all the other items in the bag of tricks, came out of a concern, originally, for such serious practical issues as the creation of wealth, the effects of taxation, and the movement of prices. Such concerns could not be dismissed as ivory-tower play. The commentaries of economists sharpened as their tools appeared to become more accurate, as measuring devices were invented, and as they opened up even more modes of analysis to handle questions of inflation, unemployment, terms of trade, cost-benefit analysis in the use of resources, and so on.

The other social sciences have much to learn from this. Economists knew how to use formal logic to link equilibrium situations to disequilibrium and dynamics—while theoretical anthropologists are still arguing that equilibrium models are incapable of development to handle conflict and change. Economists, with the aid of statisticians, developed measuring devices which they persuaded governments to use, so that they now have an impressive, if often misleading, battery of time series and comparative data—while anthropologists and most sociologists, confronted by a nonmeasured phenomenon, hide their heads in the sand and say that it *can't* be measured. Most of the things that economists now measure could not be measured until the attempt was made. Economists also knew, on the whole, how to be definite, how to give an appearance of precision and of knowing the answers.

This is a very considerable achievement for a social science, and economists have earned the influence they have. But there are illusions behind the appearance of effectiveness which also serve as warnings. There are economists who attempt to draw upon related social sciences, but they are rare; on the whole, their attempts are not very successful. Though there is much truth in their criticism, economists are perhaps too ready to blame the lack of success on presumed deficiencies in the concepts, language, and nonmathematicization of other social sciences; but even where formal models appear in, let us say, political science or sociology, there is little evidence of their consideration in economic reasoning. For an economist brought up in the rigorous school, it would seem that an idea is not an idea until an economist has invented it.

The relative success of economic analysis has had a profound effect on the general intellectual climate, even though, naturally enough, the propositions of economics that have been drawn into the general system of ideas have often been transformed somewhat in the process. (A side effect of this is the consistent misuse of economics terminology in the work of many anthropologists, who have adopted the ideas from general language rather than an understanding of economics.) It is quite true that a large area of complex argument has been specifically designed to treat issues particular to limited institutions of (primarily Western) society. Thus we get ideas such as economic behavior to imply something to do with resource management, trade, working for gain—even though in strict analysis *all* behavior is economic since all behavior is concerned with applying resources (including time and one's person) to chosen ends. And we get ideas that imply that there are economic and noneconomic (how can that be?) institutions, although *all* institutions handle resources, *all* work to satisfy wants of some sort, and even profit-making institutions have significant nonprofit objectives and implications. There is a great deal of evidence that thinking about behavior and institutions as if some were economic and some were not has blinded economists themselves, preventing them from asking questions about qualitative elements in the ends-means mix, and presenting an almost ideological and thoroughly erroneous view of the way in which firms and market oriented individuals work.

Even more seriously, the technique of dividing the world into economic and noneconomic spheres has resulted, at least in part, in the definition of certain *questions* as being appropriate to economics, and other questions as being inappropriate. This has the double effect of discouraging economists from moving professionally into such areas as considerations of the opportunity costs of religious ritual or the administration of choice for persons living in a caste or lineage society. It encourages them to put up "no trespassing" signals so that other social scientists normally don't think of considering certain questions that in the general view are dealt with in economics. (There are, of course, rare exceptions to both these statements.)

Let us take unemployment as an example. By and large, unemployment has been defined as a social ill which can be cured or remedied by bringing the operations of the real world economy closer into line with normative models (which economists do not usually think of as normative) describing the workings of a theoretical economy with low unemployment. Ideally, this should be done by the minimum influencing of one or two key factors, which by their nature are susceptible to manipulation. Favorite among these are changes in interest rates, the supply of money, the relative price of exports and imports as affected by exchange rates, changes in personal and corporate taxation, government-administered financial incentives, and so on. As time goes on, these techniques evolve and change and become a little more subtle; usually they are about as subtle, time-sensitive, and discriminatory as an earthquake.

There is, of course, evidence enough that some of these devices, under some circumstances, do have the desired effects, or at least that appropriate changes follow sequentially. But they often do not. And there seem to be situations in which a series of measures have within them counterproductive forces, so that the net result is problematic. Furthermore, the devices that are available and are used may in some circumstances either (a) work in terms of a model which in some important respects is outdated, because the real world has changed since the model was formulated, or (b) neglect operative factors that are sufficiently strong to more than counterbalance those that governments manipulate. Further, the linkages in the models may contain important connections the behavior of which is based upon assumptions that have not been examined empirically, but simply have been taken for granted. All these possibilities open up the examination of the chain of connectedness to social scientists other than economists. But they are doing very little of it.

Here is a random list of relevant topics that anthropologists could examine. There are power linkages between those who make decisions in firms and members of governments, and there are forms of communication that involve information sharing or withholding, the adoption of common or competitive stances, and the holding of individual views (one might say ethnoeconomics) about how the economy and polity operate and how firms should react to given situations in order to maximize their ends. These are real questions posed by real people—many of whom, it is true, are influenced by economists' models, but also many who are not or who may wish to ride against the tide. Can one differentiate between types of firm and types of entrepreneur in such matters? If so, what is the quantitative weighting of the various elements that in various countries go into decision making and affect outcomes?

What is there in the psychology of speculators and those who decide to buy and sell on the stock and money markets that makes market trends unpredictable? If economic theory were accurate, one should be able to predict market movements; one cannot, at least with certainty.

The phenomenon of simultaneously increasing inflation *and* increasing unemployment appears to be new. Models are being adjusted hurriedly to take into account, for example, some of the relevant new demographic factors. At the same time, other countries with superficially similar conditions have job vacancies, made up in part by immigration. It is clear that the price mechanism is being affected by a host of real conditions that are not sufficiently influenced by the standard manipulatory techniques. Putting these sorts of things together, one begins to wonder about such matters as these. Unemployment (in the sense of nonwork, reduced work, increased leisure, and independence) might be a positive goal, not an evil, for a large section of the population, made possible by welfare measures, inherited income, and new modes of living. Decision makers in firms are often less influenced by particularistic and objective market considerations than by ideology, speculative information, personal connections, and past experience. The general effects of manipulative devices are seldom uniformly global but are different in different sectors of decision making, so that multiplier or chain effects must be broken up. Each of these, and numerous other questions that bear upon the effectiveness of a given line of intervention, are more appropriate to disciplines other than economics, including anthropology.

Unemployment is not just an "economic" problem. Unemployment is a phenomenon of the real world, influenced by a chain of connectedness to other issues about which all social sciences, if they were to apply themselves, would have something relevant to say.

The point of this demonstration is not to show up the limitations of economics, which, as I have said, has gone further in many ways than any other social science. It is rather more general—to show that even those issues that seem to fall directly within the scope of a particular social science do not do so *in a bounded manner*. I shall go one step further, and perhaps the remainder of this book will bear me out: no policy issue is or can be the exclusive property of a single social science, and most policy issues can best be tackled in an interdisciplinary way.

Anthropology, the most interdisciplinary of the social sciences, most certainly cannot tackle social problems in isolation from sister disciplines.

One might then ask, in the pursuit of this joint enterprise, what is the special characteristic or contribution of social and cultural anthropology, over and above the perspective of a certain internal interdisciplinarity?

First, anthropology does not take values for granted, nor does it treat them simply as data. It subjects values to searching examination as cultural phenomena, with their own history, a certain logic, an interconnectedness, and a dynamic. Much of the most sophisticated part of this examination has to deal with the cultural expression of values and the way in which they are formed, so that there is a central thrust to deal with the key instruments of symbols, their logic, and their use in communication.

It is true that the use of the term "values" in anthropology is muddled and confused, and that the best work is usually done in technical contexts where some such concept is merely in the background rather than used consciously. The usual notion of value in other disciplines, and partly in anthropology, is of a goal, a want, a good that can be worked towards, desired, believed in, or preferred to a greater extent than others; at the lower end of the scale, there are negative values, ills, anti-wants, if you like. In all other disciplines, and in its best usage in anthropology, the idea of scale is present. This makes value a comparative and potentially measurable entity.

Where anthropology attempts to depart from this is when it searches for deeper fundamentals. One can only sum up the state of this particular art by saying that where it calls itself a search for values it is not successful and it confuses the issues. One such direction is to link with psychology and seek the causative factors that operate in the biological and mental processes. Not very much of this is done in anthropology; on the whole, anthropologists (whose data are behaviorally based) are not equipped to do very much about it except to speculate. Another direction is to subsume a large number of observations about the way things happen and statements of value judgments, and to say that underlying it all one can see these things linked to the abstract principles x or y. Therefore, the people value principles x or y, and those principles are values. They are, however, not values in the sense used before; they are almost Jungian statements of a subconscious culture or Kroeberian indications of the superorganic, neither of which is empirically verifiable. Despite the great philosophical care used by analysts such as Clyde Kluckhohn, there is a great danger that what emerges is a reflection of the observer's own point of view. A third direction is to reveal the underlying logic or philosophical principles that an outside observer can find, as psychological laws operating in the culture, through which the people think. The structuralists, such as Claude Levi-Strauss, who do this, however, do not (as far as I am aware) pretend that the laws are "valued"; they operate, they are statements of the nature of ideas and concepts as systems which can be examined scientifically—that is, with logic and empirical data.

Whatever the rights or wrongs of these positions may be, the concern with values in the context of cultural and symbolic systems goes much further in anthropology than in any other discipline. Since it is the problem of values that most puzzles and confuses the policy maker, it is possible that this is the area in which anthropology, through the construction of models explaining the formation, interconnectedness, and dynamics of value systems, will have the most original contribution to make. That time, however, is not yet.

The second special contribution of anthropology is in the nature of its empirical investigation. Anthropology does not have a monopoly of what can in short-hand be called "participant observation," and there is a crucial sense in which some anthropologists, in my view, have failed to learn what this technique is about, and have modified it to its destruction. My view is somewhat old-fashioned (I have reason to believe), but since I think that many of the objectives of research cannot be reached honestly and accurately by any other method, and since this method is most certainly central to anthropology, I had better stand up for the old-fashioned view.

First let me say that there is a great deal of enquiry necessary to any social research (including that of anthropology) that has nothing to do with participant observation. The use of official statistics, the search of archives and historical records, the administration of questionnaires, experimental manipulation of controlled groups, the use of teams to make time- and sample-controlled observations of particular interactions (market exchange, traffic movement) are all handled in anthropology, but are basically amendments of methods for the development of which other disciplines are responsible.

Participant observation is a technique in which the observer is in the most intimate feasible contact with the persons and events that interest him. Where possible, he acts as a member of the group; but where this is not possible, he contrives to have his presence accepted on the basis of social contact. The participant observer must be able to come and go within the rules of social convention, he must have a natural language of communication so that his information comes from ordinary conversation, and where discussion is necessary it is in social contexts to which the people are habituated. Such technical aids as the observer finds necessary—notebook, camera, recorder—must be known to be present (or there will be a dangerous lack of faith) and, after time, must be accepted as an extension of personality, like clothing—or else must not be used.

Now no anthropologist can depend on participant observation alone, and in some instances it cannot be used at all. At the simplest level, for example, after the detailed personal observation of a complex ceremonial exchange, it may be necessary to quickly question the key participants rather formally to get basic information before memory and accuracy fade; or it may be necessary to conduct a household survey to obtain basic information about who is who; or a storyteller may need to have his tales recorded for hours on end.

But participant observation yields the features that are the strongest part of anthropology, without which anthropology would have every reason to forget its identity and become merged with other social sciences. For the data of anthropology are built on what is very close to a living understanding of the culture and an insight into the emotive reality of natural personal interactions. There are clearly limits to this insight: sex, interior thought, those elements that the people for their own reasons wish to hide, crime (sometimes), and the conditions that flow from the fact that the observer is always an outsider, however much he is tempted at times to believe the contrary. Participant observation at the best of times is only *partly* participant.

This situation has its dangers, which indicate some of the reasons why other social sciences are on occasion suspicious of anthropology. Participant observation creates a value stance which is usually much closer to that of the people studied than would otherwise be the case, and is in opposition to the value stance of the national, the European, or the American society in which readers of the reports are usually located. Even if it does not always *create* such a value stance, it reports values that governments and social theorists often wish did not exist, because they complicate policy and challenge ethnocentric theories. Furthermore, participant observation, by definition, takes time and yields vast data of a confused kind about a limited number of interactions. This can be compensated for by linking it with supplementary, wider techniques, and by writing disciplined reports. Yet it is an irritant to those who are in a hurry and who feel that any competent science ought to have people who can go in and take the key measurements and come out again.

Certainly, this can and should be done, but it is better done with the full field report as baseline. Further, for certain kinds of questions (often the most important for policy), long-term participant observation coupled with long-term statistical collection is vital. The full understanding of an ideological or religious system (to say nothing of a consideration of its variants and distribution within a community) is simply not possible without lengthy study. At a very simple level, studies concerned with agriculture or trade or ceremonial exchange are liable to considerable distortion unless observations can cover a whole year of seasons, and unless there is some minimum further knowledge which enables one to judge how far that year of seasons is representative of others. These are two extremes of consideration, the mind and work, without which policy does not make much sense. Those who criticize anthropology for depending on long-term participant observation for the roots of data are usually confusing short-term mechanistic approaches with truth. To this extent, they are blind or obscurantist. But this is not to say that anthropology itself is without the need to develop other, disciplined, short-hand supplementary techniques, which indeed it is doing.

Participant observation sharpens a number of ethical issues about social research (which are, however, also present in the use of other techniques) which will be addressed later. But, if properly handled, it has one major ethical advantage which happens to imply a relationship between observer and people which some anthropologists find very difficult (indeed all anthropologists find some situations in which it is impossible) and which some reject. That rejection is sometimes forced—for example, in situations where the culture under study lies in the past and can only be recalled through memory. But we have a curious situation today in which there is a strong feeling among many anthropologists that the knowledge they obtain is a resource, and the people who give the knowledge should be compensated for their production of the resource. Hence, for some, participant observation is out, and payment of informants (once the standard technique, particularly in North America) is returning as the alternative. The ethical premises of this position are complex. But the fieldwork result, except for very limited and controlled areas of enquiry such as folklore or musical collection or language learning, could be little short of disastrous.

The basic premises of participant observation, apart from those I have detailed above, are mutual trust and the definition of the subject matter of enquiry through an interaction between people expressing their own ideas, values, and convictions and the "theoretically informed" scholar. In participant observation, the scholar must place himself in the hands of the people, he becomes quite dependent on them for knowledge, and they have the power to influence the weight of its parts by what they do. Clearly, there must be some kind of reciprocal element. This is seldom contractual, between patron and client, but runs all the way from creating opportunities for a flow of wealth in appropriate contexts to rendering services that originate in the anthropologist's external role and connections—speaking for and making known the position of the people studied. And let us not forget that it is sometimes the case that the anthropologist is just as much an object of curiosity and study to the people with whom he is living.

On the other hand, paid questioning, though it undoubtedly has its uses, tends to predefine the issues, leads informants to seek to please by maintaining a flow of information that has the right value weight (known by payment and by anthropologist reaction), tends to produce ideological constructs rather than behavioral data, and can lead to laughable manipulation with the attractions both of recreation and income maintenance. It should not be necessary to say this to professional anthropologists—and to sociologists who, with a little more reason when they depend on complex questionnaires, are in the same game—but alas it is.

Participant observation, with all of its weaknesses, provides a foundation for the recording of the natural expression of those values the people wish to express. Paid informants can provide good mechanical information, and must often be used. But where people—either anthropologists or those with whom they work—insist on restricting enquiry to paid information, you can be sure that the requisite basis of trust is absent, that someone is interested in selling a line, and that the results should be treated with the utmost skepticism.

It should also be stressed that the emphasis on participant observation is linked with the preoccupation that even macrostudies should be closely linked to the daily realities of social life in the most direct and intimate way possible. The goal remains, even where participant observation is not very realistic, or where it substantially restricts the field of enquiry. It is in this way also that we may begin to apply anthropology to the acquisition of knowledge in our own society. The concern with intimacy of enquiry is characteristic of some work in sociology—for example, ethnomethodology, which deals with the recording and analysis of what might be called daily human experience. It can be used in such contexts as the study of the interlinkage of values and preoccupations between the home and the work setting, of recreation and the choice of leisure, of network associations of entrepreneurs, and a host of similar questions.

The third special characteristic of anthropology, which is already substantially diffused to parts of other social science disciplines (but which anthropology cannot live without), is cross-cultural comparison, and also the study of linkages and interactions across cultural boundaries. Usually, this is thought of in clear ethnic or national terms, although there are possibilities of more subtle uses of comparison.

It is true that the ethnographic and fieldwork preoccupations of many anthropologists give the impression that they are concerned only with immersing themselves in the totality of the culture they are studying. Closer inspection reveals, however, that even here comparison usually plays its role. One may, for example, choose to compare (not necessarily in an ethnography, but in the theoretical commentary that follows) the situation of three or four communities in the same general culture, each of them, however, varying in one or more significant factors (for example, production base, external connections, degree of formal education, capital wealth). A more traditional and better known type of comparison is that employed by Robert Redfield when he developed his ideas about the folk–urban continuum. In fact, he was comparing the ideas, economy, and social conditions of highly differentiated cultures, even though the rural, small town, and urban people he considered were interconnected and were part of the same national polity.

It is because of the great importance attached in everyday living to the subtle elements of a common culture that comparison on the basis of cultural variation is so fruitful. The famous Weber–Tawney hypotheses about the link between the Protestant ethic and capitalism, though put forward by a sociologist and an historian, are in fact the result of typically anthropological cultural comparison, which led to further study and to further modification and abstraction on the basis of a consideration of the implications of other religious systems, such as variants of Buddhism and Islam.

What began essentially as an historical comparison between two religions (Catholic and Protestant) in identical political structures moved to comparisons in much more differentiated cultural and political contexts. Subsequent hypotheses, endeavoring to encompass the new materials, contained more abstract elements. Some writers would argue, for example, that the successful entrepreneurs of the type cited by Weber and Tawney were helped to save and invest by the Protestant ethic *of others*, but were themselves motivated by visions of luxury and high spending or, in some instances, by a fascination with the technical games involved in industry or business. When one looks at cases of entrepreneurial advancement cross-culturally, one finds evidence to put forward wider generalizations—for example, that a religious ethic can usually be made to *fit* entrepreneurial gain, and that where entrepreneurs establish themselves against or despite the main tide of social and cultural obstacles, they tend to be aberrant members of minority subcultures (of whatever religion) rather than conventional members of society. This is one reason why, when jealousy emerges, it is often so easy to persecute them *as* members of minority groups (Jews, overseas Chinese, African Indians).

Comparison is used, then, for two main but interrelated purposes: (1) to establish the effect of variables (a process in which historical comparison is often just as valuable as the cross-cultural version) and (2) to force a hypothesis based upon culturally limited examples into a wider and more universal theory.

Underlying this is a commitment to a form of data gathering and interpretation which is immediately apparent to those who examine what anthropologists in fact do. The first step in comparison comes when the anthropologist enters the society or subculture he is studying, since almost universally *it is not his own*. His observations and interpretations are stimulated by the fact of difference.

This is still sometimes thought of as "anthropologists study primitives and peasants." It so happens that most cultures in this world *are* primitive and peasant, so that if one were to study on the basis of a perfectly random sample of cultures, one would study more primitive and peasant cultures than others. Of course, the selection is *not* random. Anthropologists, being human, choose their careers for various reasons, which include being positively intrigued by the exotic and by the variety of man's expression, by a desire to travel and to live in other places, by a search for not otherwise easily achieved adventure, and by a *detachment from, a disenchantment with, and a critique of their own societies*. This is a very strong part of the intellectual drive that creates anthropologists (and sociologists), and it explains a great deal of what they have to say and the way they go about their business. The very first step into another culture, then, involves insight through comparison.

It is true that Western anthropologists, in their anxiety to see anthropology established in other countries, have not always consciously understood this, and have been anxious to turn native informants into indigenous anthropologists. This has provided materials of interest in their own right, but very frequently the interest comes from its eventual incorporation into a wider system. It is doubtful whether anthropologists working on their own culture can do more than make an initial record. Some have quickly turned their talents in other directions—Jomo Kenyatta and K. Busia, for example, became major political figures. But others, by far the majority, have crossed the hurdle by the very fact that they deal *not* with their own subculture, but with others, even in the same nation-state. Thus, my Swiss colleague, Gerald Berthoud, works not in his own canton of Vaud, but in the mountain villages of the Valais, where his entry was by no means easy, and was very much that of a stranger. Indian, African, Latin American, and Asian anthropologists have a world of observations to make which enables them to maintain cross-cultural detachment and insight, and through this to use comparison to add to the generalized body of knowledge. At the same time, the nature of the detachment differs from that of American or European anthropologists; the particular insights and the special contexts from which they observe add new dimensions to the total anthropological picture.

This richness of differing yet interrelated observation and interpretation has yet to be exploited to the full. In particular the very weight of numbers of North American anthropologists by comparison with others carries with it the weight of the North American intellectual tradition. It is an important task for anthropologists in other countries to use that tradition, but also to match it with insights derived in other ways.

This is most clearly understood by anthropologists, social scientists, politicians, and others in what is often lumped together as the Third World—the diverse and individualistic countries of Asia, Africa, and Latin America. At the moment, and this is inevitable until the balance is put right, it is being expressed very largely as a defensive attack on the intellectual "imperialism" of all the social sciences (by no means only anthropology), and an attempt to find creative contributions that are not as dependent on the European–American beginnings. This theme needs special attention when we deal with international social science policy (Chapter 18).

Not as frequently expressed, but just as important, are two other modes of operation. One is to make sure that non-Americo–European anthropologists have every facility to carry out original fieldwork in Europe and in America. There is every indication that fresh and critical observations will result. Canada has perhaps a better opportunity here than many other countries, since despite the recrudescence of Canadian intellectual nationalism, Canada has a much higher proportion of anthropologists and other social scientists drawn from all countries of the world (my own department, for example, contains twelve nationalities at this time of writing). Unfortunately, only a few of these scholars have yet begun to work on Canadian society itself, but a trend in that direction has begun.

The second mode of operation is to put more system into the principle by creating joint international research cooperation in which research enquiry and technique developed in one country is brought to another for replication and development. There are some limited examples of this. I am not, as later discussion will show, an uncritical proponent of community development. Yet I note with interest that Canadian applied social scientists visited India, observed community development in operation, and brought it back to the Canadian prairies to Indian and Metis communities as well as to White Canadian farmers as a research, action, and political force. This did not quite meet the criteria I have mentioned, since Indian social scientists did not come to Canada at that time, but it was an interesting step which could still lead to cooperation and replication, with results drawn from comparison. Other examples are being planned in which French and Canadian scholars will conduct joint research in each other's countries to supplement each other's techniques and to replicate research.

The special skills of anthropology, then, lie in the analysis of culture and of values, the development of insights derived from intimate fieldwork and participant observation technique, and a cross-cultural perspective which is both positive and critical. By its very nature, anthropology *must* learn to work with other social sciences; it thus has a built-in drive to work toward the kinds of syntheses that are essential to the interpretation of the human condition, and hence to the understanding of policy issues.

How can it be put to work?

PART II

A Structure of World Society

Prologue to Part II

ONE obvious starting point is anthropology's concern with social organization as a system linked to goals and values. Typically, anthropologists have approached social organization in the context of small-scale social units (even when they are part of a massive national system such as that of India). In doing so, they have developed a range of ideas which assist in the analysis, call forth the production of useful data, and establish modes of understanding.

The range of these ideas is now enormous, and it even becomes the mark of success in a Ph.D. thesis to provide yet another significant reorganization. Yet behind what appear to be a myriad of idiosyncratic theories, there are a few more general themes. I shall try to isolate those that have seemed most useful to me, and place them first in the context in which they have been created—that is, the context of village communities. This implies a certain selectivity, which is necessary for reasons of economy, but which hardly begins to tap the wealth of possibilities. In this treatment I do not, on the whole, attempt conceptual originality; almost all of it is there in the literature.

But even here it is necessary to take a few additional steps, to show that this range of ideas can be applied with profit to *all* communities, that it is of necessity adaptive to the culture to which it is applied, but that it is not culture-bound. It is also important to show that what appear on the surface to be rather esoteric and remote generalizations have fundamental significance for policy choices, for the fate of peoples and cultures which are being influenced by the outside world and by government. Many of these peoples are remote from us. They are, however, being affected by the world we live in, and for which we are responsible in some way.

And so I move to different levels of world social organization. For one thing, I want to show that some of the ideas developed in anthropology for use in villages can be amended for the analysis of world organization.

This is a matter of declaring the wider relevance of the subject, beyond that to which it has traditionally been assigned. This, I hope, will lead my colleagues to argument and research, and suggest to policy makers that there is still a great deal to do to acquire functionally significant knowledge, without which they (and we) will remain ignorant and blind.

But I have also adopted this sequence of analysis because I feel that it is essential for any considerations of public policy to link local phenomena to the world system. And it is that system which is least understood. It is more than time that we, as anthropologists, gave it some attention.

CHAPTER 3

Analysis of the Village Universe

ONE is accustomed to reading of "underdeveloped countries," the "Third World," "peasant society," "tribal groups," and even "Stone-Age man." Of course, such terms would never have been invented if they did not in some important sense identify characteristics. There is no doubt that the questions raised in the course of dealing with such classifications helped thinking.

There are, however, inherent defects in using them for anything except initial short-hand reference. In most important respects, including those that make up the very characteristics used as criteria, the classifications conceal variability. Countries are *not* just developed or underdeveloped; they contain differing elements of development which are present to greater or lesser degrees. If you take any such element, or a cluster of them, you can arrange the countries along a developmental scale. To do this, you must be very careful in your definition of the elements and the technique you use to measure. The more you do this, the more the classification "underdeveloped" becomes meaningless.

Again, if you use the term "peasant society," you are probably referring to some such issue as this: the society in question has a high proportion of self-sufficient production and exchange, but is at the same time allocating a significant proportion of its production to an urban or feudal market. All of these elements in the definition are capable of being expressed as separate variables, so that each society, peasant or not, could be described by reference to them. That is, in *all* societies there is some kind of mix between self-sufficient and external exchange activity; and in the external exchange activity there is some kind of mix between exchange in kind and exchange through the use of money. The question is, how much is there of each? This is an empirical question the answer to which differs in each case.

Clearly, then, there is a sense in which each society is unique.* Neither policy nor theoretical thought can make much headway if it builds its *principles* on each unique situation. Instead, it must seek to identify common features, to make generalizations and abstractions, and to apply these to the interpretation of the unique.

But in the real social world, the unique answers back, and so it should. This implies a dialectic between the generalizers (be they policy makers or academic theorists) and the people to whom they relate. In the course of this dialectic, if it works, two results slowly emerge. On the one hand, the policy generalizers must either soften their principles to handle unique situations, or create and work through a kind of conflict, or remain puzzled because of "intangible factors." On the other hand, the theorist also is puzzled by "intangible factors," or backs away by saying that he is dealing with an abstraction rather than the real world. Or, more productively in the long run, he moves from crude classification to other interests. These can involve detailed and unique empirical analysis or else the identification of factors that can be compared as variables between societies. The generalizations and abstractions are then concerned with the interrelationship, movement, and behavior of the variables, rather than with the discussion of *kinds of* societies.

This qualification needs to be set out at the beginning, because in exposition one needs to handle various topics one by one, and at this stage of my argument I am indeed talking in a crude classificatory way. The concern here is with "village universes." This is *not* a scientific term capable of being used to yield new knowledge. I wish to focus for a while on rural communities, but many of the things that will be said about them also apply (though in differing degrees) to other communities.

Further, it is most specifically not my intention to give a factual or empirical description of the social organization of world village communities as special entities. Consider what that would entail. The *Handbook of American Indians* runs to several volumes, and it gives but the bare bones. The *Human Relations Area Files*, which summarize pertinent social and cultural information from most known societies, fill, in microfilm, rooms full of cabinets. When G. P. Murdock classified world

---

*I am not attempting a formal definition of "society" here. A better term would be "polity"—meaning a social unit that has a unified locus of power, "society" being the same unit analyzed in terms of social relations, and "economy" the same unit analyzed in terms of means-ends choices. Such units certainly do not have to be coterminous with a nation-state, but can be a family, an organized village, a lineage, a university, or an industrial firm, to name but a few examples.

kinship systems into types, he showed that in fact no two kinship systems were th⌐ same, even according to the limited criteria he used.

In reality, village universes, in terms of the topics of this chapter, include such diverse arrangements as those of the Naga tribesmen, Hausa emirates, Fijians, Mestizo peasants, and Swiss mountain farmers. The task before me, then, *cannot be* to show that social science knowledge can here and now contribute to the specific policy issues of the world of village communities, either as a general abstraction or, for practical reasons, for each real situation. The temptation is to move to the abstraction. The only legitimate way of doing that would be to handle the abstraction in terms of almost infinite variability, and social science— even when using systems analysis—does not make such a claim.

The intermediate procedure is to talk of the kinds of issues that are relevant in various ways and at various times in the myriad of village universes.

Ethnographic treatises are usually presented in a way that shows that in a certain very real sense the village, with companion villages, is a bounded universe, and the external world has different orders of operation. The social organization internal to the village universe is presented largely as a closed system—self-contained, with its own balances and logic. This is never empirically true, and a 20th-century policy which treated it literally would be expressing its own denial. But it is a point at which to begin.

In given areas of tribal Africa, Oceania, Asia, and among the Indians of the Americas, traditionally self-contained societies with quite different social structures live side by side. The family and household, however defined, are the centers of everyday life. But a corpus of ideas, under-standings, and obligations links individual members of the family, and hence the family itself, through lines of descent and intermarriage, to others. The formal description of these lines establishes the social structure in kinship terms. The variety includes such possibilities as unilineal descent arranged in lineages whose membership is traced through paternal links, matrilineal descent in which linkage is traced through the mother but most other jural rights are held by men, and bilateral descent in which one may belong to two lineal groups, or may choose between them. Where such lineages exist, they contain dynamics for expansion, contraction, segmentation, adherence, and merging with one another, with rules and understandings governing the formality of their separateness, and interactions between them that result in overall coordination. Such elements of social structure are by no means limited to so-called "tribal" areas, but may be found in India and other parts of peasant Asia (with important additional features); a great deal of the famous "family solidarity" of the Mediterranean has analogous elements.

The lineage, in its full-fledged corporate character regulating ritual linkage to ancestors, property holding, visiting, and exchange rights between members, varies so much in its demographic base and its agreed functions that it cannot under any circumstances be regarded as, in itself, a "typical entity." The huge lineal family organizations of China have adapted to become almost states within the State, capable of being used to legitimize major modern enterprises (at least prior to communism) and to defend the concerns of members facing the foreigner overseas. In parts of Africa, the hierarchical arrangement *between* lineages sometimes led to a political dominance with military overtones. This allowed lineages to forge military units which cut across separate loyalties, permitting military action which had the effect of creating a State, with the incorporation of alien lineages of different languages. Bantu States which emerged in this way possibly had a greater internal unity and drive to territorial expansion than did the Kingdom of Scotland, whose clans remained in uneasy rivalry.

A very high proportion of lineage systems in present-day village universes did not achieve a state of large political and military hegemony at the time of the impact of imperialism (though some, as in Fiji and Tonga, were on the point of doing so). Others, through imperial defeat and influence, were transformed into relatively weak regional associations (with delegated governmental responsibilities) inside colonies, and, later, into new nation-states. In many instances the system containing the lineages is small—a few thousand, or even hundred, persons. It is structurally systematic, treating its internal relations as of a different human order from its external connections.

The concept of lineal descent implies an important ideological variable which has a number of practical manifestations. The lineal unit may be short or long in time-depth. Where it is short, new sublineages may split off with separate identities as the generations move, or they may create identities within the larger main lineage for certain functions. In Fiji, for example, there is a pyramidal structure to the lineages so that one can think of a grouping of people under the same living senior ancestor, an adherence of such groups into a large unit linked to an ancestor say three generations removed, a wider unit linked to a progenitor far off in time, and a political alliance of these last units. To simplify, the functions of the units vary accordingly. The first, as a result of inheritance and residential propinquity, deals with day-to-day village living and agricultural cooperation; the second is concerned with ceremonial relations vis-à-vis other units, the legitimation of land holding and migration, and the regulation of marriage; the third is a unit of military force and political cohesion; and the fourth is a less stable expression of political alliance.

On the other hand, in our own society, the time-depth is usually minimal—to grandparent or at most to great-grandparent. There are, however, segments of Western society where this is not quite so simple, and contemporary research (delving into areas that were once taken for granted) is continually turning up new examples. In the Valais of Switzerland, for example, the time-depth implied by membership in the bourgeoisie is very considerable, and the importance attached to rights that go with family names gives a quasilineal character to the make-up of the family units of which the bourgeoisie is composed. Further, the bourgeoisie is considered a corporate property-holding group, with highly effective rules to keep newcomers to the minimum. Recent research has turned up matrilineal linkages, though without great time-depth, in areas as diverse as the Caribbean and working-class London.

Another variable might be termed ideological strictness or flexibility. A confusing point is that there is no *necessary* connection between the strictness and precision of the formal ideology and body of rules on the one hand, and personal interaction on the other. One generalization which is so universal that it might be termed a social law is that ideologies and mythologies are used to manipulate social behavior and property rights by providing a basis for argument (even litigation, in Muslim countries or theologically controlled Catholic societies). The one truth inherent in a given ideology or mythology turns out to have many manifestations; and of course, where the basis is an oral tradition, there is even greater room for a variety of versions and changes in the basic texts over time. Thus, the strictness with which the structure is operative in a formal sense is somewhat independent of the strictness of the legitimizing ideology. Although it is often done, the one should not be inferred from the other without close empirical examination.

Furthermore, both the ideology and the operative behavior usually have elements that permit flexibility; this, again, is a variable to be sought. Present-day Fijian society, as officially interpreted and encouraged, has a much more static character than the traditional reality would warrant. The reasons for this include the vested interests of leading families who found the meaning of their élite position reinforced and changed by the entry of Fiji into world society. Then there was the administrative attempt to impose a single cultural model on what in fact was a more varied mosaic, and, of more importance to us here, a failure by some anthropologists and administrators to detect the flexible processes that are very strong, both traditionally and at present, and that are inherent in what otherwise seems to be a rigidly static and hierarchically organized society.

The following are a few indications of the flexibilities that counterbalanced the rigorous model: adoption of an adult male into a lineage, with acquisition of land rights; ability to use land belonging to one's wife, gradually obtaining inheritance rights to it; "borrowing" land from another lineage, gradually merging with it as a segment; breaking off lineage segments through migration or quarrels; warfare and conquest; the exercise of de facto influence and power by women (not belonging to the patrilineage of the male village householders), including responsibility for transmitting local culture to children. Each of the items in this list sets up processes that are contrary to the strict ideology of male authority, patrilineal descent, and transmission of property through males.

The result is that the pattern of village residence and land ownership in Fiji, as in many other lineal societies, is a mosaic of lineal holdings, with great scatter and mixture, allowing individuals to call upon a wide range of relatives in greatly differing circumstances when they wish to use or acquire property.

Note the interplay of a number of themes. First there is organization or cooperation necessary to ensure the identity and stability of the overall group or units within it against lawless intrusion, and to achieve common goals. The most widespread manifestations of this in the rural setting are land holding, ceremonial, warfare (not usually now), and, much less frequently, joint production where effort beyond that of the simple family or household unit is desirable. In interplay with this theme (Margaret Mead has called the interplay "Cooperation and Competition") is the individual, seeking to use the channels of cooperation to advance his own private objectives. In this task his goals may be quite similar to those of other members of the village universe—for example, to accumulate wealth where it is feasible and where social ethics permit it, to advance his influence and prestige, to maintain the well-being of his family, to defend it against jealousy and social and supernatural attack, to make it possible for his descendants to hold their own in the social system. If his goals differ radically from other members of the community, it is quite probable that he can pursue them only by dissimulation or by linking them in some way to the interests of his fellows.

The theme of goal achievement has been widely misinterpreted. I cannot believe that it is accurate to talk of persons bounded by the village universe as nonachievers, as some development psychologists, following David McClelland, do. This is a thoroughly mischievous and misleading approach. It is, of course, true that goals that are appropriate to a self-contained life are not necessarily those that are consistent with an expansionist dynamic. The implication is that people are bent on achieving *different* goals in different societies. To say that because one's goal is rebirth with improved spiritual standing in a subsequent life one's very considerable efforts in this direction represent a personality uninterested in achievement *in general* is analytic muddle. The important point, in theory and in policy, is the identification of goals to which people do in fact direct their attention and their creative powers. There follows from this the possibility of directing policy to the attainment of these goals or their alteration.

When social structure, social organization, self-interest, and goal achievement are put together, the theme of social exchange emerges as the network of actions and connections through which flows the social cement that holds the totality together. Because self-interest (and competition between various segments) is a major characteristic, exchange allows for the expression of conflict, but usually does so in such a manner that out of conflict comes the positive desired result.

It is now evident that social exchange must be observed and interpreted broadly if its implications are to be thought of accurately. The Western observer and the Western-educated policy maker are often likely to think of exchange as significant when it involves material artifacts or, by extension, services that come on the market. This is indeed a special and significant form of exchange, to which no one could fail to give key attention. The trouble is that it is never the whole exchange story. It often misses an element of key exchange significance, which requires accurate interpretation for policy to succeed, and in many of the rural universes with which we are dealing it is but a small part of total exchange. Thus, policy based upon material rather than social exchange may be undermined by positive forces not taken into account. Let us trace why this is so.

Social exchange, tied to communication, and hence influenced by conceptions of social structure, is simply one way of looking at social relations. Much of the theoretical discussion has been confused because, on *a priori* assumptions, the pioneers of exchange theory (Marcel Mauss, George Homans, Peter Blau) insisted that the elements entering into exchange must balance. This insistence seemed contrary to the empirical fact. For example, it could be noted that *material* goods flowed, as it were, in one direction only—pigs were perhaps observed to move on ceremonial occasions from lineage A to B to C, but not in the other direction; agricultural foodstuffs from persons of lower to persons of higher political status in the hierarchy. The search for balance at least started observers thinking about the possibility that *intangibles* moved in the opposite direction, to serve as a counterbalance.

In the examples given it was easy to note that wives, upon marriage, moved in opposite directions to the ceremonial movement of pigs, and that the circle of lineage exchange was closed, so that women moved C to B to A to C again; that in a feudal hierarchy the senior political elements provided such services as law, defense, property allocation, booty, and religious organization. In a much more intimate and personal sense, one finds that interactions are made up of combinations of transfers of "things" of different kinds—material gifts, information, elements of conversation, protection, submission, communication of emotion (love, hate). Contrary to most exchange theorists, I would affirm that these do not have to be "balanced" in any summation sense. But it is certainly the case that there must be some form of reciprocation if a relationship is to continue, and that the search for the nature of the reciprocity reveals much about the dynamics and reality of personal interaction, out of which the nature of social organization is also revealed.

There is no doubt in my mind that social exchange in this sense is the fundamental process holding societies and internal groups and organizations together. One might almost put it in economic terms (as some small-group experimental analysts do): there are costs and benefits embodied in social interaction; the cultural ideology affects the judgment of these; they continue and strengthen while the benefits exceed the costs to both parties, or until such time as an alternative opportunity contains such an increment of advantage as to pass the threshold of motivation for a change. This is as true in our society as it is in any other. In our own society we have tended to take the implications for granted, but in so doing we have neglected to enquire into potentially revealing phenomena, such as the personal connections and experiences that lie behind the choice of contractual partners in business enterprises.*

In other societies it is through the exchange analysis route that we see the reality of social process. In numerous instances we note the

---

*See my estimate of the weight of ceremonial exchange in modern society in *Traditional Exchange and Modern Markets*, Englewood Cliffs: Prentice-Hall, 1965, and the excellent empirical enquiry reported by J. Davis, "Gifts and the U.K. Economy," *Man*, Vol. 7, No. 3, September 1972, pp. 408–429.

pervasiveness of prestige as a goal. It may be attained through the *mana* attached to skill or political wisdom or through an entrepreneurial manipulation so that a large number of persons acknowledge a material, social, or ceremonial indebtedness. The debts may then be called upon to mobilize the resources for major social and religious events. We see that frequently the prestige of the individual becomes the prestige of the social group of which he is a member. Successful leadership becomes the successful call upon members of the group when required, particularly for the manipulation of ceremonial exchanges governing external relations with other groups. Marriage itself becomes a contractual element creating or reinforcing exchange links. If it is in a lineage society, it provides for a set of exchange occurrences in which prestige and expansive manipulation are prominent factors.

In these circumstances, corruption (so-called) takes on a new light. The acceptance of gifts—bribes—to affect judgments and outcomes has become an "evil" because, with the growth of the idea of objectivity in social behavior, the application of gift-giving in certain areas (particularly legal processes) was seen to enable the rich and the powerful to operate to the unjust detriment of the poor. This is a recent development of an egalitarian ideology.

Yet it does not always have the kind of consequence that goes against the cultural ideology or ethic. It has been noted in many countries that success (professional, political, and financial) has the consequence of creating a corpus of relatives and other persons who are dependent, and whose presence may in fact provide the base for the further expansion of that success. Contracts are sealed with the symbolic passage of a gift, a celebratory drink and/or dinner being but the socially acceptable vestiges in our own society; a dependent may seek services by providing others. The person at the center of all this may well become restive if the balance drains his resources; his prestige will also suffer. But if it does not, it may be an important part of his motivation to succeed and may in fact be a part of the growth dynamic. It is an extension of the village universe, but a remarkably common one.

To take another example, trade; client–patron, and debtor–creditor relations in peasant societies have often been the subject of highly critical policy comment. We all know about exorbitant rates of interest, about the peasant being in the grasping clutches of the middleman. This is such a common folk idiom that it must empirically contain truth. There is demonstrable evidence of the manner in which such relations have been used in countries such as India for the expansive acquisition of land by persons who treat it as a nonrenewable rather than a renewable resource, and hence as landlords squeeze tenants so their well-being and agricultural practice suffer. But whether it is true or not is in fact an empirical question, to be determined by examining the costs and benefits of specific acts of social exchange, their interconnections and linkages, and the dynamics that result. It can be argued (and, I believe, demonstrated) that debtor–creditor relations under some circumstances in Latin American markets—or in Africa and Asia where money lending is in the hands of alien Indians, Chinese, or Levantines—lead to client–patron relationships of a wider character. It can provide access to the supply of sophisticated equipment and sometimes to business knowledge, legal advice, and a whole range of other services. Furthermore, the lender can become more dependent on his clients than is sometimes acknowledged, for default can be serious with little recourse, and the certainty of linked supply of produce in the trading element of the relationship can be just as important to the buyer as to the seller. This is not an argument for money lenders under all and every circumstance; it *is* an argument for the removal of ideological criticism based on limited historical examples or ethnocentric views, and for its replacement by a more detached examination, in particular cases, of what actually happens.

In writing of lineages, I mentioned the possibility that they could be arranged hierarchically. This opens up intriguing possibilities for their transformation into castes and the consideration of various forms of social division as part of a single set of variables (see Chapter 7). One need not go as far as that, however, to see that the social exchange which links them can exhibit permutations and combinations containing considerable stress with schismatic probabilities. I would argue that there are fundamental differences here between (a) exogamous lineages where women marrying into them bring significant influence and property claims, (b) predominantly endogamous lineages which, however, use marriage alliances for political or property acquisition purposes, and (c) endogamous lineages. The first has built within it, through marriage, structures which hold the competing lineages together. The second two contain tendencies leading to continuous strife with the strong possibility of political and property domination and monopoly.

A revealing situation has arisen in almost the whole of the Mediterranean littoral as the result of the interplay of these kinds of forces. There was, of course, the transformation of many village universes into warlike towns and piratical trading empires, many of which continued to retain some of the key elements of their village origins into relatively recent historical times—the fierce maintenance of separate identity, the use of religion as a legitimizing weapon, political alliance and interaction into which was woven the motivations of self-interest and community prestige, symbolized by that of the oligarchic or ruling houses, and, most important to us here, major family rivalry.

There are a number of relatively common principles in the social organization of peoples in what is now the countryside of parts of Spain, much of Italy, the Mediterranean islands, Yugoslavia, Greece, and Turkey, despite all the differences of the nations of which they are a part. Family unity, rivalry, jealousy, honour and shame are emotive pawns in social exchange which have violently explosive potentialities not fully compensated for by intermarriage. Feuding, murder, and revenge have been built into the exchange.

In many parts of this world, the institutions of justice or formal law and order (despite Greece and Rome) have not grown through an indigenous evolution, but have been imposed by rulers who were alien (or seen to be alien), whose hold was seldom enduring or substantial despite the tremendous centers of civilization which were built. The almost continuous movement from one set of rulers to another assisted in the continuity of the village tradition as an expression of identity, and of hostility to alien forms of rule—an attitude which persists to this very day and makes nationalism a limited device.

Yet there are bounds to the tolerance of feud and schism; if central government were to be resisted, other devices of security, protection, dispensing of justice, and arbitration would have to be leaned on. These too were traditional. Social exchange was channeled into forms in which men gained *mana* and took respect, exercising judgment and administering society in return for obedience, gladly securing the indebtedness of others in return for support, supplies, and services. The mafiosa controlled governments within a government. That mafiosa have now become dangerous pests is a function of the way they have created international connections, with strong corporations, administering vice for profit, perhaps partly because of the gradual movement of national government into areas of administration mafias once controlled without question. The fact that mafiosa are now public enemies does not alter the equally valid fact that they were once the public defenders, and that over very large parts of the Mediterranean world processes rather like those of the traditional mafia are still the effective arbiters of order and social cohesion.

It is also true that in these countries ambitious and technically interesting projects of regional development have, more frequently than not, come into head-on collision with the traditional village universe. There has been some "development" success, but in more cases than not the village universe has taken on the appearance either of a reinforced concrete block against which the development plan rams in vain or until it shatters, or else of an open pit into which money and effort flow—endlessly.

CHAPTER 4

Policy in the Village Universe

IN CONSIDERING policy affecting village universes, there are numerous positions of observation from which to think about and judge the issues, even to the identification and definition of goals. We will eventually consider the linkage of the village to region and nation, thinking of their different interests and the exchanges taking place between them. Here I deliberately concentrate on the village as the interested party in the results of policy, and external authority as the primary provider of policy. This is close enough to the facts of the real world for an initial examination, but it is not the final reality.

A village is, almost by definition, a small cluster of residences occupied continuously by families engaged in rural, usually agricultural, pursuits. While this might be considered to be something of a norm, variations in every factor are extremely common. A strong and conscious trend in colonial and imperial governments in the 19th and 20th centuries, except where immigrant plantation villages were concerned, has been to exert pressures for social life to organize in villages according to this norm.

Residence is a key element in the chain of human ecology. Perhaps it is more a result of methods of using the environment than a cause of them, but, once established, it attains value and influences other practices, which become traditions. Inland Italian and Melanesian villages were both influenced by defense considerations and low-lying malaria to establish themselves on hilltops, rather awkwardly placed for the visits of administrators in a hurry, or for expansion, or for access to modern services such as schools and hospitals. Nomadic or seminomadic peoples tend to be small in unit population size, yet in total they must number tens of millions at this time, offending an administrator's sense of order. The very idea of residence movement and of instability of dwellings is in conflict with the administrator's need for envisaging continuity on a day-to-day basis. Further, his judgment can be alarmed by what he takes to be penury and hardness of life, and he has trouble inventing and supplying

49

medical services and education. He may erroneously think it is much simpler to turn nomadic hunters, gatherers, and pastoralists into sedentary farmers, living in accessible communities.

In North American Indian societies the forced removal of the wide land base and the destruction of hunted herds made such a movement almost inevitable, and it is difficult to imagine what an alternative could have been. Yet even today continuous village life does not seem natural, the maintenance of houses of modern materials is often ignored, almost as a protest, and there is no reason why the descendant of a former nomad should have a natural aptitude for ranching or farming as distinct from other occupations that have no place on his reserve. A few Northern Athapaskan peoples in Canada have successfully resisted such pressures. With depressing regularity, an enterprising journalist "discovers" them, dramatically castigates the government for failing to turn them into productive farmers, compares their material level of living with that of urban Canadian society, quotes undoubtedly correct figures of malnutrition or alcoholism, and organizes (for a week or two) an airlift of donated food and clothing to expiate somebody's guilt—and the matter is dropped for another few years.

Even in modern and sophisticated areas of the Swiss Alps in the Canton of Valais, the seasonal movement of residence continues to be pronounced, with families moving from river valley towns or from the highest inhabited villages to summer residences or pastures. The great diversity of occupation now available at all heights above sea level, thanks to the spectacular growth of the tourist industry and the excellence and efficiency of communications, makes it possible for some Swiss to retain traditional residence values with great flexibility and yet maintain steady income earning in a complex and highly technological society. The imposition of the standard village model is by no means an automatic and authoritarian universal; where it conflicts with significant village values, it need not be applied if other conditions can be manipulated to compensate.

Perhaps I stress this point because as a former Australasian I am accustomed to the idea of rural residences scattered on individual plots, and as an observer of the colonial scene I have been horrified at the amount of energy and conflict which once went into the banal exercise of making people live together in geometrically planned lines of buildings, instead of into other services. There is no direct linkage between the density of rural community residence and such factors as rate of increase in income, standards of sanitation, schooling (though there are some complications here), or community cooperation.

Two key variables influence the appeal of particular forms of residence to the people who have to live with them. One is the significance and frequency of the occasions on which members of the village community wish to come together. Strangely enough, the desire to hear the words of an administrator is not altogether missing from this set of interests, and has sometimes been a key motivation. But usually we are dealing with such matters as the discussion of exchange with other groups, of land allocation, of ceremonials in which elements of the village (or the village itself) play host to the representatives of other social units, of rituals connected with the health, well-being, and beliefs of the people. The Church has not been unimportant as a reason for a village cluster.

The second variable is the time and pain associated with necessary movement. Village people can, to us sedentary city dwellers, tolerate an extraordinary amount of walking or riding in everyday conditions. A two-hour mountain walk to an agricultural plot or a five-hour walk to a mountain pasture is not an uncommon routine. Thus, it is not surprising to see secondary residences in or closer to the sites of exploitation; if they are established, the amount of territory tapped from a given village can be geometrically increased. Further, given this capacity of movement, schools and other services do not have to be established in a continuous community permanently occupied by total families. They may be located in central positions to serve scattered homesteads almost as easily, and, if necessary, accommodation of a simple sort can be provided for overnight sleeping.

The desirable residence pattern is closely linked with the pattern of land use, in turn related to land ownership, in turn related to social structure and its ideology. I suppose that it is natural that governments—confronted with a bewildering multiplicity of ethnic situations, as almost all of them are, and desiring to have a stable and predictable base from which to work—should give a priority to land organization.

The kind of situation that imposes itself dramatically upon the consciousness of the Western public is one in which a large working group is dispossessed from direct ownership of agricultural resources. There are several main varieties of this condition. The most common and perhaps most noteworthy is the one in which peasant agriculturalists, through processes of indebtedness, wealth inequality, the exercise of brute force in acquiring land, or movement out of indigenous enclaves, are tenants of big and often absentee landlords. Egypt, parts of the Sudan, India, Latin America, pre-communist Russia, and early Industrial Revolution England come to mind. It is said, with truth, that the relations of landlord to tenant are such as to discourage productivity and to reduce the peasant farmer's return to subsistence levels, which create poverty and prevent adequate care of the land as a renewable resource. But the *mere* redistribution of land to peasant, private or communal, property does not necessarily create a wealthier agricultural class or remove poverty or create an increased supply of produce for national use. The examples of Russia, Cuba, and until recently Chile give one cause for thought. Redistribution is in fact ineffective unless it is accompanied by other reforms linked to motivation, marketing, and technology. Further, it may settle so many persons on the land that the benefits of other reforms may not be realized, in which case it can only be effective if accompanied by a parallel movement of persons *away from* the land.

Similar principles are relevant where the land pressure is institutionally different. Many years ago, P. T. Bauer showed that peasant rubber production was effective, more flexible, and more economical in many respects than plantation production. His demonstration was debated and is not fully accepted in all quarters, but it has enough truth to warrant serious attention in those countries that aim to create more equitable property bases, and that are dependent on plantation cropping. A major point of Bauer's classical argument was that because peasant agriculture was thought in official circles to be *less* efficient, it was all but ignored in policy considerations—research, financing, market support, and the like. If the question at issue becomes the break-up of *existing* plantations into peasant units, it is at least possible that the new population will be marginal in production terms. In any event, the success of the redistribution will be highly dependent on the provision of support services within a peasant, rather than a plantation, framework. It is not easy for economists and technical officers to become peasant- rather than plantation-oriented, even when they are perhaps motivated by revolutionary ideologies.

Another situation in which the peasant is removed from a direct individual relationship with production and income is when he is incorporated into a communal production enterprise. This should be distinguished from a cooperative, which can be based on individual land holding, effort, and reward. There is no clear evidence that fully communal enterprises are necessarily more effective than individual ones. The primary variable seems to be the force of the ideology to which the members of the commune are committed. In religious communities in North America (Hutterites, Doukobours, Mennonites, Amish, and a few secular "back-to-earth" movements) the strength of the ideology has created very effective enterprise. In Israel there has without doubt been success, although some are now arguing that commonality has gone too far for some kibbutz members, and that the dynamic could wear off. In Russia, where communal enterprise was enforced on a large scale, the ideological dynamic was only partial, and the passage of generations has still not brought the kind of commitment that provides a reliable motivation.

Finally, it must be admitted that the most dramatic increases in rural income and farming productivity have come in colonialized situations in which huge areas of territory were settled afresh through the brutal and enforced removal of populations and an insatiable pioneering greed, which resulted in the assemblage of large land units to which technological innovation and business practice could be optimally applied. The Argentine, the United States, Canada, Australia, and South Africa are the obvious examples. Brazil and Colombia are attempting to get away with a similar policy today in rather different conditions, in which one factor is the outcry of a small section of world opinion. Nobody can seriously and openly advocate such a policy today if it involves enforced population movement; but if the predominant concern is a radical improvement in income per capita, and if the major existing resources are agricultural, then the basic lesson (long ago pointed out by Colin Clark) is significant. Too many people on the land, and dependent on it, can stand in the way of its improved utilization.

The above instances are the more dramatic ones. Far less dramatic, much more routine, but with consequences just as significant, are the attempts to rationalize land use through registration and the manipulation of taxes and incentives. The kind of registration we are thinking of is that which affects peasant proprietors or subsistence agriculturalists in shifting cultivation. Another variant is where there has not been individual cultivation, leading to the identification of land "belonging" to North American Indian tribes, and the allocation, in artificial ways, of reserves.

Because such techniques raise issues that are more difficult to comprehend, I shall outline an example known to me through my own research. I have already referred to the flexibilities of Fijian social structure in practice, and the manner in which administrators attempted to define it as a static system. The same sorts of attitudes carried over into land registration, established very early, in part to defend Fijians against alien encroachment and in part to ensure that income from the rental or sale of land was properly distributed. The various Commissions that enquired into land ownership throughout the country held meetings in which they talked with villagers and identified the social units claiming ownership in specific, named, pieces of land. But the Commissions operated with the notion that there were basically three levels of lineage—the *vanua*, or maximal lineage, which held general rights of suzerainty and in traditional times organized defense, the *matanitu*, or major lineage, traced back let us say four or five generations, possibly with branches in a number of villages, which was the effective administrator of the named land areas and could, by agreement, transfer and allocate even outside the *matanitu*, and the *i tokatoka*, or minor lineage, usually grouping families linked to living brothers, the individual members of which used and laid use-claim to specific parcels of land. Inheritance was thought of as being strictly in the patrilineal line with egalitarian distribution of use-claims (including those made by women) but primogenital transmission of authority over the *vanua*, *matanitu*, and *i tokatoka*. The heads of *vanua* held important chiefly titles and came to be something of an aristocracy from whom heads of even wider political units were chosen.

Now, Fijian land is seldom alienated outright, but a great deal is rented to non-Fijians. All rents are arranged, collected, and distributed by the government. Periodically, officials visit the villages, read out the list of rents, and allocate them in proportions fixed by law to the senior *individual* representing each of the lineage units linked to the rented land according to the 19th-century registration. What that individual does with the rent (that is, whether he holds it or distributes it) is his business. It is interesting to note, though, that this process, carried out in the name of tradition, has introduced a form of income which increases the wealth distance between the leading families and others.

But this system only operates in connection with rentals. Technically, transfer of ownership may be registered, but in practice this is seldom done. The result is that with the passage of generations, the land register has become a static document, used to legitimize an earlier state of affairs which in some instances even oral tradition has forgotten, and having little relationship to actual land use and the interests people have in their rights.

In practice, the following processes have operated. Some landowners give historical explanations of why the original Commissions made factual errors (nonappearance of witnesses, illness, intrigue); under these circumstances the rent once paid to the registered owner is quietly transferred to the "real" owner. Some *matanitu* have grown in status to become *vanua*, and others have declined for demographic or even land-loss reasons to become *i tokatoka*. In some parts of Fiji the functions associated with each level were different, but these variations were not on the whole recognized by the Commissions; they still continue, however. After one or two generations, men (using the land of a grandmother or other female ancestor) have acquired rights equivalent to a *matanitu* or *i tokatoka* within a *vanua* to which their *matanitu* did not formerly belong, thus conflicting with the patrilineal descent theory. There have been numerous transfers of parcels of land for material and ceremonial considerations. Thus the actual mosaic of land use and land ownership at its various levels is now quite different from that entrenched in history by the register, and the law governing the register does not correspond to the social reality.

This in itself is not important, except as a symbol of the difference between official social interpretation and the everyday lives of people. It is, however, potentially important if steps are to be taken, as indeed they are, to encourage the more effective use of land for peasant-style cash earning purposes or for partnerships in nontraditional enterprises, such as tourist resorts, land development, or even mechanized agriculture. There is now on the books a classification of land type, with the possibility of differential taxation according to whether or not the land is being used in accordance with its capacity. These measures imply accurate identification of the owners and users, if they are not to create social schism based on false accusations of responsibility. Further, they are designed to increase the effective use of land; if they work, they will presumably link land use and, in Fijian terms, ultimately ownership to productivity. But present owners are not necessarily producers, so that if the policy is effective, land transfer is inevitable. At the time of my research, there were complex rules governing the rental and alienation of land to non-Fijians, but these were only traditional mechanisms—not reflected in official recognition—and there was no governing law to handle rentals or alienation between Fijians themselves. Fortunately, Fijian society went on in its own way, paying little attention to the land law except at rental time; otherwise, economic growth would have been even less than it was.

Fiji also happens to provide a very good example of ways in which the "ethnosocial science" of administrators can create dangerous mythologies about social processes and their effects upon initiative and production, with resultant socioeconomic policies which actually damage the ability of the society to accumulate and expand its production. I cite Fiji again because it is well known to me, but the principles underlying the example can be repeated in many parts of the world.

Over the years the Fijian Government lived with the notion that Fijian society was static and tradition bound. It did not detect the flexible mechanisms I have already mentioned, and it did not see accurately that the principles of stability and hierarchy were counterbalanced by, and indeed could not have existed but for, equally strong drives toward individual accomplishment, within and making use of the system. There were tremendous prestige and material incentives for families to exert claim to lineage leadership, and enough ambiguity in the oral tradition to enable them to legitimize almost any step once taken. Those steps involved using social, ceremonial, and material exchange to mobilize on significant occasions the interest and support of relatives and friends, however tenuous the kinship connection. Success in this kind of entrepreneurial endeavor inevitably led to an increase in the social wealth and status of one's lineal group, with multiplying effects resulting from successful in-marriage and a widening circle of claims and responsibilities.

Particularly in modern times, individuals could transform this process by making use of some of the same forces to acquire, in a gentlemanly and ceremonial way, land and labor, and even equipment, from others who had it at their disposal, and by so doing to combine factors of production in an expansive dynamic. Admittedly, in most societies of these kinds, from peasant America to Africa and much of Asia, there were specific accumulative actions that were acceptable and others that created jealousy, ostracism, and even punitive ritual (sorcery). On the whole (there are major variations), accumulation that brings benefits to others through some form of distributive process—ceremonial, gifts, sharing—can be tolerated much more easily than a process in which the beneficiary indulges only in personal conspicuous consumption. Further, the very distribution of the benefits creates a supply of those things the enterprising individual needs.

The official response to this situation was argument and confusion. There were those who saw the network as repressive, who believed it was all one way and that whoever managed to get ahead materially would have wealth stripped from him. Those who thought this way, who failed to see the need for entrepreneurs to obtain the resources to work with from the social system, created the image of the individual farmer, the sturdily independent man relieved of *communal* pressure and obligation. They influenced government to provide incentives for the independent individual farmer by formally and legally relieving him of communal obligations. But the measure of the confusion is that the communal obligations that in effect were excused by these provisions were *administratively*, not traditionally, imposed. That is, the individually registered farmer no longer had to turn up for community school building, road clearance, and the like. Technically, if his chief were looking for assistance to build a residence as a lineage status symbol, or if his close relative were mobilizing ceremonial whales' teeth for use in a marriage ceremony, the independent farmer was under no *legal* obligation to participate. But participate he normally did, because it was *in his interest to do so*. He still needed the return support of others for everything from farm labor, to help in house building, to the marriage of his daughters. He might pay wages, but the wages and the relationships were definitely modified by previous social exchange.

The other side of the argument was put forward by those who *did* detect the value of community linkage, and who felt it should be built upon. It seemed to make production sense (in that it provided an opportunity for tapping the inherent social processes for joint effort) and to make distribution sense (in that all might share from a given result). The form this took varied a great deal, from formal cooperatives to enterprises run by Fijian government officials in the name of a particular group, to more or less private group projects. Insofar as the direction was one governed by official intervention, it was usually based upon *village* membership in the enterprise.

This approach, too, had its defects. In the first place, the mosaic of residence patterns had the result that many villages, while having a certain cohesion, were composed of rival lineages, and that lineages also had their residence spread over more than one village. So the village seldom reflected any traditional corporate entity. Furthermore, residence in a village by no means implied an equality of interest or aptitude in productive behavior—it usually turned out that perhaps three or four families out of a dozen or twenty were the interested parties. (In one region, in order to advance banana production for export marketing, banana suckers were distributed evenly throughout the population linked to production units. Production certainly went up, but as the result of the actions of about twenty producers out of a potential of several hundred. Production would have gone up even further if the distribution had been channeled to those who were motivated.)

Thus, while the traditional mechanisms of social organization based upon socioeconomic exchange do imply a form of cooperation, they do not necessarily imply that the networks have the same boundaries as residential units (i.e., villages). Indeed, the traditional village is characterized by such an intimacy of relationship that any incident of conflict, dispute, or tension has severe emotional repercussions which can inhibit and disrupt the type of corporate day-to-day organization that is implied in a production cooperative. This is not always so, but it is highly probable, and it accounts for failures and disappointing levels of success in many parts of the world. It is only on occasions of major motivation that many village societies can in fact pull together. On the other hand, if the cooperatives build on voluntary personal membership for technical village issues, as with a specialized marketing agency or an arrangement to provide an essential service such as an irrigation supply, friction can be accommodated.

In other words, it is naive to conclude that a residential unit, because it is physically visible and because its people live together, is a harmonious and cooperative whole, capable of new forms of productive endeavor. The creation of such units as a deliberate act of policy demands much more careful analysis of who in the community has what interests, how these tie together and are manifested in social processes, and, as we shall see, what the real linkages are beyond the apparent village boundary.

The point of view underlying the preceding remarks is consistent with the perspective that the identification and interpretation of enterprise in its technical sense is a complicated and difficult matter, and that much current thought is overly simplistic. The entrepreneur as manager is to be found everywhere, for management is a major aspect of all human behavior. We need to manage to be able to survive. The need, from the viewpoint of policy analysis, is to distinguish those forms of management that lead to differing results.

One school in the study of entrepreneurship singles out the aspect of management that is innovative. The true innovators—those who take the first step first—are a tiny proportion of the management population in any society. Much more common is the act of repeating an innovation made by someone else—that is, the process of diffusion. This is a different kind of innovation, consisting of the ability to learn and adapt, rather than to create something that is original. If we watch the activities of middlemen rather than industrial producers (and if we accept the observations of some social psychologists such as George Katona, who have looked into these matters), we can see that many managers prefer to live a secure and stable life, and that a high proportion really want to keep adaptation and innovation to the minimum necessary to maintain a livelihood; new ways are too disturbing and troublesome.

If this is true in our own society, despite its ideology of infinite change, it is unrealistic to expect entrepreneurial miracles in societies where that ideology does not exist.

Further, there is a very simple set of propositions linking demography to communication and innovation which is capable of accounting for the empirical differences in the rate of innovation between different societies without any ethnocentric recourse to such mystic factors as "n-Ach," an innate drive to achievement. The basic proposition would hold that the rate of innovation is a function of the size of the body of knowledge available in a culture and the rate of communication. This proposition is in turn based upon the observation that all innovations must be incorporated into the existing body of knowledge to be effective and applicable, and that the overwhelming number of innovations is based upon new syntheses of existing bits of knowledge. On sheer statistical probabilistic grounds, innovation is a function of the volume of interaction between the bits.

The act of innovation is thus inevitably a much slower and more difficult task in a village universe than in other more complex societies. The range of knowledge is more limited to begin with. The number of people who hold knowledge and are in interaction is small. The rate of communication, by comparison with more complex societies, is relatively slow. Although oral communication can be speedy, this is not the same as oral communication plus mass media.

Since I approach the matter in this form, I differ fundamentally from those of my colleagues—including anthropologists—who characterize village, rural, and nomadic universes as essentially repetitive and unchanging, a view strongly endorsed by the so-called "substantivists" such as Karl Polanyi, George Dalton, and Marshall Sahlins. On the contrary, given the limited opportunities and chances for change, such universes show considerable potentiality for innovation and adaptation. It is true that, where knowledge and opportunity severely limit the possibilities and motivations for change in the material sphere, the innovative movement is channeled into other spheres, such as religion and even social relations. This was strikingly demonstrated for New Guinea religion by one of the first and most thorough observers of that scene, the policy anthropologist, F. E. Williams, who described traditional adaptations of cult behavior. Furthermore, it is the only possible explanation of the tremendous variety of religious ritual, ceremonial, social organization, and art forms, linked nevertheless to shared basic principles and themes, which occur in contiguous regions in tribal areas throughout the world. And it is a major part of the explanation of the transfer of effort from actions oriented toward material advancement to religious and cult innovation in poverty-stricken areas where opportunities for secular economic and political organization are nonexistent or repressed.

If policy acts on the assumption that individuals are conservative and uninterested in innovation or entrepreneurial management to degrees greater than that in some other society, you can be fairly sure that it is based on uninformed guesswork. On the other hand, policy cannot operate in small-scale societies on the assumption that innovation and entrepreneurial activity will *automatically* occur with the extraordinarily high frequency that may be needed to establish rapid growth, or that when it occurs it will be visible in forms that external policy makers can easily identify.

Thus, not only is it possible for an entrepreneur producing for the cash market to call upon labor and other resources by traditional, nonmonetary means, but he may interweave what in the West would be called his business and his personal interests and accounts in such a fashion that they simply cannot be disentangled. The interweaving may thoroughly confuse the outsider's interpretation of what is going on and of the general effects and implications. An interior hill villager, for example, may run a trade store for which he has to pay a license; both the license and the small physical building will identify the enterprise to the outsider, and its lack of expansion and dynamic may be traced to lack of business acumen. However, despite the license, the motive behind the trade store may be little more than convenience to the owner and those around him. The store represents a local stock, which saves people a trek of many miles for small items; it is a convenience—a service—rather than a true business. And the payoff to the store operator may not be in this case transactions for money and profit, but rather a combination of the facts that his family gets its own supplies at cost, and his service and function are recognized by reciprocal social exchange of a quite different order.

I have observed such conditions, for example, in the activities of a small Papuan boat builder who produced sailing vessels for sale. He did not keep very good accounts, and those he did keep did not distinguish his business from his domestic operations. Some of the cash from the sale of the boats went into needed manufactured supplies, but a great deal went into feasts, presents, and what might be described as something of an "open house." It was impossible to find from the accounts themselves any hint of a financial nest-egg, a rate of profit, or financial capital investment. Yet there were numerous indications of substantial, if not fanatic, business expansion. Over the years, boat building on an increasing scale, saw-milling, trade store operations, and fishing for marketable shell were established. The feasts, presents, and similar activities were one major way of rewarding workers and partners and keeping the interest of a wide range of community residents involved. The only real "key" to the profitability of the operation was its *expansion* in an operational and physical sense.

Under such circumstances, it is easy for observers to be hasty in their judgments. It is also easy for enterprise partners coming from different social or ethnic backgrounds to have conflicts of motivation with far-reaching effects on the conduct of business. One technique to bring modern methods and capital into productive use within the rural universe is to create a partnership—one side providing capital, knowledge, and marketing arrangements, the other providing the operation at the production level. This is a technique which can overcome many problems of property and law, and it often has a highly educative function as well.

But there are also trouble spots to watch for. The example I frequently cite in this context is that of a well-known Fijian manganese mining partnership. To the Fijian owners and miners, the ore represented a capital sum to be dispensed gradually for the foundation of alternative enterprises that would carry on after the ore was exhausted, with a proportion going into capital for social purposes such as housing, and school and medical buildings. To obtain capital for tools and an access road, and to gain access to accounting skills and marketing, the Fijian group entered into a partnership with a major overseas organization interested primarily in manganese marketing. To this second partner, the objectives were quite different—namely, to work the mine for maximum production at the time of highest prices. If the mine were exhausted, they could move onto other suppliers. Further, their interest in profit was tied to marketing, not to production: they could even afford to take a loss on the production unit. They therefore used their influence and legal power to try to force the Fijians to accept a huge capital input to work the mine quickly, but the Fijians resisted with the suspicion that they might end up with a loss, and because it was in conflict with their skills and policy.

It could be argued that the Fijians might have achieved a similar result by selling the mine outright and investing the proceeds. This is true, and indeed they might have been better off in some ways. But at that time in their experience they felt in greater control of physical than of financial manipulation, particularly since in Fiji there was no adequate investment market. Whoever was correct in the long term, the Fijians had the right to make their decision, and learn from it, in terms of their own objectives;

their partner had to be patient and understanding. (The subsequent history of this particular enterprise was not so happy.)

This example links with other differences of view between government and village. A great deal of the policy must be governed by national, if not international, considerations and standards. The appropriate degree of "give" or flexibility to allow for unique village interests and conditions is always a problem. One of the most significant achievements of 19th- and 20th-century colonial governments was in the field of law. In rather different ways, the British, French, and Dutch established new bodies of law, mainly on the metropolitan model, for handling new issues such as commerce, industry, and public service, for creating a new territorial basis of order (courts, the control of violence), and for dealing with problems occurring between nonindigenous persons or persons from different cultural and conventional backgrounds. But behind this was a substratum of customary tribal law which governed civil relations and a wide range of customary duties. Considerable ingenuity was shown in handling such law through codification in some cases, through civil case law developed with the assistance of lay assessors, and through introducing decentralization of courts, local responsibility, and variations in court procedure. While administrators tended to refer to such systems as preserving and respecting traditional values to the maximum possible extent, nationalists sometimes regarded them as a brake on reform. Empirical studies have shown, however, that in most instances very substantial changes followed. Local courts, for example, might be given responsibility for enforcing minor laws that had their origin in national rather than local policy: the outcome in cases of conflict of laws was not to be taken for granted; appeals from local courts to superior courts often meant dealing with judges who had a different set of principles and even transferring from one system of law to another. These issues and problems still exist.

Again, there is an uneasy relationship in policies dealing with rural services, such as roads, schools, and medical facilities. If one starts with the needs, ideas, and resources of the rural people, one obtains a very limited plan of action, which national and international considerations almost certainly overrule. Sometimes the result is to introduce a dynamic which the local people willingly accept. Very frequently they fight it or tolerate it. Sometimes the reasons are lack of understanding and communication. Just as frequently, the local people have grounds to believe that the policy does not in fact meet what they consider to be their needs. They may know this directly (the road goes between two major centers, but does not wind into their agricultural lands; the school site is subject to flooding; the proposals of the agricultural officer do not fit their rainfall or land-use conditions), or they may sense it because of an absence of obvious link-up. It is no secret that tremendous efforts have gone into the design of school curricula that have special meaning and use for particular rural conditions, to replace the unreality of taking "Dick and Jane" into the bush. But it is still no secret that, figuratively, Dick and Jane (and rote learning, and uninstructed teachers) are still widespread, in conditions where elementary bookkeeping, applied biology and anatomy, or soil science could be useful and broadening. Again, what are rural people to make of the indirect value of an anti-malaria campaign, established because of a world eradication program decided upon by the nations gathered together in solemn World Health Organization conclave in Geneva, when they feel they have learned to live with mild malaria and have been asking the government for years for a simple dispensary to deal with urgent illness and midwife care for childbirth, both impossible because national resources have been diverted from deepening the structure of permanent local medical care in order to give the required counterpart support to the plethora of international programs?

A social scientist thinking about these kinds of issues and engaged on empirical field investigation on the whole knows what to look for if he is at all sensitive and not ethnocentrically bound. He gains this knowledge not, at least at the moment, from formal training, though clearly what he has learned of comparative systems and the theory of processes and interactions will give him a major start. He gains it just as the administrator or policy maker does, through experience and, above all, through learning that some of his cherished ideas do not work very well. His experience is often—but by no means always—more intimate than that of the administrator, more systematic, and more inclined to see the village from its own center rather than from that of the nation. This may lead him to be too much *parti pris*, too emotional, intemperate, and unable to balance the issues that national policy must balance. But the intemperateness may come from sheer anger and impatience when, perhaps after *twenty years* of such experience, he sees the same errors and mistakes being made time after time in different parts of the world, sees the weak being dispossessed from Australia to Brazil, sees village universes with real values being pushed and squeezed quite needlessly.

A danger is that, as he thinks about these things, solutions appear that seem to be sensible and rational, and that become stronger when moral fervor is added. But there is absolutely no guarantee that solutions that seem *right* to the social scientist will in fact also seem *right* to the people concerned, and even less that they will seem to be right to the people three generations hence. The social scientist who appears to be the savior today may well be cursed tomorrow. In that respect he bears the same risk, when he advises or deals with policy, as the administrator or policy maker himself.

The primary question must be, who takes the decisions, who bears the responsibility? This cannot be the social scientist. As social scientists (and, while we may preach, as individuals and professionals), we must beware of deciding, except in two fields. These are in standing up for our ability to carry out investigation and to make the results available; and in standing up for the existence and creation of responsible institutions that can, in fact, make the decisions.

In other words, the basic policy task is one of creating political structures through which rural people can express their wishes, enter into bargains with wider regional or national institutions, and, above all, *resist*. Resistance against pressure, if patient and firm enough, usually brings changes in the nature and objectives of that pressure, and enables bargains to be reached that represent reasonable compromise. At the moment we frequently have either complete resistance and no movement, because fundamentally there is no communication, or because the communication is based on a complete lack of comprehension of the respective premises; or we have overwhelming pressure which, however, very often misses its objectives because it has not been thought necessary to develop an accurate analysis.

Very frequently, the first task of the social science adviser to people and to government should be linked to the creation of local political institutions. Once they are in being, it becomes possible for subsequent social science analysis to be placed before *both* people and government. Since even here social scientists do not have perfect insight or knowledge, and since discussions they may have had with the people about the future may well have a certain air of unreality until the time of decision comes (at which point the balances may move substantially), such advice should normally be presented in terms of alternatives. Then consequences may be seen, and choices more realistically made.

CHAPTER 5

The Village Extended

VILLAGES, as many of the earlier remarks have shown, are not self-contained entities. A point which is a little less obvious is that they may not even be the appropriate units of organization for all the activities relevant for policy.

One of the more significant factors bearing upon this condition is the effect over generations of marriage external to the village. One can consider this dynamically by illustrating the case of a village founded by a single family, assuming the ceremonial structure to be patrilineal. The creation of that one household-residence already has external connections of some importance. Unless the foundation were the result of a serious political breach, the family head will have patrilineage connections in at least one and possibly other villages. But every marriage, on the assumption of exogamy, brings with it a connection with a different lineal unit *additional to* the patrilineage. Thus, the foundation family already has a link with the lineal unit of the founder's mother and the founder's wife; and quite possibly of the founder's brothers' wives and of the founder's sisters' husbands; and, if you want to go on counting, as the founder himself does, there is the small question of the father's siblings' spouses and the father's wife's siblings' spouses.

As the generations pass, the village is likely to be populated by the families of sons and grandsons of the founder, who import wives and, with them, social connections with their lineages. The daughters, on the assumptions used here, themselves move out; and while some of the marriages may be reciprocal, some may not be—creating yet further possible links.

The founder or his sons may accept in friendship the immigration into the same village of an alien lineage that has land nearby. On those occasions in which the village does act together as a corporate whole, it may thus make use of the connections of the immigrant lineage as well.

The example does not imply that all village universes are based on this kind of social structure. But the interplay of residence rules, marriage rules, and inheritance rules obviously has significant effects on the kinship linkages used by people to further their interests. Since social organization in the anthropological sense consists in the sum of the functioning of these links, their content also shows the way the social system works (together, of course, with such additional linkages as friendship and separate political power, if any). Even in societies where lineage in depth is not a factor, the same sorts of connections—on a smaller scale and supplemented by others—constitute the permutations and combinations of social connectedness.

Sometimes the rules and expectations tighten up the system so that it is a little less open-ended—for example, through the use of circulating marriage between defined lineages so that the choice of lineage for a marriage partner is strictly limited and defined. But, however this may be, simple arithmetic and empirical observation both show that the range of connections is surprisingly wide.

Where the choice is open, the possibilities in the selection of a marriage partner are enormous, and the calculation in terms of material and prestige considerations going beyond the personal attraction of the partners is highly complex.

Since it is through such connections, once founded, that social exchange flows, it follows that any village in such a society will consist of inhabitants whose preoccupations will be largely external. Inhabitant A, for example, will have the possibility of calling upon his own resources and supplementing them with others drawn from his lineage members both within and outside the village, plus those of, let us say, twenty or thirty affinal (that is, through marriage) connections. Such on-call capital may lead to the flow of labor, objects needed for ceremonial purposes, small local manufactures and handicrafts, and sometimes even cash. The choice of which link to activate will depend on such matters as whether the call creates or expiates a debt, whether the channel has been used before (leading to expectations of a successful result), whether there is amity between the individuals, and whether the person called upon has the specialized resource or skill that is in question.

By making such calls, inhabitant A creates liabilities, which make it possible for his exchange partner to call upon him in turn. Further, if the channel continues to be activated, at least up to certain points of balance, it will become an expected channel for calls. If inhabitant A has, for example, a serious ceremonial obligation, the rest of his village may cooperate to mobilize the activity. Each resident makes use of his own particular channels, justified by linear ethos, to do so. Similarly, if inhabitant D, let us say, has ceremonial obligations, inhabitant A may assist by calling on his own partner once again. Of course, inhabitant A has many partners for a variety of purposes, and it could even happen that partner X calls on inhabitant A for a particular service or object that inhabitant A cannot personally provide; however, to meet his feeling of obligation, he may call upon inhabitant D or upon partner Y or Z to put the transaction together. It should be noted that in present conditions the transactions can be in cash or in manufactured objects as well as in traditional items.

Out of these possibilities of connection certain lines may be more emphasized than others because of geographical propinquity, closeness of friendship, political alliance, or rules that emphasize one kind of connection over another. In examples known to me, it is possible to put a fairly rigorous boundary to marriage movement around a defined group of villages, and it then follows that this boundary governs the practicability of normalized day-to-day cooperation. Outside that boundary, special institutions are brought into play, such as trading expeditions, seasonal ceremonials, or highly ceremonialized individual trading partnerships, if external connections are needed. In other societies, with a larger scale culture, one can draw such a boundary statistically as a matter of emphasis, and even on occasion find clusters of villages that turn in on one another for most of their concerns.

These principles are worth examining in particular cases where policy is being developed, because when they are given concrete expression they indicate the nature of partnerships and cooperation and define structures that may be present. No one starting from these principles and applying them to Fiji, for example, could have regarded the individual village unit as a suitable base for the creation of a mandatory production cooperative or community development scheme. He would have noted that the individual interests on which productive cooperation must be based do not necessarily cover all village members, and that those who do have such interests have like-minded partners in other villages. Thus, a more successful form of productive cooperation would be one in which membership was voluntary and confined not to a single village but to a cluster as a minimum. He would also have noted that community development, if linked to such things as self-help building of community facilities, would always imply the ceremonious provision of services and cooperation by inhabitants of *other* linked villages. Thus it might be that community development would have more success in the long run if it involved a cluster of villages, each one helping the other in turn.

Patterns of cooperation, then, should be sought beyond the village as well as within it. The assumption here, however, is that there is a cultural homogeneity (though sometimes the relevant connections do cross variations in religion, dialect, symbolization, and the like).

Nonlineal peasant societies, though exhibiting many of the above qualities in modified form, also have external connections of considerable time-depth that are based on a greater specialization of function, hence differences in cultural viewpoint, and often major differences in culture as well. Trade, connections to a wider religious organization such as the Church, and interactions with national political power are traditionally characteristic of peasant societies. It is interesting to note that the "modernization" of tribal and lineage societies is creating the same sorts of external links—so much so that, except sometimes in social structure and in the traditional basis of agriculture, there is less and less analytic difference between tribesmen and peasants. What is said about peasants can almost always be said about tribesmen in modern conditions, though the reverse is less true.

While there may be a representative of the religious or political order and even a trade store in or close to the village community, the significant pattern is for trade to take the peasant to the town or city. The marketplace, in one form or another, becomes a worldwide phenomenon, and associated with it is the possibility of a range of subsidiary activities. The marketplace may be a central locus of activity where peasants offer produce for sale. Mixed with them may be more permanent vendors (as in Europe or the larger Latin American markets) who buy stocks from peasants and otherwise act continuously like shopkeepers. Around the formal marketplace are likely to be stores that buy produce from peasants, at lower prices perhaps but with the certainty of a sale and hence perhaps greater returns. They compete with the market and supply goods in the reverse direction in addition to cash, capital, and advice. Such areas are also convenient sites for lawyers, letter-writers, herbalists, doctors, and clinics.

While the persons with whom peasants interact on such occasions may (or indeed may not) speak the same language and may have originated in the same culture, the peasants are by definition in contact with a different world, controlled by values with different goals. The mere trade contact does not necessarily imply movement of ideas between the two parties except for limited functional purposes. Yet this communication *may* exist. It is my contention that in Fiji despite a political ideology that insists that the races are separate, the Indian and Chinese storekeeper and money lender, and the Indian peasant farmer and truck driver, have, largely unconsciously, done more for the acculturation and agricultural and business education of the rural (as distinct from the urban or professional) Fijian than two generations of primary schooling. The condition that has made this possible, which is not present in many otherwise similar circumstances, is the intimacy of informal contact that is associated with commercial transactions and propinquity of residence, so that house visiting and exchange of languages (but not intermarriage) is common.

Migration to the towns from the villages can be assisted by the cultural experiences of marketplace trading; where there is such a connection, the cultural shock involved is modified. But rural–urban migration is not by any means limited to such conditions.

The issues of migration are of great importance. The town end of migration will be examined more systematically later. Here I am concerned with migration as an expression of the outward-looking village universe, now a contradiction in terms.

In Oceania, Africa, and Latin America, rural–urban migration has been the subject of concern from the 19th century at least, and now it is an issue for examination everywhere. Much of the concern has been linked to the obvious poverty of urban conditions and the apparent inability of towns to absorb a high proportion of immigrants. In some areas, towns have been White alien settlements, and the influx of rural peoples has been seen as a social threat (this, however, is usually limited to racist societies such as South Africa, or to former colonial administrative centers).

Viewed from the village perspective, however, the issues are not as clear. In many parts of the world the rural areas that are yielding migrants are undernourished. Production on the land is actually held back by the presence of unwilling or inept farmers, or more able farmers using (but underutilizing) inefficient labor. The town, to protect itself, creates an invisible underemployment, inefficiency, boredom and lassitude, anxiety, and malnutrition in rural areas. Society tolerates it because the visible elements are far removed, and in any event most of the ills are less pressingly visible than they would be if they were concentrated in cities. In the modern world, even in the modern Third World, it cannot be assumed that the man born in the village is thereby an effective farmer or that this is where his interests would lie if he were given other opportunities.

Much of the inherent criticism of migration studies applied to thought about village interests has shown another side of the coin. The kind of enforced migration associated with slavery and South Seas kidnapping was selective in terms of attracting the ablest and physically strongest people. Indentured contract labor (which replaced enforced labor in Oceania and Africa) or longer term arrangements which permanently moved Indians, Chinese, Indonesians and Vietnamese to many parts of the world tended to remove the ambitious and innovative at a time in which, had other conditions been right, they might have made a contribution at home. Where they returned to their communities, they brought a little inflation, disturbance, and new routines, they had difficulty in settling down, and so forth. While it is true that some villages found themselves short of productive manpower for traditional purposes, it is doubtful whether this was a long-term result, and it takes fairly subtle investigation to be sure of the balances involved in any given case.

It is certain, however, that ethnic enclaves of people of rural origin are common in towns, and that often they are associated with particular villages, groups of villages, or cultures in large, multicultural societies such as Ghana or Nigeria. As the generations pass, the enclaves come to have their own urban character and identity, but many of them continue to act as hosts and magnets for a mixture of temporary and permanent migrants.

Thus, from town to village there are established pipelines of communication outside those of "normal" commerce and administration. (Indeed, it would be very unusual for transactions along such familial pipelines, which might be quite voluminous, to enter into trade statistics.) The villager obtains a kind of security when he visits the town: for short visits, he does not have to find probably nonexistent commercial lodgings; he has a base from which to become a permanent working townsman. In return, he is likely to supply quantities of produce with which the villagers in the city supplement their wage-purchased diet, and he is available for ceremonial assistance such as help with the return of the dead to their natal communities. The continuation of the link gives the urban villager the sense that he can return home on retirement, where his pension or savings will go further, or if life in the city gets too rough.

The importance of this last point can be judged by a contrary example. The Indians of Canada are now residentially concentrated in villages located on reserved land; there are, however, numerous emigrants from the reserves. Up to a point, experimental emigration for short terms is encouraged by this system. But, after the passage of a certain period of time, the emigrant is deemed to have lost his rights in the reserve, which is communally held. This means the loss of a traditional home, a break in the line of inheritance, the loss of a share in reserve income if there is any, and the loss of certain tax privileges. While life on some reserves can be extremely depressing, the depression is counterbalanced by its shared nature—there is some kind of kinship and community support, and there is a comfort in traditional land, the continuation of ceremony, and one's place in the movement of generations. Urban Indians have a great deal to overcome in the course of migration, and ethnic enclaves have been of only limited help, though efforts are now being made to give them coherence, visibility, and, in some instances, political strength.

Rural–urban communication is, of course, much wider than that which travels along kinship pipelines, and we shall have reason to show that it is not all one-way. A great deal of the communication the villager receives is irrelevant, at least to his immediate concerns, and it is not easy to know how much is stored for future use. Perhaps the fastest movers are music and oral language. Urban examples of these can be used to indicate modernity, sophistication, being "with it," for the village is by no means impermeable to such influences. Transistor radios are common, but they are one-way, and the villager does not control the content. Programs handling serious rural concerns—agricultural marketing, rural health, techniques of production, success stories—may strike him as interesting, but not within his sphere of action, his power, or his possibilities; yet there is conversation about them, and presumably something remains. Communication the other way (for example, by telephone), which is capable of individual use for specific immediate concerns, is rare because it involves capital equipment and outlay and the persuasion of a bureaucratic organization to make the investment. Similarly, it is usually relatively easy to get a letter *into* a village—friends pass by the post office and pick up neighbors' mail, or a bus or a truck helpfully drops letters off along a route. To get mail out the other way is much more difficult, since not only does the letter have to be placed with the local post office some distance away, but a stamp must be purchased, and the problem of knowing how much to allow for, and giving it to one's friendly "agent", is precisely the small important thing that stands in the way of action. It may be possible to bypass the postal services effectively—I once was in a position to notice a highly intensive exchange of letters in the Solomon Islands, carried by canoes and passing travelers and indeed by political agents, at a time when the internal postal services could hardly be said to have been functioning at all (and were also politically distrusted). The intellectual and organizational effort that went into correspondence reserved it for the most important occasions. Letters can acquire some of the *mana* and mystique of the occasions that they describe; they can be treated with a respect and their message accredited with a force that is rather different from those situations in which letters are daily events.

The cultural separatism which underlies the above remarks is itself a variable state of affairs, and seems to react largely to a combination of sociopolitical status and the ready availability of communication *for individual use* (as distinct from the political attempt to establish a policy). Let me give two examples as a hesitating move toward the examination of this idea.

In both instances, begin with a relatively self-contained village community, in touch, as we have seen, with neighboring villages, but untroubled by the inroads of the industrial revolution, imperialism, colonialism, nationalism, or any other of the great 19th-century movements that nonhistorical social scientists are now treating with such moral indignation. Place each of these communities in the middle of the 19th century.

Community A is on a seacoast, and has seen something of European settlement at a distance; indeed, its people are beginning to feel the effect of the "isms" because a commission is at work creating a boundary to the lands they may use. Since there still seems to be plenty of forest to hunt in, and as they depend a great deal on sea and riverine fishing (which has not yet been restricted), there seems little cause for alarm. By 1880, a small settlement of White entrepreneurs and Asian laborers, and a railway line, have been established eight or nine miles away. Ninety years later, before this settlement has celebrated its first centenary, it consists of over a million people, and its port has the largest turnover of any for 3000 to 5000 miles of coastline. The middle-class, suburban residential area has filled up the intervening miles, and the property (small though it is) of village A acquires value for residential development, which takes place.

During the same period, village A has gone through a severe population decline, then has begun to reassert itself demographically and psychologically. Many of its members have resisted communication with the encroaching city and have turned to nearby villages of similar culture, spread over miles of inland ocean and islands, for personal and cultural reinforcement. Communication could not, however, be avoided. As a result, learning took place with village children attending urban schools, with fishing adapting to capital-intensive modern technology, with some adults acquiring significant professional jobs and taking a part in city affairs, and with the village council learning to speak for its members in dealings with city and national institutions. Within this framework, members of the village pursued their individual interests. The framework came to be an intelligent device for the administration of affairs for the common good and particularly for the exploitation of common resources and services.

That in itself was not enough. The social reality was that those resources had to be used in a manner that also protected them from outside encroachment. It would have been only too easy for the people to have handed over responsibility to the government or to an outside developer without themselves retaining an interest or exercising control. I am sure that such a course was tempting, since most productive activity was individually organized, and the village could have been broken with schism.

That this was not the case was probably due to two factors. The very scale and speed of urban development meant either complete defeat as an entity or vigorous reaction. The reserve, with all its defects, provided a base from which to fight back. Linkage with other villages not quite so hard-pressed (though some were, and those reacted in the same manner) gave strength to cultural reserves. Education and available advice were sufficiently varied and intensive to offer choices and answers. The second factor was that out of the cultural base the people were able to find creative traditional outlets which at first helped carry them over the worst periods by giving a focus for action and commitment. Then, as fortunes rose, increased confidence enabled the people to use their cultural strength to forge cohesion, reinforce their belief in their identity, and to go further in their dramatic and religious creativity. Ceremonial winter dances and spirit initiation, which linked the villages of the region, were not tame tourist performances (sometimes put on for show or money in these very same villages) but were private community expressions to which the White man was *not* welcome except as a privilege under special circumstances.

The special circumstances of intense communication across the boundary and intense but different communication within the boundary, coupled with almost unbelievable but successfully resisted pressure on the boundary itself, determined the outcome.

Village B, on the other hand, is situated on a mountain valley shelf, 4000 feet above sea level. At our starting point it was organized in a commune with two *endogamous* subdivisions which also had political functions. Some land and resources were held and administered on behalf of the whole community, but much was individually inherited and administered. There was a small town, 1500 feet or so in the valley below, but no road, and the trails were steep. Cultivation was greatly influenced by the season, variations in altitude (governing vines, crops, and pasturing), and the supply of water by age-old wooden aqueducts.

About the turn of the century, a first road-like trail was built from the valley to the second level of pasture above the village, but bypassing it by over a mile, since the pasture area had been discovered to be highly suitable for health sanatoria and tourism, and a transcontinental railway in the valley below began to make such investment a paying proposition.* A small mountain railway, again bypassing the village, came some years later. Hotels, hospitals, and shops were established on the plateau, which became frequented by literati and a fashionable worldwide clientele, including royal heads of State.

At this time, the villagers themselves began to be involved in enterprise other than their traditional agriculture. It is probably the case (history is not clear) that some benefited from the initial bankruptcy of the promoters and bought their way into investment at cheap rates. That chance, however, affected only a few, and the remainder first became involved in such enterprises as mule packing, guiding, small retailing, and construction. To obtain an education beyond a primary level, it was necessary for villagers to leave home. A few of the more ambitious (not necessarily in monetary terms—at least one person followed this path in order to obtain church organ lessons) walked down and up, to and from the small town below, where some specialized instruction was available.

By the 1930s—as late as that—better roads were constructed, the mountain railway was doing a thriving business, and bus services and the railway line in the valley brought upper-level schools, professional services, and newspapers into daily contact. The schedules and prices were such that it was possible for young people to attend classes in the regional capital some distance from the small valley town. In two to three hours they could be in a variety of important national cultural centers and the home of major international activities of worldwide interest and importance, with the choice of four universities. In four hours they could be in major cultural and commercial centers in other countries. They became the beneficiaries of a first-class automatic telephone, television, and radio network; combined with one of the world's best postal services, it made it possible for them to order a component for the operation of their enterprise in the morning and have it arrive from almost any part of their country by afternoon, or the next day at the latest.

Today, the bulk of the village residents are involved in either full-time

---

*The first, English, investors, however, went bankrupt.

business or professional activities connected with the development of the summer–winter tourist resort, or a combination of such activities with a highly modified but still present agriculture and pasturing. The population includes construction entrepreneurs, bankers, architects, hoteliers, and merchants. The village shares the exploitation of the tourist resort on the plateau with other villages of its commune and with four other communes. It still runs separate communal properties. It is extremely difficult, but not quite impossible, for nonvillagers belonging to the same nation to gain access to village or communal property, or to become members. The dual organization persists. Marriage links with other communities carry with them highly significant social exchange ties. Traditional cultural interests are kept alive, partly through the existence of special organizations. In the same general region there are village communities that have not benefited either from the intensity of capital investment (in which foreigners have played a major part) or from the communication network (some being cut off by snows in winter months), so that it is possible to make direct comparisons.

The germs of interaction and movement in village B were certainly present at the turn of the century, and the interest of foreigners in the *mise en valeur* of the plateau property created a new conception of the available wealth and its possibilities. But the real developments came in stages: in the 1920s and 1930s with communications which the people themselves as well as their visitors could use and in the 1960s with a quantum jump in information movement, professional education at last paying off, and a major rise in foreign interest and investment which the local people were in a position to utilize and, up to a point, control, either directly or through partnership.

The point to stress, however, is that this major shift in culture and professional competence, though beginning earlier, carries the time dimension of fifty, and in some senses twenty, years. The speed of change was made possible not so much by some kind of differentiated indigenous base, but through the combination of highly effective communication which *individuals* could exploit and capital availability for allocation to a major local industry—tourism.

I have deliberately not located these two examples until this point, because their naming suggests ideological interpretations rather than factual ones, and it is important to get to the fundamentals. Village A is Musqueam, situated adjacent to the city of Vancouver in British Columbia, Canada. Its people are of Indian Salishan culture, shared by other villages on the mainland, on Vancouver Island in the vicinity of Victoria, and in many parts of the State of Washington.

The prototype of village B is Montana-Village, above the township of Sierre in the canton of Valais, Switzerland. The tourist area it has exploited is known as Montana-Vermala-Crans. The description could apply just as easily to other nearby villages such as Chermignon-dessous or Randogne, except that the first road passed by the outskirts of Randogne.*

An objection to the Swiss example may be that it is unfair, for a comparison that deals with world village communities, to draw lessons from a village that is part of a highly integrated, and unquestionably wealthy, and technically advanced nation-state. I differ on a number of important grounds of principle, which should be stated. The first is that Switzerland was by no means always rich; her wealth and technical achievement are of relatively recent, but very rapid, foundation. In the course of that achievement many areas of Switzerland were left behind; for others, emigration, enlistment in foreign armies, and the most abject rural poverty have been thoroughly documented. While their own resources and limited trade gave a certain steadiness to the level of living in the Valais mountain villages, and while some were drawn into the active world orbit through the opening of the Simplon Tunnel and the St. Bernard Pass (much earlier than Montana), some are *still* isolated socially and economically and others have completely died or become depopulated (particularly in the Tessin).

If one took as a baseline the year 1820, it is very doubtful whether one could clearly say that the level of living of Swiss mountain villages was higher in sum than that of the Indians of Musqueam. Indeed, if we glance across the map of Europe at that time, it is most unlikely that the level of nutrition, housing, education, and perhaps health of rural peasants in parts of England, Ireland, the Scottish Highlands, Switzerland, many parts of Italy, or the Balkans was as high as that of the villager of Fiji, Polynesia, Thailand, Ceylon, Indonesia, many parts of India, and possibly some parts of Africa. This, indeed, is still true of quite important areas of Europe.

But the point is that Switzerland did develop centers of industry and technical perfection (often in rural areas or small towns), and thus by the late 19th century there was a network of communications of ever-increasing importance, spread over the countryside as well as linking cities. This made it possible for many villages, when they were ready, to plug into the national network and to participate in national growth,

---

*For the type of consideration mentioned here, see Uli Windisch, "La Communauté de Chermignon-d'en Bas," *Annales Valaisannes* (Sion), 1970, pp. 105–146.

changing professions, livelihood, style of life, and some modes of exchange in the process, with minimal residential upset.

The linkage of village to the wider world inevitably raises questions of control, authority, and influence—in short, power. This again may be looked at from the viewpoint of the village or from that of the nation: it is the first view that we are considering here. In the examples I have given above, Musqueam's first position was essentially one of resentful hostility to external power, which had the effect of at least adding to the symbolic separateness. Musqueam was not strong enough in itself to carve out an independently creative future, but in its ceremonial and other links with neighboring Salishan communities, prestige, influence, and authority in traditional forms retained a continuity. Experiments in instrumentally oriented power forms (for example, the Band Council) went on, and the time came when spokesmen for the people were able to exert internal coordination on secular business matters and to deal with national government agents as advisers rather than as bosses. In effect the law provides a considerable independence for communities such as Musqueam, *provided* that independence is backed up by a political determination to stick to one's objectives and resist dictation. Other Indian communities, subject to the same law, have in some instances knuckled under. If they once give in, they become dependent on the bureaucracy of the Indian Affairs Branch, and it is extremely difficult to recapture the initiative without expressing conflict, so vicious are the effects of misplaced paternalism.

The Swiss example is, of course, the classic instance of decentralized power, and it might be argued (though I am not sure that it could be proven) that it is the continuation of decentralization that has *forced* the communication system into its effective patterns and given the spread of commerce and industry its typically decentralized pattern as well. There is no great Paris dominating the country here. There are signs of change, with a greater federal weight against the cantons and communes in the regulation of commercial activity, and clear signs in the communities referred to that the federal weight, at least temporarily, is conflicting with commune initiatives.

In other words, both the examples selected had local political power which they were able to exercise in self-defense and for creative purposes. In the one case, most elements of the political power themselves had to be created, and their use learned; in the other, they were inherited.

Such power is always at an intermediary level between the village and nation. There is no such thing as a village political authority, when part of a national system, that is either completely autonomous or completely subservient. Village authority, whatever its form, cannot be purely internal, for any internal authority creates a situation that bears on relations with the external world. Similarly, there are always limits beyond which people will not willingly obey an autocratic power, and an authority that appears subservient must amend its actions to bear this in mind. In extreme cases, such as enforced dispossession of a people, no village authority in itself could possibly enforce the order without the intervention of outside power—that is, without giving up some element of its authority.

I stress this point because, in a great deal of commentary today, the exercise of power is treated in absolute terms. The impact of ideological considerations in social science has had the effect of obscuring the advances in the analysis of law, and power, which have been made over the past twenty years. The creation of political entities that can represent a people within a total system, and that handle the checks and balances characteristic of that system, is now called "co-option." The exercise of external bureaucratic action, even in support of village policies, and particularly when there is an ethnic or professional distinction between bureaucrat and villager, becomes "colonialism." We shall have occasion to look at these points again more closely. Here, it is perhaps worthwhile to point out that if this is so, almost the whole world is co-opted and colonialized—and a good thing, too.

One of the complicating factors in the power game consists in the influence and authority of what might baldly be called "alien impactors." These are nonvillage people whose profession and mission in life it is to intervene in village affairs and change its lifestyle.*

I propose to examine some of the assumptions and modes of action of

---

*One characteristic tack in "critical" anthropology and social science is to complain that village studies typically neglect analysis of the "impactors." The complaint is also typical in that it neglects the evidence that does not suit the stance. Malinowski made this a central part of his conception of the study of social change, and the work of Godfrey and Monica Wilson in Africa and of Ian Hogbin and Lucy Mair in Oceania involved frank and critical observations which hardly made them popular. My own Ph.D. thesis in anthropology, published in 1954 as *Changing Melanesia: Social Economics of Culture Contact*, and my 1950 book *Island Administration in the South West Pacific* both pay particular attention to the analysis of the special characteristics of "impacting" European agents such as missionaries and administrators. At a much more subtle level, the work of K. O. L. Burridge (for example, in his book *Mambu*) is particularly revealing in the analysis it provides of nonindigenous thought and activity. These are merely a very few examples of a much wider literature. "Critical" anthropologists may, if they wish, disagree with such analysis, which is by no means uniform; but when they deny that it exists, they reinforce my impression that they lack historical perspective.

the impactors as part of the later general analysis of action itself. Here it is only necessary to register a few salient features.

Despite the decline in formal colonialism, the number and range of alien impactors has increased manifold; while many of them have learned wisdom through careers of genuinely selfless service, the quantity of sheer brash arrogance has increased unbelievably.

The traditional impactors consisted of missionaries and administrators. In some colonial systems, a combination of political philosophy and, more important, a shortage of funds and manpower kept the involvement of administrators at a certain distance. The resultant "Indirect Rule" had at least the virtues of giving a greater weight than would otherwise have been the case to village decisions and speed of change and of forcing the growth of local political and jural institutions. I am old enough to have talked with individuals who have lived through the transition from fear to civil peace, and who have seen their horizons open from a few miles of thick jungle to islands and continents. The speed with which colonial administration brought about that change, in conditions in which force of arms simply would not work in any literal sense, is testimony to the village universe's yearning to be at peace, with an interest in wider humankind. It also represents possibly the greatest cultural and social achievement of the past century—a largely unheralded world revolution as important in its consequences as the Industrial Revolution.

Some initial missionary impact was equally devastating, and reinforced the concern for peace and tranquillity. But sometimes the tendentiousness and aggressive sectarianism, repressed by social controls in the home country, burgeoned overseas into social schism and full-scale violence. Paradoxically, missionaries, because of their closeness to village society and because they saw themselves as moral and spiritual leaders, only too easily identified themselves with God and righteousness. In retrospect, in those communities (the Northwest Coast of North America, and Polynesia, for example) where they gained a combination of temporal and spiritual power, they overdid the destructive use of it. In some instances, doilies and tea cosies became more important than understanding and tolerance. Yet, despite isolated instances of near total cultural destruction, the power of the village to retain some of its ideas for a generation or two was very strong, and the germs remained for later cultural flowering in a more tolerant age.

The missionary went through considerable transformation, even before the death of colonies. He came from a wide variety of backgrounds: working-class, urban districts; French, rural peasantry; good schools and bad. There was a curious mixture, varying in faith and order, of European peasants who were in many respects all too close to the people with whom they were dealing (and sometimes resented it) and intelligent, cultivated men of considerable creative power. Only in more recent years were these creative powers systematically trained and directed toward understanding. But always there was a substratum of perception, which sometimes seemed to create great theological models, as abstract and removed from village reality as mathematical economics statements, but much more often turned to the recording of language, the search for indigenous ideas, and a human laying on of hands.

The missionary had neither the resources nor the skills to do the job the administration at first tended to leave to private enterprise: to create networks of village schools, medical facilities, and the like. But for very large regions of the world, they were the pioneers of education and medicine; by mobilizing public opinion and engaging in fierce if amateurish legal battles, they did much to secure the end of forced labor, the improvement of migrant living conditions, and an end to violence. They were not always successful, and a few—as is the way with the organized Church—temporized in the present in the hope of future salvations; the worst examples of this are now in some of the land-hungry areas of Latin America. The modern missionary, in his person and his message, is now a very different person, on the whole and with some exceptions, from his 19th-century brother.

The third element in the triad is often thought of as the trader and businessman. In fact, however, it tended to be the non-European trader— Chinese or Indian perhaps—who penetrated into villages. (A major exception was North America, where, even today, the White-run Hudsons Bay trading posts strongly resemble the little trade stores of Oceania or Africa in social and economic roles.) European plantation owners and large ranchers had little demonstration effect; they even tended to employ nonlocal or immigrant labor, so that these kinds of connections were circumscribed. Yet, clearly, from their counting houses in the towns, Europeans pumped imports into the country and provided export connections which laid foundations for indigenous interest in economic growth and the capacity to pursue it.

Perhaps just as important, in many parts of the world, trading came to be defined as an alien occupation. This need not have been so. It was a curious accident of history, as the comparison between, say, Ghana (with strong indigenous trade in certain areas) and Uganda shows. The identification of trade with particular ethnic groups is always potentially explosive, since it focuses jealousy, frustration, ambition, and aggression on readily identifiable targets.

In some parts of the world, however, the European presence was colonial in the classic sense of the term. The new lands were settlement lands, and there was great variation in the degree to which the incoming settlers added aggression to the weapons of competition or merged into a tropical countryside. This kind of invasion certainly added notable dimensions to the patterns of social contact, communication, and potentialities for schism and political action. It would be quite possible to feed indices of variables linked to such factors into a computer and come out with the highly varied results represented by pre-independence Algeria, Tasmania, New Caledonia, Brazil, Rhodesia, and Angola. It is unlikely that such an exercise would have any effect on anyone's policy.

Today, in most parts of the formerly colonial world (and, of course, in countries that have been politically independent for lengthy periods, as in Latin America), the alien administrator has been replaced by political institutions and indigenous civil servants. The more recent independences usually gave a tremendous drive to do things that had village impact, and particularly to push education, agricultural change, and rural services out into the countryside. What needs to be said, however, is that this is *still* very much an alien set of operations to the villager—it comes *to* him from analyses and points of view which he usually has little or no part in forming; it is brought by men and women of different educational background, cultural predispositions, motivations, and objectives. The results are still dialectics and syntheses.

To this system have been added some extremely interesting new roles, which have now spread almost worldwide. The first is that of the international technical adviser, who often deals with rural matters from the headquarters of a Ministry or who works in the field. Far from reducing the impact of an alien presence in rural areas, independence and the growth in international aid have greatly increased it. It is now, however, no longer based on the push of a single metropolitan culture; it comes from varied cultural and political sources. This, frequently coupled with relatively low levels of relevant experience, reduces the sharpness of the impact and can create village-level confusions (imagine, for example, a Swiss aid expert followed by a Chinese). Nevertheless, it raises interesting questions about the long-term impact of confusion seen as the presence of a variety of ideas in competition. If one stops looking at the aid process as a handout of previously formed knowledge and methods, but rather thinks of it as an injection of knowledge out of which future thought and applications grow, the impact of muddle might turn out to be highly significant. In the meantime, however, the villagers may well be going through a period of puzzlement.

Added to this now are the substantial bodies of young international volunteers who tend to be shipped into rural areas to do their good works. The level of commitment, understanding, intelligence, and flexibility of such young people is extraordinarily high, and a considerable proportion achieve concrete specific results and perform useful service.* They obviously lack experience, which limits their utility as general impactors in accord with policy objectives. But they interact at different social levels and in different ways with the village populations, so that their indirect effect is rather different from that of the senior technical expert. Sometimes, where they are employed as self-directed *animateurs* or community development leaders, their inexperience and occasional youthful brashness can create effects that are the reverse of helpful, and resistance (even conflict) can be the result. Also, their use as instruments of conscious change is dependent on the way in which responsibility is structured, part of a more general question we shall examine in Chapter 13.

There are other examples of impactors on the current scene. *Animateurs* in francophone and some Spanish-speaking areas, community development leaders elsewhere, are a special brand of administrator. Youthful short-term volunteer parties, such as those invading Mexico from the United States every summer, provide another kind of international contact. And, of course, there is the professional revolutionary, who warrants particular treatment (see Chapter 15).

There is an interesting and significant characteristic of *all* those forms of human impact. Every one of them involves relatively well-educated people who come from a context of urban influence. In some instances, the individuals may have been brought up in a rural environment, but they are in a minority and the context in which they work is urban-defined. In some instances, they believe they are saving or developing rural values; they do so, however, out of a reaction from urban experience.

The city is fond of telling the countryside what it should do. I do not know of instances in which village people have offered to help cities out of their difficulties or to revolutionize them.**

---

*An excellent and balanced summary of Peace Corps involvement is contained in a review by William Mangin in the *American Anthropologist*, Vol. 74, No. 4, August 1972, pp. 983–984.

**Chinese agrarian communism might be offered as a possibility. This does not really stand up, except for those periods in which it was indeed a rural-based movement, excluded from the cities. The leaders are by no means peasants in origin or in point of view; while they are forcing rural experiences upon some city dwellers, their attitude to the traditional rural values is one of apocalypse.

CHAPTER 6

The Urban Contribution

THERE is much talk today of the ills of city living. Each issue (of pollution, overcrowding, crime, or transport) raises policy questions which cannot be answered except through taking value positions about the costs and benefits of city life. These in turn sometimes involve stereotypical ideas about urban living, with insufficient imagination directed toward the numerous variations in style that are possible and that have existed. Again, those who are caught by rural poverty and who think of the city as an instrument of upward mobility will be prepared to pay quite different costs from those who already *have* a satisfying urban existence which may be threatened.

Many of those who are pessimistic about cities continue to live in them and would not live elsewhere. This in itself says a great deal about their continuing value, and suggests that the contribution of cities is an important element in world social organization. The countryside is bound to cities in many different ways, city life with all its variation has a certain international quality, and it is in the cities that many of the most significant influences upon national government and organization have their origins.

Despite the considerable research attention that has been devoted to cities, and the extraordinary wealth of historical and comparative data that has been examined, there is little agreement about the dynamics of formation and movement. One problem is the very richness of the data and the labor required for their mining. Another has been a tendency until recently to see the city as an organism separated from, rather than integrated with, its hinterland and the surrounding socioeconomic districts, a tendency which is being corrected under the influence of geographical studies and attempts at comparative classification of rural–urban systems. A further problem has been that the proper theoretical considerations that have guided the search for materials have been unduly influenced by *a priori* theory and value preconceptions. Recent sophisticated systems models of the movement of urban characteristics have seldom if ever been free of the last two criticisms. And like the rural village, the city is not a uniform phenomenon, so that any *general* theory or understanding must eventually be able to account for quite different outcomes by playing with the variable force and timing of elements. In view of this it would be presumptuous of me to opt for one of the current theories rather than another as a matter of established truth. My task is different: to put forward something of a personal synthesis, identifying the kinds of general issues and factors that need to be elaborated by research if we are to understand the dynamics of particular cities in ways that may give us influence over their future quality and density.

One of the least satisfactory areas of knowledge and investigation is probably the one most basic to policy. What is it that turns cities into magnets for population attraction—or, in rare cases, population repulsion? Why, in other words, do people come to and leave cities?

The first, and classic, answer is that people come to increase their income. This is a "pull" factor, which may be the obverse of a "push" factor—namely, poverty, famine, or dispossession in the countryside. Rural poverty and famine, if endemic, are most unlikely to be helped by movement to the city. Where they occur, the city, in its physical arrangements and to some extent its occupations, is rather like a rural community on a larger scale. It can only support the inflow through a supply of the foods produced in the country. The same number of mouths must be fed, and migration in itself is unlikely to relieve poverty or famine. The relief will come only if the city can embark *immediately* on industry or trade that does not drain rural resources but creates an inflow of profit from abroad or from other areas where poverty and famine are not endemic. If the city is already embarked on industry, the issue is largely a distributive one. It is unlikely that a city can immediately employ large quantities of new labor quickly, but the already employed labor may be able to support some of the immigrants and may be more likely to do this if they are physically present rather than removed from sight in the villages.

Dispossession, on the other hand, may entail a restriction in rural population growth or a revolution in rural practices. Each of these conditions can have the effect of maintaining, even increasing, rural agricultural yield at the cost of under- or unemployment. Part of the motivation for movement can be the loss of rights to rural production and income (as with enclosure) or the inability to use them fully, with attendant prestige loss. The city may not clearly be better, but it is not much of a loss to move there, and an opportunity may be seized.

Both city and village can therefore be "over"-populated in relation to employment and income. But because of the differences in their character, and the continuation of some social exchange links, each continues to support the other. Indeed, in many parts of the world, even today, *the city is subsidized by the countryside* in important respects in the years prior to the establishment of sufficient industry or commerce to enable the city to support its population from its own income. For example, commercial and government wages paid to indigenous employees in Port Moresby, the capital of Papua–New Guinea, in the early 1950s were a fraction of the level required to purchase food and rent for a family at the lowest nutritional levels. The survival of families (despite high levels of tuberculosis, rickets, and other deficiency diseases) was made possible by two conditions. In many instances, families remained in rural communities as suburbs, living within kinship networks and using family land. In others, kin channels provided a flow of food to the urban dweller for which he aimed at compensation over time. Sometimes the compensation was monetary and sometimes the urban worker became a link for entrepreneurial activity (for example, by acting as agent or principal for the trade of village produce).

While this account refers to Port Moresby at a particular stage in its history, its essence is repeated in many parts of the world, including Africa and Asia. It is merely a variant of peasant marketplace movement, only in this case with at least one kin representative established in the town. The kinds of facts involved have important implications for labor and wage legislation, link to conceptions of housing policy (very seldom do public housing arrangements conceive the importance of rural visiting, and sometimes they even forbid it), are in complete contradiction to the idea of controlled visiting passes used in some parts of the world for "White" protection, and are significant for the nascent growth of enterprise in *both* rural and urban areas.

But this conception of movement drive is still limited. One gains the impression—when visiting or reading about the *bidonvilles* and shanty towns of Latin America, Africa, and Asia—that a very high proportion of the population is speculating with its lives. Sometimes this can be misleading; the slum areas have a continuity and a life of their own that pass from one generation to another, and the mere physical impression does not denote unemployment. Oscar Lewis' "culture of poverty" is relevant here. But problems are exacerbated when the *bidonville* area and population are rapidly expanding, sometimes against harsh government measures to put a stop to it.

Even here there is a certain dream of a steady income and rising expectations. But the statistical unlikelihood that this will come in any dramatic manner does not make it a dominant draw. The people who move are not fools, and they do have information. Studies showing steps in the processes of communication and decision, linked to linear programming models and conceptions of "strategy", have begun; one may expect to know a great deal more about this in the future. But what we know now indicates that nonemployment considerations must play a very great role. These include a complete difference in *material* living style from the country, with a change in the nature of the services with which one lives (water, power); an increased intensity of social interaction, in both work and recreation, but with a greater relative freedom of norm; new sights, sounds, and sensations; new ways of spending leisure time; the stimulus of ideas, varieties of religion and politics; and organizations that give a possibility for individual influence, authority, and power.

Within this context, survival and advancement depend not only on employment and perhaps rural support, neither of which may be forthcoming in individual cases, but on tapping into a distribution system and on using ingenuity to purvey one's labor and other talents. In some instances, social welfare and public aid, for example for housing, are an important part of the distribution system. So too is the linkage with already established figures in the city; wage and entrepreneurial income are spread.

But a most important part of the context (and this too raises significant principles for village development) is the rate of circulation of *everything*. Classical economic theory talked of people "taking in each other's washing," a process to which the division of labor contributed. The more people do things for others, for a return, the faster the medium of exchange circulates, and the greater the productive effect of a given quantity of monetary wealth. The intensity of social relations in a city gives considerable opportunities for this process to be expedited. It is extremely difficult to devise research techniques to investigate the implications of the quantity of money and its rate of circulation under such conditions (although it is surprising how little attention has been given to the issue). But there is evidence of great ingenuity in the way new city populations seek outlets for their imagination and energies in providing, even inventing, services for others. This is not merely tapping into a distributive system by gaining access to the more conventionally earned regular incomes of others; the activity also directly adds to the value of enterprise and increases the rate of circulation of money.

Many governments—alarmed at the costs of providing services, at direct evidence of poverty, and at the possibility of social and political unrest—try to put a brake on these processes, or at least on their superficial manifestations. They do so by trying to restrict movement to the city, by regulating city behavior (e.g., through passes) so that it has unattractive elements, by demanding evidence of employment, and by forcing investment in housing rather than in other more productive things. Most of the policies of this kind are based on the premise that employment opportunities must exist *before* migration into cities is permitted.

This premise probably puts the cart before the horse. Had such policies been in effect during the Industrial Revolution, or even in the Middle Ages, they might have led to even greater and more destructive explosion than resulted in fact from the presence of volatile, poverty-stricken, alcoholic, politically susceptible, and violent, underemployed crowds. At least until such a question is answered definitively, one should pay more attention to the dynamics of the current situation in cities, and one should balance the effects. It is quite possible that cities having apparent unemployment, large sections with low monetary income, and *a magnetic pull effect* contain vitality and creative forces which are missed in official analysis (but which the people know or sense) and can only be revealed by enquiry sensitive to the possibility.

It is also clear, at least to the anthropologist, that conventional inventive social science, while it has had a great deal to say about new forms of productive, commercial, and bureaucratic organization, has had very little to say, as yet, about alternative modes of distribution. Yet these may be fundamental to the approach to unemployment or underemployment, where enquiry shows that these are endemic (see Chapter 19).

Popular social analysis about many institutions is bedevilled by crude ideological thinking about the implications of size. Large corporations, large universities, and large cities are attacked because their ills are traced to size itself. This sort of ideology has at least the merit of challenging the alternative view, which was used to legitimize the almost unrestricted expansionism of the 19th and 20th centuries—namely, that size brought with it economies of scale, more concentrated and coordinated power, and an opportunity to extend rationality to a greater range of activities. But size itself is never an isolated variable, and the effects of size upon organized life depend on the way in which other elements in the institutions work.

In cities, for example, large size may be said to tend toward anonymity and impersonalization. But this is never fully true, and the weight of the factor depends in turn on patterns of communication. Thus, for example, one could argue that for all cities there is a basic interaction between the inhabitants of a residential unit—let us say an apartment—and between each of these inhabitants and the service units of the city (hospital, store) and contacts at places of occupation (school, office, factory). From this point on, variations emerge in striking ways. In some cities, or for some families, the social world may be restricted to the basics. In other conditions, there is interaction between a number of households linked by occupational contacts. In yet others, the links between households are independent of occupational contacts. Sometimes the number and range of continuous social interactions are in fact greater than those which would be normal in villages of the region.

Further, the possibilities of chance contacts with acquaintances are not as limited as the idea of the impersonal city would imply. Even in the largest of cities, individuals move in habituated ways, and a high proportion of such movement (for shopping, commuting, recreation) can be predicted on the basis of past behavior. The paths of movement crisscross, setting up increased chances of contact. (Writers of detective novels and thrillers have sensed this; their characters, located in New York, Paris, or London, usually seem to know the "hang-outs" and patterns of movement of other characters.) Even complete strangers visiting a large city are aware of the rather weird sensation of running across a friend from the home town by chance in a public park, a square, an art gallery, or a cinema. The low statistical chance if one treats the city as composed simply of randomly moving people is replaced by a much higher chance if the movement is not random.

Thus, the city cannot be said to be impersonal (unless for visitors) except in the sense that *over and above* one's personal links one meets individuals one has not met before, and there is a huge range of human activity going on which impinges on one's senses without personal connectedness. In the rural areas, such nonconnected activities are for the large part outside visibility or perception—in other faraway villages or towns. This is also true in the city, but you are nevertheless surrounded by known activity that has nothing to do with you. There is a social environment which impinges on your senses without creating social interaction. This is interpreted by some observers as reducing the individual's scale, and increasing his anonymity, as releasing him from social bonds or losing him in the crowd (depending on your value premises).

But here, too, physical–social arrangements change the reality. There is a world of difference between those large African, Asian, and old European cities, which are rather agglomerations of *quartiers*, and some of the modern cities of North America and Australasia. The *quartier* is a relatively self-contained neighborhood (containing all necessary facilities for its existence), over and above which there may (or may not) be imposed other centers for specialized functions, drawing together a set of occupational or commercial interests from each of the *quartiers*. Such arrangements are even known in North America, and some partial redevelopment of them is taking place through the interactions nucleated around neighborhood shopping areas, churches, and the like. But the special characteristics of the *quartier* are the intensity of neighborhood interaction—the village writ large—and the very low level of contact with other parts of the city which a high proportion of its inhabitants may exhibit.

Quite opposed to this concept is the existence in cities of areas organized around highly specialized part-time activities—a financial district of tall buildings linked together by telephone, almost uninhabited at night (City of London or Toronto, so different from financial Geneva), a night-lively recreational district revealed to be sleazy and hung-over the next morning, a suburbia when children are at school and both parents at work.

One may see the difference in philosophy applied to the construction of new apartment areas in, on the one hand, cities like Bangkok, Geneva, and to some extent Paris, and on the other hand Vancouver, Toronto, and to some extent (though this is changing) the outskirts of London. In Bangkok and Geneva, there is a high degree of integration of services into the apartments (laundry, dry cleaning, newsstands, coiffeurs, cafés, banks, restaurants and bars, and recreational facilities). Some of the French examples have gone even further, with the integration of apartment areas and multipurpose American-style complete shopping and commercial facilities on a very large scale, so large that the neighborhood character of the Bangkok and Geneva examples is lost. In Vancouver and Toronto, on the other hand, largely as a result of planning rules, and in the English "new towns" of the late 1940s and early 1950s, functions are separated so that the shopping area does not impinge on the quiet and serenity of suburban homes. The same sorts of rules apply to apartments, with the service and commercial conveniences removed to nearby but distinct locations. Partly as a result, such conveniences have not developed, and certainly the neighborhood–congregation aspect is played down.

Which style of living does one choose? Which is the better city to build? The reality is that the building and conceptualization of the arrangements is on the whole *not* normally done by the future inhabitants. Have you ever heard of a large-scale developer obtaining his clients *before* he builds and *then* building to their specifications? This is not very likely, save for large corporate partners. So people on the whole express their preferences after the building is complete, and then move for considerations (price, pressure) that include substantial compromises and adaptations. At least some suburban areas (despite packages of rules and regulations) and *bidonvilles* (despite poverty of resources) do give residence occupiers some room for self-expression and creativity in their constructions.

As for the authorities—architects, planners, promoters, and city councils—on the whole their plans seem to be dictated by intelligent guesswork (as to the state and wishes of the market), their own aesthetics, organized pressure groups, and profit-making or tax-producing self-interest. There have been a very few studies of the value premises of some of the groups who actually do the building and authorize the physical relationships.* Much remains to be done to link such values to the real aspirations and mixes of interests of expected inhabitants.

Further, one wonders about the extent to which inhabitants' views of their own values are themselves affected by the ethnosocial scientific theories presented to them. For example, to what extent were North Americans *taught* that suburbia was an environment that would reduce tension and produce a peaceful family life, a haven from the battles of income earning? Opinion has largely swung the other way, producing a different ethnosocial scientific theory; but to what extent do the new popular beliefs correspond with social processes? If we find out and know about those processes in various parts of the world, what effect will that knowledge have upon the dynamics of popular belief, changing the validity of the processes before our very eyes? Even when we feel we do know about the processes, there are still difficult value balances to sort out, and one often doubts whether urban authorities and advisers have the skill or the legitimacy to do the balancing. When, for example, does a neighborhood become a ghetto?—or when we use such terms are we mainly engaged in manipulating language as an instrument for political objectives? What value does one ascribe to the desirability of separate

---

* In addition, there is a schematically interesting project carried out by the social scientists of the Musée des Arts et Traditions Populaires in Paris, who undertook research designed to identify and integrate the interests of potential tourists with traditional regional styles for the construction of tourist centers in the south of France.

identity and self-determination to the parts of a city, as against the desirability of coordination and the corporate structure of the whole?

At this point one comes to the political structure of the city—the way in which considerations of power and influence, expressed both in formal authority and informal pressure, lead to decisions and consequent action. Here the balance between localized, professional, even private interest, and the concern for the overall good and for coordination of services and economies is crucial.

It is here too that we can see interlinked roles for the social scientist as investigator, as inventor of social systems, and as policy adviser. While the middle role—that of inventor of social systems—is to some degree mixed with the other two, it consists of tasks that, on the whole, social scientists eschew. I have done some of it, and realize the considerable air of unreality that accompanies such an exercise (see, later, Chapter 16). Nevertheless, to be effective, policy advisers must stay within or very close to the system they are observing. This restricts the slightly utopian act of inventing social structures, although sometimes it can lead to the total unreality of anti-rational "revolutionary" statements. There are possibilities of intermediary inventions, which indicate drastic alternatives without implying total social and political upheaval. While it is unlikely that they will be directly accepted, they become incorporated in the issues to be examined, and some amendment of them may come into being.

The reason for mentioning this here is that the field of public administration and political representation for city government (and indeed for regional government within nation-states) appears to be more than ready, in many parts of the world, for imaginative social invention. Much social science activity goes into describing and understanding existing systems, "activist" social scientists become involved in pressure group citizens' organizations for one cause or another, and advice may be given for modest changes in political structure or for the better operation of the existing machine toward certain ends. Yet very rarely does one see this kind of experience translated into a normative attempt to define the organization that might have some hope of running the city better in terms of the desires of the inhabitants.

It is beyond my task to attempt this here, and in any event resulting solutions will be particularistic. But at least some indication may be given of the types of situation that suggest that inventive thought in this field could be useful. In some instances cities are run by nominated officials who may have some independence from centralized government or may be given decentralized powers. City government becomes administration, handled by a civil service. In other instances there are divisions of labor and authority between officials representative of central government and elected officials and councils. In yet others, the central government removes itself from direct involvement in city affairs, channeling its funding influence by law or negotiation to responsible city authority, directly elected, and contenting itself with the establishment of an overall framework of law within which policy works.

Many of the newer rapidly expanding cities are plagued with the problem of moving political boundaries, which, once established, become hard and fast. *Barrios* and *bidonvilles* located on outskirts may have no early linkage to the city electoral system, and may in fact be outside the formal boundaries. The apparent social and economic gulf between the established and the mushrooming parts of the city make it extremely difficult to conceive of a unified policy or one that serves both sections of the population equally. Other cities expand in fact, but not necessarily in political form, to overrun surrounding units of local government. The difficulties, compromises, and many failures in attempting to create or impose metropolitan government when such overrunning occurs are legion.

In part such difficulties come about because each of the overrun units believes itself to have its own character (which incorporation into the metropolis will change) and because, of course, taxation and accountancy predictions are always capable of challenge and debate. Metropolitan units that are in effect federations of former local governments usually contain local bodies which are most uneven in wealth, population, area, and objectives. Sometimes this would be easier to achieve if the main nucleus could split itself up prior to federation. To give an *imaginary* example, if each of the *arrondissements* of Paris had its own elected and responsible council, and if Paris city government consisted of a federation of such councils, it would be easier to incorporate neighboring units of local government into the federation as these became urbanized. On the other hand, if Paris were nonfederated, it would be rather difficult to incorporate Vincennes, Neuilly, St-Cloud, or Sèvres without solving serious issues of relative power and flows of expenditure.

A modification of this kind of approach is to be found in ward systems. Some of these are restricted to defining areas within the city from which representatives are elected, on the theory that this creates balance and the representatives can be spokesmen for the local point of view. This does not provide, however, the type of bargaining power that would come if the ward had its own elected council with statutory authority and some administrative responsibility. The individual ward representative system has also on occasion been criticized for leading to corruption as a result of the lobbying bargains to which it can point.

Dissatisfaction with city (and other local) forms of government is now quite widespread, and perhaps more visible through the effervescent emergence of local citizens' groups. Formal voting on issues still tends to be uncommitted and low, in part a reflection of the feeling that the issues preoccupy the politicians and the political citizens rather than the ordinary inhabitants, partly because inhabitants' concerns are even closer to home than the seat of city government, and partly because the structure seems somewhat removed from voting influence. There are, I am sure, other reasons as well, but these are the ones that seem most directly relevant for the structure of the organization.

In addition, in some instances there is a movement of power and authority *away from* city government and into the hands of other groups. Urban community development, for example, has been a movement that has frequently sought out the leaders of voluntary organizations (such as chambers of commerce, churches, and welfare groups) and banded them together into a powerful and influential structure. The new unit— permanent or temporary, formal or informal—has then taken on the formation of policy and even some of its administration. Such a develop- ment implies a serious criticism of the effectiveness of existing city government, but it also weakens it. City government tends to be treated as "just another group," or a service that is "over there"—part of the environment. The community development organization cannot get along without city government, since from time to time it must deal with such material things as sewage systems or rehousing, or must work within established legal structures for aspects of social welfare.

Community development in this form (of which there are a number of examples in the United States) has the philosophical and tactical advan- tage of building upon voluntary participation (and sometimes increasing it), but it has the curious effect of partially bypassing and weakening the democratically elected decision makers, the mayor and council. It has an advantage in that such lobbying as goes on contains a greater proportion of open and responsible pressure than that which occurs under other circumstances behind closed doors. But where the balances lie is hard to determine, at least *a priori*.

Another way of seeking participation, but with retention of the elec- toral process, is to decentralize functions still further. Although I once worked out some of the implications of this as an exercise in social invention during an enquiry into the provision of recreational services in communities in the Vancouver metropolitan region, I do not know of instances where this approach has in fact been tried, and I can see several reasons why it should not be—complexity for one. Hence, the discussion remains in the realm of the imagination.*

It was quite apparent in the course of the study I undertook that householders, despite the fact that they lived in quite small but urbanized communities, felt distant from the decision making of local government. They also felt that the particular services in question, though provided on a very high standard, were removed from their day-to-day needs. Only one or two multipurpose community halls could be built, and many of those interested in recreation could not be bothered with the movement and the formal arrangements that were necessary for their use. An additional approach, which would not destroy the function of community recreation services in a few central locations for those who did participate, seemed to be indicated. This pointed to the provision of services within very easy walking distance of homes, which in turn meant the identification of the facilities in which small neighborhood groups could be interested—daytime playlots for children, simple structures for indoor games, skating rinks, and the like (all the things that in some other countries are provided for by combinations of pubs and street games). These were precisely the things that local government, interested in bureaucratic structure and capital-intense service provision, was not ready to imagine.

In turn, such an arrangement is fundamentally established on the principle of very small-scale identification of need and on participation. The study suggested the identification of neighborhood blocks (rather easy to do in this particular group of communities because there were obvious geographical division points) in which close-to-the-people services could be run by local committees. This, in turn, suggested that local government could be built up from such committees—either by election out of the neighborhood blocks or appointment from the committees themselves—and that certain kinds of administrative funds could be allocated to the committees for their direct expenditure.

Whether such an approach would work can only be determined by trial in appropriate circumstances. Certainly, the funding of local action programs in the United States through locally controlled organizations

*It is possible that the street committee system of present-day Peking is comparable.

has run into serious criticism. It seems, however, that this is not the same sort of approach in any event. The linkage of such organizations with formal local government was, almost on principle, very tenuous indeed. Once again we have the tendency, which seems common in the United States, to create something that *rivals* anything that can be called a government. But the scale of funding, the enormity of the job to be done, the atmosphere of distrust, the possibilities of corruption, and quite cynical political manipulation on all sides, also must be taken into account.

Behind the generalities I have discussed lie some of the same concerns that anthropologists customarily deal with in rural settings. It is tempting to approach city problems on a massive scale, with a necessary bureaucratic apparatus. But, as in the rural areas, the large bureaucracy must in the end come to terms with individuals and small segments of population. To do this successfully requires advance analysis of conditions, sensitive to local nuances, rather than ideological, *a priori*, or universalistic asseverations. Individuals, groups, and subcommunities are linked in networks of mutual interaction and dependence, which must be mapped and understood for each urban unit. The significance of the map will be governed partly by the city's connection with other areas and sources of power, from hinterland to nation. To complicate matters further, the population is likely to be in flux, and even if there is stability and continuity in a demographic sense, there can be no guarantee that values and the balance of interests will be unchanging. Can the bricks and mortar that give physical form to the life and character of the city be modified to reflect the changing values?

Urban anthropology, which can address itself to some of these issues, began its life in Africa with the study of migrant labor in mining towns. But it is now an important subfield of the discipline, building on studies in India, Latin America, Europe, and North America. The orientation still tends to be toward ethnic enclaves or poverty groups, but the full impact of the anthropologist's perspective will not be felt until there are more sensitive, detailed studies, which link work and family, pressure groups and values, neighborhoods and power. The sociologist's normal techniques of sampling and the use of surveys need extending, but they also need to be supplemented by the more sensitive concerns of the anthropologist with cultural processes and small-scale observational examples. The challenge for data, knowledge, and comparative understanding has enormous consequences for the organization and manpower of the social sciences, which we are far from handling effectively.

CHAPTER 7

Elements of the Nation-state

THE 19th century was a time of nationalism—of the unifying and creation of nations as independent political forces riding on the revolutionary waves emerging particularly from France, and inspiring indigenous national leaders. Nevertheless, nation-states pre-dated this great European and American movement, for example the United Kingdom, France, Spain, Portugal, China, and Japan. By a kind of extension of 19th-century ideology, the later achievement of independence by colonial peoples is interpreted as part of the push of nationalism. School interpretations, as I well remember them, tend to be built on some such concept as "The Age of Nationalism" or the "spirit of nationalism," in which the force of peoples of common ethnic and cultural background to unify themselves politically against outside domination almost attains the quality of a mystic independent variable, controlling the actions of heroes almost against their will.

In fact, despite its apparent central place in history, the idea of "nation" is misleading and ambiguous, and the unifying of peoples of the same cultural heritage in a common political territory does not stand up to examination. It was not cultural unity that forged the nation-state—it was the other way round. National unity is strictly political, symbolized by a central "independent" (this word will be reexamined in the next chapter) government, almost always bringing together peoples of *different* cultural heritages.

First, let us consider the idea of nation. The original idea is very old in human civilization, although it was not apparently adopted into the French and English languages until the revival of classical knowledge in the 11th and 12th centuries. The word is derived from the Latin *natio*, associated with *birth*; it was the concern with common ancestry that brought the use of the word "nation" into being. Political states in Roman times were empires—only barbarians were nations. Empires worked through the domination of peoples; barbarians might in time dominate

96

too, but their most evident characteristics were *tribal*. Even the Roman world was more complex than this, but the distinction (particularly as associated with the word "nation" as it was first used) was important. However, the idea of common birth could only be mythological, so that it extended to imply a birth into a common culture, which, as one dictionary puts it, revolves around history, language, religion, and economy. An anthropologist would add other features. In this sense the word "nation" was used even in the 18th and 19th centuries, when it was supposed to be colored by the lights of modern trappings to refer to tribal peoples in America, Oceania, and Africa.

Indeed the modern nation-state is by no means conceptually necessary for the self-centeredness and independence of the "we" of a tribal nation and the "they" of the external world. One does not need government as we know it to get along perfectly well with a feeling of identity reinforced by kinship, and ceremonial and social exchange, which puts an effective boundary between "us" and "them." Indeed, there are many peoples now *enclosed within* nation-states who retain their independence in this sense, who are left alone to varying degrees, and who seem to be quite happy to be ignored.

However, conditions arise in which the isolation is not so happy. One set—which clearly operated in Europe, Asia, prehistoric America, and Africa—was the impermanence of the cultural boundary as a political defense. It was of little help against an aggressor determined to obtain land, slaves, cattle, or loot. Indeed, the mythological history of almost all cultures refers to the dispossession of neighboring peoples as the primal claim to ancestral legitimacy.

It is important to note that such violent interactions incorporated foreigners into the tribal system only as individuals or chattels. But there came times when political genius or the pressure of events suggested other solutions. At the point at which the principle "destroy thy neighbor" was complemented (not replaced) by the principle "incorporate thy neighbor," we had the beginnings of the modern nation-state.

One does not need to go far back into history to observe this. Largely as a reaction to external White aggression and threat, African Bantu tribal groups in the 19th century had to make use of sophisticated strategy to defend themselves. That strategy included the colonization of border areas by specially created military-economic units, for which tribal manpower was insufficient. Members of other tribal groups were conquered or entered into alliance, and in either case were incorporated into what came to be called kingdoms. With the entry into the political unit of groups with differing languages and cultures, ordinary tribal arrangements no longer sufficed as a basis of political unity. An additional impetus was given to the forging of new administrative devices and ways of securing the operational loyalty and internally centered interactions of the new members.

Government, with its secular administrative overtones, was born through the need to establish devices that dealt with the issues of handling peoples of *different* cultures. Government was not necessary under conditions of tribal cultural unity.*

Once having identified this principle, one can see that *no* nation-state of any effectiveness is based on unicultural origins. Certainly, one culture usually predominates, though even here a division of labor is associated with different cultures. Sometimes the ideal of cultural unity gives a certain superficial force to the emergent dominant culture and, as in the case of the United Kingdom and modern France and Germany, there comes to be a single culture which, with some distribution of emphases, far outweighs any other variant. But these cultures were forged *after* the creation of "national" administration, not before it.

To hear nationalists speak of England, France, or Germany now, one would think that the unity of their cultures had always existed, its origins buried in prehistory. Certainly many elements of the dominant cultures have prehistorical antecedents, but in these instances clear cultural dominance only dates back from five to thirty generations, which is a very short period of time. England was, before central government, a mass of warring tyrannies, some based on languages and political power alien to the island. The Norman Conquest, which ultimately created England as a political force, was not undertaken in the name of cultural unity. Only the Napoleonic conception of full centralization, with Paris as the Mecca, extending the notion of unity to an intellectually imposed, relatively static language created the politicocultural phenomenon that is France. In the United Kingdom, the troubles of Ireland indicate the fragility of the unity concept; and Scottish, Welsh, and Cornish cultural manifestations have political and social significance. In France, despite centralization, there is far less unity than appears on the surface, and a Canadian troublemaker would have no difficulty in gaining revenge for de Gaulle's "*Vive le Québec*

---

* The importance of the transition to a state in which secular administration supplants or overlies unities based solely on social exchange cannot be overemphasized (though this is not to deny the use of social exchange mechanisms within a context of standard administration). It has often been pointed out, for example, that charismatic religion succeeds in becoming a political force only if there is an administration standing behind the religious message.

Libre" in Brittany or Basque country. On a nonpolitical level, regional cultural differences are considerable and very much alive.

The three great examples of national creation in the 19th century were Germany, Italy, and Greece. Germany was brought to heel by Prussian dominance, the definition of what it is is still not settled, its regional differences are now recognized in the West by a federated structure, and its official written language has only recently been imposed over dialectical variants. The cultural differences of Italy are much greater than the crude north–south dichotomy. Although (despite differences in style) one would hardly notice it now, the Sicily that gave Garibaldi his unifying toehold was linguistically and culturally as different from Rome as was Alexandria. In fact if not in principle, Greek nationalism in the 20th century has been a history of unity through the exercise of force; as an example of the national ideal, the less said about Greece the better.

The methods and philosophies that nation-states have used to handle the issues of multiculturalism have been widely different. Such differences are among the most fundamental indices of their qualitative character. In almost all instances, until very recent history, the State has operated with the notion that uniform culture is the ideal, and continued multicultural expressions are to be thought of as quaint anomalies, nuisances which must be borne, or threats to national unity.

The policy of Nazi Germany, extended and inherited from that of Prussia (though with very different class implications), does not need, nor does it bear, description. Weak, but still vicious, expressions of similar policies covered most of Eastern Europe up to World War II, and from time to time, both Czarist and Soviet Russia gave vent to similar activities. The dominance over minority cultures through their identification as scapegoats, their persecution, and their ultimate removal—almost never entirely successful—has been characteristic of pogroms through the ages, but the past two centuries have seen ultimately refined versions. At the present time, a few of the newer States, of which Uganda and Libya have been the most prominent examples, have shown signs of moving in the same direction.

A variant which was as drastic in its day as anything perpetrated in Nazi Germany is part of the brutal colonizing history of overseas Anglo-Saxon settlements, in which the United States and Australia share first prize. The deliberate cold-blooded destruction of the Tasmanians differed from the Nazi concentration camps only in that men and women were hunted and shot instead of being imprisoned and gassed; that the Australians seem to have lost the act from their consciousness, whereas the Germans are engaged in expiation; and that in the German case the hysteria and brigandage of the events were placed in the context of a legitimizing political philosophy. On mainland Australia and in the United States some of the threatened cultures are still living, in the latter case thriving and becoming a major part of the tide of guilt which pervades American thought.

There are yet other variants of cultural suppression. Apartheid separates, through legal and political action, members of one culture from another, giving each a defined set of roles and limiting interaction to contexts such as master–servant, patron–client. The South African view of this is easily attacked since it is accompanied by a deliberate racial philosophy, and is a matter of total national policy. Elsewhere, similar conditions exist as a result of social pressure and class distinction, without the necessity of special legal provisions, though these may be intermixed. Many would argue that the Black, the Chicano, and the Puerto Rican in the United States, the Maori at one time in New Zealand, and the Algerian in pre-independence Algeria, experienced similar conditions. They did, but there are still nuances, and one can see that the cultural barriers sometimes have openings, so that boundary interactions and mobilities can be expressed as matters of degree.

It is also possible to have a national cultural domination that does not necessarily express itself wholly in political or commercial domination. The philosophy of France—both internally and as applied to civilized man in former colonies—is that of "one culture" in an even more pervasive and uniform direction than has ever been achieved elsewhere. This has involved centralized cultural administration (what other country would have a group of Cabinet Ministers signing *décrets* governing the correct use of the French language, imposing it on civil servants, and enjoining the citizenry to follow suit?), and to some extent the relegation of numerous, and in some instances quite powerful, regional cultural forces to the status of folklore. (In European intellectual thought generally, as evidenced by the organization of academic studies, there is an almost universal distinction between "culture"—with a national and middle-class bias—and "*argot-patois*" and "folklore"—with regional or working-class implications.)

It is perhaps of interest to compare the mythology and practice of French and Anglo-Saxon cultural advocacy. There is a popular view that the French have been more tolerant than the English in matters of race relations, both at home and in their colonies. There is also a view that the English in their colonies did more to encourage, or at least to allow, indigenous political and cultural self-expression. The French had the imperial philosophy of spreading French civilization, but at the same time keeping it pure. The English believed in "Indirect Rule" and ultimately in Trusteeship.

Such differences certainly existed, but they seem to be in the realm of political philosophy and formal statement rather than in that of direct results. The formal centralism of France, inherited from Napoleon, was more evident than the behind-the-scenes centralism of the Colonial Office. The separation of the élite of French culture from the *autochtones* was much greater than in English colonies, and has been carefully nurtured into the present by continuing French influence. This had the effect, however, of maintaining important self-contained indigenous cultural units that were different in form but nevertheless similar to the results of Indirect Rule. The sexual and social tolerance attributed to the French was largely the result of large numbers of working class and peasant settlers admixed with indigenous people, but it was more sexual than social, and (as Algeria and racial incidents in metropolitan France show) it did not stand up to crisis or pressure any more than with the English. It is also doubtful whether there has been much difference between the French and English treatment of colored colonials, and now of the representatives of new nation-states, who have been educated at higher educational institutions in France and England and have acquired the associated sophistication and metropolitan culture.

Both England and France have thought of the culture for which they were responsible as moving in a single direction defined by social and cultural leaders. Since World War II, England has loosened up its conception somewhat. The influence of able men and women of provincial or working-class background as they have moved into positions of cultural creativity or administrative power (and into universities) has increased the melting-pot aspect of English society, though by no means destroying the influence or dominance of a certain cultural layer. In France, the influence of the *grandes écoles* is much more rigorously established. The United States and Australia (despite—in the latter case, particularly—a strong weight in favor of the dominance of an Anglo-Saxon culture) perhaps express most consciously the ideals of the melting pot. The immigrant tends to be seen as contributing to national life by merging with it and suppressing (at least in his children) his traditional cultural heritage, although at same time transmitting those little bits of it that have "value" as a gift to his host community.

The melting pot works, but it does not work completely. There is a strong tendency for immigrants to be attracted to communities where there are people of similar background, at least for important transitional periods. Such "poles" are cultural rather than national, and are sometimes linked to exporting communities in the homeland. Thus, a high proportion of the Japanese community of Canada came from a village significantly called Amerika-Mura, and northern Italians do not generally choose to live with Sicilians. It has been noted, too, that once these clusters start forming, they become operational. They develop services and functions that keep the external–internal communications moving and assist in further migration (sometimes in both directions). Also, members of the community turn to each other for professional, artisanal, and commercial services, thus creating the processes of "taking in each others' washing," which we have already seen to be so significant for economic viability.

Despite the melting-pot philosophy and its undoubted influence and dominance over the whole, cultural differentiation remains within it and is even reinforced. Further, curious differences begin to emerge where migration results in continued cross-border communication. There are not sufficient studies of the impact of migration on home communities, particularly when there is the expectation of the return of the emigrant. The huge scale of contemporary international labor migration in Europe is now seen to have created more or less *permanent* continuing communities of non-national immigrant labor, so much so that a group of European countries has recently called upon UNESCO to begin a program of investigation and advice connected with the educational problems of children caught up in the process.

It is well known that migrants frequently establish a pattern of remittances to relatives at home, or visit their former communities to display wealth, assist churches, or even to retire. But this has been interpreted largely on an individual, or a one-generation kinship, base. Current phenomena suggest that a greater revolution may be occurring. Whole classes of Spaniards move to Switzerland to spend time in the hotel trade—not to stay in Switzerland, but to return to Spain with new, saleable skills. Northern Italians have moved to North America and have returned home disillusioned or with capital to invest as they judge that Italian conditions open competitive possibilities. Communities in labor-exporting countries in Europe (paralleled by Japanese labor demand exerted in Asia) are becoming differentiated from their nonexporting neighbors as the influence of the to-and-fro movement manifests itself.

The greater intensity and new roles of migration are thus creating differences within the exporting nation-states as well as the receiving ones. Further, there is a sense in which the culture of China, India, Italy, Portuga., or Yugoslavia is not coterminous with the national boundary, but extends through real connections internally into other "nations."

One further major variant needs to be examined. This is the case in which cultural difference within the nation-state is regarded as positive, to be encouraged, and to be allowed political expression, provided it does not threaten the existence of the political unit. In one form or another, this situation now influences the culture of a considerable number of nation-states.

In Switzerland, cultural pluralism is linked to the symbols of language and religion. The cultural boundaries do not necessarily coincide with the political boundaries of the cantons which make up the Confederation, but the considerable decentralization of power even to the commune level makes quite subtle differences in way of life a possible basis for organic unity. The politicization of cultural differences is leading the canton of Berne to move reluctantly toward a separate status, perhaps ultimately cantonal independence, for its Jura region.* At the same time, there are cross-border regional links: contact between the people of the French and Swiss Jura, or between the people of the valley of Hérémance (Switzerland), Chamonix (France), and Aoste (Italy) is based on close cultural affinity. (Because of its French cultural base, the Val d'Aoste was one of the first areas of Italy to be accorded a degree of regional administrative autonomy and because of Italian slowness is establishing cable television in French from France and Switzerland.)

In Canada there are two layers to the issue. A political primacy is given to the autonomy of a French and English political-cultural base. The geographical location of the two cultures, however, does not coincide with the Provinces, which have regional autonomy, and beneath the provincial level, unlike the situation in Switzerland, the units of local government have neither the cultural autonomy nor the political strength of communes. So that, within the Provinces the position of English and French minorities is not normally deliberately expressed through the medium of local government.** While special attention is accorded to their position, in many respects they are little different from settlements of the mosaic of other cultures that serve to make up Canada—Ukrainian, German, Scandinavian, Mennonite, Hutterite, Japanese, Chinese, Sikh, Italian, Portuguese, Indian, Eskimo, Austrian, Greek. Such communities

---

* This was achieved by referendum in 1975.
**There are some exceptions, such as French-speaking communities near Winnipeg.

do not expect to have administrative autonomy (unless they form local government units by accident), but they might well do so in time. While there are definite and strong forces within Canada pushing for the absorption of such communities into the French or English melting pots, there are probably even stronger forces in the other direction. Canada has not settled on its path, but the attachment to multiculturalism may well win out.

These are issues that require settlement in almost all the newer nation-states. In many they are complicated by the lack of a single *lingua franca* (yet Switzerland is evidence that this is not an insurmountable problem) and by the colonial (and in some cases still unsettled) artificiality of the national boundary. It is, however, remarkable what a boundary, however artificial and apparently unreasonable, can do to provide a focus on internal unity of administration, and a sense of cohesion, unity, and conjoined fate.* Further, in some countries the tribal or cultural minorities have internal political structures that differ substantially from those of their neighbors in conception, operation, and modes of adjustment to new conditions. It would be difficult to imagine greater differences, from this point of view, than those between the Ibo and the Emirates of Nigeria, the Bantu and non-Bantu peoples of Uganda, the peoples of North and South Sudan, the Hill Tribes and the plainsmen of Thailand, West Irian and the Menangkabau inside Indonesia. One could go on and on.

In addition, the presence of such groups constitutes a tremendous challenge to nation builders, because (as tragic events have shown us) many internal cultural units are large enough to carry independent political status and they can opt for it, leading to revolt and civil war. In part the first task of a government is to create a civil service and administration which gives outlets and power to representatives of diverse cultures and enables them to work together despite major differences in orientation; if not, it must provide some other solution.

There is no single solution. But it has become apparent that the multicultural State is going to be the most common for many years to come (if not forever), that it will govern by far the largest proportion of the

---

* I recall noting the same phenomenon in internal administrative units in such countries as the Solomon Islands or New Guinea. The linguistic units can cover very small populations and, while a Swiss-type commune would be possible theoretically, the poverty of administrative resources makes the viable local government unit larger; hence, it is not uncommon to find several linguistic groups linked together and subscribing to a "district" unity. The identification with such artificial "districts" is often surprisingly intense.

human population, and that many countries that consider themselves to be unicultural may not be able to continue to do so for long.

At this point one may raise some questions about the nature of social groups as components of a political nation-state. In considering manifestations of social structure on a large scale, and identifying group differences within that structure, analysts have tended to concentrate on a few major types. We have, for example, societies in which differences are expressed through lineage arrangements, others in which there is reported to be a caste system, and yet others in which social or economic class is the differentiating force. Others, such as those we have just been describing, exhibit parallelism of political autonomy, subject to a central coordinating mechanism, containing units each of which has its own structural character. The tendency is to treat each of these types as separable constructs, with little connection between them.

One can, however, treat them as variations on a set of themes, in which case the differences of result may be great but the differences of process not so great. This may be put in conceptually dynamic terms. It would be relatively easy to manipulate lineage systems in such a way that they became caste systems. All that is needed is to give lineages strong incentives to retain property in order to accumulate it in their own hands to the exclusion of others, and particularly to the exclusion of affines. Following this step, one shows that it is to the advantage of the lineage in this process to become endogamous instead of exogamous. At the same time, one grants symbolic and if possible administrative status to the now endogamous lineages on a hierarchically differentiated basis. We then have castes.

If instead of conscious manipulation we write social, economic, or historical forces, something like this occasionally happens. The reinforcement of "chiefly" families by colonial administrations pushed in this direction.

More important, however, is the analytic status of the comparison. Only three variables are involved, and all of them represent boundary interactions of the groups. If a is an index of property transfer across the boundary, b an index of marriage across the boundary, and c an index of flows of political and religious services and authority such that hierarchical differences can be observed, then the difference between lineages and castes is not so much a matter of *kind*, but of *degree*. Actual human societies could in theory be described by weighted indices.

This indeed is what happens in practice. A perfectly noncaste lineage system would have high a, high b, and low or zero c. A perfectly caste-like system would have zero a, zero b, and high c. Any real system will be found to be somewhere between these extremes (there is, for example, considerable and growing evidence for Indian caste mobility).

We can also perform the same sorts of exercises for linkages between other social structure "types." To do so effectively, we need to introduce a few additional variables. These include the expression of corporate identity through political, administrative, or religious acts; the size of the units considered as a proportion of the total polity; the rate of cultural and idea communication across the boundary; and whether the flows of transfer across the boundary are conceived to be hierarchical (up or down) or parallel (across). Class can then, for example, be thought of as being akin to caste, but with much greater mobilities and boundary transfers; or akin to lineage, but with not only greater transfers but a difference in their significant across-boundary direction. Furthermore— and this is a fundamental qualification to the utility of class as a current concept in any but a distributive sense—it is very seldom the case that social class has *any* corporate identity. Similarly, parallel cultural groups in multicultural situations can be analyzed to exhibit a great deal of variation in the nature of the boundaries and the rates of transfer across them. It can be shown that these are variants in factors we have already set out for groups making up other types of social structure. The variable of corporate identity, of course, has a controlling role to play.

I should not hide my bias and opinion that the tremendous stress placed upon the identity of social classes, and their function as forces of social movement, is misplaced, and has served to distort a great deal of the analysis of social processes. Once we open up the question of internal cultural boundaries, and consider the *variations* in the phenomena that relate to them, we find ourselves dealing with a much more complex and empirically real mosaic of human organization. Indeed, we must introduce an additional variable, which is the degree to which the cultural groups in question are *role-complete*—that is, the degree to which they encompass the total roles expressed by their individual members. Classically, a lineage tends to be role-complete, enclosing the whole world of its members, although modern lineages may be less than this since, for example, its members may trade or work across its boundary. On the other hand, a political party, a church, or a business enterprise in a modern capitalist community is a good deal less than role-complete.

So, then, a nation-state, conceived of as a social system, is composed of a large number of group elements, all of which have boundaries which set them off one from another. But the boundaries are never entirely closed on all fronts, and the dimensions of movement across them provide the cements which tie the State together. An important quality associated with adaptation is the degree to which the boundary movement can be said to represent an *articulation* of the parts, one to another. That is, for example, do changes in the movements across the boundaries, including the passage of resources and information, bring about adjustments in the behavior of the receiving group?

This question is fundamental to the efficacy of many theories of economic, social, and political systems as guides of policy. It is no use, for example, to rely on multiplier or demonstration effects if boundary transfers do not in fact take place, or if, when they do, the decisions of organizations or the behavior of group members do not react or adapt. Yet the strange thing is that indices of such important phenomena have not been developed, statistical services do not monitor them, and sociologists and economists are more interested in putting together indices of *results* (per capita income, rate of crime, number of telephones per household) than of processes.

It is more important to our understanding, and to the accuracy of social policy, to be able to monitor changes in phenomena such as the circulation of ideas within and across group boundaries, changes in the flow and direction of transfers, and the adjustability of decisions.

CHAPTER 8

International Connections

IT IS not difficult to see that an anthropological perspective can be useful for the analysis of national cultures and of the social organization that reflects disparate interests within them. This is, in effect, the construction of a mosaic, and the observation of social and cultural relationships and exchanges within and across various kinds of boundaries embraced by the national polity.

Just as we noted that tribal, lineage, and rural peasant systems are seriously affected by the national scene, so we consider more systematically the interactions that occur across national boundaries. We shall now be thinking of the World Society, and taking a step toward the consideration of the world as a single social system, with its own policy and social organization. In the last chapter we noted some of the conditions that modify the idea of the nation as a self-contained homogeneous unit.

The power of nationalism as an ethnosocial science idea must not be underestimated. Indeed, from now on it will become increasingly apparent in my argument that social scientists themselves have been influenced, mostly unconsciously, by this idea. The thrust of commentary in the social sciences is strongly in the direction of thinking about international affairs as relations between States. Even commercial interactions tend to be seen through the perspective of such data as trade figures gathered on a national scale to record movement across the national boundary. Only recently has there been much formal attention given to the worldwide activities of individual firms.

The field is ready for anthropological attention, with the cooperation of other social sciences. It requires a continuation of small-scale analysis, carried out at the location of national boundaries to observe connections across them. It further requires the forging of new techniques to enable us to handle data referring to social exchanges (in their cultural, economic, and political manifestations) on a world scale. And it involves studies in which the anthropologist observes a web of connectedness from a center that he defines in non-national terms. When these things occur, we will be able to see more clearly that the concept of the world as consisting of a finite number of social organizations, each carefully bounded within a national political system, is false, misleading, and dangerous as a premise upon which to build world policies.

National unity itself can be dependent upon external relations. The German, Italian, and French Swiss of the early 19th century had little in common, and it is not long since the cantons were engaged in the extremely bitter religious war of the Sonderbund. The sense of national unity came as a result of the fear that individual cantons would lose their autonomy if they were swallowed up by the aggressive nationalisms of France, Germany, and Italy; because the German majority proved farsighted in extending political and cultural rights to the minorities; because it suited the European powers to have a neutral country sitting astride their lines of communication; and because the Federation was divided in such a way that no single canton was large or wealthy enough to dominate the others. Now that the threat from European nationalisms is no longer pressing, it is becoming a little more difficult for the Swiss to use external threat as a unifying force, and their interests turn to increased cooperation. How increased cooperation will balance with the creation of new myths of external threat (e.g. from foreign labor), or how the reduction in the power of such myths will affect national unity, remains to be seen.

The Canadian example offers instructive contrasts. The Provinces are gravely unequal, so that the rest of Canada sees Ontario and Quebec as dominant in both commercial and federal political life. An imperial threat from England or France is not taken seriously, despite a few French pretensions.* By far the greatest threat, because of its size, its involvement, and its economic power, is that of the United States. The Canadian Government (and some other authorities) is indeed seeking mild counterbalancing influences from Europe and Asia. But the English have not yet had the wit to create the myth that says resoundingly to the French, "We need you to protect us." In the absence of such a myth (it is there, but very softly), the French can view the English as an instrument of the American threat.

The situation would be very different, I suspect, if France and England were more aggressive, and if Russia decided to claim an influence over the

---

*This may change. During its visit to Quebec in 1975 the Académie Goncourt was surprised to find its visit interpreted as an act of cultural imperialism.

descendants of its former citizens. Then Canada would have more reason to adopt a Swiss solution, each element in the population flying into each other's arms to maintain a modicum of independence *from each other* as well as from grasping neighbors.

Migration, with continued communication, creates pockets of influence and contact, and even dual loyalties and citizenship. The Swiss, for example, have an assembly and association of Swiss living abroad; they earmark funds for social security support and for insurance against some of the dangers of living in insecure countries; expatriate Swiss have been discussing in their own assembly, with federal officials, questions of military obligation, Swiss taxation, the right to vote, and representation in the federal parliament. Some of the rights and duties apply to Swiss families who have been away for generations and who have citizenship in the countries of their residence.

This situation may be extreme, but in one form or other it is more common than is generally realized. Dual citizenship, or what amounts to it, has been receding, however, to the detriment of the breadth of human rights. Citizenship in the British Commonwealth once meant the transfer of the franchise automatically on changing residence, and it was the basis of negotiated taxation and social security reciprocities, as well as guaranteeing freedom of movement and protection as a citizen. This is no longer the case. The Dominions introduced restrictions in the name of nationalism, and the later development of the Commonwealth as a multicultural association caused the reinforcement of barriers. In many respects this step backward is against the tide of history, although the Commonwealth was clearly not quite ready to take up the opportunity to lead the way to international citizenship. At the other extreme is the narrow, rigid, but intensely held conception of nationalism in the United States, which— while expecting foreign residents to fulfill certain civic obligations and while inducting young Canadian residents into the armed forces— nevertheless until a few years ago considered it a crime that could result in loss of citizenship for a United States citizen to vote in a foreign country, to accept foreign official honors, or to serve a foreign government in any official capacity.

We have also noted border cultural linkages. Many of these came into prominence as new nations were being constructed in Africa, Asia, and elsewhere, with somewhat artificial boundaries. The highly exaggerated claim of the Sultan of Ternate to footholds on the New Guinea mainland was used by Indonesia to legitimize an imperial right and heritage. It brought into Indonesia a vast area which has far more by way of cultural linkage with the now independent country of Papua–New Guinea on the other side of the artifical border. The troubled northern provinces of Thailand are partially inhabited by tribesmen of migratory habit who moved into the present Thailand *within living memory* and who have kinsmen in Burma and China. The political boundaries that divided the indigenous cultural groups of Togo and Cameroun were based on colonial history and the acquisition of the language of the governing power as a *lingua franca.* Subsequent boundary adjustments with the neighboring States of Ghana and Nigeria had to take both indigenous culture and European language affiliation into account—the combination pushing toward federal solutions.

These kinds of examples have been fairly well publicized and can be repeated throughout the world. Others have been matters of ordinary livelihood for generations. They normally come into prominence only when they are dramatized for political ends, as with German and Italian pre-War expansionist claims, or where (as with the Swiss Jura, the Basques, or the Italian Tyrol) the cross-border links become the unit for demands of regional autonomy, often focused on the nonrecognition of cultural (particularly language) differences, in forms valued by the population (education, political expression). But the phenomenon is common and significant.

Indeed, it can be argued that it is a feature of borders everywhere. Given its geographical position, how could Cyprus be anything but a combination of Greek and Turkish populations? The long border between the United States and Canada is characterized by intermarriage and kinship links, as well as by occupational similarities; and one segment of the population—Indians—has the right of unrestricted crossing with customs privileges. I have referred to one example of Alpine regional culture linking Switzerland, France, and Italy. This can be repeated *ad infinitum.* Almost all rural border areas of Europe contain examples of "customs free zones" within which peasants may exchange produce without customs control. Town groupings such as Geneva–Annemasse or Basle–St. Louis–Weil link agglomerations in two or even three countries, giving rise to a corps of *frontaliers,* i.e., persons who cross the border every day to work, to border-crossing trams and buses, to shared airport facilities, and even to municipal tax-sharing arrangements. Weekly town markets in one country are frequently served by sellers from another.

The strange thing is that such arrangements are not taken into account by the proclaimers of cultural nationalism. The boundary is a much purer thing when imagined by the citizens of a metropolitan capital than when seen in reality by the people who live beside it.

International cultural patterns are well known to be significant. Unfortunately, only the fairly obvious appear to have been studied, and then primarily through consideration of such phenomena as linguistic borrowings, with relatively little sociological or anthropological attention given to elucidating the channels and mapping the diffusions.

For the newer nation-states, and some of the older ones, the issues have been complicated by the discovery that a national identity can be built on multicultural foundations, so that while the national *lingua franca* may be a foreign language (or an indigenous language spoken by a minority), the vitality of the regional cultural expressions becomes a matter of national significance. A group of Asian scholars meeting recently unhesitatingly identified the preservation, expansion, and communication of oral tradition and indigenous arts as being the primary scientific field that would contribute to national unity and development—not, as might have been expected, studies of economic processes. Despite this, foreign languages are of key importance to the communication of knowledge, in both directions.

There seems little doubt that English may be dominant as a transnational medium. French is fighting a rearguard battle based on its traditional role. It is in danger of being killed off by the linguistically unintelligent policies of the *Académie* and the French Government, who are doing their best to identify the language with France and to use it as an international political lever, which creates adverse reaction. They are also standing in the way of its adaptation. Anyone who has heard the language used in international exchanges knows that it is effective only through the occasional use of anglicisms and other borrowings. Anyone who has watched the translation of social and political statements into French knows that the traditional claim to precision and clarity is nonsense, and the feat can only be achieved with either loss of meaning or considerable and confusing circumlocution or borrowing. (This also applies to a surprising degree in ordinary language: compare, for example, the available French and English vocabularies to describe degrees of heat or cold. There is an interesting ramification of this vocabulary limitation in French when analysts come to describe an economy as being "overheated": they must use a different idiom to talk of "warming up.") All languages have such limitations, but English has proven a past master at the art of borrowing. *Unofficial* French is also highly adaptable, and the French survival as an international language may be as a result of a Swiss, Canadian, or Belgian revolt against the dictates of Paris.*

Other languages also have substantial claims. Spanish is, after all, the primary language of a huge continent, leading to a diverse publishing industry, which (despite political controls) moves pamphlets, translations, monographs, and treatises of all kinds of persuasions, to say nothing of literature and children's comics, across the national boundaries. German, although it has lost its pre-War status, is still an important mode of communication for everyday contact in much of Eastern Europe. Cantonese will open doors for you in every one of the many parts of the world where there is a Chinese community. Russian and Mandarin are of immense political importance; Malay, Swahili, and Arabic operate well beyond national boundaries; and Japanese is an increasingly established second language for Asian commerce.

The transfer of ideas and cultural influence is not, however, dependent on the penetration of language. The translation industry is immense and, perhaps for the first time, is beginning to bring about flows in more than one direction. This is particularly evident in children's comics and books, and not quite so evident (but destined to grow) in television. American comics still dominate the world supply, particularly as used in the daily press. But they reach their public in translation, and that works both ways, so that European satirical comics such as Astérix, Tin-Tin, and Lucky Luke now have a growing international audience linked to cultural and political values. Eurovision is responsible for the cooperative production, translation, and distribution of a wide variety of television programs. The number of East European and Canadian films shown on European television is high, quite possibly outnumbering American programs. For obvious technical reasons, the movement of theatrical productions from one language to another is limited, but there is increasing movement when languages are shared. All these forms carry ideas with them.

Music, which seldom requires translation, is the primary international mover. It is interesting to note the way in which presentable syntheses of indigenous musical styles have added popular exotic elements to the international musical world, and, as fashions, have penetrated national entertainment industries. The more intelligent national popular music has leant heavily on borrowings and inspiration from abroad, and yet has been able to retain national themes. The interactions have not created merely a

* French cultural (as distinct from official) opinion is sometimes more open to this consideration. In 1973 the first dictionary was published, for school use, giving full weight to French usage outside of France, as distinct from *patois* or localized dictionaries.

banal lowest common denominator (although that is present) but have increased interest in national musical expressions, in syntheses, and in what may be regarded as "international ethnic" music.

There seems, then, to be little real evidence that international cultural movement *destroys* national or ethnic culture, except in limited and special instances. The overwhelming result of the contact is to increase the variety, the richness, and the vigor of expression. Even what appears for a while to be a heavily commercialized cultural imperialism creates reactions and eventual retaliation by reverse movement. Only the United States, because of its sheer size, and the Soviet Union and China, because of policy as well, are relatively impervious to reverse cultural influence (for the United States there is an important exception of reverse influences directed to the intelligentsia). This is no doubt to their loss.

Political movement and contact across national boundaries is no new phenomenon. Indeed the Communist International in its heyday was much more ambitious, universal, and even sophisticated, than the rather clandestine and shame-faced operations which take place today. The growth of nationalism as an operative myth has put nonofficial international political movements on the ideological defensive. Yet at two levels they are clearly and distinctly effective, in new forms.

One is the official regional association of governments for cooperative action and policy coordination. In its formal supra-national organization, this will be discussed in the next chapter. But there are many transitional steps short of modifying national authority. The Organization for African Unity, the Organization of American States, the interaction for consultation between Australia and New Zealand, and the host of bilateral discussions that lead to agreements or treaties are cases in point. No State exercises its sovereignty in isolation, without reacting to influence.

At the nongovernmental level, political parties are in consultation across boundaries, but it is doubtful whether this has more than the most informal of effects on policies.* On the other hand, the mutual influence and support (though rivalrous, chaotic, and episodic) of revolutionary activist movements, the use of transboundary military bases, the supply of arms, finances, training facilities, and ideas are clearly international. Paradoxically, the limitations of formal governmental nationalism are at the root of the ineffectiveness of government response—relative to their apparent control of power, since effective response often requires action

* Perhaps this is changing. Note the effectiveness of Mr. Helmut Schmidt's address to the British Labour Party Congress in December 1974 on the subject of Britain's membership in the EEC.

across boundaries that governments have not yet adapted to the new situation.

The influence and interaction of the labor movement across international boundaries have been checkered. The growth and rivalries of international labor associations make these less effective than they were in the formative days of trade unions, when international moral and political support was most important. A great deal of the technical function of trade unions is handled by the International Labour Organization—for example, technical assistance with regard to the formation of unions or cooperatives, and developing legislation in accord with international conventions. It is the ILO rather than the unions themselves which carries this flag, although since the ILO is not predominantly a "labor" instrument, the union world still retains a separate interest. That interest, however, is very different from having a central responsibility, and in many instances the major unions of the communist or capitalist world do not have more than a passing involvement in what goes on in the rest of the world.

There are signs of change. The so-called "international unions" crossing the Canadian–US boundary are now the subject of highly critical appraisal as the Canadian members and public become increasingly restive about the dominance of US policy within them. This, however, is an unusual situation. The more noticeable trend is the tardy reaction of unions to the growth of multinational companies, and the slow realization that multinational operations can be used to play off national unions against one another. The widening of the European Common Market is giving stimulus to effective, rather than token, cross-national union activity, which is easier to achieve when the partners are not so disparate in size and power as is the case with Canadian–American unions.

At this point we come to the multinational corporation itself. If ever there were a need to identify (as a matter of prime policy interest) significant breaches in national boundaries, the multinational corporation would provide the example. Contrary to some current rhetoric, this is not a new phenomenon. As not only radical commentators have long pointed out, it has its origins in imperial expansion and in colonial activity. One should also add the example of early banking houses and the Mediterranean trading cities.

Indeed, before World War II, left-wing scholars and politicians had the same kind of fun pointing out the political implications of company linkages, both nationally and internationally, as is now exercising radical commentators. The interests and activities of Standard Oil or the United

Fruit Company in influencing United States policy and the political affairs of smaller countries are, in principle, not exactly news. Nor was Firestone's control of Liberia's destiny. Such companies often operated in a context in which other countries were nominally independent, did not have the will or the technique to fight back, and would not have been able to mobilize effective international support if they had.

While American companies frequently worked outside the formal jurisdiction of the United States, European companies had a different relationship to political power when there were colonial interests.* In the first place, several trading and plantation operation companies—more particularly in Africa and Asia and, for the Germans, Oceania—had evolved from a situation in which they had been given the rights and responsibilities of political administration. Many companies had been direct colonial administrators. On the whole, this situation did not last long into the 19th century, and although Belgian colonial operations continued to have much the same status, elsewhere colonial administration tended to be set up by branches of government which had a combination of protective and developmental points of view, in various mixes.

On the whole—and this is grossly simplified—the developmental role was thought of as creating law, local body functions, and commerce (which was considered to be of alien stimulus). One task of colonial government was to administer that alien stimulus in accordance with metropolitan nationalist predilections—i.e., by restricting it to enterprises which belonged to the governing nation. This was not always achieved. In addition, colonial administrations—and this was reinforced by their creation to supplant commercial government—had the task of preventing abuse and of holding the reins of power to counterbalance that of aggressive private enterprise.

Despite this, the power balance nearly always worked in favor of the extraterritorial firms, which increased considerably in number and in breadth of operations. There was a sharing of values between administrators and company officials and a tendency to see national companies as efficient by comparison with indigenous enterprises—to favor them in policy matters. The companies' strongest card was political pressure at home in the metropolis, a pressure which was particularly effective in

---

*The following remarks are based partially on personal observation in colonial administration from 1943 to 1946, plus archival research relating to British and French territories. See my *Island Administration in the South West Pacific*, London: Royal Institute of International Affairs, 1950, and *Changing Melanesia*, Melbourne: Oxford University Press, 1954.

France, Belgium, and Holland. In Britain it was also strong, but very much modified by the political line that colonial governments, however directly ruled, were *governments*, that the voice of those governments must be listened to, that their spokesmen were accustomed to being independent and to resisting political pressure, that colonial governors frequently had personal political connections in England, and that the Church, working in the colonies, occasionally brought effective pressure to bear. Companies by no means had it all their own way and frequently fought last-ditch but losing battles against paternal authority. That authority was, however, limited by its very paternalism, by the lack of a social climate that it could recognize for use as a source of responsibility, and by absence of the kind of imagination and knowledge of economic dynamics that we take for granted today.

In terms of sheer size, measured by capitalization or value of sales, such colonial companies were on the whole small even in pre-War times. Exceptions were Unilever (an example of spider-webbish vertical and horizontal integration going far beyond mere colonial interests) and Royal Dutch-Shell (which was more like Standard Oil than the United Africa Company or Jardine's in the Far East). It is only recently, for example, that the famous South Seas trading firm of Burns, Philp and Co. has reached the upper brackets of the Australian league (still well below Broken Hill Pty. Ltd.), and it has achieved this not through its Oceanic expansions but through massive diversification into Australian enterprises.

South America evidences perhaps the greatest continuity in the interaction between alien firms and national governments and interests. Despite examples of the nationalization of alien firms elsewhere, and of course their complete post-War takeover in newly formed communist countries, nowhere has the operation of alien enterprises received such consistent political analysis and attention. This is in part a reflection of deep entrenchment over the decades, including identification with indigenous social elements that are the object of revolutionary attack. (It is no accident that this was also the case in the Congo, and was the source of the bitter strife.)

Here, and in other countries where a move to nationalization has occurred, targets have tended to be banks, as symbols of foreign financial manipulation; monopolistic trading companies, which have been in a position to manipulate the terms of trade through price and wage depression; plantation industries, seen as encouraging alien rather than local enterprise, or as competing with peasant land use, and also as exporting profits; and, above all, extractive industries. While many of the examples above are of binational enterprises (in their operations if not their ownership), with some extension to embrace groups of neighboring countries, the extractive and agricultural marketing companies are a little more typical of "multinational" companies in contemporary usage. They often operate in a number of countries to obtain raw material, and may sometimes be able to play off one operation against another. Their profit structure is divided among subsidiaries so that they can afford to have losses in one area as long as they are counterbalanced by profit elsewhere, and they sometimes elect to do so. Governments attempt to gain control, sometimes completely as in Allende Chile, and Saudi-Arabian oil, and sometimes by retaining foreign management interests and skills, as with Bougainville copper. In at least one instance (New Caledonian nickel) the importance of the extractive industry is such that the metropolitan government has held onto colonial rule in order to avoid the bargaining issues which inevitably arise.

The attempts to take over or control local operations of the industry are usually justified by inequitable power and income considerations, and by the adoption of company strategies that are not in the national interest. When governments design their controls with the concept and in the name of nationalism *alone*, however, they miss perhaps the most important half of the story. The success side of such companies is frequently dependent on their operations that *do not take place* within the jurisdiction of the government concerned. It is this fact that caused, prior to 1973, a slowing up of the inevitable Arabian oil takeover. In other instances (e.g., Zambian copper) it has been possible to operate the internal processes with independent success. It is still questionable, however, whether that success would have been greater if a multinational structure had been salvageable.

This may be an open question. Further, even if it were to be shown that multinational conglomerate structures are sometimes more effective than bargaining between units divided on both functional and nationalistic lines (producers and sellers, marketers, purchasers and users), it is often in the national interest to gain national control *first*, before moving into international arrangements, if only to defend the nation against the untoward manipulation of the internal units. That this is a real danger can be dramatized by the actions of Canadian subsidiaries of American firms acting in terms of United States *political* policy, in *opposition* to Canadian policy, by denying sales to the People's Republic of China or to Cuba. There was also the case of the United States vetoing the sale of a

Canadian-built civil research submersible to the Soviet Union because it contained technical equipment of American origin that was on the US list of exports prohibited to communist countries.

Nevertheless, what we have been considering so far is but a very small part of the tip of the multinational iceberg. The major multinational companies go where the markets are, and are not as much concerned with developing countries as the examples so far cited. They operate between nations, and take the nations where they find them. The *sales* of the top *non-American* giant (Royal Dutch-Shell) are almost ten *billion* dollars; of the second (Unilever)—six billion; of the third (Philips)—three and a half billion. American-based firms are substantially larger. There are at least twenty other firms with sales of over two billion. Bank assets of over fifteen billion dollars are not uncommon in Britain, France, and Japan, as well as the United States. The budgets indicated by these sums are far greater than the budgets of most national governments represented in the United Nations. They are also many times greater than the budget of the largest international organization—namely, the United Nations itself—or even of the whole United Nations family of organizations put together.

The classification "multinational" is extremely rough and in some instances a misnomer. All firms engaged in external trade enter into liaisons with other firms abroad, which give rise to linkages of less formal character but similar functional result than those of technically multinational firms. By entering into supply or sales contracts, they move money, affect employment, and have an interest in influencing policies. In some instances, they can switch sales or purchases between countries if the policies of the one are displeasing. In such activities, their power is not often monopolistic, but groups of companies acting in concert or as cartels—either as suppliers or as buyers—can have very similar results. Sometimes governments emerge as power-partners, particularly where international pricing or quota agreements are involved; sugar, coffee, cocoa, rubber, shipping, air fares, to say nothing of oil, are but a few of the instances in which national companies concerned with international movements of goods or services are deeply affected by international negotiation, and in turn deeply affect the conditions and policies of nation-states.

The multinational company is merely a more dramatic and perhaps powerful example of direct relationships. The multinational company tends to treat the world as composed of national States which are little different from States or communities within a single country. Where a national company will feel free, within the law, to upgrade or downgrade production plans, to switch production from one State or city to another, to consider material advantages and tax relief in locating operations, and to move money about to gain the best returns, so too do multinational companies—but on a world basis. Just as national companies are sometimes constrained by costs and movement frictions from altering production locations (from depressed areas, for example), so too multinational companies are often tied into particular countries that they would prefer to be out of. It should not be forgotten, then, that what can be said about multinational companies can also be said about national ones, in terms of both national and cross-boundary effects, albeit in different styles and contexts.

Some multinational companies are accused of using their influence to interfere in the internal policies of countries by expressing direct wishes for labor or social legislation, by financing and maintaining political parties, by threats of withdrawal of capital or expertise, by influencing the men in power. This sort of thing is not unknown inside nation-states, and indeed it raises serious issues about the sovereignty of the elected authority (if it is elected) and the nature of political power. While some States (e.g. in Central America) have governments which are unwilling or unable to exercise control, and in some instances even welcome financial and other enterprises that are being excluded from other countries for malpractice, the attention now being given to multinational companies is largely due to the repercussions of the newly found *effectiveness* of Latin American controls. The occasional fighting back, as formerly the case of Chile, and now of Arab oil, is the dramatic exception rather than the day-to-day rule. The increasing sense of effectiveness puts control apparently within grasp, but not fully so.

Publicity and calls for research and study have gone out to almost all the relevant international agencies. Thus, the International Labour Office, from October 26 to November 4, 1972, held a meeting that laid plans for an examination of the social consequences of multinational firms, the results of which have since been reported. (Within the debate, some participants also objected to the operations of multinational union federations in their country.) Resolutions at the 1972 UNESCO General Conference and at the United Nations General Assembly also made specific reference to multinational firms.

The effects of decisions are most obvious in production; the decision to close mines or to alter output has profound effects. While national companies may make the same decisions, and both types of company are subject to the same internal law, the fact that the multinational decision *may* be taken outside the country makes it less bearable. Multinational companies are also in a position to add insult to injury by switching the production to another country. Thus, recently, Ford moved production of a car destined for export to the United States from Britain to Germany, and General Motors reduced still further its production of the British Vauxhall in favor of the more competitive (in the British market) German-made Opel. That these were rational decisions in the face of suicidal labor activity is reinforced by parallel increasing interest of English car manufacturers in *becoming* multinational by moving substantial production and assembly units to Belgium, Spain, and Holland and leaning more heavily on continental suppliers of parts. Nevertheless, when such decisions come from firms seen to be controlled abroad, tension and hostility are created.

Another field in which the effects of multinational firms is as dramatic, but in which the attribution of responsibility is not as easy, is money movement. The past five or six years have seen huge increases in the weight of money movement for speculative advantage at times when fixed exchange parities seem out of line. It is no exaggeration to say that all monetary crises of recent years have turned on this point. The massive movement of money, as money managers arrive at the same judgments and decisions, is on such a scale as to put unbearable pressures on governments. The 1973 ten percent devaluation of the US dollar was forced by money movement linked to undervaluations of the German mark and the Japanese yen, and the stubbornness with which the two governments refused to revalue upward.

The ethnosocial science revealed in the commentaries was extremely interesting. As a nonexpert in the field, I certainly cannot tell which points of view represented the more accurate notions, but it is first of all clear that there *is no agreed* monetary theory that applies to policy resolutions, or even, beyond a certain superficial level, that provides explanations. M. Giscard d'Estaing, then the French Minister of Finance, could hardly refrain from rubbing his hands before the TV cameras, since the United States used a gold price as the measure of devaluation, thus reinforcing his theory and policy of long standing that gold is of predominant importance. Yet, in the normal course of events, anyone who has related Paris prices to prices in other countries, through the medium of exchange conversion, knows that even before the recent devaluation French *consumer* prices were internationally out of line. The simple classical theory that would relate the international values of currencies to the status of prices is clearly overlaid by other factors. Because of later exchange movements, these comments no longer apply to the France of 1974, but do apply, with more strength, to Germany and Switzerland.

By the same token, commentaries in the *Economist* indicated that the effect of devaluation on American competitiveness in world markets is severely limited by a relative lack of demand response to price changes for the most important products, such as grain. In other words, lower prices will not cause much more to be sold, and one might even predict that for some products the foreign currency earnings could in fact drop, if sales did not rise more than the devaluation 10 percent. Further, the devaluation came at a time when the US balance of payments had been in a healthier state than for months previously and when the German terms of trade were predicted to be entering the weakest phase for the same period. Theories based on these factors are pretty shaky.

The timing was also closely linked with Vietnam peace accomplishments. While there was still considerable doubt as to the effectiveness of the peace arrangements, there was little doubt about American withdrawal and about such facts as the ending of selective service. In the intelligent newspaper and journal commentaries I have read, this was regarded as a great psychological boost for the market, and indeed the US market indices did rise. But they did not *jump*, and I could never quite understand why the market, as distinct from the population relieved by war's end, would react in a bearish manner. For my own hypotheses would be that (a) rightly, or more probably wrongly, money managers would have the view that cessation of US hostilities *and* selective service together would mean a reduction in armament demand, with depressive effects on the economy; (b) this trend was not counterbalanced by any other expansive policy since President Nixon was at the same time cutting back on other activities such as massive social service programs; and (c) the timing coincided with the movement of Europe into a much stronger competitive and political stage with the entry of Britain, Ireland, and Denmark into the Common Market.

But the fact is that *nobody knows* in a systematic way what factors did influence the money managers. Could it possibly be that they were increasingly influenced by bank reports and financial newspaper accounts of disparities in currencies, made three to six months before? Could it be that some were influenced to act in a hurry and belatedly before conditions changed? Then as soon as the news got about, and particularly as governments made disturbed noises, all the other managers hurried to cash in, like flocks of sheep pressing through a narrow defile with expanded pastures at the other end?

And who, in any event, *are* the money managers? Many of them undoubtedly are concerned with the placing of multinational corporation funds wherever there is a profit to be had, until such times as they are required for other operating purposes. Some are handling portfolio investments on an international scale, and see the chance of a quick gain. In both these cases, it is clearly an advantage to have close international connections, preferably subsidiaries, through which one can work quickly and quietly, and make use of intelligence gathered internationally. But one does not *have* to be structurally multinational—an ordinary large national corporation may be in the same position; but in so reacting it undoubtedly creates connections that make quick, effective movement possible. Once again, there is not a great difference between the multinational and national concern.

This last point is emphasized by the onset of the 1973–4 oil crisis. The huge sums generated by inflated prices have been skillfully redistributed from multinational companies to national financial organizations controlled by Arab and other oil-producing governments. These in turn are developing new consortia for the investment of the proceeds to replace the former multinational operations. The Arabs and Norwegians in particular are faced now with choices of the kind referred to in Chapters 4 and 5. For example, they must decide, as did our Fijian manganese producers, whether to extract quickly and invest returns in enterprises they do not control, to extract more slowly, thus guaranteeing a steadier return, to use investment power to gain some control over foreign economic policies that affect them, or to seek short-term political capital. It has been pointed out, for example, that Arab financiers are now in a position to create chaos by holding prices high until other countries invest in expensive energy alternatives, and then to slash the high prices (which they can afford) to bankrupt the new energy enterprises. Britain's North Sea oil, and with it Britain, would be exceedingly vulnerable to such a tactic. What has happened in oil can, with varying degrees, happen with other commodities. The interplay of national political interests and those of the wider world society is now more visible. Pricing, trade, marketing, and production are now more clearly than ever subject to an economy in which political and social strategies loom large in the calculations of cost and benefit. We can no longer pretend that the analysis can be limited to the field of economics.

Multinational firms are not, in any event, a single species.* Such a concern might, like Ford, completely retain its major policy decisions in the country of its incorporation and headquarters, with executives in charge drawn from that country. Others, like General Motors, may be divided into highly competitive units, almost like independent firms, with unit management a mixture of central and local origins. Others, like Nestlé, may have centralized policy and management training facilities, but may draw in top management for the central board from all the countries in which it operates, thus truly internationalizing it. The location and structure of decisions—the most important political characteristic—is not determined by the word "multinational."

Similarly, the world pattern of multinationalism is changing rapidly, and it is by no means an exaggeration to say that most members of the public would be thoroughly surprised to know that firms they had long regarded as being thoroughly national and part of the national heritage of initiative were in fact foreign owned and controlled. Until that fact becomes known, or unless it is accompanied by a high profile (ITT, Hilton, General Motors), members of the public are not normally concerned. Can one recall, for example, a fuss being made about Canadian or Swiss control of dominant elements in the US food preparation industry?

In the absence of genuine international government, control is exercised by national governments with national considerations in mind. As we shall see, this may be severely modified in the European case. But the French are still reacting with alarm at past threats of US takeover bids, and are watching with some trepidation as established British firms (such as J. Lyons or Burtons) enter the European food and clothing industries, either through direct intervention or takeover. The Common Market is facilitating and giving an ideological base for such moves, but its structure is not a necessary condition for them, as Swiss commercial policy has been demonstrating for decades. Indeed, the Swiss model could provide a useful set of principles to be examined by small countries lacking physical resources but well off for management and the ability to attract and mobilize capital, such as Hong Kong and Singapore. There is no reason why multinational companies should not at times be established as indigenous enterprises in developing countries, contributing somewhat to a correction of the overweighted trend in the other direction.

One cannot fully tell what the evolution is likely to be. One can, however, hypothesize that the solutions are sometimes improperly or

---

* There recently have been a number of studies of multinational firms that provide data on this kind of point. For example, see M. Z. Brooke and H. L. Remmers, *The Strategy of Multinational Enterprises*, London: Longmans, 1970.

unimaginatively restricted by national interests, whereas international considerations—if backed by international government—might yield more productive results. This is part of the subject of the next chapter. But, by way of preparation, let me show the frictional implications of nationalism by putting forward a highly unreal but, I think, instructive example.

In the recent dollar crisis to which I have referred, one can imagine a different set of reactions. Let us assume, for example, the massive flight of dollars to Frankfort and Tokyo, together with central bank purchasing intervention. Let us assume, however, that the central banks have the authority to sell or lend unwanted dollars to a public institution or a consortium of private institutions that have as their function the investment of migrant funds in the country of their origin. Under these circumstances, the flight of speculative dollars to Frankfort and Tokyo would be counteracted by investment and share purchase in the United States. At a simplified level, this would counteract the speculation and bring money transfers into equilibrium, although it might well set off internal money market adjustments that had more complicated effects. However, the point of the example is to show its political unreality rather than its economic unreality. The United States Government and public, thinking of themselves in nationalistic terms, would probably react by creating legal barriers, seeing foreign governments as being behind the reverse movement. Nationalism is not interested in the free play of market forces, even when these may be in the world interest.* While it is normal for such adjustments to occur *within* a country, governments do not admit the conception that the *world* is the equilibrium unit, in this sense.

Nationalism is too strong for the needs of the modern world. It is rapidly becoming destructively dysfunctional, not in the sense of provoking wars but in being inadequate to deal with the real issues confronting mankind. Whether this can be seen in time to create the international institutions and mechanisms that we desperately need is, alas, an open question.

---

* My example may be put to the test. In 1973, following the crisis, the United States Government indicated the probability that regulations would be eased to permit the increased inflow of capital. It was expected that this might lead to the repatriation of the overseas activities of some US banks. However, easing of the national regulations was not based on the premise or expectation that there would be deliberate acquisition of American stocks and property on the basis of regular foreign government policy. By 1974, the whole situation changed still further, with the beginnings of massive Arab and Iranian oil money recyclage which included large investments in German, French, Canadian and US utilities and equities. The Western world is now bracing itself to be at the receiving end of policies it has for so long adopted toward less powerful countries.

CHAPTER 9

Supra-nation

NATIONAL government is an artificial and deliberate creation. Its forms are set by constitution makers and organizers of bureaucracies. But within them, "natural" social forces are at work that create policies, modes of operation and relationships which give life to the constitution and go beyond it. One has the feeling that the practical men who create the organizations and structures have learned very little about them, despite sophisticated political and philosophical education, since the days of the French, American, and Russian revolutions. Certainly, the Gaullist Constitution of the French Republic, though, at the cost of tremendous strain and crisis, perhaps accomplishing what its imaginers thought it should, would seem nightmarishly incompetent (as well as ideologically false) to the great constitution makers of the 18th and 19th centuries. It is ironical that the French with their intellectual anti-Americanism should have adopted the unstable and friction-creating elements of the US Presidential system. The British constitution makers who advised colonies on their road to independence were incredibly blind to the experience of non-British countries, some of which had invented careful and objective electoral devices to ensure the protection and cooperation of ethnic components. The blindness was quite in contradiction to the supposed British genius for political imagination.

If these matters are difficult at the national level, if experiments and learning are still—belatedly—going on, it is not surprising that the techniques to create legally binding international policies based upon supra-national administration leave even more to be desired. They are at an earlier stage of evolution; they contain greater elements of artificiality and deliberate design; the social and political forces that overlay the formal links are in some respects more difficult to study and to comprehend; their modes of change are so unwieldy as to be almost nonexistent; and those who hold the power in them do not really want them to be effective.

126

Therefore, what follows is (in terms of social science) even more "critical," more personal, more normative, and more imaginative and speculative than the remarks of previous pages. It is, nevertheless, based on a certain experience and low-level ad hoc knowledge and observation, more particularly of organizations in the United Nations family, which is the main grouping to be considered here. My knowledge of other international experiments—the institutions of the European Common Market, OECD, the Commonwealth Secretariat, and so forth—is either superficial or based solely on written materials.

In the selection of examples, and their analytic treatment, personal experience has been the guide. But, in addition, the principles underlying the comments have a loose theoretical unity with the interpretations used in previous sections. On the one hand, the international organizations are part of one world—what happens in them is often deeply and subconsciously affected by human aspirations and experiences at other levels of organization. On the other hand, the men and women, the political cabinets and diplomats, and the technical professionals who operate and guide them are responsive to the same kinds of pressures (and the game of social and political exchange) that govern human life in other contexts. There is room, therefore, for the use of similar modes of analysis at the broadest level. There has, of course, been a great deal of the more remote type of formal calculation of decision-making strategies in the international context. This, however, is but one example of the possibilities of extending analytic thinking from one field to another, and is not suited to my present purpose, which is more critical.

It is, incidentally, significant that social science has been neither used nor greatly developed for applications to the total conception and structure of national or international government. (An exception to this is a certain growth of independent constitutional, legal, and organizational consultation, more particularly in connection with developing countries.) Established governments and international organizations tend to use social scientists in relation to predetermined policy, and for parts of the whole rather than for the whole itself. Of course, some of this gets fairly close to raising fundamentals that affect the whole. Within the United Nations, the Jackson Report on the organization of technical assistance was closer to the central issues than might have been expected from its terms of reference. Since technical assistance happens to be a major unifying concern of the whole United Nations family of organizations, what happens in relation to it has a fundamental impact. Nevertheless, there are times when a critical total overview, looking at the wood rather than the trees, is due. This, it appears to me, is one of those times.

All non-Comintern nation-states, I think without exception, behave in ways designed to guard their national independence. In dealing with the issues of the inter-nation, they do so in their sovereign right and through negotiation, partnership, or conflict, which recognizes that right in others (even though one may make moves to subvert other governments). A partial qualification to this is the exercise of judgment by the United Nations that may "call upon" a nation-state to take, or desist in, certain action, or the reference, usually after treaty prescription, of a matter of dispute to the International Court of Justice. We all know, however, that the United Nations is little stronger in such matters than was the League of Nations. There are many loopholes in the Charter and in the applicable resolutions that are built in by nations defending their independence. These then enable member States to argue that a sanctions resolution, for example, is illegal because it is directed to an internal matter; or, even without doing this, to more or less openly flout the resolution with impunity. Such resolutions are not necessarily right, nor just, nor effective; they are almost always ignored in some crucial aspect, as resolutions bearing upon Rhodesia and the Middle East conflict amply illustrate. Even treaties that refer matters to the International Court are not always observed, although there seems to be a somewhat better record of submission to its findings. However, in 1973, for example, Iceland refused to appear to argue its case on fishing matters, although a treaty with Britain and Germany stipulated the competence of the Court. In other words, if the matter is important enough to a nation-state, it almost always behaves in terms indicating that its national interest and independence take precedence over the conflicting international interests or opinion.

However, members of the public, who are also obviously members of nation-states, are becoming rather more directly concerned about the way decisions taken outside their country affect them. It is possible that pressure may grow from within nation-states in the direction of securing modifications of behavior that will allow international policies to be formed more frequently and more successfully. In order to protect the myth of their independence, nation-states show a strong preference for bilateral or multilateral agreements rather than a subjection to a rule or directive laid down by a supra-national authority which can be swayed by power blocs. The issues, however, are so important that it is doubtful whether they can ultimately be solved satisfactorily without the parallel evolution of supra-national institutions. The development of the European Community in this direction, despite considerable nationalist rearguard action and the patchwork nature of the institutions, is indicative.

The catalog of international issues for which nationalism gets in the way of final solutions is immense; I shall list only a number of the most important and representative.

One does not need to stress the current concern for environmental quality and the supra-national implications of the distribution and movement of air and water. The United Nations family of organizations has responded quickly to this world concern, each one having significant programs related to it. The United Nations Conference on the Human Environment reported directly to the General Assembly, which approved a broad program of work to be undertaken by a new organ, called the United Nations Environmental Programme. The work will include monitoring, studies, public information and communication, and reports on the environmental situation. The Programme has a Secretariat and a Governing Council. It will no doubt become an agency for the administration of technical assistance and similar Development Plan funds; I am sure, if other such organizations are a guide, that its Council will adopt resolutions from time to time calling for concerted international action or goals. In all of this it is a standard United Nations organization, the strengths and weaknesses of which will be examined shortly. At this point, it is sufficient to note that the enabling resolution makes it quite clear that "international co-operative programmes in the environment field must be undertaken with due respect to the sovereign rights of States...."*

There is a network of international treaties and law, more particularly where *rivers* cross national boundaries or flow between them, that provides for the cooperative exploitation of river basins and, particularly, enjoins compensation or remedial action where the resources available to one country are damaged by action taken in another. This applies to rivers as widely separated as the Danube, to some extent the Rhine, the Mekong (until war made cooperation well-nigh impossible), and the Columbia. But, for the most part, international concern based on nationalism is limited to the concept of damages and traffic control, whether the point at issue is water, air, or the ionosphere.

For a program of preservation or administration of the upper atmosphere, in the interests of controlling satellite traffic or preventing damage to the outer layers, however much other nations may meet and talk about it the final action is likely to be a result of agreement between the United

---

* Resolution 2991 (XXVII) of the United Nations General Assembly at the 2112th plenary meeting, December 15, 1972.

States and the Soviet Union, reached in accordance with their own national interpretations of their own (and world) interests.

The control and operation of communications satellites have been based on the notion of property control, with corporate exploitation and shareholding partnerships, arrived at through bargaining between representatives of nation-states and of the communications organizations within them. A world communications policy, owned and administered in the name of the international community in the United Nations framework, is excluded. It pays to be a member of the Club.

Public opinion is becoming more concerned about the pollution of the seas, which in fact no one controls. Each nation-state contributes to that pollution through discharges from its rivers and through treating the sea as an infinitely large garbage dump. This, however, is but the latest and most fashionable concern. The administration of the sea and of the sea beds has become a matter of major political interest. Fishing rights, free access to marine passages, and control of actions between persons on the high seas have long been subject to various forms of agreement and the operation of a considerable body of national and international marine law. This, however, no longer suffices. National governments are taking unilateral steps to declare their competence over increasing areas in terms of national property. Three-mile fishing limits have been extended to twelve, and are now being extended even further; rights to the exploitation of the sea bed are being developed as it becomes practical to draw oil and minerals from it; concern with the new scale of pollution from damaged vessels is extending the areas of shipping control. Every year brings new developments. As in the North Sea, bargains may be struck to delimit boundaries. Still, a great deal of ocean remains fundamentally uncontrolled and unadministered, and the extensions of national control have an ad hoc and "let's see if we can get away with it" flavor. Ultimately, the power rests on the crude threat of embarrassing force, as Icelandic incidents have shown.

It is not an accident that the obvious solution—to place the oceans, beyond an agreed offshore limit, in the hands of an *effective* supranational administration—is the last thing that governments want to conceive of. The idea was simply not discussed at the Caracas Conference of 1974, which instead devoted itself, unsuccessfully, to national bargaining reminiscent of the 19th-century carve-up of Africa. Such an administration could not operate without supra-national powers; as it became effective, it would have to call into being adjustments in other parts of the international machinery to establish a rule of law and probably of sanctions. At present, the exchange payoffs between governments enable them to gain apparent short-term benefits, though the world as a whole pays the cost.

If the seas represent a challenge to administrative ingenuity, the control of international air traffic is an example of the near breakdown of international mechanisms. On the high seas, shipping "conferences" act as cartels to control aspects of commercial operations between specific countries or ports, and national governments restrict the free flow of "bottoms" by various mercantilist regulations linked to access to ports.

Air traffic is in some ways much more complicated. Passengers and cargo on international routes are forced to tranship from one line to another because national governments consider routes to be entries and exits from their territory; they license and control them accordingly. Very few countries give unrestricted or liberal traffic rights to airlines to "fly through" with multilateral patterns. This tendency is further emphasized by the use of national airlines as status symbols; a country is almost not a country if it fails to have an airline of its own. It must then be protected, and the only firm way of doing this is to ensure, through bilateral agreement with trade-off bargaining, that it gains rights to carry international traffic.

However, in another sense the whole international network is a single system, which must work through complex timetable and fare coordination, as well as control in other matters. Until recently, governments unanimously passed de facto control not to the International Civil Aviation Organization, which deals with technical matters (and is a member of the United Nations family, thus therefore implying the possibility of transferring sovereignty to a developing supranational authority), but to the International Air Transport Association, which is a private coordinating cartel of airlines. Even countries that in principle have anti-trust and anti-cartel legislation gave this system their blessing. The fare part of the arrangement can be threatened only by operators outside the cartel. When this happens the initiative is returned to governments, which recognize national and airline interests as paramount, rather than international and customer interests. The last thing that any government is going to suggest seriously is that the ICAO be given mandatory regulatory authority on a supra-national basis.

If there had been any effective move in the direction of international control, one would have thought that hijacking and violence in the air would have been the signal for action. The only body that has seriously been reacting in this sense has been the International Airline Pilots'

Association, which seems to have understood that it is against the ideological interest of national governments to take measures that would inevitably imply some degree of non-national control and modification of sovereignty. The Association, in 1973, took the theoretically correct steps of placing the matter before the United Nations and using their strike powers in such a way as to try to push national governments toward concerted action. They did not succeed because (as we shall examine in more detail) the United Nations itself is dominated by national concerns, and very rarely rises to a supra-national challenge, and national pilots' associations were in some instances easily dominated by the influence of their national governments, and broke away from the concerted action. Also, national governments had other interests—for example, relations with Arab States, or complex concerns with Eastern Europe—which made them unwilling to arrive at international agreement which would have tied their hands and forced them to take embarrassing action. The agreement between the United States and Cuba does, it must be admitted, pave the way for other possibilities. Once again, a solution that might imply supra-national control of national policies was ruled out of court. It is unlikely that the International Airline Pilots' Association will gain greater success until it can rally public opinion for international action *against the will of* the national governments. If it could succeed in doing that, even on this one issue, it would have made a major contribution to the slow development of supra-national institutions—which is precisely why it will be opposed.

The use of arms and violence as political weapons for civilian terrorism, guerrilla freedom movements, and the like, and armed repression through military intervention (Czechoslovakia) and internal fascism (Uganda), raise sets of questions about international social control that can no longer be handled on the basis of the policies of single States with the effectiveness that is required. On no subject is the political opinion of the world more divided, at least when justifications are being put forward and remedial action avoided. What is to one group the legitimate use of power is to another anarchy or blatant imperialism or nazism. The United Nations Security Council, which is the formal international instrument of control, consists of representatives of nation-states who vote for peacekeeping only when it is in their own national interest, whose members supply arms to warring or repressive factions, who are seldom called in question (even theoretically) when arms of their national manufacture are found in the hands of combatants, who keep international peacekeeping forces weak and starved of funds (by comparison with the importance of the job), and who take the major initiatives to settle disputes as far as possible outside the machinery of the United Nations, which they make sure is not equipped to handle them in any event. The major powers lead the way in resisting any major developments that would limit their sovereignty in this vital area, preferring the tortuous methods of trade-off negotiation, and considering the risk of continued violence to be less costly than the modification of nationalism. Even the concept of United Nations peacekeeping itself (which spilled over into the conception of the Vietnam international inspection mechanism) is based on an intermediary function which is not intended in any way to be superior to the national rights of the conflicting parties. The dangerous weakness of nationalism is revealed in crystal-clear form by the failure of governments to be able to handle terrorist attacks on innocent parties or between factions, more particularly when these have international ramifications.

The handling of questions of migration and citizenship is not at this point a subject of danger and threat, but it does have explosive elements and, from the point of view of the civic and social position of the individual, the recent increase in restrictive devices and measures seems to be turning the clock back away from advances that were made after World War II. This is particularly noticeable in formerly liberal countries such as Britain—largely as a result of the confusions that surround the large-scale sudden immigration of ethnic groups.

There are two features that make migration a matter of potential international rather than purely bilateral concern. One is the way in which racial persecution sets in motion inhumane chain reactions which undermine the ethical and moral position of nations with severe consequences for their own integrity. The other is the fact that questions of population and wealth distribution are getting to the point at which they will soon no longer be resolvable by national actions in national terms.

The Ugandan move against Asians may seem to the world to be a tragic and regrettable incident, but trivial in terms of world concerns. No greater mistake could be made. Consider the following. The first Nazi pogroms against Jews were mild by comparison with the final eventual "solution." None of the countries whose public expressed horror at the events officially accepted more than a handful of refugees. Switzerland, the country of traditional refuge, went so far as to ensure that the German government identified passport-holders as Jewish or not, and denied entry to Jewish passport-holder refugees. Prominent Jewish leaders in France made speeches urging that the situation not be made worse by intemperate criticism of German leaders. The United States took care to make certain that their expressions of disapproval had no material effect in terms of trade. Having succeeded in their first comparatively mild pogroms, accompanied by outright thefts of property, the Nazi leaders knew they could go as far as they liked without danger of interference. They retorted to expressions of disapproval: "You have no moral basis for your disapproval since you will not accept the Jews as immigrants yourselves."

What happened to the Jews also happened to others, who became displaced persons persecuted at home, with passport renewals refused, trapped by continually moving boundaries, living a life of dangerous and clandestine movement from one country to another.* Europe's population of displaced persons was treated with unbelievably bureaucratic inhumanity. Lesser countries began to follow Nazi practices, and, until war actually began, the moral resistance of the free world was thoroughly sapped by its own compromises.

The Ugandan events are having the same kinds of results. Faced with President Amin's racial persecution of Indians, the rest of the world bent over backwards to describe it as a matter of economic class and citizenship rather than race and ethnicity, and to keep remedial action as far away as possible from the likelihood of causing pain to their own countries. Only Britain and Canada came anywhere near responding in terms of solving the problem at a cost to their own countries. Britain, which bore the brunt, was then forced into a set of restrictive migration policies, and served notice to the world that henceforth they could not be counted on again. France, the supposed bastion of tolerance, admitted *not one refugee*. Switzerland, which has been accepting small numbers of Tibetans with some success, opened its doors to but a handful. Some Indians lost all citizenship rights as they left Uganda, and are still in refugee camps administered by the United Nations, separated from their families in some instances.

The persecution of Ugandan Indians was treated by the world community of nations as *an internal national matter* for Uganda, which countries could protest on an individual basis but which was, by definition, ruled out of United Nations competence for intervention. No mechanism existed for enforcing an alteration of Ugandan policy. Since Britain has now backed off, only Canada retained a moral position by its actions that would enable it to protest without hypocrisy. Other States have now

---

* E. M. Remarque, *Les Exilés* (The Exiles, Liebe Deinen Nächsten) is a moving evocation which in my view should be required reading in all countries.

been given effective notice that in the world of the civilized 1970s internal persecution is their own, national, affair.*

This situation bodes ill for the future. One can assume that there will be some increase of persecution and that, to defend States against these "dangerous" unfortunates, migration restrictions will increase, except in special circumstances where there is need for large-scale, low-status manpower or where capital and skill can be transferred. This means, on the one hand, that any move toward the creation of world citizenship (accorded, let us say, by a United Nations organ certifying complete mobility of political and social rights) is a pipe dream. On the other hand, it also seems to rule out or delay the acceptance of measures linked to the redistribution of population and wealth.

It is usually stated that the current population explosion is having exponential growth effects and that the areas of greatest population growth have the lowest incomes. It is also stated that the gap between the rich and poor nations is increasing, except for a number of significant examples where rapid measurable growth has occurred. Each one of these statements hides a series of important qualifications and modifications that can change their significance; so much so that I do not wish to imply a personal adherence to the statements in the above simplistic form or to the consequences I am about to state (see Chapter 18).

However, if the above model is treated at face value, as it often is in public discussion, there is only one theoretical solution. Nation-states are notoriously chary about introducing population policies to save the world, particularly in circumstances in which they see manpower as an essential defensive instrument. It is indeed remarkable that China, India, and Japan have overcome this deterrent to population restriction to a considerable extent and have been able to introduce control policies. But, while they once represented major population growth, checks in their growth rates are matched by increases elsewhere. A first step toward effective world population control is a formal and enforceable world policy, which will *not* be created by nation-states alone.

Further, nation-states (which could, for example, be taxed for popula-

---

* Uganda is unique only in that persecution and emigration are part of the same policy; the world is currently full of deliberate persecution of ethnic minorities, which rarely receives the kind of publicity or protest that moves other governments or international agencies to take cognizance. Current events in Chile are creating more stateless persons. It is curious that while events in Cyprus made world headlines, newspapers do not consistently follow massacres and warfare in Kurdistan, Baluchistan, and parts of Africa and Latin America. Recent African commentators have been making the point that Amin's persecution of African Ugandans is going on unprotested.

tion growth by an international agency) will resist controls all the more while there is the implication that population control is being required of poor countries in order to maintain the increasing material advantages of richer ones. Migration from poorer to richer countries is possibly the easiest and most effective way of increasing *world* economic growth, since in principle it brings people to a climate of enterprise and expansion. If it is to be reasonably effective, however, it would have to be on a scale that would at least have the initial effects of reducing the increase in the *per capita* GNP to near zero, although the total GNP would then increase perhaps faster than before. There would also be delays in the effects since it would take time for migrants to adjust and begin to make their contributions. However, if begun on a sufficient scale, such a policy could be expected to have the following additional consequences: a reduction in population growth rate attributable to those families that migrated, an increase in per capita productive capacity in those countries where a significant population proportion migrated, an increase in the rate of development catch-up (on a per capita income basis) partly due to a slowing down in the rate of growth of per capita income in the richer countries matched by increased productive capacity in the poorer ones, and a slowing up of the net reproduction rate as the world policy begins to bite. Unfortunately the world lacks the institutions to ensure the creation of such a policy and the adhesion of nation-states to it.

Finally, to complete the catalog, passing reference must be made to the issues of commercial interdependence that were raised in the last chapter. The recurring monetary crisis is not only subject to the confusions of differences in the economics being used by the practical men but is inevitably bound to the concept of national control of national currencies. Painfully, in the 19th century, nation-states brought their currencies under national control (instead of leaving them to the decisions of regional authorities or private enterprise) and the process was hastened and carried further in the 20th century by the creation of central banks and other instruments of centralized monetary policy. It is inconceivable now to imagine the situation that would exist if Britain, Canada, the United States, or Switzerland had different internal regional currencies in variable relationships to one another.

In some senses, the world is in that position now. Regional adjustments are not really allowed, because nation-states have the responsibility for seeing that all is well within their boundaries. The idea that population, capital, and resources may flow freely across national boundary lines, and thereby bring about adjustments that are rather similar to the adjustments taking place within national boundaries, is only just being revived in

Europe. But it is still conceived of within an exclusive boundary; as it revives, it is in some respects being threatened because of the national interests of countries such as the United States which are outside the system.

Furthermore, even in Europe, the notion of an international operating currency to help make the adjustments (analogous to those made through the use of a national currency) is still far away. One wonders what would happen to international commerce and balances if, over and above national currencies, the United Nations or the World Bank issued its own currency as legal tender in all member States.

As for the multinational companies and the international unions, it is becoming clear that their exercise of power requires an increasing degree of international control and regulation, and the provision of international law applicable to their needs. Once again, the European community is, within its own sphere, engaged in developing instruments of facilitation and control, which are likely to provide invaluable lessons should United Nations agencies ever achieve similar mandates.

To sum up, nation-states, through the use of present methods, are inadequate for the task of handling world affairs. They are a fact of world political life, and will not be supplanted. One does not expect world supra-national government to come overnight. Except in the sense of the great autocratic empires of Asia and Europe, mankind has not yet devised a system of world government that is compatible with modified national units. In the hope of facilitating a slow movement in this direction, one should perhaps critically examine the way in which our existing world government—the United Nations—works, with perhaps side references to its more cohesive regional analog—the European Community.

The United Nations itself was originally designed with problems of post-War security in mind. It was at the time thought, with some reason, that the greatest danger to security lay in conflict between the Big Four—the Soviet Union, China, Britain, and the United States—and that their respect for the moral force of the United Nations would, because of their size and power, be purely voluntary. Great authority was thus placed in a small quasi-executive Security Council, which could not take decisions unless the Great Powers were in sufficient agreement not to use their veto. There was no realistic possibility of mobilizing force in such a way as to ensure compliance with a United Nations resolution if a large power chose to ignore it.

Since the formation of the United Nations, the power balance has changed. Japan certainly has Great Power weight, and suggestions have been made that Japan increase its level of financing in return for a veto-carrying seat on the Security Council. West Germany and France are of the same order of power as Britain, and they are increasing relatively, while Britain may be declining.

Furthermore, the attention given to security of the Great Power conflict variety is substantially reduced by comparison with that given to other problems. Smaller-scale conflicts, with the potentiality of leading to world conflict, are the order of the security day, and the Great Powers have learned at least to exercise restraint in dealing with them. However, they still tend to see such conflicts in terms of the effects on the balance of power, and on the position of power blocs, so that initial reactions tend to maintain divided viewpoints. The point of view that gains majority support among non-Great Power members tends to be emasculated or vetoed unless the powers are divided. In any event, the national vote game is usually played with a substantial number of members voting to win, on grounds influenced by ideology, alliance, or regional interest. Only a major technical and political reform could turn the Security Council into a controlling, instead of a winning, organization. At present, its members behave very much as lineages in conflict seeking to restore a status quo with which they can live and as a result of which they can reestablish social contact.

More important still, it was earlier recognized that many other types of activity had within them the seeds of conflict. For this reason, among others, the United Nations became concerned with human rights, development and technical assistance, the level of social welfare, trusteeship (originally inherited from the League of Nations), colonialism, and population. New programs were added that were not justified by reference to security in the old conflict sense but because of their importance to the general fate and well-being of man—the latest being the concern with the environment.

The above list is merely indicative and does not include those programs which are solely housed within one or another of the specialized agencies. The formation of the list is a response to international need as expressed by at least a significant number of nation-states. The instrument for expressing this need, and creating the executive organs, is the General Assembly of all member States, which constitutes the fundamental legislature of the United Nations. The role of the Assembly as a defining and enabling organ has steadily increased, since it is possible for groups of States to put together their common interests and establish a policy; the chances of finding such a group which could obtain benefit from concerted action are quite high. Most voting members are relatively poor and regard themselves as the net recipients of technical assistance. Also, therefore, once technical assistance was invented, it became a major objective of most voting members to ensure a maximum flow, as far as possible under their own control; as each area of concern was added, technical assistance and development aid were written into its core.

In fact, the United Nations now is at least as much, if not more, an organ for the development of knowledge and policies that can be used for technical assistance, and for communication and technical assistance itself, as it is for security in the narrow sense. This in part explains the weight attached to the publication and distribution of reports and to the otherwise unexpected size of its research and documentary interests. Its staff has an academic as well as an administrative orientation, and within the network a considerable range of research institutes and activities are supported.

On the whole, though, the instruments that the United Nations has at its disposal are rigorously limited. Peacekeeping operations, a relatively late development, are financed by voluntary contributions of nation-states or levies over and above the regular budget, many of which are said to be in arrears, mostly for political reasons. A nation-state may be drummed out of membership for failure to pay its regular dues, but the practice has been to exercise extreme tolerance, and a large number of big contributors pay late. After the war, the United States paid the lion's share of all contributions. This was understandable in view of the distribution of the productive capacity of the world at that time, but the temporary expedient has been allowed to drift. By no stretch of the imagination can it now be argued that Europe and Japan are unable to pay their way in the same manner, mainland China has entered, and several developing countries are now in a good position to make more substantial contributions. Moves by the United States to reduce the proportion of its contributions are in fact overdue, should result in a healthier balance of contributions, and should not be attributed to petulance or irritation.

On the other hand, while the poorer countries might in theory concentrate their votes for higher expenditures, there is no way they could make such a resolution stick if the main contributing countries (or even a few of them) decided to boycott its implementation. This, at worst, could result in the destruction of the organization, and at best in suspicion and cold-shouldering. Hence the countries that have most to gain have, at least on the surface, moderated their influence, language, and financial voting behavior.*

* This is changing, with the new power of blocs led by the more confident Arab States. A reaction may be in the making. The improper politicization of UNESCO has, for example, caused Switzerland to reduce its financial contribution.

The result is a budget (1968 figures) of $128 million, 42 percent of which was allocated for technical assistance. Any programs beyond this figure (such as peacekeeping) implied voluntary contributions; indeed, some voluntary contributions are included in the figure.

I simply ask the reader to reflect on the size of this sum by comparison, for example, with the budgets of universities in the United States and Europe, the bilateral technical assistance programs of OECD members, the capital controlled by any major bank, the civil service wage bill of any of the top 75 percent or more of member States, or the major charitable foundations in the United States, to say nothing of the great multinational companies.

The central element in embryonic world government is quite simply starved of funds. Programs are added to its responsibilities yearly. Unless, as with the environment, they are tied to additional, *voluntary* funding, they cannot be supported since such increases as are allocated to the regular budget are nearly always swallowed up by standard cost of living adjustments.

Yet the irony, and the cynically manipulated fact, is that the wealthier countries continue to demand improved results, point to certain inevitable wastages that in some instances they themselves create, and threaten budget reductions if greater efficiency is not achieved. To anticipate a little, a financially starved organization is always less efficient than a properly budgeted one (it cannot achieve the required outputs, and much of its energy goes wastefully into exercising ingenuity to make ends meet); governments complain immediately when the supply of documentation is not forthcoming, yet also complain about its volume; and governments have insisted on a structure for the total family of organizations that inevitably leads to a disproportionate amount of time being spent on liaison and coordination. The contributing governments have been responsible for insisting on these policies, yet complain at their effects on output. Since government policy is set by reasonably intelligent men, one can only assume that there is something more substantial behind the contradiction.

And there is. It is simply that, to the wealthier and more individually powerful countries, it appears on the surface that they retain more influence and power by actions undertaken outside the United Nations framework. This is especially clear in the vital area of development assistance. There is argument as to whether multilateral or bilateral assistance is most effective (see Chapter 13), but the difference is most certainly not in accordance with the relative weight of multilateral and bilateral contributions. The sixteen countries making up the Development

Assistance Committee of OECD (containing the most important donors), according to one interpretation of the figures, provided $1386 million in multilateral aid in all forms in 1970 including projects outside the United Nations system, as against $6562 million in their own bilateral programs. They rated their own programs six times more importantly than those of the United Nations.

In theory, the United Nations international civil service should be apart from, and above considerations of, the policies of nations from which they are drawn. In fact, a very high proportion of them are; indeed, my own impression is that, apart from one or two of the specialized agencies, the staffing is of an extraordinarily high caliber. Much of the morale dates from the days when the United Nations was first formed—when it attracted some of the most intelligent and idealistic brains of the world, who genuinely shaped ideas and policies on the basis of perspectives and social science theories that were substantially *in advance* of those present in academia, to say nothing of national civil services. For the first ten to fifteen years, the United Nations was perhaps the most fundamentally innovative of the world's bureaucracies.*

This situation has changed, and in some respects was not intended. The rules governing appointment to the service are based upon national quotas; while these are sometimes stretched, they are there as a basic consideration. Senior positions are expected to be divided among the most prominent nations. An increasing number of appointments are made *on temporary secondment from* national civil services, so that it takes a very strong man indeed to ignore his own bureaucracy's policy. Some countries, to make up their quota, provide less competent candidates, because they have a real shortage of qualified people from whom to choose, because their more qualified experts are indispensable, or because they regard the United Nations as a good place to dump those who are under a cloud. This does not alter the fact that those in the key majority are dedicated, independent, and brilliant—but it gives them at least an additional 25 percent burden to carry.

If national governments had been genuinely interested in detached international operations, they would not have introduced national quotas. Quality would have been the only criterion and permanence of career would have been of key significance, with loyalty to the organization.

Add to these comments the observation that, particularly of late, the most significant arms and peacekeeping developments have taken place with relatively minor United Nations involvement, and one is inevitably

* For a less optimistic view of some of these issues, see Shirley Hazzard, *Defeat of an Ideal*, Boston; Little, Brown, 1973.

drawn to the conclusion that nation-states, particularly the wealthy, are extremely suspicious of allocating power to the United Nations family. There is, of course, the argument that the United Nations has not developed the instruments that would make security manageable. This, however, is the direct responsibility of the nation-states governing it, for they have avoided making proposals in this direction. There are also good reasons for skepticism in this field, if not in some of the others, for it is here that political blocs vote together and outcomes tend to be linked to their voting size rather than to rational argument or detached control.

Nevertheless, outside of security matters narrowly defined, the United Nations family has a great deal of responsibility which it can potentially exercise. The members of the family are a varied body of unequal partners, whose identification, formal organization, relations with one another, and relationship to the United Nations itself are so complex as to require specialized study merely to describe it. Only the barest outline of the most salient features relevant to the present discussion will be attempted here.

Many of the most significant agencies are completely independent of the UN General Assembly. This arose largely because the model of the preexisting International Labour Organization (founded in 1919) which had independently coexisted with the League of Nations was used to establish additional organizations charged with specialized sectors. In addition to the ILO, the International Telegraphic Union (1865) and the Universal Postal Union (1874) carried on from earlier days. In the six years from 1945 to 1950, most of the fields that governments consider to be of importance were covered by the international organizations. Those years saw the establishment of FAO (agriculture), the International Bank for Reconstruction and Development, the International Monetary Fund, UNESCO, the International Civil Aviation Organization, the General Agreement on Trade and Tariffs (which, despite its name, is an organization flowing *from* an agreement), the World Health Organization, and the World Meteorological Organization. Others have been established since.

Each one of the above organizations has its governing body (made up of representatives of member States), which is formally completely independent of any one of the others. It would be unthinkable, in current practice, for the United Nations General Assembly to *instruct* such a body. It may strongly advise, and there is machinery which makes its influence significant, but most of the above organizations are sovereign international bodies. Further, the number and list of member States differs for each one.

It will be noted also that the sectoral divisions differ along lines that are familiar to most national governments; they correspond to a common model of departmental responsibility within government, although the model is by no means uniform. It is, however, normal for UNESCO affairs to be handled by Ministries of Education in consultation with Ministries of Science and Culture, for WHO matters to be handled by Ministries of Health, for FAO matters to be handled by Ministries of Agriculture, and so forth. United Nations matters are normally handled by Ministries of Foreign Affairs and, in coordinated States, such Ministries also keep a watching brief on the international "political" implications of the specialized agencies. These crop up surprisingly frequently; innocent-looking resolutions on the study of racialism, the admission of Rhodesia, technical assistance in Jerusalem, or the control of narcotics open up a Pandora's box of political pleading.

In addition to the above, there are numerous agencies that were set up by the United Nations General Assembly and, while administered by independent governing councils, are considered to be subject to it to varying degrees. Control can involve the ultimate right to revoke the constitution, or the receipt and critique of reports, or more specific policy directions. Among the better known of these organizations are UNICEF, the UN High Commission for Refugees, the UN Development Programme, the World Food Programme (with FAO), and UNCTAD (the United Nations Commission for Trade and Development). The new Environment Programme has been set up in this way.

The dangers inherent in an organization based upon a proliferation of high-powered independent international organizations were quickly recognized to make up the Achilles' heel of the United Nations. They can be summarized as follows.

At the beginning there was no location of responsibility, either in the international organization or in most nation-states, for an overall view of the total operation or for its coordination. The very small budgets (in 1968, for all these groups taken together, $462 million, of which 50 percent was technical assistance) were spread thinly over conflicting and duplicated programs.* To take one example, the ILO, UNESCO, WHO and the United Nations Bureau of Social Affairs, which are all concerned with

*In 1972, while attending a limited specialized session of the UNESCO General Conference, I calculated roughly that the costs to member States of providing for representation at that meeting, neglecting costs to UNESCO itself, was at least 50 percent of the UNESCO budget for the sector being considered. Quite independently, a colleague unofficially and very roughly estimated that it probably costs member States $2 million to be represented at the General Conference, plus $5 million a year to maintain permanent delegations in Paris. These figures taken together are equivalent to 10 percent of UNESCO's regular budget, and there are other elements in the decision-making operation that are not included.

rural well-being, each became involved with the problems of rural maleducation and stagnation. Each then began to use interrelated concepts such as fundamental education, organization for rural welfare, and measures to increase rural employment through self-help, which ultimately came to be dealt with under the catchall of community development, which in turn has evolved into a concern for internal regional development. It took years for each organization to learn what the others were doing, and to work out agreements dealing with sectoral responsibilities within overall policy; even now the competition and the jealousy between agencies continue. They are reinforced by sectoral jealousy and lack of intersectoral communication *within* the nation-states. The Department of Public Health of a given country is not going to gain much in terms of its own national program and stature if it persuades WHO to hand over responsibility for rural nutrition to FAO, which then deals with the country's Department of Agriculture, boosting its programs to the detriment of the Department of Public Health. This is a concern that is characteristic of all bureaucracies and has been built into the very structure of the United Nations family at the most extreme level.

Yet the nation-states that allowed this elephantine organization to grow in this way used the weaknesses *they themselves had built in* to criticize and belabor it. They accused the international administrations of being power hungry, jealous of prerogatives, competitive and empire building, and wasteful of the resources that were so generously (*sic*!) provided. This point of view is reflected in speech after speech and in all the organs, particularly from representatives of those who were paying the bill— countries such as the United States, the Soviet Union, France, Britain, Australia.

Naturally enough, the secretariats, particularly in the United Nations, reacted, but their powers were limited and they could not get at the roots of the difficulties. The best they could do—and it was by no means an insignificant best—was a patchwork job.

The most significant proposal, which involved a fairly strong member government commitment, was the establishment and expansion of responsibility of the United Nations Economic and Social Council (ECOSOC). The Council is in effect a subcommittee of the General Assembly, and its most important decisions and recommendations are ratified in the Assembly. It is generally responsible for an overview of economic and social affairs, which may include almost anything apart from security matters. There is no inhibition about debating matters that crosscut the interests of particular specialized agencies, and the influence of ECOSOC has been less dramatic but extremely important in the move to more effective world government, certainly in the 1960s.

ECOSOC, however, has limited powers. It may make some decisions related to the continuing supervision of existing programs which the General Assembly has agreed should be its province. For any new initiative, it must persuade not only the General Assembly but also the governing councils of those specialized agencies into whose field the matter projects. It cannot, however, interfere in the independent pro-grams of the specialized agencies. It cannot, for example, at least at the legislative or governing council level, prevent UNESCO, ILO, WHO, and FAO from each adopting dramatic world policies that might conflict with one another, have the effect of distorting national priorities in developing countries, place a strain on the available international funding, or other-wise create confusion and sometimes false hopes.

But ECOSOC does have two weapons—one of which is very effective, so much so that I suspect that it is responsible for reactions against an increase in its authority. The effective weapon is through its influence on the United Nations Development Programme and technical assistance operations generally. While coordination has slowly increased by stages since the beginning of UN technical assistance in the late 1940s, it was still inhibited by sectoral rivalries, the competitive sovereignty of the specialized agencies, and the undermining of the coordinating machinery by agency and sectoral interests in the field. The 1969 Jackson Report,* carried out on behalf of the Inter-Agency Consultative Board of the UN Development Fund, resulted in discussions in the Enlarged Committee for Programme and Coordination of ECOSOC, and in ECOSOC itself, which in turn resulted in the strengthening of the general authority of ECOSOC in technical assistance matters with the UNDP as its agent. This included—a most important matter as we shall see in Chapter 13—the strengthening of the role of the United Nations Resident Rep-resentatives as coordinating officials for the work of all agencies in the field, insofar as technical assistance programs and policies are concerned. While this is still by no means perfect, and specialized agencies still symbolically budget their technical assistance programs according to their own view of the relative significance of various sectors, they must be much more careful about considerations of coordination.

The other weapon consists of a rather confusing coordinating machin-ery, which, it is to be hoped, may be more effective and rational as a result

* R. G. A. Jackson, *A Study of the Capacity of the United Nations Development System,* Geneva; United Nations, 1969.

of the Jackson Report. In addition to the two relatively high-powered and general policy committees mentioned in the previous paragraph, there is a day-to-day coordinating committee known as the Administrative Committee for Coordination. This is an interagency series of committees which meets on specific technical subjects to "clear" actions and programs that particular agencies are about to be engaged in. The participants tend to be the persons responsible for the technical area in the agency concerned, and it is in these committees that charges of "poaching" can be aired, cooperation offered, and information exchanged. The participants keep one ear on the technical questions and the other on the jurisdictional ones.

This divided concern, made mandatory by the insistence of government representatives on the economies of coordination, and exacerbated by the independent sovereignty of the organizations, diverts a great deal of the available manpower from substantive creativity. On several occasions, in front of international civil servants, I have estimated (and not been challenged on the estimation) that each administrative division in each of the international organizations must have a minimum of the equivalent of two to three posts devoted to liaison functions within the UN family itself. Each technical seminar or conference of experts, for example, is likely to draw into it "observers" from related departments and agencies. This load is, of course, spread among officials, but it constitutes a priority in their activity which they cannot avoid. On balance, it is more than likely that governments, by their insistence on coordination at the administrative level (while failing to insist on it at the policy level) are adding to costs and reducing output.

No national government would itself operate this way, in its own internal activities. It is, of course, a byword that government departments in nation-states are competitive and empire building and that coordination is labor consuming. But that tendency is counterbalanced to some degree in most governments by the existence of some effective centralized responsibility for total policy—for example, a cabinet. It is this feature which makes national government possible.

On the other hand, the United Nations operates with each "department of government" (the specialized agencies and their functional equivalents) responsible to a different sovereign "electorate." It is as if each department of a national government were responsible to a separately elected legislature and a separate system of law.

In theoretical conception it would be fairly simple to transform the United Nations system into one of unified world government. One could, for example, conceive of the General Assembly as the supreme legislature and the Economic and Social Council as an executive, an enlarged cabinet but without portfolios, perhaps. The governing Councils of the specialized agencies, and of the programs that have almost agency status within the UN, could then be transformed into smaller, more executive, business trustees and watchdogs, with their legislative authority transferred to the General Assembly and the Economic and Social Council. The secretaries-general would then constitute an executive cabinet, unless the Economic and Social Council elected to allocate portfolios of responsibility (not particularly easy when members are spokesmen for particular nation-states). Such a system would enforce coordination of policy and would relieve junior international civil servants of trying to coordinate uncoordinated policy by administrative acts, knowing that their own Councils were breathing down their necks in competitive fashion.

It is, of course, not likely to come about in this way. The involvement of the United Nations system in security, and the existence of a very small number of extremely and disproportionately powerful States that are determined not to subordinate their independent force and influence to the decisions of a conclave, are two facts that alone would be sufficient to put a sharp brake on any movement of the United Nations to become an effective world government. Indeed, at least while security matters remain paramount, and perhaps also while there are such disparities of wealth between countries, it is possible that world government as real government could come about only through either the domination of the system by a relatively small number of powers acting in close concert, which would put the smaller countries on the defensive, or by some impossible-to-foresee breakup of all huge countries into smaller independent units. If the United States, the USSR, and China consisted each of five countries instead of one, the manageability and the evolution of the United Nations in the kind of direction envisaged above would be more probable.

On the other hand, there is still the possibility that the smaller countries, particularly as they increase their share of the budget as against that of the Great Powers, will come to seek greater executive effectiveness for the United Nations at least in economic, social, and cultural matters. At present their national interests are to maintain national independence at all costs. This maintenance of political, social, and cultural lifestyle is seen, falsely as we have noted, to be a matter of maintaining political boundaries as a friction reducing the flow of influence across them. Moves to restructure the United Nations may be more practicable once this fear can be assuaged—once it can be shown that supra-national government is indeed the only real way of controlling those very influences and that national governments are basically power-less to control their destinies on their own. It is significant that the challenge of creating an organization to deal with environmental issues was not used as an opportunity to increase effective action; instead the same old pattern of quasi-independence added yet another group with which all the existing groups had to establish liaison. This indicates more than anything else that the world does not yet really see environmental matters as the crisis for humanity that is so often used in rhetoric. If it did, governments would not be able to tolerate the construction of such a weak vessel, even in the name of their own sovereignty.

A more encouraging sign is the direction of development of the European Community though this is subject to vicissitudes. Despite the divergences of European countries, and the centuries of strife which lie behind their formation and their relations one to another, there has existed a deliberate will to emphasize common issues and to solve them together even though views about the solutions may initially be very far apart. The Community has evolved through first tackling a number of limited issues—coal and steel rationalization—and then, by means of the Treaty of Rome, developing a skeletal administration which could inter-pret the clauses of the Treaty in ways that would bind member govern-ments to particular actions. Effective policy legislation, broadly linked to the Treaty of Rome but interpreting it very widely, is arrived at through meetings of relevant Ministers of the government cabinets of the coun-tries concerned. The Common Market aspect of the Community is reflected in the existence of a powerful cabinet of Commissioners, each with a departmental portfolio, located with the civil service in Brussels. The Commissioners and their civil service are intended to be above nationality; however, there is still strong national rivalry in the allocation of powers between the Commissioners. In addition the civil service has many of the same problems as those of the United Nations system, except that there is no sign that any government as yet uses it as a "dumping ground"—its functions are far too important for that, since they impinge very closely upon all aspects of national policies. The facts that policy is decided by discussion between direct representatives of governments with powers of commitment, and that the Commissioners acting together can bring departmental and sectoral interests into the same sort of harmony that exists in nation-states, give the operation an enormous strength.

There is also a Parliament, which theoretically has influential powers.

These, however, have not on the whole been developed, partly because the Ministerial committee system ensures the adhesion of governments to agreed policy, and partly because the Parliament did not adequately reflect the dominance of France and Germany prior to the entry of Britain, Ireland, and Denmark. The dominance of two parties, relatively speaking, in a small group of six countries was inhibiting. Now there are three large and powerful countries in a community of nine, the three have sufficiently divergent views that a steady ganging up against the others is unlikely, and this, combined with individual veto powers, makes the community a more balanced enterprise.

In addition, an important judicial machinery has been provided. Elements in the system are able to impose fines on governments, firms, and individuals, and in fact do so for breaches of agreed rules governing their conduct, particularly in economic and human rights matters. On a number of issues, particularly human rights, it is possible for appeals to be lodged before the European Court from decisions of national courts or to bring certain cases more directly to the European Court. Furthermore, Community law takes precedence over national law and must be recognized as such in national courts.

In Europe, supra-national organization is already effective as government; it is patchy, hesitant, unsure of itself in some areas, but remarkably confident and determined in others. With all its limitations and uncertainties, it is indeed true international government. Despite argument and protests to the contrary, the nations concerned are learning the essential steps in preserving the essence of national identity and individuality, while joining powers for the common international good. This may be a more important direct experiment, in the long run, than the history of the United Nations family to date—if only because it may demonstrate to the United Nations that supra-national government is practically possible, and does not mean the loss of the part of national identity that is of importance.

PART III

Movement in the Social System

Prologue to Part III

POLICY is by definition change oriented. It works to stop changes, to promote them, or to channel them. In so doing, it seeks to find elements in the social system that can be manipulated. Anthropologists might stress the quality of familial interactions as having a bearing upon divorce rates and living styles. This may be interesting, but unless the observation can be translated into a form suggesting, for example, that a change in family allowances, in taxation, or in social work guidance will have some predictable effect, there will be little by way of policy implication.

On the other hand, the machinery of government is used to bring about results. Those who use it and design it have those results in mind. This implies that they hold an ethnosocial science theory that contains the causative links, and that this theory must be embedded in assumptions about the way society works. This study is not an account of the ethnosocial science assumptions and theories that are embodied in actual policies. Such accounts are long overdue and, to be informative, should be compared with the theories present in the social sciences themselves. The intention here is rather to set out those anthropological perspectives, consistent with the general line of my argument, that can serve as one example of an anthropologist's background of thinking.

I have tried to sketch an outline of world society, from the village universe to the United Nations, and to stress a number of themes that are embedded in anthropological analysis on the one hand, and on the other represent major questions to which anthropologists, among others, could address themselves. But anthropologists also work with more general theories of social change, which attempt to establish, for example, the manner in which ideas and cultural expression change, and the processes by which social issues establish a dynamic leading to altered forms of society. We saw in Chapters 1 and 2 that there are a number of ways of looking at such matters—for example, with evolutionary, ecological, or cultural change perspectives. There are thus a number of competing

153

theories, and even different theoretical languages. Within the total body of the subject there are countless theoretically informed empirical statements covering almost the entire gamut of social life.

In this Part, I shall distill what I believe to be some of the more important themes that anthropologists are using to understand social and cultural processes in general, and that seem to me to be significant if policy makers are to have a reasonably accurate knowledge of the world they are influencing. The themes are examples only; there are others I could have chosen, but it is not my goal to set out a complete theory of social change. While the statements are subject to argument, they are not particularly original, and may be found reflected in many specialized studies, except for a few concepts and terms I have introduced to clarify my own thought. In a way, these themes constitute some of the essential assumptions that applied anthropologists need to use and examine.

CHAPTER 10

Innovation and the Genesis of Ideas

ANY public policy is based on an implicit or explicit theory of the way society works. When policy does not work, at least in the way its designers foresaw, the implicit theory has been defective. When policy does work, the implicit theory *may* be right, and social scientists would do well to examine the reasons why.

Indeed, social scientists have paid far too little attention to the ethnosocial science of public decision makers—to the task of revealing the conceptions that politicians, managers, and civil servants have about the nature of human interaction and the social structure and organization within which they work. The comparison between conceptions used in the real world and social science theory, if made deliberately and pointedly, could be stimulating to both.

One theme of importance to both worlds consists in the movement of ideas and symbols and the ways these are combined to make structural artifacts—conceptions, theories, propositions, values, works of art, machines, tools. The influence of popular philosophy, and many naïve social science constructs using the name of philosophy, have contributed a confusion to our ways of looking at these things. Naïve materialism or naïve idealism give causative prominence to material nature on the one hand, or to man's thought on the other. It would seem that materialism has its greatest weight when we consider the origins and nature of man himself, for the biology of man is there to be seen and examined, and we do not know when, under what circumstances, and by what mechanisms, thought (as we know it) was formed and how it relates to the biological base. (This last set of issues may ultimately be solved, but the when and where of origins may be forever lost.) Certainly, the methods of anthropological ethology, while interesting and enlightening on some points, do not and cannot get at the fundamentals.

But to apply materialism to a one-way causative sequence in the contemporary social world, or indeed to any social world man has invented to our knowledge, is to run headlong into trouble. It is a matter of debate whether abstract ideas can exist without some material referent. There is, however, no question but that abstract ideas emerge out of a consideration of material phenomena. Even mathematics begins with the observation of singularity and plurality, angles and lines, relationships, sets, exclusions and inclusions, and a thousand matters that, in their axiomatic or definitional base, are drawn from the real world. The constructs built upon such foundations may move a long way from empirical reference, but the base is there.

Similarly, use, recognition, and manipulation of the real material world is made by man through the generalized identification of its parts—that is, the real world is given symbolic meaning. Until iron is identified and given a set of characteristics it is not incorporated into social use. Trees, herbs, animals, and pieces of machinery are given symbolic status; those symbols and ideas are part of culture; and their existence makes it possible for man to transmit knowledge about use from one generation to another, from one social group to another.

There is little difference, in principle, between the movement of ideas and the movement of physical things, or the change in the use of ideas and the change in the use of things. It is often difficult to make any distinction, on a clear-cut basis, between means and ends. What are ends in one context are means in another, and means frequently attract the same value attachments as so-called ends. When Marshall McCluhan proclaimed "the medium is the message," he was almost right, but not quite. A message comes to be *allocated to* the medium, in the sense that artifacts *of all kinds* must have symbolic meaning before they can exist as social phenomena and that meaning changes with use and context. This is true of a machine, a television set, and a poem. The meaning attached to the artifact can alter the meaning of any message allocated to it or carried by it; the same words spoken on the telephone or written in a letter carry less urgency than when conveyed by a telegram. But, while the medium can influence other elements of the message, it does not *dictate* the message it carries.

Nevertheless, and I think unwittingly, McCluhan brought materiality and symbolism together. Although the details of his manifestos are not very helpful, and the fact that he has not thought the implications through has made him stop at points where other scholars have gone much further, the public is now ready to see what the relationships may be. Ideas are disembodied artifacts. If you have a system of ideas, it may be changed in the same way as a machine—that is, by altering or substituting its parts. If an alteration is not consistent with the existence or the workings of other parts, it may be necessary to transform each bit until in effect the total system is replaced by another.

Policy is such a system of ideas.

Further, material artifacts, carrying their symbolic worth, are only valued if they are given a context. The same thing is true of ideas; new ideas, or new groupings or systems of ideas, may lie dormant, unused (just as is the case with an unidentified mineral) because their linkage to other relevant knowledge is not accepted or recognized. What seems to be rational policy to a reformer is not interlinked with existing policy, nor does it replace it, because its value is not recognized or because it is *seen* (rightly or wrongly is irrelevant) not to be consistent with other already established elements of action. How many magnificent, humanitarian, welfare-oriented, technical assistance projects, how many fine ideas of volunteer *animateurs*, how many fierce projects of political reformers have failed on this very point!

Again, material artifacts, carrying their symbolic meaning, are physically moved from one place to another in order to be combined for new use. Car parts are manufactured in one country, shipped to another for assembly, and the car itself is shipped to a third for use in domestic living; small pieces are made for assembly into alarm clocks, then they are warehoused, retailed, and placed in bedrooms—having a changed meaning in each context. The directions, speed of movement, place and mode of assembly, and linkage with other artifacts to constitute an assembled context are all variables. It is the same with ideas—most popularly seen at this time as "information" but by no means limited to so-called facts or data. Ideas are conceived—made, if you like; the more abstract, generalized, and penetrating they are, the more the process of creating them differs from that of the manufactured assembly line. Nevertheless, there comes a point at which they are recognized, given circulatory value, and become part of the currency of thought. Then they may be moved, always through the intervention of some physical means, whether through speech and audition, writing, or on-line computer. They are assembled, ordered, logically interlinked, combined and recombined; their logic, order, and combination (even when the links are only intuitively known) require identification and recognition. This is not an automatic process any more than the recognition of the utility of a tool is an automatic process.

Just as we can speak of a fund of capital or a pool of equipment, so we can speak of a fund or a pool of ideas. I have already suggested, in relation to the so-called conservatism of some societies (p. 59) that acts of innovation are to some degree a function of the size of the pool and the rate of idea-circulation. This is a statistical statement based on the probability of new conceptual arrangements (and remember that physical inventions are conceptual arrangements) emerging from populations whose distribution of intellectual powers is similar. While we do not have firm evidence that such distributions are in fact similar, the richness of human culture suggests that they probably are. (The contrary "evidence" of intelligence tests in certain situations, leading to the famous controversy over genetic versus environmental causation, is not relevant here [see Chapter 18], since one thing intelligence tests do not succeed in doing cross-culturally is to measure "intellectual powers.")

It may be thought that since this is a probabilistic statement the whole question of innovation and change may be safely left in the hands of chance, and that policy need not (indeed, cannot) be concerned with the matter. Such a conclusion would, however, distort the meaning of the generalization and would be contrary to other aspects of experience.

In fact policy can encourage or inhibit growth in the pool of ideas arriving from external sources. Further acts of innovation are embodied in members of the population in a selective way, so that by identifying them and encouraging or restricting their creativity, policy may change the rate of innovation. And an innovation, to be culturally significant, must be accepted and put to use in some segment of society, so that policy may open or close the channels of acceptance and diffusion, encouraging innovation in certain directions and closing its acceptance in others.

We have noted some of the circulation frictions represented by boundaries. I doubt very much indeed whether ordinary people going about their business are aware of the extraordinarily high number of ethnic groups distributed throughout the world. Although the Human Relations Area Files of Yale University number distinct "cultures" in the hundreds, that census does not even begin to enumerate, for example, the totality of ethnic groups in Canada or Australia or Switzerland, where a "Ukrainian" or an "Italian" culture is rather different from that of the ancestral homeland.

Further, the concept of cultural grouping, as linked to the notion of "multiculturalism," goes beyond ethnicity as normally approached. Within the same "ethnic" community, there are often major differences of culture—for example, differences based on religious affiliation carrying over into education and moral emphases, or upon wealth distribution as between *barrio* or slum dwellers and the rich of Palermo or Latin America, or upon political ideology as in present-day France or Chile.

A question at issue, then, will be: should policy endeavor to open or close movement of ideas across defined cultural boundaries? Paradoxically, the closing of the boundary may be advocated by those whose motives are highly humanistic in the interests of preserving the richness and variety of culture. There is a large and genuine fear that the use of modern communications to link the whole world will result in the creation of a single world culture (a global village, to use McCluhan's term), destroying minority cultures in its cannibalistic expansion.

I do not wish to be a prophet. But it is necessary to correct the balance of factors that influence such fearful predictions and, by setting out some modifying influences, to suggest that we need much more monitoring and research before we can be even approximately sure of trends. New technologies are providing certain worldwide distributions, which in the past existed only in bounded communities. Cross-national artistic influences have already been mentioned. At a more mundane level, you can now go into stores in any countries that do not have import controls and find in speciality sections almost the same range of brand-name products and durable foods. But—and this is the significant point—even where this is so, the population *as a whole* does not participate in the new opportunities. Such possibilities increase the range of possible choices, and thus increase the potentiality for the existence of subcultures within the nation. Some of those subcultures are outward turning, finding their stimuli and contacts from similar (but seldom identical) subcultures in other countries; others are inward turning.

It is, in fact, probable that the world range of subcultures is increasing. This state of affairs is not inconsistent with the possibility that a certain level of world homogeneity is also being forged—greater linguistic understanding and an increasingly shared tolerance, even encouragement, of cultural difference.

Indeed, such an outcome can be derived from a consideration of the fundamental propositions more readily than the expectation of a single, universally shared culture. If you take the permutations and combinations theoretically possible from the existence of the main cultural variations available in the world today, the number of combinations must considerably exceed even the large number of ethnic groups and larger number of subcultures present in the world. The great variety of subcultures has been based upon relatively limited availability of cultural forms. The more populations are exposed to additional possibilities, the more new cultural forms will emerge.

No amount of technological communication will replace certain intimacies of human social contact. Whereas the connections and groups that result will often be localized, changes in communication will give regional or world subcultural connections. These have not been absent in the past, as is shown by the distribution of overseas Chinese and links between religious communities in various parts of the world. That there is force behind this trend is evidenced by the considerable increase in experimental communal living and in new religious groupings (particularly among the now-young in the Western world) and its stimulus by selective contacts with the Orient. This is *not* a transfer of Indian culture to the West, any more than television and satellite communication has changed India (or, for that matter, Japan) into Western models. In both parts of the world *new* subcultures have been formed.

Some writers have suggested that growth, development, and cultural change can be linked to the existence of presumed cultural "orientations." Usually underlying such a statement is the idea that a population has acquired a "character" that predisposes it for or against certain lines of innovation.

If the proposition were that a person brought up in a given culture will have his perceptions molded by that culture, and that his actions will be rewarded and punished by it so that he will tend to direct them in certain ways rather than others—*and that this set of influences is specific to time and place*—there could be little argument, but it would not tell us much. We would then have to find out empirically just what the educative and ideological influences are, and which rewards and punishments lead in which directions.

In fact, almost all such theories go further than this.* They tend to imply that populations acquire characters through the pressures and boundary limitations of culture exercised particularly through child-nurturing and the formative years of education. What they do not say clearly are two things. First, what is the permanence and/or malleability of the system? They tend to favor permanence, despite overwhelming evidence to the contrary, evidence that in fact destroyed the national character school in anthropology. Second, when an orientation principle has been discovered or revealed, what is the flexibility in the *choice of ends* to which it is applied?

Thus, for example, it is really quite silly to say that one culture is oriented toward achievement and another is not; all cultures are oriented toward achievement, maximization of some values, minimization of

* Examples are David McClelland's achievement orientation, Everett Hagen's socialization theories, and the national character studies popular in anthropology in the 1940s and 1950s.

others, and efficiency. Where they differ is in the *selection* of things to achieve, maximize, and minimize, and the values that enter the calculation of efficiency in terms of both benefits and costs. If you place a high value on sleep and arrange things so that you achieve a way of life in which the opportunity to sleep is maximized at the cost of things like work or an expensive food intake or driving a Rolls-Royce, you may indeed not be opting for "material progress," but no one should have the ethnocentric temerity to call you inefficient or non-achievement-oriented. You have effectively achieved what you wanted—sleep.

Policy arguments based upon assertions that such orientations are absent are absurd and miss the point. The point is to analyze the goals of the society—a much more complicated task. Politicians within that society may then well wish to change those goals, finding that some of them are incompatible with, let us say, material progress or democracy, which they value more. They must then determine how to link goals so that they become drives and incentives, or they must calculate the strength of the opposition to their proposals.

In this context, religion and ideology play an extremely important and much misunderstood role. Religion in particular can operate as a paramount goal, or there may very occasionally be a system of ethics that limits or dominates action. Out of such systems may grow specific positive or negative enjoinders, taboos, and modes of calculating preferences and values. In fact, *absolutes* of a permanent kind are very rare, even in the most dogmatic religions. Religious purity is seldom evenly distributed in a population. Society can allocate certain functions to separatist sects (a dangerous solution, but common). And, religion and ideology must always be *interpreted*—an act which provides almost infinite possibilities for change and rationalization, if there is sufficient incentive. Buddhism, so often said to be other-worldly, has been shown in its impact on the day-to-day life of villages to be capable of a high degree of consistency with rational, even expansive, material calculations.* After all, Thomism and Jansenism played a part in the development of Catholic theology, and the battles now going on with a very substantial number of dissident churchmen are as much institutional as religious.

* The pious men and women entrepreneurs (non-Chinese) of Bangkok would laugh at such a theory and show, in very sophisticated ways, how their activity is consistent with other-worldly ambition, just as the church-going, church-supporting business leader would do in our society. We are too inclined to draw major inferences from apparent statistical correlations (Buddhism correlates with low per capita managerial effort, it seems) and fail to put the correlation to the test of the opinions and actions of individuals. Note, however, the dynamic interpretation of Buddhist society, when constructed from the observation of individual behavior, in the work of Edmund Leach, S. J. Tambiah, Melford Spiro, Manning Nash, Tissa Fernando, and Michael Ames, for example.

At the same time, it is surely legitimate for societies to decide to keep change away from certain cultural emphases, to impose limits on innovation, and to keep life "simple." In some contexts, this in itself may require a considerable degree of adaptability as new forces impinge. In all societies, certain kinds of innovation—let us say, in sexual mores—are considered illegitimate or punishable, and other innovations may be made, but may fail to secure social acceptance and thus diffusion.

It should be obvious that to determine the creativity levels of a culture one must be careful to identify the subjects and channels of creativity recognized by the society itself. There is little doubt that European and North American society channels much of its creativity into the exploration and use of the material world. It still, however, concerns itself with artistic and religious innovation, though those fields are often identified as nonconformist, even bohemian, whereas material innovation is highly respectable. This emphasis tends to blind us to the dynamic thrust of other societies. For example, I recently watched a highly intelligent Swiss TV program dealing with artistic movement, making the often repeated point that "90 percent of the world's innovations have been made in the 20th century," and correctly linking this to our interest in material culture. It is indeed true that *the rate of innovation* per period of time is very high indeed, and that the joint impact of a highly educated population, an immense pool of interacting knowledge, and rapid (though still surprisingly limited) rates of communication contribute inevitably to this result. Nevertheless, the statement quoted above must be taken with a considerable grain of salt, revealing as it does the failure to give credit where credit is due for nonmaterial innovation.

Take note of the following. Almost all religious ideas now extant were created before the 20th century. With the exception of minor vocabulary additions, all languages—and there are hundreds of them—were created before the 20th century, and many of the earlier creations have now been lost. A high proportion of musical forms, some only now being utilized in contemporary music, were in existence before the 20th century. The foundations of modern logic and experimentation were laid before the 20th century. The world was almost fully explored before the 20th century. One should not confuse the current *rate* of innovation in certain *selected fields* with the *total* body of innovation created by man.

Indeed the present rate of innovation would be impossible were it not for the gigantic buildup of previously created knowledge and ideas.

We have seen that the process of creativity is linked to the rearrangement of previous knowledge, including speculative ideas and aesthetic expressions. Very occasionally, discovery of an entirely new fact or principle may occur, but it is only made use of, intellectually, if it can be related to what has been known or imagined before. The process of creation, then, consists fundamentally of the capacity to reorder existing symbols (items of knowledge, ideas, principles, aesthetic components), which implies a capacity to question the existing order. The creative person seeks flaws in the existing arrangements, logical inconsistencies, the possibility of reversing aesthetic statements, questions that have not been answered; or he may simply play with present arrangements arriving at new combinations that please him or make some other sense.

The social function of a potentially creative person can be restricted for a variety of reasons. The society may be oriented toward relative stasis; high premiums may be placed on the existing order of things, and intellectual games may have to be undertaken within specific rules. Melanesian art and religious expression did not go beyond certain intellectual boundaries; it would take much more study to determine whether it would have been possible to use the stock of conceptions in ways that crossed the boundaries, and therefore whether the restrictions were truly imposed culturally or whether they were restricted by their inherent nature. The restriction, however, did not prevent cultural innovation within those rules, and this resulted in considerable regional variety, temporal cult changes and experimentation, and numerous other innovative outlets.

Again, certain kinds of innovation may go too far for the current values of the society, and may carry the social costs attached to intellectual pioneering, or religious or community nonconformism. In many respects, the successful innovator, whose activity results in adoption and diffusion, knows how far to go, senses the acceptability of the change, or is a persuasive leader and entrepreneur as well.

Deliberate policy can do little directly to influence the degree to which a society encourages or discourages creativity, but it can do a great deal indirectly. A first step is to influence family values, intellectual horizons, and the school—that is to say socialization and junior education. The two processes are closely interwoven, although some contemporary educators (mistakenly following and distorting Dewey) try to separate them. Despite the millions of words that have been written on educational theory, few societies as such have provided their citizens and educational agents with clear statements or mandates defining the role and function of school and family. It is indeed a tricky matter.

Both school and family are concerned with socialization—the first primarily as an agent of the wider community, the second in its own terms. In this situation there is bound to be a difference of view as to where socialization should lead, except in a completely regimented society. In a nonregimented one, it is important for the State to define the socialization goals of the school, and the role and authority of the teacher, and to determine the degree to which parents should directly assist in the definition of the goals. To what degree, and in whose name, should teachers overrule parental goals? If they do so in the name of the wider society, of broader horizons, of changing needs, should it not then follow that teachers lose their professional autonomy, for should they not be answerable to the body politic for the substance and direction of their influence? By the same token, where can one find a justification for a teacher reversing and conflicting with the moral and ethical goals of the parents?

Yet, depending on the degree of cultural pluralism in the society in question, teachers in conformity with one group of parents may be in conflict with another. Should policy lead then to a pluralism of school systems, with choice among them for the parent?

Such questions cannot be left to the implied and haphazard answer of the individual teacher in the classroom or the policy of an individual headmaster, who have their children in captive audience. In the absence of social science knowledge on which to base rational policy decisions, the professional body of teachers may well have the best available basic information, apart from the political expressions of the parents and public. But as a professional body their action to force governments to accept one policy as against another would, if it took place, be an arrogant usurpation of the responsibility of family and polity for the socialization goals of the community.

There is a tendency in this direction in some countries. It comes about in part because sometimes the total body of teachers is the largest reasonably educated group in the society and is naturally frustrated and resentful when it believes that educational policy is inadequate, or is not meeting the needs of the community. Under such circumstances, as informed citizens, teachers do have a role to play in exercising influence—but not by monopolizing the socialization role or removing decisions from the public authority. Schoolteachers are not *self-appointed* agents of social change.

It also comes about because of a reverse confusion. Many advocates of educational reform* have noted that the school's socialization role

---

* Post-Dewey educationalists Paul Goodman, A. S. Neill, and Ivan Illich are some. See my *Towers Besieged: The Dilemma of the Creative University*, Toronto: McClelland and Stewart, 1974, for more extensive argument on this and the following points.

includes the communication of conservative values through restrictive disciplir.ary techniques, and they see this as being in conflict with the task of opening the creative child's mind and skills to his capacities. There is a tendency in such writing to equate socialization = authority = restriction = bad and creativity = freedom = anti-discipline = good, and to see schools and teachers as being concerned with the former and needing to be concerned with the latter.

I have somewhat (but not much) exaggerated the equations as handled by more moderate and realistic commentators; but some, such as Ivan Illich, go much further into the realms of non-logic, anti-rationality, and Orwellian fantasy. There is, of course, good reason for the popular appeal of some of the fantasy theories of education, primarily because the *critical* statements contain strong elements of truth. There are indeed schools where rote-learning replaces thought, where the curriculum has no social meaning, where teachers conceive their main role as being to keep a disciplined group out of harm's way for a few hours, where creativity is punishable, and even where teachers use their authority to impose social values in conflict with those of parents.

Nevertheless, to stress creativity *alone* is to miscast the school's role. If the school is to stress creativity, it is because (and only because) the society has determined that children should be brought up to be creative. Within the school, creativity then becomes *one of* the goals of socialization, to be developed and balanced alongside others. It is never the *sole* objective.

Furthermore, creativity is by no means always the result of free-form daydreaming. That does occur. But basically it is a caricature. At some point, the daydreaming must relate to order, and the child must learn to identify and find knowledge and technique, to organize it (aesthetically or scientifically), to communicate his thoughts about it, and to put such dreams as he may have, not into the melting pot, but into form.

In this process, not all children are creative; for some, the act of creativity is a threat. Certainly, creative children are not equally so. It does them no service to be told that they are creative if in fact they are merely muddling around, engaged in precocious fantasy, with self-indulgence the sole measure of value. Under the influence of some current educational theory, this is happening, and it is only the later ultimate discovery of discipline and a sense of relatedness which rescues the appallingly miseducated creative youth. Unfortunately, it must be said that some of those who sense that all is not well in education are making things worse in Western society with muddled theories of socialization and creativity. One hopes that educators in other countries will see through the banality and superficiality of much that is receiving popular acclaim—but the signs of this are yet to be made evident.

There are, thus, a number of elements of action that comprise innovative creativity: learning facts that are placed in the context of relationships and systems; questioning or challenging; placing the questions in forms that lead to problem-solving action (invention, experiment, composition); identifying the relevance of the solution or the new synthesis in terms of its conceptual bearing upon existing relationships and systems— that is, by what it has to communicate; and then the communication itself to society, the world of scholarship, the world of the intellect, or to practical men.

The way in which individuals arrive at and combine such elements of creative action is highly variable, as are the motives and psychological impulses. Human beings cannot exist without *some* element of creativity in their make-up for each time they confront a new experience they must draw upon their fund of knowledge and their talents to reach an interpretation and devise new responses. However, the experience and the response may be new to them, when they are not to society; the individual has been creative, but his creation is personal and does nothing new for society itself. He has not added to the cultural stock, although he has personally acquired a little more culture himself.

If a society has set out along a path that requires or emphasizes innovation, it has in fact said that private personal creativity is not sufficient, and it is looking for those forms of creativity that *add to* the cultural stock, which implies identifications of relevance and communication. If it were rational about this—and no society in human history has truly thought out the implications of a policy designed to maximize creativity—it would establish or encourage institutional arrangements that enabled culturally creative individuals (that is, those individuals who go through some aspect of *all* the steps mentioned above) in their personal development and activity. Society would not expect all individuals to act in all these ways and would be prepared for individuals to arrive at and discover their mature creativity at different ages.

Most societies do not take special steps to encourage creativity; it happens anyway. Some do, by implication, through the creation of funds for the support of research and the arts, and by a commercial and industrial structure that is open to creativity and provides support for its results.

In the school it is possible for sensitive teachers to see and encourage the beginnings of creativity, but usually at this stage the act of creation cannot be known to be a part of a drive that will lead the individual to add to or revise the stock of culture—the pool of ideas and artifacts that society needs and uses. Children who are creative in school may use that skill entirely for their own personal benefit, learning to enrich their lives, and being intelligent in picking up knowledge and carrying out tasks.

Creativity is carried a stage further in institutions of higher learning, but these are of very different kinds. Some are geared to the conveyance of preexisting knowledge and the development of defined skill; technical institutes, and industrial arts schools fill this bill. Creativity is not necessarily absent from such institutions, but the emphasis is upon learning materials and skill-drilling. New ideas are treated with surprise and have to fight the system to emerge. The justification for such institutions is to fit people into social niches; they are employment oriented.

Many universities throughout the world have the same character. They demand, particularly of undergraduates, rigidly prescribed regurgitations of knowledge, and justify themselves to the taxpayer by producing expected numbers of professionals to fit the usually wrong labor requirement forecasts. Often they carry out this task as a public function controlled by government departments, perhaps even as part of them. They inevitably contain creative people, since this is the only place for them to go, and there are no other ways of earning a living. Creativity, immature though it may be, is placed in molds that cannot suit it; conflict is an inevitable result. The employment model for universities leads to misunderstanding and clash.

While universities by no means have a monopoly of creativity, they are the only institutions yet invented that have in a rigorous sense the gestation and encouragement of mature creativity as their primary goal. But that goal is not understood by many governments, by many university administrators and professors, or by many students—and very few universities establish the goal as the criterion of their policy and success. This does not mean that in fact universities are not creative; they are indeed. But their creativity is often limited, confused, and inhibited by a failure to concentrate on the provision of appropriate conditions, in itself due to a failure to identify creativity as the dominant aim or to analyze its nature.

In the course of writing on this subject I have reviewed most of the literature that has appeared in the past few years criticizing and analyzing universities. Quite a number of such works do attempt to set out what it is that universities are supposed to be doing; but nearly all use the mechanical organizational criteria of undergraduate and graduate training and research. Of course, these imply creativity. But if the objective is also to turn out given numbers of professionals, and if the argument is that these professional subjects belong in universities because their subject matter is complex and because they belong there traditionally, then the creative implications can be overwhelmed by mechanical approaches to education. These revolve around the absorption of given quantities of knowledge—the assessment of results according to hours of study or units of credit, so that the success of the institution is measured by the numbers, not the quality, of the graduates. Only one recent writer, the French sociologist Alain Touraine, has come close to seeing the function of the university as being concerned with the *expansion of culture* (in its broad, intellectual, sense).

In the wealthier countries, many students, professors, and activities that find their place in universities are not creatively oriented. They do not produce innovation, the development of innovative modes of activity, or anything more than static professionals who go into life and promptly lose any creative impulse they might have had. Many students who would otherwise become creative are seduced by the university's own propaganda to the effect that a university degree brings a job. These kinds of goals should, in my opinion, be removed from so-called universities; no professional school should be in a university *unless* it is based upon the development of aptitudes for questioning and answering questions that will carry on into later life.

Serious though this matter is in the richer countries, it is much more so in those poorer countries that have embarked upon a policy of growth and development. It is no exaggeration to say that in such countries the need to encourage creativity permeates every corner of social, economic, and political activity. There are features about this process that sharpen the difficulties.

First, technical skills are lacking in the requisite quantities and emphases. Technical institutes and universities are therefore quite properly directed to such areas. But unfortunately a great deal of the effort goes into the acquisition of the technique as heretofore developed in alien contexts. Mechanical learning, though by no means universal, is startlingly frequent.

Second, there is a "recipient" culture which has its own validity and into which new knowledge must be fitted. That culture is without doubt under considerable pressure to change and, as we have seen, does not have to follow a purely Western model. But its existence and value mean that the incoming or newly created knowledge must acquire a special flavor which cannot be borrowed directly from abroad.

Third, the technical knowledge and skill must be applied in new contexts of the natural world, as well as in society and culture. Biological principles may be much the same, but the local flora, fauna, and geological conditions are distinctly not.

The challenge, then, is for creativity *par excellence*; but the emphasis on "employment" and "practicality" tends to underplay the significance of fundamental (as distinct from applied) knowledge and of reflective innovative thought as distinct from crammed, nonrelevant facts.

In many countries the particular form of universities tends to be stifling and counterproductive. Fortunately, it takes more than that to hold creative people down. The wealth of ideas in the nonuniversity sectors, and as university people go into the challenge of everyday life, is remarkable. It is simply too bad that in so many cases universities are not contributing in the manner that they should. And, if I may say so, it is symptomatic and discouraging that UNESCO, in its work on *university* affairs, has consistently emphasized the mechanical and underplayed the problems of creativity.

CHAPTER 11

Resources and Their Management

THIS chapter will focus on management, as an element in social dynamics, rather than on the presence or absence of resources themselves, because obtaining, identifying, and using resources is a management act. Further, I shall use the term "management" rather than "entrepreneur" because the latter term has changed its significance in economics to the point at which it is either so narrow as to be almost useless for policy analysis, or else is wrapped up in semantic argument, the meaning changing with the use.* A manager is someone who combines resources through the use of organization involving more persons than himself. This leaves open the question as to the degree to which the manager is dynamic, repetitive in his acts, expansive, profit-taking, risk-taking, willing to innovate in his enterprise by learning from others, innovative in the sense of doing things that have not been done before, or carrying out his management in a nonmonetary or nonprofit framework such as an army or a civil service. All of these characteristics are variables.

In its intellectual aspect, management consists in recognizing characteristics that can be ascribed to resources—both material and nonmaterial. These characteristics are used as bases for synthesis, combination, and movement. The purposes of such manipulation are not uniform: in some contexts they appear to be profit maximization; in others expansion; in others the steady administration of a policy; in others personal aggrandizement; in others to win a game.

Management is thus dependent on cultural symbols, information and communication, as treated in the last chapter.

Policy tends to treat management as an aspect of property. Managers are persons who act on behalf of property owners, and, it is argued, their

* For a discussion of the way in which economists moved the meaning of "entrepreneur" from "manager" to that very rare bird, the person who innovates, not for himself but for society, and the limited applicability of this approach, see my article "The Cultural Milieu of the Entrepreneur: A Critical Essay" in *Explorations in Entrepreneurial History*, Cambridge: Harvard University Research Center in Entrepreneurial History, Vol. VII, No. 3, 1955, pp. 146–163.

motivations, activities, even efficiency can be linked to the type of property ownership which is relevant, and the relationship of the management to the owners. One ideology would hold, for example, that civil servants are less effective managers than department heads of large private enterprises, since rewards and sanctions differ. Another would argue that when workers own the property and govern the manager instead of private property owners directing him, the manager will do things better. Another point of view is that if indirect management is stripped away so that individuals own the property communally as workers, then management can be vested in workers' committees. Alternatively, large estates can be broken into peasant holdings, and each peasant becomes his own family-manager. In these last two instances, it is said, society is not only more equitable but more efficient, since management is directly related to self-interest, expressed as workers' ownership.*

There is no doubt that in certain circumstances, which would be difficult to define, changes in ownership can result in changes in effectiveness according to output or profitability measures. Sometimes the circumstances are in accord with the above propositions, sometimes they are the opposite. But no empirically verified theory has emerged to cover general situations.

Indeed, how could it? We are dealing with human beings, not automata, and the act of management deals with human beings within the organization with relations outside it. The complex of social exchange involves many more motivations and interests than the mere movement of one physical item into an association with another in order to produce a product. No one has even yet shown, empirically, in the whole literature of economics, or in the sociology and anthropology close to economics, that there is a universal or even common drive toward maximization of output or monetary profit. Sometimes that drive does exist, as a kind of intellectual game (I have seen it at work with Howard Hughes style fanaticism in New Guinea indigenous enterprise). But in the vast majority of instances, individuals, including managers, act to maximize a combination of payoffs of which increased output and profit are only two. Security and the quiet life are just as important. Perhaps the well-being of workers plays a part. Friendly relations with other firms may have a determinate role in guiding a manager's actions. The possibilities are endless.**

---

* An interesting and critical comparative approach to some of the issues is contained in René Dumont, *Socialisms and Development*, London: André Deutsch, 1973.

** Two popular explorations of some of the sociocultural manifestations of management, which make amusing reading, are Martin Page, *The Company Savage*, London: Cassel, 1972; and Graham Cleverly, *Managers and Magic*, London: Longman, 1971.

It should not be surprising that if management and property change, so too will social relations, social exchange, and the maximization calculus. But this will not necessarily be in the direction of a clear-cut drive to increased output or profit; it may be the opposite.

The material ideology of Western society leads to value judgments about such results, particularly when a change in ownership may increase certain satisfactions (seldom specified in the political credo) at the cost of productivity, and the country concerned loses ground in the race of competition toward "being developed." The irritation comes when the Western countries find themselves paying out because policy has confused equity of ownership, constituting a new society, with a material millennium, and the resultant loss of output has to be made up with food imports, capital subsidies, and the like.

Furthermore, despite the clear evidence to the contrary, the more popular and less reflective interpretations of economic growth talk in terms of "availability of resources," by which is meant primary material resources, within the political ambit of the potentially developing political unit.

What management does is to *control* resources. The model of owning physical resources that are located on one's land, putting them to work, and shipping off a product to some other location is implicit for a great deal of thinking on the subject. But, of course, this is only one model; there are innumerable other possibilities.

Promoters and merchant bankers are managers who, among many others, seldom work in this kind of way. Their operations suggest a different model—namely, the symbolic identification of some possibilities in resource 1, owned by group a, located at x; the possibility of linking it to resource 2, owned by group b, located at y; the formation of group c and the juncture of resources 1 and 2 in the hands of group c in location z.

The value of stating the model in this way is that nothing need be predetermined. Any constraints and predeterminations can, of course, be allowed for, but until they are discovered and identified one has no grounds for implying them. The resource may be highly abstract in nature (funds), very personal (skilled professional labor), or may be physical raw materials or semifinished products.

The important element is control. In modern society, the control can be fairly indirect—that is through influence in the form of professional advice, which is usually paid for. More permanent control, however, does not necessarily imply "clear title." Contemporary society has devised scores of ways of dealing with combinations without "clear title"— through minority partnerships, directorates, and the use of indebtedness.

Though the instruments are more sophisticated, and although current economic ideology is formulated and presented to the public in ways that indicate that social contact in business does not affect the impersonal market, nevertheless the networks of relationship and social exchange are not very different *in kind* from those that operate in so-called primitive society. The Melanesian who wishes to gain prestige, to manage a complex production act (the manufacture of a canoe or the building of a house), or to mastermind a complex ceremonial does so by calling upon the services of others. He does not *own* them, in the sense of physically possessing them or unilaterally deciding on their fate. He does not necessarily have a medium of exchange accumulated as in a bank and then dispensed. What he *does* have is a network of credit—that is, of obligations to him—and a fund of trust and credibility which enables him to call on services. This fund is his true wealth, and is part of the explanation of why people on $10 annual income (as world statistics tell us) in fact not only survive but operate. Such a system works in one form or another in every society in existence.

It is also at the basis of our own economy. We are so accustomed to accounting for wealth in terms of the abstract monetary value attached to physical objects plus paper certificates that have exchangeability, that we neglect the underlying principles. Perhaps, to make myself clear, I should coin a new term—*command wealth*. This consists of the value of those goods and services that you can control, that you can bring into action, that you can command. Under some circumstances, you can do this, even though you are in debt to the full value of the things you command. In other circumstances you do not own a penny of the property, but you have legal rights of control. Command wealth is power and influence, expressed through the control of the property and actions of others.

Public policy tends to handle these issues indirectly. It may circumscribe, limit, or attach conditions to property rights, but, for example, the management of a large steel production and distribution concern requires very similar attributions of command wealth whatever the political ethos may have to say about it. It juggles with the things that people who exercise varying degrees of command power do and the rules under which they do them. But political approaches to the issues of management do not normally recognize the universality of the processes in question.

When the issues are recognized, the special position of Japan, Switzerland, Hong Kong, and Singapore—all countries with a dearth of natural resources other than people—as growth centers is no longer strange and anomalous. The art of the game is in movement. Emigrant

Swiss established agencies, entrepots, and networks throughout the world; hoisted bales of cotton over alpine passes and established major industries, not in the primary Swiss towns but in such otherwise out-of-the-way places as St-Gallen, La Chaux-de-Fonds, or Baden. The Swiss made maximum use of *social* contacts, established through kinship and friendship networks of immigrants and emigrants; these were the effective communications links of the time, as they still are with many beginning entrepreneurs in other parts of the world. But the Swiss, more than any other nation, quickly learned the lessons of communication and have made of it a key passion. Coal stoked the fires of Britain's industrial revolution; it also stoked the fires of the railways and steamboats. Not all the coal in the whole of Britain would have established an industrial revolution if it had not been moved, and if the products that came from its energy use had not been distributed throughout the world on the basis of laboriously contrived movement of information.

Regional associations, even today, reduce the issues of physical movement. The entry of Venezuela into a consortium of Andean countries brings a capital supplier into a group hungry for nonimperial funds and sufficiently diversified to make movement of products interesting. On the other hand, both the United States and the Soviet Union have so far failed to solve the fierce problems of land transport that face them; if Europe begins to outstrip them, it will be due in no small measure to superiority in land communication.

The manager today, however, does not have to be in the United States or the Soviet Union, Europe, or Japan to make things work. His center of operations may be Athens, Nicaragua, the Bahamas, even the New Hebrides (although, despite its entry into the role of financial haven, the last example is a little farfetched, precisely because of the backwardness of its communications with the outside world). A small group of men, meeting in a beautiful but modest building in Vevey, Switzerland, has great powers of control and command (powers that they wisely decentralize) over a high proportion of the distributed foods of North America. A company situated in Liverpool moved papers and accumulated legal rights over other companies and established patterns of communication in the 1970s that gave it a near monopoly of China's thirsty cotton trade, (nearly 40 percent of the world's cotton movement) and, in close association with other companies of a variety of nationalities, reestablished Liverpool (in the 20th century almost as far away from any "natural" center of physical cotton accumulation as you can get) as the world center for cotton trading. All this was done in a matter of four or five years, through the skilled and judicious use of human contact and communication.

Hong Kong has made the utmost use of the skills of its population for manufacturing, where transport costs can be reduced to a small proportion of value. Both Hong Kong and Singapore are making serious bids to be world centers of financial exchange and regional command posts for cross-boundary management.

Reflecting upon such indications, one might make a number of observations about policy priorities.

First, many developing countries are at a serious disadvantage, not because they lack resources or even management skills, but because those skills are not linked to the international contacts that would open up opportunities. It took the Japanese decades to learn this lesson, and even now they suffer from certain restrictions of a sociocultural order and from political suspicion. African countries, in particular, do not have the attitude to immigration, or the emigrant connections, to fulfill the functions of establishing trusted contacts which have been so invaluable to other countries. Latin America, the Caribbean, and Asia are much more fortunate in this regard, and it may be that Africa will make faster leaps forward the more it develops continental communications, rather than links directed to so-called metropolitan powers.

Second, the creation of a several-tiered effective communications system, for all types of communication, is one of the greatest needs of developing countries, and is an area where technical aid can be of most use, provided that the network can be maintained physically and financially.* In many countries, communications systems are founded, often with World Bank or bilateral foreign advice, on the proposition that a country's income is dependent on its export of primary raw materials. The hinterland is linked to ports in a limited and selective way. Subsidiary trade and activity is connected to the almost riverine flow, but cross-connections that may be important for the internal gestation of management and commercial growth may be missing or distorted.

---

* P. T. Bauer, whose work I admire because it usually challenges accepted positions with good reason, disputes priorities being given to communications infrastructure. I think he is quite wrong in his opposition here. I have seen with my own eyes the ways in which peasants enter management activity—commerce spreads, agricultural productivity can increase, markets can be opened up, and ideas flow faster, all as a result of the creation of a twenty-mile dirt road. I have also seen perishable banana crops destroyed because the same road was not macadamized or sealed, and it washed out at crucial dates. The effects of a communications infrastructure are not automatic, since they can be misapplied. But the evidence for their deep effects is overwhelming.

Such a communications system needs to be several-tiered because the needs of sections of the population differ. A sophisticated Swiss-type system may work wonders for local industry, with the coexistence of high technology and tradition, but this is dependent on the parallel development of education as well. Further, the costs of use may be such as to rule out its handling by peasants who are struggling to find ways of manipulating the market. For them, the localized and flexible bus and bus–taxi services so common in Latin America may be more effective, provided that they can be linked to agencies that can be caretakers of precious cargoes. Again, it is inefficient to have a road system without other modes of communication in support; the great advance of railways was at least in part because they were also the first channel of telegraphic communication. A network of telephones, radio-telephones, and posts to which the public can have easy and cheap access is crucial. Yet it is often one of the lowest priorities because it seems to be a "service," a luxury, rather than the most fundamental of resources.

Third, it is often said that sophisticated communications are too advanced for most poor countries and that the appropriate technology, and hence communications system, has to be cheap and technically simple—and in other words slow, inefficient, with very limited spread. This may or may not be valid. But it requires investigation with the alternative hypothesis in mind—namely, that just as North America and Japan benefited from the technical expertise of capital-intensive technical innovations of England and Europe, by coming late and improving on them, and just as Germany actually benefited technically by having its old 19th-century factories reduced to tragic rubble, so the now-developing countries should *not* be saddled with inadequate and out-of-date communications systems, but should make the fullest use of the latest technical knowledge, specifically adapted to their conditions.

Let me take one example. It is costly and physically difficult to establish good technical libraries in, let us say, five major centers in Nigeria or Thailand, or twenty-five in Brazil, to take three of the most go-ahead developing countries, two of which are of major population and resource importance, and all of which have a distinct possibility of reaching a present European level of living by the end of the century if not before. But if a number of developing countries with similar space problems moved in the direction of establishing central library-archives with computer retrieval and on-line reading and print-out connections to regional centers (perhaps with a tie-in to the provision of national market and similar information), then the chances are very high indeed that the new technology would become financially feasible. In this crucial area the developing countries would be several steps ahead of their more conservative developed brethren, tied as they are to conservative networks.*

Similar remarks apply to telephone exchange systems, railway track and traffic-control equipment, radio networks, air traffic layout, and so forth. In each case the special circumstances of the countries concerned, the availability of power sources, and the distances and population distribution involved create new problems of design. But, whereas at the village agricultural level or even in small artisan industry, the technological challenge may be to introduce the simplest ingenious improvements, for national communications and similar systems the appropriate act is to move as far as is economical into the technology of the 1980s.**

The internal communications issues of management are embodied in organization. There is still considerable disagreement in the literature as to whether the formal arrangements of organization—that is those that can be set out in an organization chart, for example—have much bearing upon operations. The amount of attention given to them in any organizational planning suggests that the normal theory is that they do.

An organization chart does have important symbolic meaning. By setting out responsibilities and relationships, it focuses on the origin of information and the directions in which it must flow to enable members of the organization to adapt their behavior. A policy established in a Board of Directors is communicated to management and translated into specific directives, which become the mandates for action. Information about the context of the action (markets, labor conditions, equipment supply, and so forth) and about the action itself (production levels, accidents) goes up, down, and sideways in the hierarchy.

However, a chart does not normally take cognizance of related

* Among the reasons for high costs of such systems are (a) the demand for components (e.g., television reader-printers) is not high enough at the moment to warrant assembly line production, and (b) in older countries where such systems are being studied the old network of line communication creates hair-raising difficulties of modification. A concerted demand from developing countries would change item (a) substantially, and they do not have equivalent item (b) problems with which to contend.

** Electronic communication linked to computers makes it possible for persons in Zurich, let us say, as part of their normal everyday conduct to place commodity orders—including futures—in New York or London, the whole transaction taking seconds. It would be interesting to know what geographical points are linked in this manner, and how the skew of their distribution affects the ability of investors and firms in the developing countries themselves (which produce the commodities at issue) to participate in the ownership market, which is, after all, a different thing from productive use. If there is such a skew, an alteration in international communication patterns might be a most important objective for developing countries to pursue.

variables which can be of fundamental importance. By setting up a form of organization, the management indicates the way it expects the group to work. In fact, it is most unlikely to do so in the predetermined way. Here are just a few of the factors that intervene. As management decisions are communicated downward, they are rephrased and interpreted, and they change their meaning. The information that flows to management can be misleading, erroneous, or selected and arranged in ways that miss the conditions that would otherwise suggest an adaptation of behavior. The formal channels of communication turn out to be cumbersome or inhibitive for reasons including personal relations or the tiresomeness of the reporting routines. Users of information may thus set up their own channels or use devices to get at the matter quickly outside the confines of the chart. The *real* organization network is very seldom what the chart, the myth, or the political ideology states.

When this is accepted, the way is open for empirical investigation of differences between different kinds of real organization, as they affect management and the use of resources. There are conditions in which one form of hierarchy rather than another makes a considerable difference, particularly if there is an ideological commitment to one rather than another. This can affect morale, but its most common effects are upon the legitimization of juridical rights over property—for example, with holding companies or with lineages that are, to some degree, corporate property holders.

But a great deal of this is embodied in myth and ideology rather than in fact; the crucial variable is contained in the question, do the members of the organization work together? By extension, is the organization composed of complementary parts which adjust to each other's needs and changed conditions? In the jargon, do the parts of the organization articulate one with another? Almost any form of organization will work if articulation takes place smoothly; the best looking organization in the world will not work if there are articulation frictions. Sometimes the conditions of physical work dictate or strongly influence the type of internal relationship that is likely to articulate best, but usually a considerable variety of solutions is possible.

As an aside, one may remark that the problems of a formal organization in this respect have considerable similarity to the problems of articulation of any *group* of such organizations. Together they constitute a social system, or social organization, and the mode of operation is established around the interactions and responses of each to each: articulation, adjustment, exchange, cooperation, competition, conflict.

Recognition of this way of posing the problem, and of looking for answers, reduces the significance of a commonly held myth—that the type of organization characteristic of nonindustrial societies stands in the way of material progress and modernization. There are two parts to such an assertion.

One is that existing organization cannot be adapted to new functions and must in some way be modified or swept aside. In the days before women's liberation, for example, it was commonly asserted that matrilineal societies could not administer cash-oriented agricultural production on the grounds that an important incentive was the possibility of family inheritance, and that this was best recognized in patrilineal (if possible, primogenital) land and crop transmission. Some small movement from matriliny to patriliny has in fact occasionally been observed. But there is nothing inevitable or necessary about it. If people *believe* that it is proper and right to inherit property from the mother's brother rather than from the father, one destroys incentives by altering the system to patriliny, while there is no inherent disadvantage in one form of transmission over another. Much more important is the question of whether the inheritance involves a parceling of the property into uneconomic units, for this does raise questions of property concentration or, alternatively, cooperation in property administration. There has been a considerable revival in non-Western-style family units in urban settings in India and Africa, where the early migration to the towns had destructive effects initially. Further, commercial and industrial organization in such countries as pre-communist China, Japan, Taiwan, and India contains many valuable and productive elements of traditional organization.

The other part of the assertion is that existing organizations do not do the jobs that are needed and that the national infrastructure lacks important elements. This is much more likely to be true. Where are the credit facilities? Do city banks know what it is to be a village farmer with suppressed wishes to expand into commerce, to educate a son as a public works engineer, or to acquire additional land? Who is going to look after regional population and environmental interests during the development of a winter sports tourist facility? In the absence of locally based enterprise, is the government simply going to say "no" to external promoters? Do peasants have to carry their own produce to market, in the absence of a system of consignment and agencies? Is commercial security beyond reach because of the lack of locally available legal organization?

Issues of this kind, down to earth though they may be, are of major importance in the articulation of the national system as a whole and in the ability of its managers—from the humblest peasant to the most sophisticated production chief—to adjust to changing conditions. It is in this sense that organization must be considered to be a major element in the resources available to a country. Anthropologists have all too seldom directed their attention to such issues.

Points of the foregoing kind give a particular significance to judgments about "optimum size" or "optimal form of organization." It is probably the case that there is *no such thing* as optimal size for an organization, even if its objectives are fairly strictly defined. What can be said more accurately is that, for any given size, there are some modes of operation that are more likely to work effectively than others (given technical considerations) and that there are some that may lead to breakup. It was not size in itself that caused the breakup of major American journals such as *Look, Life,* and *The Saturday Evening Post* but a financial structure in which advertising demanded mass circulation but did not pay the costs of it, and a change in public taste which management did not recognize in time.* Mammoth firms in private industry, whether multipurpose, production- or commerce-oriented, or holding companies—show a considerable variation in effectiveness at all levels of size. The small businessman can fail to inform himself properly of local market conditions and, by locating in the wrong place, he may fail; the head of a giant multiple combine may save himself from such errors because they cancel out, but a single key mistake in his financial judgment may multiply through his structure before he discovers it—the pack of cards comes tumbling down.**

One of the factors at work in some notorious instances is that growth dynamics hides the fatal flaw from attention. Once growth hesitates for a moment, the flaw—particularly if it is a financial one—reveals itself, and management (unequal to the task) cannot recover. (One day a daring iconoclast will write a systematic empirical account of management error—the hair-raisingly destructive decisions that are taken with devastating effect in "private enterprise" are often at least as damaging as similar errors in the public service, although I suspect that the latter occur less frequently.)

But if a social scientist were to say (within the hearing of top

*On these points, see J.-L. Servan-Schreiber, *Le Pouvoir d'Informer*, Paris: Robert Laffont, 1972.

**The tangled history of IOS, to say nothing of Rolls-Royce and well-established firms on the New York Stock Exchange, have provided juicy but worrisome headlines for some time. Amusing stories, with slightly different twists, are contained in Andrew Tobias, *The Funny Money Game*, London: Michael Joseph, 1972; and Norman C. Miller, *The Great Salad Oil Swindle*, Harmondsworth: Penguin Books, 1966. But ITT seems only too effective, see Anthony Sampson, *The Sovereign State of I.T.T.*, Greenwich: Fawcett, 1974.

management in General Motors, Ford, Nestlé, Unilever, Shell, or Brown-Boveri) that there is an optimal size, he would be ridiculed for his *naïveté*. For what these and many other organizations have done is to show that there are ways of establishing internal units and structures to fit specific tasks, and to relate these cooperatively or competitively with variation in independence and coordinating mechanisms.

Such organizations, of course, have accounting mechanisms at their fingertips which provide yardsticks for performance. Though they can be misleading, they simplify the task of judgment. But the adequacy of such financial yardsticks for other sectors of human life is severely question-able even with the beginning development of cost-benefit analysis. How does one measure the effectiveness of an army unit, of a school, of a university, of a government department? Measures can be devised, but so far they have always distorted. In their absence, how can one decide whether size has any bearing on performance? The judgment is basically subjective, out of the experience of dealing with such organizations and out of descriptively evaluative studies.

Here are some of my own subjective hypotheses.

1. A university, to take an example, can be extremely effective at any size, provided it has the ability to organize its component units, to decentralize certain decisions, to define its roles in accordance with the size, to obtain resources commensurate with its objectives, and to retain in its component units a sense of unity and purpose. If there are differences in quality between the universities of Oxford, London, Harvard, or California, they are *not* due to size.

2. A university is usually a more efficient and smoothly running enterprise than a private company, and it produces less dissatisfaction among its "consumers." It so happens that university students are better organized than consumers of private company products and make more noise about their problems, many of which have nothing to do with the university. Private companies, however, continually deliver defective produce, make accounting mistakes, fail to rectify errors readily, and get themselves into the most ridiculous hassles.

3. There are wide differences among bureaucracies in different coun-tries. But, on the whole, a bureaucracy is at least as effective, and sometimes more so, in its given tasks than indigenous private enterprise in the same country. Nevertheless it sometimes achieves this at the cost of adaptability—that is, by imposing an unnecessary or undesirable stasis.

4. The effectiveness and adaptability of a bureaucracy has less to do

with its size than with its management and the degree to which decentralization of judgment is necessary and achieved. It also depends, of course, as with other organizations, on the flows of information, their utility, and the adjustments which result (or fail to result, as the case may be).

Perhaps we should be astonished that so many people have shown themselves to be adept at complex and difficult management. It is a major source of hope that, despite the incredible folly of so many decisions in all sectors of human interest, the skills of managerial judgment are widespread in all countries. Sometimes it is the infrastructure, the experience, and the opportunity alone which are lacking.

CHAPTER 12

Of Change, Conflict, and Resistance

ANALYSTS who deal with the *practice* of change and persons who are directly engaged in trying to bring it about tend to make use of naïve and simplistic theories. It is true that social science theories do not produce unified and agreed-upon statements about change which other analysts or persons in neighboring disciplines can pick up like a bag of tricks. To get the theory, one has to work over the materials and establish logically linked principles that appear to have some empirical verification.

One would have thought, for example, that theories of economic development, which are concerned directly with social change, would have established themselves in well-founded schools of thought about the subject. Not a bit of it. Even those economists such as Hla Myint, Sir Arthur Lewis, P. T. Bauer, and A. O. Hirschmann, who have sensitized themselves to the importance of "social and cultural factors" much more than most of their colleagues, write as if a theory of social change does not exist. Everett Hagen, at least, had the courage to try to invent one.

The practical men, trying to "induce" social change in the field, find resistances where (according to their analysis) the advantages of change should have been so obvious as to be automatic in producing results. But they aren't and they don't.

In the worlds of thought I have just been citing, there are two lines of approach. Certain optimists, who have had lucky experiences, who are very far away from the field, or who are linked to revolutionary political dogma, say that it is just a matter of opportunity. All you have to do is to provide the opportunity by building a road, establishing marketing, improving fertilizer, introducing birth control, or sweeping away the oppressing classes or the foreigners, and you will have widespread response. There is a little truth in such positions.

Certain pessimists (or those who have learned that people who receive "opportunity" do not always think of it in the same terms as those who provide it) hold that the bias of many cultures is conservative—that they contain forces that are in opposition to change and that simply cannot be overcome, however strong the "opportunities" might be, without at least direct attack over long periods of time. There is some truth in these positions also.

It is interesting to note that authors who believe themselves to be fighting about such issues are often saying basically the same thing. Gunnar Myrdal, in *Asian Drama*,* holds that Western nations changed their cultures very slowly over the centuries to accommodate the changes of the agricultural, commercial, and industrial revolutions, and that it is unrealistic to expect Asian nations to change their way of life almost overnight. Indeed, since a great deal of the problem lies in the field of religious "attitudes" (here comes the sacred cow of India), it doesn't look as if the needed changes are going to be brought about very easily. Yet the need is for even faster change than occurred in Europe. From that point on, the problem—stated to be crucial—is ignored.

P. T. Bauer, in his most recent book,** argues with Myrdal whenever he can, and is correctly and devastatingly critical on many important issues. He attacks Myrdal for apparently thinking that the age-old attitudes don't matter very much and will be swept away as nuisances of custom when progress takes place. But then Bauer lists, on numerous separated pages of analysis, social and cultural phenomena that stand squarely in the way of material progress. A typical quotation (p. 78) should be made at length, since it sums up not only what Bauer has to say but much of Myrdal as well, and indeed almost every commentator; there is agreement, apparently, on the data, but disagreement on what it means:

> Examples of significant attitudes, beliefs and modes of conduct unfavourable to material progress include lack of interest in material advance, combined with resignation in the face of poverty; lack of initiative, self-reliance and of a sense of personal responsibility for the economic fortune of oneself and one's family; high leisure preference, together with a lassitude often found in tropical climates; relatively high prestige of passive and contemplative life compared to active life; the prestige of mysticism and of renunciation of the world compared to acquisition and achievement; acceptance of the idea of a preordained, unchanging and unchangeable universe; emphasis on performance of duties and acceptance of obligations, rather than on achievement of results, or assertion or even a recognition of personal rights; lack of sustained curiosity, experimentation and interest in change; belief in the efficacy of supernatural and occult forces and of their influence over one's destiny; insistence on

---

* Abridged edition, New York: Vintage Books, 1972, e.g., pp. 49–50 and 68–69.
** *Dissent on Development*, London: Weidenfeld and Nicolson, 1972, Cambridge, Mass.: Harvard University Press, 1972.

the unity of the organic universe, and on the need to live with nature rather than conquer it or harness it to man's needs, an attitude of which reluctance to take animal life is a corollary; belief in perpetual reincarnation, which reduces the significance of effort in the course of the present life; recognized status of beggary, together with a lack of stigma in the acceptance of charity; opposition to women's work outside the household.

This list could of course be extended greatly. Moreover, the attitudes and aptitudes discussed here are not surface phenomena. Over large areas, with huge populations, especially in south Asia, some of the prevailing attitudes and beliefs most uncongenial to material advance are so deeply felt and strongly held that they have become an integral part of the spiritual and emotional life of many millions of people, probably hundreds of millions. Enforced removal of these attitudes or beliefs, or even energetic attempts in this direction, would probably result in large-scale spiritual and emotional collapse.

The sacred cow of India is mentioned in a footnote. But at least this is a sympathetic account; it attempts to confront what are seen to be the issues, not merely (as with Myrdal, and many theoretical economists) sweeping them away as an irritant.

What such authors are saying, however, is that growth and development are of paramount importance; a society that chooses goals other than these is *ipso facto* resistant to change.

Several issues must be sorted out. One is that the society might be very open to change that is consistent with the values expressed above; material progress is not such a value, but (it might be said) give us new paths to righteousness and a life integrated with spiritual values, and environmental unity, and the leisure for family and human interaction, and we will consider following such objectives. If that is the message, would-be reformers had better be very careful indeed, for that too is the message now being preached by radical leaders of the West. Growth is no longer the holiest of holies.

Another issue, as I have already shown (p. 43), is that many of the philosophical preferences stated here, even in southern Asia, are capable of being linked to material progress. The goals are not necessarily even directly opposed, except occasionally for special classes of society or on particular ritual or educational occasions. Even charity is a most significant redistributive process that is a useful device in a rapidly developing society where it is impossible to employ everyone at equivalent wage rates—in other words, where the act of development bears unevenly on the population. Indeed, its absence might place an absolutely intolerable burden on social institutions.

Again, sometimes religious and philosophical issues do change dramatically and quickly. Some writers have pointed out that if material and social conditions build up frustrations to the point of revolutionary intolerability, one of the most effective forms of drive is messianic, charismatic leadership attached to *new* religion. It seems evident that this occurs, not in the most poverty-stricken or oppressed areas, but where there is a dramatic change in conditions of life—for example, through dispossession, or where there is a considerable increase in justifiable hope almost but not quite within grasp.* If it were true that the road block were religion, however long standing, then I would say that south Asia was one big barrel of social dynamite. But the socioeconomic condition of Buddhist and other-worldly countries is far more complex, and the factors explaining peasant choice are far more mundane. While theorists may be excused for mistakenly identifying religion as the problem, since the control of variables is indeed difficult, the practical man has no such excuse. He finds that his prescriptions misfired. He does not blame himself, or the fact that his analysis may have been faulty. He seeks explanation outside himself, in the religion of the other fellow. Religion, laziness, and preference for leisure become the scapegoats.

I would be more inclined to accept such accounts of social and cultural impedimenta if I had not seen so many sacred cows destroyed, both in theory and in practice. Bauer does not, thank goodness, raise the old hoary fairytale of the "extended" family standing in the way of progress, although that is still a strong enough myth to be part of ethnosocial science in some quarters. But many of the above assertions, while they *can be* operative, are not *necessarily* so; the trick is to know when, and to avoid promoting them into absolutes. I have lived among people who were described in all the official literature, *without any exception*, as having a leisure preference, being happy-go-lucky and lazy, being uninterested in material progress, deriving satisfaction and prestige from ceremonial and ritual, turning beggary into a destructive institution, being at one with nature. But as I came to know them, I learned what should have been obvious: that smiling hid pain, that people were capable of long and sustained physical labor in conditions that no European would have tolerated, that they were always concerned with the real-world future for themselves and their children, that daily life was a round of stress and battle that no concern with the hereafter could possibly remove or counterbalance except in the lives of the saintly, and that there were flexibilities and payoffs in the ceremonial, charitable, and religious world that had distinct importance for the genesis of material benefit.

*The writings of E. Hobsbawm and Peter Worsley are leads into this fascinating topic, which (despite its esoteric appearance) is one of the few major social themes on which there is a wealth of historical and comparative data, and also good explanatory and predictive devices.

The ethnocentrism of scholarly judgments about important institutions—avoiding the analysis of linkages with other aspects of the
social and cultural order and almost, it would seem, the deliberate
shutting of one's eyes to the vast wealth of analytic and descriptive data
about what actually goes on in social relations, particularly in so-called
conservative villages—is quite appalling.

Let us turn to some of the ways of approaching movement and
dynamics.

The oldest, and in some ways the strongest, approach to this topic in
anthropology is evolutionary theory. The label conceals a considerable
variety of approaches. Basically, it is concerned with accounting for the
transformation of one social system into another through the combination
of internal and external forces.

Nearly all evolutionary theory which bears that label is *ex post facto*,
deals with relatively long time periods and major changes, and for good
reason avoids extrapolation to account for current events. The earlier
evolutionary theories, under the influence of Darwinism, were applied to
such issues as the contact between cultures with the survival of the fittest
and to tracing the history of human society. This last task was undertaken, as in biology, by comparing structures and functional forms and
deducing historical-evolutionary relationships on the basis of structural
equivalence. One result was to "establish" an evolutionary sequence
which roughly ran—hunters and gatherers yield pastoralists yield agriculturalists yield townsmen yield nation-states. . . .

To those who were interested in changes occurring before their eyes,
from the late 1920s, this was a most unsatisfactory formulation. In the
first place, it was based upon a set of classifications linked to modes of
production. But the societies one could study, as Raymond Firth force-
fully pointed out, were in most cases *mixtures* of the types, and there was
little real evidence that such mixtures represented an interruption of
movement from one type to another. Further, elements of social and
cultural life did not always correlate very well with the production types;
one can find matrilineal kinship structures in a wide variety of productive
settings, for example. Again, historical data did not always agree with the
sequence; the statements as to how the sequences occurred were, in the
absence of good data, often wildly imaginative and unverifiable, and
incapable of being applied in a predictive manner to social change as
observed in the field.

The reaction against evolutionism, and the quasi-history on which
much of it was based, was strong, particularly in Britain. But it has been
revived again, particularly in the United States, largely through the efforts

of Julian Steward, who broke through the restriction of unilinearity. Although there is still a great deal of predeterminism in the evolutionary exercise, in theory it is possible for evolutionists now to say that the outcome of movement will be variable, according to the mix of internal dynamics and external forces working in and on the sociocultural structure and organization. The evolutionist still tends to think in large terms and in relation to ideal types of society. His growing concern for the *detail* of social change, however, brings him much closer than before to the social change theorists who grew up in opposition to evolution in the 1930s. Indeed, many present-day American evolutionists are using almost identical techniques of analysis to those advocated by Malinowski in his uneven posthumous book on *The Theory of Social Change*.

Despite this coming together of the two movements, there are still some difficult and unfortunate hangovers from the older evolutionism. For example, one of the silliest but most persistent controversies in anthropology is that between the so-called "substantivist" and so-called "formalist" schools of economic anthropology. The substantivist school, given an ideological lead by Karl Polanyi, divides the world into redistributive, allocative, and market economic systems. While such a taxonomy, though hardly adequate for the thousands of historical and extant social systems on record, has an advantage over the pastoralist-agriculturalist typology in that it is based on socioeconomic exchange relations and the exercise (in different ways) of power, it fails even more in the task of providing connecting links. For it explicitly denies that there are *common* forces and mechanisms between the types. I have shown elsewhere* that this denial is erroneous because it is based upon naïve rejections of abstract economic and sociological conceptualization, and hence fails to ask relevant empirical questions. But the main point here is that, in its own terms, it does not create the *links* between the systems that would enable change from one to another to take place. On these issues, Polanyi wrote as if the whole world of economic development did not exist (despite his earlier interest in such matters) and the Great Transformation was somehow lost.

It is remarkable how this essentially élitist if not racist theory has been taken up by radically oriented social scientists looking for an intellectual cause. It is probable that if Polanyi had lived he would have responded to the objections by modifying his viewpoint, or at least adding dimensions that would take care of the objections. His numerous followers, however, do not. Thus we have the curious situation in which Marshall Sahlins,** in

* In *Traditional Exchange and Modern Markets*, Englewood Cliffs: Prentice-Hall, 1965.
** *Stone Age Economics*, New York: Aldine–Atherton, 1972.

most ingenious and valuable elaborations of the redistributive idea, builds in some of the current wave of European neo-Marxist jargon and talks of certain of these societies as "precapitalist." But he does this in the same breath as demonstrating that the whole spirit and functioning of the societies in question is contrary to capitalism, has no possible relation to it, is thoroughly opposed to it, is of a quite different order. This is eating your cake and having it. On the one hand, something precedes capitalism—that is, is capable of changing into it; on the other hand, there is no possible connection. At least Marx himself provided a theoretical dialectic as a mode of linkage.

I do not think that this kind of paradox is a necessary feature of evolutionism in social science, but it is sufficiently common for me, at least, to disassociate myself from that particular label, at all costs. I see every reason to support the view that human society and culture are capable of almost infinite variety and of almost infinite permutations and combinations; the directions of change are themselves much more numerous and creative than any theory that is evolutionary in the classical sense can possibly master. Straight statistical probability would probably give a better prediction of change than current "laws." But that is not good enough, because we know that there *are* limiting factors, that there *are* forces that influence human choice and creative change, and that these would skew any probabilistic theory.

Current theories of social change, as I think of them, are also based on a reaction against two other major influences in anthropology—namely, functionalism and structuralism. Here the reaction is not so much one of disagreement but of asking questions that cannot be put easily within the functionalist or structuralist framework, although both may be adapted and brought together to be homologous with social change theory.

The older Malinowskian functionalism based its analysis on a search for the operative reasons for the phenomena under observation. If there were head-hunting or female circumcision or a binary counting system, the significance could only be brought out by disposing of the notion that these were strange esoteric phenomena resorted to by queer people dominated by irrational convention. It was then necessary to follow up the leads which would show that the phenomena "fitted" neatly into a cultural pattern by supporting needs or objectives which had been established in other parts of the culture, which helped to constitute a logical and psychological whole, and which "worked" to established ends (established, that is, by socialization and social control processes).

This is now so well accepted as an approach that it is difficult to see how great an intellectual revolution it was; yet it is not too much to say that the kind of interpretations which Malinowski and parallel thinkers were able to put on cultural behavior laid the foundation for intercultural tolerance, provided the essential drive and techniques for intercultural understanding, and enabled the public to see (almost for the first time) the richness and value of alternative cultures.

Malinowski himself had basically only twenty years to make his impact. There are signs in his posthumous work of unresolved issues and of new worries, though not all of these were taken up by his followers or those who created subsequent divergences of thought. The weakness of functionalism was paradoxical; it tended to allocate value to everything observed. It had no techniques to establish what was more or what was less value. It did not yet ask questions about the possibility of dysfunctional (a term introduced not in anthropology but in sociology) aberration, or what one should do analytically with the phenomena of Hitler or President Amin. If all was truly functioning, why change it? How then did change occur? Was it only as a result of outside pressure?*

There was, of course, the possibility of adopting a functional approach in an algebraic rather than a normative sense, and indeed much of this was buried in the empirical and conceptual work of all anthropologists. Such work only made sense if *relationships* between phenomena could be established or postulated. It is at this point that an extraordinarily interesting divergence emerged, quite different from that in other social science disciplines, which later intellectual historians will have great fun in accounting for (the present radical view that it can be accounted for by imperialist, capitalist, conservative, intellectual bias is just not good enough).

The essential property of an algebraic relationship is that if there is a movement in the value of one term the relationship describes the effects of that movement on the other terms. The testing of the validity of such a relationship *can only be carried out in the context of movement.* Only when y in fact moves can you determine whether the reaction of z or x is of the kind or degree that your theoretical relationship has stated.

It would be wrong to suggest that no such relationships exist in anthropology. They abound. But there was almost a deliberate movement to avoid them. The natural testing ground of such hypotheses would have

---

*Contrary to the views of many present anthropological commentators, who do not seem to have read Malinowski's posthumous work or that of his students such as Godfrey and Monica Wilson, Malinowskian functionalism did *not* ignore external influences on society during the process of change, and it did *not* fail to ask questions about the nature of the impinging society. The intellectual assumptions of functionalism *forced it* to begin moving in this direction, since only in this way could widespread change be accounted for.

been in the field of social change. But the anthropologists who regarded themselves (justly) as the theoretical contributors to the discipline almost completely ignored social change. It was regarded not as the central core of the theoretical apparatus but as something on the fringes.

This came about partly because of the need to establish and determine *structures* in societies and cultures without recourse to teleological functionalism. Algebraic linkages were put in static form, with the later introduction of equilibrating mechanisms. One of the first developments of the latter was in the use of the notion of reciprocity, following Marcel Mauss, to create system out of the network of social exchange, a point of view which has been used extensively in the previous chapters of this book. Some applications of this point of view revealed interesting empirical data about such phenomena as marriage exchange, and the equilibrating mechanisms involved, and the relations between power and service in a variety of social contexts.

But with the arrival and application of other forms of symbolic logic, structuralism, as it developed, was able to use such techniques as set theory to reveal underlying logical relations in cultural phenomena; culture, even society, could be seen in highly abstract terms as embodying logical links. There appears to be an argument (or, if you like, a bias) in the structural approach toward the revelation of relationships that are persistent over time and that continue to have validity independent of the content expressed in reality.* Thus, for example, one can determine an abstract structure of relations which apply in mythology, and which by extension could apply to that kind of mythology which in these pages I have called ethnosocial science. This, according to the structuralists, makes it possible for societies to change content while maintaining known relationships. As Pierre Maranda has said, the question being asked is "how do societies maintain themselves?" How, at the same time, can they allow for change?**

This, in certain respects, is precisely the question raised by Myrdal and Bauer at the beginning of this chapter. Structuralism, in principle if not in fact, provides part of the answer. Thus, Japan can maintain certain kinds

---

* See Pierre Maranda, "Structuralism in Cultural Anthropology," in Bernard Siegel, ed., *Annual Review of Anthropology*, Vol. 1, Stanford: Annual Reviews Inc., 1972.
** The perceptive reader will see the analogy between this method—providing an abstract and logically sophisticated *foundation* for cultural action—and (a) previous attempts by philosophically and psychologically oriented anthropologists to determine fundamental cultural orientations, themes, and the superorganic, and (b) Jung's collective unconscious. De Saussure, Piaget, Propp, and Levi-Strauss were and are operating different techniques with quite different formulations, yet (dare I say it?) structurally their search is similar.

of relations and ideological reasoning in the vastly different behavioral context of modern industry and bureaucracy. This destroys some of the argument that wholesale revolution or change is necessary to bring about major alterations in way of life and in the definition of performance.

On the other hand, Myrdal and Bauer are still left, as are all of us, with the following questions: (a) When does structural change *itself* occur? (b) When do conditions make it *necessary* for structural change to occur if other objectives are to be attained? (c) Since structure is partially defined in terms of "perpetuation" (to use Maranda's term), how can one judge the permanence or impermanence of a relationship (that is, whether it is or is not in fact structural)? On the last point, surely the mere ability to describe the relationship abstractly or in terms of set theory is insufficient as grounds for establishing perpetuation or permanence.*

The study of *social change*, as I understand it, is in some senses more ambitious, and in others—more down to earth. It does not make the prior assumption that any specific society *x* must inevitably change into *xy* or *y*. It leaves open the possibility that one may predict the movement of a total society in a given direction if one knows enough about the society and the pressures within and upon it. This cannot be achieved through typology, but only through a total operational model of the society itself and a conception of the way in which the internal and external factors bear upon each other.

Nor does the study make the prior assumption that any given sector of society or culture is more or less predisposed to change on theoretical grounds; revolution can occur in mode of production, use of power, religion, or ideas associated with education. If there are some areas of rapid change and blocks in other areas, the differences are due to particular characteristics of the society itself, acquired through history and cultural adaptation, plus variability in the pressures to change. At this level, no general prescriptions can be made, and only deep enquiry guided by these principles can have success. Needless to say, despite vast bodies of data, the existence of the key information is seldom systematic enough to enable us to be sure of the sequences of causality, at least sufficiently to rule out alternative hypotheses to those that are presented.

---

*In other writings I have argued that such phenomena as "permanence," if they are to imply a fundamental attachment of the society to them, or a strong "valuation," must be tested against pressures to change. The elasticity of resistance could give clues to valuation, but it is extremely hard to estimate, let alone to measure, and it is impossible to do so where pressure variation cannot be seen empirically. But in the absence of such an exercise, statements that such and such a set of principles is more stable in a given culture than another can only have a temporal meaning; any functional meaning attached to it can only be conjecture.

Marxism comes closest to meeting the criteria set out here, which is one reason it has such a widespread intellectual appeal. However, it does not quite do so since it gives necessary preeminence to material conditions in the causal chain. In fact, it is possible to retain a great deal of Marxist theoretical structure, particularly when applied to questions prior to the 19th century and to the 19th century itself, and to modify the conception of the interrelations of conceptuality and ideology on the one hand and materiality on the other, to give a much more flexible approach—and to find justification for this in the Marx and Engels literature. But to do so defeats the spirit of materialist philosophy.

Further, the entry of the notion of class as both prime result and prime mover in transitions surrounding the entry and departure of capitalism, and the erroneous notions of "primitive" society, and hence the antecedents of the modern world, have given Marxism a set of baggage which it doesn't know how to get rid of. Present-day Marxists and neo-Marxists are trapped into a set of conceptions which can be shown to confuse and to mislead when applied uncritically to the present-day world, which the initiators of the movement did not know. I have already, for example, criticized the concept of "class" (see Chapter 7). The use of the term in the Marxist sense as a key to the explanations of change in contemporary Asia and Africa simply confuses, because the realities of social organization are bound up with interest and action groups having very different implications. This can be argued around, particularly when it is necessary to do so to create ideological unity, but that is not very helpful.

Thus, a great deal of social change study concentrates on what might be called low-level empirical data, the observation of the way in which specific changes in social institutions can be linked to known social processes and to specific forces that operate upon them. But even here, higher level generalizations, often banal in their simplicity (and hence frequently and mistakenly left unstated), serve to provide a framework for the analysis of the observations and the construction of hypotheses.

The first step is to postulate, for the society in question, a given set of descriptors covering such fields as culture, social structure and organization, political arrangements, resource recognition and use, choice mechanisms, and external relations. It follows that if the set of observations to which one is addressing oneself is severely limited—let us say, to watching what happens when administrators endeavor to introduce a new technology into a village community with or without parallel changes in market conditions—it is possible to limit the descriptors as well. But in our present state of knowledge, it is extremely dangerous to do so prematurely; most "field" predictions have failed precisely because the set of descriptors used omitted to include an important element which only appeared important after the result.

One can then endeavor to trace the paths of choice that are open to people living in the situation. In doing so, one can arm oneself with a set of strongly supported (but also debated) general principles, some of which are sufficiently general to be held to be social laws.

A change stimulated in one part of the society or culture has ramifying and multiplying effects in other parts of the society and culture which can be traced step by step, and which in some cases (on the basis of past and comparative experience) can be predicted with a high degree of certainty. Much work still has to be done to sort out the *kinds* of relationships and linkages that exist and the conditions under which they are operative. This is important for the advance of general theory, but for most conditions ordinary empirical analysis, if thorough enough, is sufficient for policy considerations.

Where perceived ends *are seen to be* incompatible, conflict, synthesis, and adjustment will occur with a view to making them compatible (Law 1). This is a dynamic equilibrium involving such processes as dominance and competition; the concept of incompatibility implies a disagreement that is seen to *require* resolution. (In real societies the new "equilibrium" may in fact never be reached, since before it comes about new factors have intruded. This is not an argument against the concept of "equilibrium," as some anthropologists naïvely maintain, because what the notion does is to give a direction to the movement observed and this direction can be confirmed or denied. Note the comparative use of the notion "dynamic equilibrium" in economics.)

Any change in conditions (i.e., resources, knowledge, potential goals) will bring about equilibrium adjustments toward a state in which the achievement of goals will be maximized in an optimal economic way (Law 2). It is most important that this statement be interpreted *in terms of the culture involved*, and that the calculations be open to *nonmaterial* as well as material elements. The operation of this law has sometimes been denied, but such denial has always involved failure to include the nonmaterial as significant or the ethnocentric use of values.

Choice, whether it be of means or ends, is within the range of perception open to the persons involved. This is stating the obvious. But it is incredible how often this particular piece of obviousness is overlooked. Where the range of perception changes, the range of choice changes to a greater degree (Law 3), since choice is linked to the permutation of conceptual elements.

The values assigned to elements in the choice context are influenced by an ethical context, the linkage of particular elements positively or negatively to other goals, considerations of influence and power and of social control acting on the individual, the *perception* of the opportunity to act and of its consequences (Law 4).

Some of the above generalizations (for example, Law 2 above) have been denounced as tautological and circular. The only way of telling whether a goal is valued enough to result in action is to see whether action is in fact linked to such a goal. This is true. But there is nothing in that statement alone which says that the valuation is sufficiently strong or its nature sufficiently known to constitute a predictor for future action. Other elements must enter this judgment, such as a consideration and assessment of the place of alternative opportunities or ends in relation to future action, and an analysis of the ways in which potential goals (seen through the expression of hopes and aspirations) relate to the field of action.

Further, the tautology results *in a search*. The balance of factors is *not* self-evident; no one can make the calculation as well as the person who has to do it and act it and live it. The analyst, governed by his own sociocultural (perhaps even political) predispositions, and by a limited knowledge of the society in question, usually does not see the costs and benefits at first glance. In trying to repeat the calculation, with methods as close as possible to those used by the people concerned, he fails to solve the equation. He must search for new elements to which the actor is consciously or unconsciously giving weight (for perception in the sense we are using it here is often taken for granted by the actor, and so "buried" until it can be brought to the surface). Or he must admit that his thoughts about the way the people weighted their values were somehow wrong (and he must find out why).

Finally, the failure to use the principle thoroughly results in practical errors of interpretation. This is by now well documented, and even economists (who should be experienced in using the calculations) fall down on the job because they are not accustomed to the cross-cultural implications in the calculation. Then, instead of trying to find out what *should* go into the calculation, or borrowing that knowledge from anthropologists, they shrug it off as a bad job: "culture is getting in our way."

I shall simply elucidate with some simple examples drawn from a recent research report.* The reader will be able to pick up thousands of similar examples from the literature for himself, most of them lying unexplained because of the failure to use this form of analysis.

In approaching the explanation of the incidents, the author sees three factors bearing upon the exercise of perception: communications affecting information about alternatives and consequences, questions of trust which color the information and the judgments, and differences in resource control that affect judgments about practicality and opportunity.

First example. "The goal in this case was simply the introduction of a shaped hearth and chimney to facilitate smokeless cooking, and hence improve the working conditions of housewives. The unforeseen consequence was that a proliferating army of white ants ate away the thatched roofs. These ants had previously been killed by the smoke, but under the new arrangements could multiply unmolested." The result was a breakdown in trust as well as increased poverty, leading to resistance to further well-meaning advice, even where perhaps this might be better founded.

Second example. Chemical fertilizer was introduced, but information was lacking about its proper use, and about some of the complexities in the variables. The result was, in some cases, underuse so that no improvement in yield was evident; in other cases, use as a replacement for animal manure rather than in combination, so that the nutritive quality of the soil deteriorated instead of improving. A further result was breakdown in trust and declines in yield. These results were not counteracted by the demonstration effect of rich farmers doing the work properly; ideological considerations intervened to provide other than technological explanations for their success. Distrust of this kind put blocks in the way of cooperative action to purchase new styles of farm machinery.

Third example. Local political power was linked to persons whose interests were against the land allocation policies of government. Thus,

One critical example of such monopolization is the failure to use village common lands, now controlled by the headman as elected leader of the village council. Some years previously a government order required that these lands be distributed free to landless families. This order, however, conflicted with the interests of large landowners, including the headman himself, since it jeopardized the supply of cheap agricultural labour.... The result is that, years later, it has not been implemented in full in any of the five villages. One village council controls 250 acres of arable land, sufficient to provide subsistence landholding for all landless families in the village.

---

* S. M. Hale, *Rural Development Projects in India, as a Problem of Choice Behaviour,* Working Paper Number Three, Vancouver: The Institute of Asian and Slavonic Research, 1973.

In such examples, one fails to find the absolute sway of cultural conservatism as an unexplained or unchangeable phenomenon. Self-interest, worry, doubt, traumatic experience, faulty analysis, power used in a competitive drive for comparative advantage—these are the much more common and the human grounds which are at the basis of change and nonchange. The theory that fails to take them into account in their own context of reality will need to resort to cross-cultural caricature or to large sounding phrases about the inevitabilities of human destiny.

PART IV

Styles of Action

Prologue to Part IV

IF ANTHROPOLOGISTS or other social scientists are to involve themselves in either the examination or the support of public policy, or indeed its criticism, it behoves them to pay attention to two major themes. First, they should know how the action system works, particularly through the intermediation of "action agents"—that is, persons who have acquired the authority to devise actions and to persuade people to do things that are consistent with policy. Second, they should know how the work of the social scientist is affected when he adopts an action role, and how it relates to the interests and opportunities of the numerous groups involved.

Radical social scientists have been quite right in drawing attention to these kinds of issues, but they are quite wrong in saying that anthropology, at least, has overlooked them. I have pointed this out, to some extent, in Chapter 4. For example, during graduate work at the London School of Economics in the late 1940s, I participated in seminars on social change in which a great deal of attention was given to the analysis of action agents as social phenomena. In those years I wrote a small book on colonial administration in the South-West Pacific, and found that I could not do so without asking the following questions: Who were the alien authorities in commerce, government, and missionary activity? Were they "typical" of the societies from which they came or did the new setting establish new and different codes and expectations? The work was superficial, not at the highly focused but more controversial level of O. Mannoni's *Prospero and Caliban*, which gave a psychological thrust to the analysis.

In addition, as a student writing on social change in Melanesia for a Ph.D. thesis, I found it quite impossible to deal with the topic without considering similar questions more deeply. Take the issue of forced labor in the Pacific—"black-birding." How did it pay? What prompted men to engage in it? Why were they violent to the point of destroying populations—the source of their trade? What bodies of law and ethic

201

governed the conduct of the Royal Navy? Why were the missionaries unable to bring successful court cases? Why, later, did other missionaries arm adherents and engage in fratricidal war with rival sects? What drove the first administrators to establish law, and why did it take the forms it did? How did the indigenous people establish leaders and figureheads to cope with this curious chaos which had descended upon them? Later writers have corrected much of what I wrote and have filled in gaps, particularly from the historical record. But the point is that these questions were not irrelevant to anthropology, and they were raised; nor were they atypical. They were fully justified, theoretically and intellectually, by the thrusts that had been given by predecessors such as Malinowski and Herskovits, and by the anthropologists' reaction to the theses of colleagues from other disciplines, such as Boeke and Furnivall, whose notions of "the dual economy" and "the plural society," however simplified and erroneous, could never have held the attention and position they did if the authors had not based them on an examination of the social character of groups in conflict.

Although the arguments continue, this is much in the past. For the present, where do we look?

In what follows in Part IV I shall limit myself to cross-cultural situations, and shall not pretend to intrude (except occasionally) into the question of action agents in highly industrialized societies. (Part V will be closer to this issue, in the consideration of values.) I shall draw on personal experience, and events I have observed in the field or that have come to my attention in the course of action-oriented analyses.

My object, however, is not to repeat studies about action agents themselves, which have been and are being made: How do technical assistance specialists view the world? Who are the Peace Corps volunteers? How have science and liberalism (to say nothing of "independence") changed the missionary? How do officials of independent governments differ from those of colonial rule? Those questions can, for the moment, be left to specialized monographs.

My task is rather to treat of the ways in which personal action to achieve goals, more particularly by agents who do *not* belong to the culture in question, relate to principle and theory.

One point, however, does need to be made about the social scene as a whole. Many of the countries with a colonial history, striving for development, now have an infinitely higher proportion of aliens than they had in the days of restricted colonialism. Further, the variety of agents has increased even more dramatically. The latest country to change in this respect is Australian-administered Papua–New Guinea, now achieving independence. Until the late 1960s, the Australian administering power was completely jealous of its prerogatives. Despite the serious dearth of skilled training, without a single university graduate in the indigenous population until the late 1960s, it refused to make use of multilateral Fellowship aid available from the United Nations' family. This has changed, and there are now UNESCO, World Bank, and United Nations missions dealing with developmental questions, and also a thriving young university.

In almost any developing country there are alien groups competing for influence, to greater or lesser degree under governmental control and sufferance. Political missions, diplomatic representations, military advisers, youth service volunteers, missionaries, technical experts, educators, agriculturalists, industrialists, economists, planners, short-term missions of inspection, financial advisers, and a wealth of others (not to mention private speculators and commercial men) from scores of countries, operating under a wide variety of rules, regulations, assumptions, cultural backgrounds, and political and ethical objectives all abound. It is no joke. It takes specialized concentration for the host country itself to know what is going on, and to develop methods for keeping the patchwork quilt together, and to keep it according to specification.

Into this bewildering array of social and cultural forces steps the social scientist. What does he see? Only a part of it. To whom does he talk? That is crucial. To whom does he report? We had better watch that. Can he cope? I wonder.

CHAPTER 13

The Process of Technical Assistance

DEVELOPMENT assistance or development aid, as expressed in official overall statistics, consists of the value of transferred resources from one country to another, the purpose being to contribute to the development of the recipient country. This includes programs which have very different implications. For example, private capital investment, perhaps at reduced terms or perhaps in operations that have major local control (but nevertheless investment for all that) may be included. Military aid, aid for dealing with problems of refugees, and aid to relieve the impact of famine or cataclysm may also be included, although what the contribution to development is would require analysis. Contributions to capital infra-structure of a physical kind (the construction of a dam or a highway system) by direct grant or by repayable loan, even where the construction may be carried out by foreign firms who repatriate their fees or profits and a proportion of senior wages, are noted. So also is the provision of technical advice and training—through the work of visiting experts, contributions to research and educational institutions, and the provision of Fellowships for study abroad.

United Nations Second Development Decade strategy, influenced by the Pearson Report, has suggested that the economically advanced countries provide 1 percent of their GNP for development aid. The countries of the OECD Development Assistance Committee provided 0.83 percent of their GNP in combined private and official funding in 1971; of this, only 0.30 percent of their GNP was in the form of outright official grants. The remainder, presumably, involved some form of repayment obligation.

Technical assistance, more narrowly conceived, consists in providing help to improve the technical infrastructure and operations of the society. It should specifically exlude emergency "handouts" or profit-making investment for private gain, but should include equipment and personnel provision. No country provides figures that are truly rigorous and comparative; to get at that requires original research.

It is obvious, however, that only a small proportion of what is called development assistance is in fact development oriented. I cannot tell you how much, but my guess would be of the order of 50 to 60 percent. That which falls into the category of technical assistance, public and private, is probably a good deal smaller.

One of the difficulties in making the judgment is that a substantial part of development assistance does *not* in fact develop anything except the small sector of personnel exchange that is involved. When an expert is withdrawn (in some instances having achieved little), he is immediately replaced by another, that is, he has not helped the society to do without him. This example should not be regarded as typical, but it is sufficiently common to affect our judgment about the validity of the official figures if they are to be taken as representative of a functional situation. They should not be.

In what follows I shall concentrate my remarks on quite a small area of the whole operation—namely, the provision and operation of technical assistance *in human terms*, which is the area I know best. But many of my remarks will be applicable to other areas, particularly when I come to discuss criteria for judging whether a particular operation is contributing to development and, more importantly, to social performance.

The ethnotheory (or, if you like, the mythology) of development assistance is predominantly as follows.

Development is good. The disparity in wealth between nations is an evil, both in itself and because of the human suffering, the waste of human capacities, and the social tension it causes. If developing countries are left to themselves, the disparity will continue to increase and the problems will grow as well, perhaps even increasing international tension and the likelihood of armed conflict. Technical and developmental assistance are therefore necessary to give an additional thrust and increased access to a resource base. It is in the interests of the richer countries to provide this.

In providing such assistance, two propositions have rival weight. One is that technical assistance and development aid should be administered multilaterally, to provide for better overall coordination and to act as a brake on possible political manipulation on the part of the donor country. The other is that such aid should be administered bilaterally, since this is deemed to be more direct, more efficient, and more convincing to the taxpayers who provide the money.

Whichever mode is chosen, most countries (there are some exceptions) and most international agencies subscribe to the following principles. The first is that aid must not be imposed—it must be wanted, and hence must be applied for. The projects making up the aid must also be wanted; furthermore, they must fit the specific objectives of the country concerned. Hence, the aid-receiving country sets the priorities, defines the objectives, and selects the projects. Projects will not be established on the initiative of pressures from the donor country.

The reader who has consulted Chapter 9 will recognize that the mythology of development assistance is dominated by the mythology of nationalism and national independence. Everything possible is done to remove from sight, but not from the reality, the facts of national interdependence.

The reality is much more complex. The reservation that is most obvious to the public comes at the beginning, with the proposition "development is good." The fact is that development might or might not be good. Critics, particularly in the richer countries, are saying that it is not good, because it "distorts" values toward those of a consumer society, it involves destruction of the environment, it often increases wealth inequalities, and it may even involve a higher world population. In some contexts village people, by their opposition to particular projects, have shown that they are not willing to engage in the act of development at any price; if there is to be development, they wish to choose their own mode, and sometimes they don't want it at all.

Nevertheless, such a stance is all very well for those of us who already have an infrastructure for sophisticated supply and the wealth to make it work; some of that may be diverted to improvement of environmental quality and social justice. In most other countries the problems are more severe. No attack of a positive nature on these issues is likely without substantial income increase. The destruction of the environment through erosion caused by improper agricultural practice is extremely widespread and is often a function of poverty and lack of an infrastructure that can provide knowledge and research. Poor towns are often destructive of health and morale. These kinds of issues cannot be tackled on the basis of "stop growth" and "stop development."

Some of the countries in the middle are proposing that the issue is not development versus values, but development for and with values, of social importance. They are inclined to resent the pure environmentalist as being anti-humanity, and to protest against the kind of development that is based upon blatant resource-use and profit-making. Out of the internationalization of discussions resulting from the Western-oriented and simplistic assumptions of the Club of Rome and the MIT projections (see Chapter 19) more balanced proposals will undoubtedly be made.

It is my contention that the balance of such issues can only be resolved in the case of particular countries by linking change to the idea of performance, as I have presented it on pages 13–14. We are dealing with human satisfaction as defined by human beings, and it is they who must decide in the end on the answer to the following question: Does development bring increased or decreased satisfaction? What kind of development is likely to represent an improvement of the state of affairs in my eyes?

The disparity in wealth between nations may be an evil, but it is not to be taken at face value. The statistics on which such comparisons are made are extremely misleading.* A great deal of the material production that occurs in the subsistence or nonmarket sector of the economy escapes record. This omission distorts the interpretation of the significance of trends; a drop in market production, for example, may be more than counterbalanced by an increase in subsistence production, distributed through the social network. Even in Western, nontraditional society, this is a factor. Statisticians in developing countries usually *try* to make an estimate of such quantities; in Western countries they do not even try. Yet variations in *bricolage* and self-help in Europe and the United States, and the continued value of subsistence activities in many parts of Europe, are substantial quantities. A distinguished statistician has held that errors in per capita income statistics for developing countries may be of the order of *several hundred percent*. Indeed, if some of the figures were taken literally and translated into real rather than monetary income, the individuals concerned *could not be alive.***

Beyond this major problem lies, once again, our familiar challenge: performance. Statistical manipulations (despite some determined theoretical work by sociologists and real-welfare-level-of-living economists) do not as yet measure a large number of things that are important to large numbers of people; a quantitative summary comparison of the achievements of people living in quite different cultures is so far impossible. Per capita income comparison is no guide to the satisfaction or dissatisfaction

---

*One of the best accounts of this, which should be required reading for all those pondering development questions, is contained in P. T. Bauer, *Dissent on Development*, London: Weidenfeld and Nicolson, 1972, pp. 64 ff.

**D. Usher, *The Price Mechanism and the Meaning of National Income Statistics*, New York: Oxford University Press, 1968. The study primarily deals with Thailand (for which I can only record substantial personal agreement with the subjective judgments) together with comparative material.

people may have with their way of life. A comparison between the behavioral and the potential *profiles* of the relevant culture may yield an idea of the level of performance, but no set of statistical devices has yet been devised that will summarize the level of performance for a given country at a given time, or, still less, compare such performances. Analyses, whether politically or scientifically motivated, that pretend to affirm a clear situation or to be precise, should be immediately suspect—this applies to 99 percent of them. There is a lifetime's work here for ambitious young scholars. In the meantime policy must be based on *some* assumptions.

A further factor affecting our judgment about wealth disparity is the rather rapid movement of a number of countries into the world league of the "better-off." One can discount some (but not all) of the examples of oil-rich states because of their oligarchic nature and the consequent forms of distribution within them. In some respects this is an external political judgment rather than an internal one. One can also argue that in the case of Thailand, which has not yet reached the status of "not being poor," at least some of the advance has been due to extensive American military expenditures within that country, although that would be to neglect the substantial push upwards which occurred before the expenditures reached their recent levels. In all developing countries there are serious pockets of more or less large numbers of people who are poor by any standards—but that is true in the richer countries as well.

Given all of this, the familiar idea of an increase in the gap is subject to caution. In many parts of the underdeveloped world, the figures we have show that per capita income has grown faster than in the United States for a long time. One can no longer overlook the potential, just-around-the-corner entry of Brazil into the league of the economically well-off, or the position of Iran, Taiwan and Mexico as pace-leaders. The communications limitations and population heterogeneity of Mexico and Nigeria are likely to produce tension-building inequalities, but the signs are that Nigeria (partly thanks to its oil) may be the first Black African nation-state to make the breakthrough.

The "facts" upon which these judgments are made are as liable to challenge as any others; once again, no judgment has been included about satisfaction, happiness, or political justice. Nor is it to be accepted offhand that even an increase in national disparities is unacceptable if, *for the bulk of the people*, the increase in level of living and of satisfaction is large enough to be known, seen, and savored. This might be quite acceptable, let us say, for the next twenty years, *depending on the country*; after that point, who knows? Europe and Japan by that time may be putting more of their income into environmental and other satisfying sectors, and less into multiplying investment; the United States has already basically slowed down its rates of growth. Several countries on the "almost-there" list could in fact catch up at that time, in their own value terms.

This then raises serious issues about the costs and benefits of developmental aid. I partially disagree with P. T. Bauer, who says in effect that developmental aid is necessarily distorting, and that developing countries will be better off if they are self-reliant in such matters as were the countries of Europe in the 19th century. Many of his observations are correct, and he is right to criticize the popular mechanistic formulations of the Pearson Report, the vague and imprecise conceptualization of Gunnar Myrdal, and the writings of those economic formalists who play with inapplicable assumptions. (But we all suffer from these limitations to some degree.)

It is only partially true that Europe "got there" without aid, and took a long time over it. The basic infrastructure of connections was there prior to the 19th century, and was a crisscross of countries. Switzerland moved into orbit, as I have mentioned, on the basis of the importation of ideas and skills, and the use of these in a worldwide network; once it began, from a wealth base quite as low as that of many underdeveloped countries, and with just as big a gap in education, it moved very rapidly. One can argue that France has become "big league," in the sense of spreading its development internally and exchanging an ethos of consumer-oriented growth for the traditional complaisance, only in the 1960s. Of course, it began from a strong base.

It is also true that the genesis of much growth is and has to be internal. It is out of internal ideas (and the exchange of the fruits of productive activity internally) that wealth, capital, the will to move, and the expectation that change is feasible will come. Too much unsought dependence in part creates the wrong attitudes.

Nevertheless, developing countries do have major new obstacles to overcome, and these suggest in part that technical assistance has a role to play. First, as I have pointed out, they lack the connections created by migration patterns (this is not completely true; there are *regional* connections in Africa and Asia which could be used). Technical assistance creates connections. Second, the patterns of linkage still tend to be metropolitan-oriented, usually to the old colonial power. Technical assistance can break and modify this monopoly. (Some metropolitan powers, particularly France, fight this through the use of a linguistic and cultural mystique, as well as in more down-to-earth terms.) Third, it surely helps to get the communications infrastructure established. Fourth, in some cases a communications infrastructure, and other technical investment, has to be much more complex than was the case in the 19th century, costing more, and requiring a support of skills and technical knowledge which was not present then. (An extreme example: nowadays the opening up of New Guinea or Northern Canada is unthinkable except on the basis of air connections which must be designed specifically for the terrain. Roads and railways may come, but they will be much more costly than was the case in Europe.) Fifth, technical innovation must be based on largely imported knowledge, at least initially, and will always require highly efficient international communication. It can no longer be built from the local scene up. The imported knowledge is only a base, it is true, for it must be amended and adapted; but it is essential, and it creates the requirement for support research and educational institutions on a scale not present in the beginning of the 19th century.

If you want to make your statistics look good, you call all of this development assistance. Yet some of the forms in which it is provided are damaging, at least in the short term. Most projects, however, have a benefit factor, sometimes not that which the project designers anticipated. Certainly, if the technical assistance element can be strengthened and concentrated with a clear analysis of the ways in which the effects can be maximized, so much the better (and 1 percent of the rich countries' GNP would be more than enough). At the moment, one must allow for perhaps 50 or 60 percent wastage, and one must argue that this is a reasonable price to pay, if men and nation-states remain the way they are. For a realistic change in this figure requires a change in modes which would threaten the concept of nationalism.

Let us now move a little more closely to the mechanics of aid giving and receiving. Despite what the myth says, the reality is two-sided. Receiving countries apply for aid projects, true enough. But donor countries and agencies do not necessarily agree to provide the projects requested. Their decision on whether or not to support a project is governed by *their own* analysis, and they all maintain large staffs to carry it out. The analysis has three main parts: the effectiveness with which the aid project is likely to be carried out, as the donor country or agency perceives it; the agreement or disagreement of the donor country or agency with the receiving country's assessment of the "significance" of the project (this is seldom stated bluntly, but obviously donors avoid getting landed with insignificant projects, and find excuses to enable them to be selective); and the degree to which the project fits the general aid-giving policy of the donor party.

Thus, a donor does its best to determine whether a project is likely to carry through (a judgment largely based on past experience), the realism with which the project is put together, the nature of the resources the country itself is putting in, and the cooperation that is available from counterpart professionals. It may decide that although the project is not likely to succeed, it is desirable to have a finger in that particular pie since, if it does not, somebody else's finger will be there, and after all a failed or only partially successful project can lead to a further sequence of projects, giving the donor a kind of property stake in the operation.

The judgment of "significance" also has several parts. One is political. Does the project reinforce the donor's moral, economic, or political position vis-à-vis the country concerned? This is without doubt the predominant consideration in most (perhaps not all) bilateral programs; the stronger the donor country, the more intense this factor. It is reinforced by international rivalries, particularly by the big powers (US, USSR, China), those countries that would like to be, or those that have intense preoccupations with their international position (France, Israel). For countries where that factor is not so strong, real or imagined internal pressures may bring about a similar result. Canada's aid is based on two principles: "since we are a detached middle power, everybody loves us" (untrue), and "the public will support aid only if it brings economic benefits to Canada in the form of market influence" (probably untrue, but blatantly exercised, with some signs of recent modification).

A second judgment of significance is technical. While this seems straightforward, it is often not so. Technical appropriateness can often be determined only, perhaps, by an initial expert visit. There are strong motivations for an expert to recommend a project in terms that will be understood, or at least accepted, in the donor country, so that it may be continued. An expert who recommends against a project may run a serious risk of making himself persona non grata with one of the parties involved. In fact, technical appropriateness is often a function of flexibility, since local conditions are often liable to change the analysis as they come to be known. One of the features of earlier concepts of aid was that this was not "cricket"; a contract was a contract. Most donors now recognize the need for flexibility, and they expect the conception of the project to change as it progresses.

A third concern is connected with the donor's ethnosocial science, and in particular his development theory. However, on the whole bilateral donors do not have theories that are consciously applied, except for very crude attempts at cost-benefit analysis (that must at this point in their nature be crude because of urgency and lack of time). In fact, each donor operates with built-in assumptions, often prejudices, sometimes influenced by expert feedback or discussions with development agents. Some bilateral donors do this more than others, and the multilateral agencies are swamped with studies and often a considerable amount of in-house expertise. The crudest assumption is that any provision of capital is developmentally and politically beneficial if it can be seen. The second crudest assumption is that any change in technology in a more sophisticated direction, which can theoretically be linked to increased output, is justifiable (in fact, the technology may destroy output, may create damaging spin-off effects, or may be just unworkable.) These two assumptions are still applied, and the materials fed into the cost-benefit in-house studies reflect them. But, fortunately, they are often misleading when applied—in other words, the benefits turn out to be important, but not as planned. Nevertheless, the evaluation of technical assistance effects falls far short of what could be achieved, and will be treated positively in the latter part of this chapter.

The judgment of consistency with aid-giving policy is of crucial importance. Aid, in the sense we are using the term here, is by definition government to government. This opens a considerable temptation for political leverage, which has led the Americans, French, and Chinese (to take three examples) to use aid as a screen for intelligence operations, to suggest and agree to projects that have the effect of supporting some elements in the government at the expense of others, and to think of it as an adjunct to military influence in certain cases. Again, some countries define their aid program in terms of a narrow approach to *economic* development, and consider other sectors only if they can be seen to support economic growth directly. The international multilateral agencies each have (over and above their aid programs as such) programs of international action endorsed by their governing councils as global strategies to be financed from the regular budget or by voluntary contributions. Thus, for example, the World Health Organization has had a malaria eradication campaign, and many other world goals; UNESCO has had world campaigns for the reduction of illiteracy and regional campaigns to achieve universal education for specific periods of time; and so on. Such organizations, chronically short of money, endeavor to guide technical assistance into a supportive role for their overall objectives.

The Canadian International Development Agency has a somewhat technological approach to development and aid. It is interested in dams and machines, engineering, and the transfer of technology, and it knows how to handle these. Recently, its Director announced the laudable objective of taking into account the "social implications" of projects. A committee of the Social Science Research Council of Canada, realizing that this was not as simple to handle in practice as to state in theory, offered to help in developing techniques of evaluation and analysis, in assisting recipient countries to create institutions that could analyze the social implications *in situ*, if such assistance were necessary, and in locating social scientists in Canada who could provide appropriate knowledge for the Agency itself. The Agency was interested only in the last point; it is most likely that "social implications" will, as usual, be put in the rag bag of miscellaneous materials to be brought out for an occasional public relations dusting, or treated technocratically as an element of such social sectors as education, welfare, and population policy.*

The significance of these kinds of issues for the development assistance myth is as follows. A donor agency has its own ideas and policies. Donor countries have their own staffs in recipient countries, usually attached to embassies. Multilateral agencies have their own traveling representatives, some regional offices, and (more effectively nowadays) the office of the UN resident representative. One of the major tasks of these officials is to make clear to the officials of the donor countries just what kind of aid is available and what kind of applications are likely to be approved. It goes further. Since there is competition in the field, the officials often behave as salesmen, telling the country concerned—in polite and carefully chosen words—that if they want funds for technical assistance, the donor country is particularly interested in seeing that it is spent in defined sectors (police, education, electrical power), but not in others (perhaps computer technology or the social sciences).

It is, of course, the recipient country's privilege to ignore such advice. If it does, it is likely to find itself tagged as inefficient, politically unstable, or what have you. Further, and more important, departmental and internal rivalries within the recipient country create competition to *get* aid. There are numerous contexts in which the presence and the reports of aid experts do not in themselves add new knowledge—or, if they do, this is a by-product of the real function. The real function is to be there, visibly, and to write a report which can be quoted; for the presence of the expert

*However, since the above was written the Agency has established an imaginative Non-Governmental Organizations Division which is supporting the work of international social science organizations.

is a part of the battery of weapons that a particular department can use to gain internal support for its program. Thus, an Education Department, a Public Health Department, or a Police Department can say to the Cabinet, the Central Planning Office, the Premier, or the President: The expert provided by our friends has drawn our attention to the fact that our proposal would help us meet our obligations to attain certain standards endorsed by Resolution of the relevant World Body. If his report is endorsed, it will require so many hundreds of thousands of baht or rupees or dollars to implement. However, we are given to understand that if his report is endorsed, and only then, we will get 5 percent of the funds from the expert's agency, and if US AID likes it, an additional 40 percent will come from them. Please, in the next budget of the country, supply the remaining 55 percent. Such a line of argument can improve the internal bargaining position of the Department concerned.

I am not introducing this example to undermine the importance and significance of technical assistance; I do so simply to bring out the reality rather than the myth. Given the circumstances of the countries concerned, and the way technical assistance has become a competitive political operation, these results are inevitable and natural. Furthermore, they are functionally valuable since, without this kind of support and argument, the Departmental chief involved would probably never have achieved his project.

In an extreme form this could lead to chaos, and in some instances in some countries almost identical projects (community development is a good case in point) have been supported in the hands of different competing ministries, with different competing sources of external aid. Let me say again, competition is not necessarily bad, and lack of order is often one way of arriving at an ultimate solution. I am *not* an advocate of rigid centralized planning. I am *not* criticizing developing countries for their departmental divisions; each developed country has its similar departmental confusions (both internally and in supporting external policy) and each of the multilateral organizations has its departmental rivalries.*

But only the strongest and toughest countries can resist the blandishments to the point at which there is coordinated policy. One of the main reasons for this need is the fact that every dollar of aid involves a number of dollars of local financial, material, and personnel support and back-up.

---

*I have watched with amusement, for example, the way in which an FAO project, let us say in fisheries, immediately leads to the arrival of staff members representing, let us say, forestry or water resources, anxious to get a project for their department "inscribed" in the country concerned, so that their presence can be seen and maintained and their energies can be evident.

The most successful aid is catalytic. Some key element is introduced, probably costing relatively little money: a leprosy-control expert, an expert in rural literacy campaigns, a prosthenics expert, a three-man team to design a technical institute. It is after his impact that the fun begins. The leprosy campaign involves four hundred technicians and buildings and supporting services; the rural literacy campaign involves an institution for retraining teachers and funds for special rewards and equipment for rural service; the prosthenics program requires local counterparts, experimental workshops, additions to hospitals for exercise space; the technical institute requires expensive, imported machinery and instruments, the training abroad of instructors.

A country must take these factors into account, must allow for them, and must decide on priorities among them. Yet if it does not do everything at once, in line with all the great international resolutions "calling upon member states," it will be tagged as unprogressive, perhaps even reactionary.*

Two corrective principles have been established. One of the most important influences of United Nations technical assistance has been to gestate institutions and methods, adapted to a country's system of government, for coordination and control of aid inflows. A few countries have been so successful in this that their interdepartmental cooperation is substantially superior to anything to be found in many Western capitalist countries short of the cabinet level. They are, however, very much in the minority, and the principle and the institutions are still subject to the influences mentioned above. Quite often planning is, and must be, little more than a summation of each department's goals, perhaps controlled by an overall limit or an *a priori* assignment of values to each department.

---

*I must say I become annoyed at the manner in which aid agencies—and they all seem equally guilty—take full credit in propaganda sheets for programs in which they are involved. UNICEF tells you of the tremendous world programs for which it has been responsible. It does, indeed, provide an essential and invaluable service, particularly supplying support equipment and personnel that fall outside the normal definitions of aid programs; hence, its catalytic effect and the great morale boost of its support to men and women who are working against desperate odds cannot be overstressed. That in itself is achievement enough. But to imply, as many of the hand-outs do, that the whole program was due to UNICEF is usually so much nonsense. Similarly WHO quite cheerily claims credit for controlling diseases; it certainly helped, and that help was essential. But the blood, sweat, and tears (and the innovative ideas) are most likely to have come in greatest quantity and at deepest emotional cost from the personnel of the country itself, together with parallel and supportive aid groups, and at the cost of alternative programs of great importance. Officials in the recipient countries swallow their resentment with dignity and allow "experts" to take credit, even for innovative ideas that counterpart colleagues have produced and put into effect. Why should good and invaluable work be tarnished by hypocritical and hurtful public relations claims?

The second corrective idea is to secure coordination among donor countries at the level of the recipient country. The techniques for doing this are varied. The size of the aid program required for India, for example, has brought into being a consortium of the major donors who cut up the pie into slices for which they will be responsible; but this is only at the level of the larger strategy. Representatives of the countries of the OECD Development Assistance Committee regularly meet, and the UN Resident Representative usually participates in such meetings in each recipient country. One has the impression, however, that the motivations for *bilateral* aid giving are not fully aired, and that much aid is given under the table, as it were, largely because of the increased and rather blatant involvement of US AID in political and strategic matters.

Following the Jackson Report on the Capacity of the UN Development System, the position of the UN Resident Representative as field coordinator of the proposals and projects of all UN agencies and the strengthening of the UN Development Programme as the agency that contracts UN assistance to individual agencies for particular technical purposes should have brought about more serious linkages in multilateral assistance. The Jackson Report refers also to the gradual buildup of staffing for the UN Resident Representative, who is charged with producing a total "country programme" for UN Development Assistance by the creation of junior positions (with expectation of promotion) for persons experienced and qualified in developmental analysis. Between the lines, one sees that the expectation is that the UN Resident Representative himself will in time come to have such knowledge and expertise, in addition to his administrative and diplomatic qualifications, at a very high operational level.

If the Jackson Report recommendations are being followed through in fact as well as in principle, the results are likely to reinforce still further the inherent superiority of multilateral development assistance over bilateral, or limited consortium, types.* It is too soon to make judgments about the practical effects; no doubt the proposals, like all such ideas, are being affected by budgetary considerations and the continuing rivalries of organizational power.

It is also true that multilateral assistance programs still have weaknesses. Where men and women of differing nationalities work together as a team (or where a director of one nationality is followed by a colleague of

---

* Unfortunately, power bloc votes are now succeeding in introducing political considerations even here. Note the effect of decisions in the 1974 UNESCO General Conference upon the supply of assistance to Israel, and probably to other countries of the Middle East.

another), the chances of misunderstanding and conflict are high as a result of differences in perspective and training. In any event a high proportion of experts have a touch of the prima donna in their make-up so that conflict is not entirely absent from bilateral programs either. Again, the present complexity of international organization makes coordination, check-outs with governments, personnel selection, and the like relatively slow.

Despite these kinds of drawbacks, there is little doubt that if all countries would put their funds into multilateral pools, the developmental (as distinct from the political) effects of development assistance would be immeasurably enhanced; this improvement would be doubled if some measure of movement toward the coordination of the specialized agencies along the lines laid out in Chapter 9 were achieved. Multilateral arrangements permit the recipient country to express uninfluenced preferences for particular experts from particular countries, remove the force of economic imperialism associated with bilateral capital supply and construction contracts, and provide a cushion against undue political influence. The type of country programming envisaged in the Jackson Report—in which the officials of the country provide priorities and project definitions and discuss the interrelations of these with the UN Resident Representative and his staff for forwarding as a coordinated package to the UN Development Programme—gives development assistance a much greater chance of increasing its strategic impact. At present, the impact can be relatively limited by the much greater volume of bilateral aid, even from single countries such as the United States and many others, with bilateral aid programs pulling in opposing directions. Furthermore, a major multilateral program, if dominant in its volume and weight, would have a greater chance of gaining experience and coming to grips with the nontangible serious issues of "social implications" and the quality of life.

There are continuous and complex processes for the evaluation of the impact of technical assistance programs. Most of these are concerned with the evaluation of *projects*—that is, the operational units linked to specific contracts. Evaluation tends to take objectives of the project as stated, and to see the project as a unit. It may ask the questions: Were the objectives technically realistic? How did the project tie in with its immediate social and economic context? This would be an unusually broad evaluation, but cost-benefit analysis does at least point to some of the answers. From then on, the questions have to do with the project operations: Were the right men in the right place? Were the costs kept down? Was the timing as anticipated? Did the recipient country provide counterparts and back-up services? Were the clauses of the contract fulfilled? Did the project reach the objectives set for it? And, sometimes, what is known about the broader effects of the project? Did it stimulate or disturb the neighboring sectors of activity?

This, of course, is not enough for those who wish to know more about the way projects interact with the movement of society, economy, polity, and culture. Most of the information about the significance of projects from this point of view comes from scholars and commentators external to the official evaluation process, since it involves lengthy techniques of investigation and subjective or qualitative observations that do not fit the administrator's desire for speed and apparent precision. A high proportion of the observations, even in such sensitive works as Kusum Nair's *Blossoms in the Dust* or such theoretically rigorous books as A. O. Hirschman's *Development Projects Observed*, give their attention to the way in which the project was not "fitted" to the culture so that all sorts of things went wrong with its operation, or else culture is seen as getting in the way of progress or of the project's implementation. Kusum Nair does, however, raise fundamental questions: Should the project have been started in the first place? Was it really a contribution to the improvement of the lot of the people? In many cases, her answer is negative.* Hirschman deals with World Bank projects. Since he respects the World Bank, he hardly questions the choice of project itself—that is taken for granted—but he does give weight to the importance of unplanned spin-off effects.

However important the design of a project may be to its success or failure, even more important is the first question that has to be asked: How does the project fit into strategies of change and improvement? The donor countries can conveniently bypass this question because the responsibility for deciding upon it is technically that of the recipient country. However, if donor countries do not show an interest in it, several things can follow. One is that the recipient country does not itself have the techniques and expertise to raise and answer the question, so that the choice of project is on its part haphazard or political, and it puts itself in the hands of the political and social objectives of the donor. The other is that the project may create profound disturbance of a more intractable kind than the problem it was set up to solve, and may increase short-run misery. The famous post-War groundnuts scheme of East Africa was the

---

* Technically speaking, her book is not about technical assistance but about government-initiated projects in general. But similar principles apply.

first major and dramatic example of this kind. Mechanized agriculture with huge land exploitation units was rapidly and brusquely imposed on a traditional society. The result was destruction of the top-soil, breakdown of nearly all the highly unsuitable machine equipment, thorough upset of residence and work patterns, creation—temporarily—of a proletariat, and misery and frustration all round, with agriculture going back to square one until the basic research could be done.

Thus, both objectives and design have profound linkages with social conditions, and no policy will be successful unless, intuitively or explicitly, the decision-making authority analyzes them. If the analysis is intuitive, this is done through political sensitivity and innate knowledge of the world in which one lives. It is for this reason that, however much scholars may produce schemes of analysis, the fundamentals of decisions must be taken by public representatives of the society involved. The scholar and expert may provide help, but there is no escaping the ultimate responsibility, and the scholar and expert have neither recourse nor legitimate objection if their proposals are set aside or fundamentally modified.

As a scholar, I shall set out some of the ways in which criteria for the significance and relevance of projects may be approached. Much of what I have to say is general. While it is introduced in connection with a discussion of technical assistance, it can also be used in connection with the selection of any official projects.*

I have mentioned that one way of judging social performance is to ask to what degree does the existing effective demand level (or profile) relate to the potential demand profile. The technical jargon I have introduced refers to the behavioral profile of culture and the potential profile of culture in order to broaden the concept into cultural areas that economic language does not normally take into account. The question then is: to what extent does a project move effective demand so that it is closer to the potential profile of culture?

To put it simply, does the project help people get what they want? But it is not a simple question with a simple answer, and it can seldom be approached just by asking people "what do you want?" and then designing a project accordingly. A philosophical or abstract response to

---

*What follows is a restatement of propositions put forward in my article "Evaluation of Technical Assistance as a Contribution to Development," *International Development Review*, Vol. VIII, No. 2, June 1966, based on experience with a team charged with evaluating the total impact of the technical assistance operations of the United Nations family of organizations in Thailand.

the question may be quite different from the action response; for the action response always embodies costs, and the choice of what people aim to achieve will change according to the assessment of the particular costs involved.

To give even an approximate answer to the question involves a deep knowledge of cultural parameters, of ways in which people assess costs, of how they perceive advantages, and what the differences between different groups of the population amount to.

The paradox may well be that, as the project is completed, the demand situation may certainly be improved, but the movement may also extend the breadth, complexity, and intensity of the group of unsatisfied desires, hopes, and ambitions. This is not to be held as a criticism of a project, if the first condition is satisfied; it means in most cases that the people have moved from one stage of possibility to another, where the possibilities are greater than ever.

The last point may be elaborated by saying that there will be a contribution to both development and performance if a change in effective demand makes it possible to move some items in the potential profile closer to fruition, so that they become goals for further action. From the developmental point of view, such a state means that the project has added a dimension to the take-off base and given an opportunity for more complex behavior. From the performance point of view, people are closer to getting more of what they want.

A project will also contribute to development if it helps to increase the range of resources used and the range of commodities produced (provided such increased ranges are justified economically), or if it removes bottlenecks in the system of resource use and production. In the first instance, increased development is present by definition, since there is an increase in the organic complexity of the system. In the second instance, increased development is linked to the improvement in the working of the system and in its possibility of moving further.

In neither instance is there necessarily an improvement in performance. Increased ranges may not correspond to the desired profiles (it has been argued that planning that interferes with market choices is liable to produce this result), and increased productive capacity may go in the wrong directions in terms of popular ambitions.

If a project contributes to an increased division of labor or to an increased complexity of organization, it is by definition developmental. It is helpful to performance only if that increase in complexity is weighted in favor of optimal production (if you like, keeping costs down) and to the satisfaction of wants identified in the profile. As we shall see in the next chapter, this proposition is particularly relevant to the judgment of community development and self-help schemes, but it also applies in other contexts.

A project contributes to both development and performance if it increases the pool of knowledge available to the culture and/or if it increases the capacity of members of the society to generate new knowledge and improve their problem-solving skills. This is particularly relevant to technical assistance, since it has been argued that this is the fundamental area of useful intervention from which all other possibilities follow.

In practice, several major confusions often obscure the evaluation. For example, an expert arrives and brings knowledge, but he goes, and takes it away again—that is, he fails to transfer his knowledge. An expert comes and acts as catalyst, but his indigenous colleagues are the innovators in fact. The expert's record will likely claim credit for the development. The conundrum is, would it have occurred had he not come? I would argue that in some fields 75 percent or so of innovative developments happen in this kind of context. The expert trains counterparts in static knowledge, or local experts go abroad to institutions which consider the job to be merely to fill their heads with the latest gimmicks. There is a short improvement in the pool, but there has been a failure to develop creativity—an innovative dynamic. This is distressingly frequent and a major criticism of training institutions and operations in many contexts. Note the discussion of education, innovation, and communication in Chapter 11.

Projects that increase the velocity of circulation—both abstractly in the form of ideas, and physically in the form of things—increase development and are likely to have effects that increase performance. I have discussed the reasoning behind this proposition in Chapter 10.

Projects will contribute to development—and indirectly to performance, since they will improve available means of doing things—if they help create institutions which accomplish functions that have hitherto been lacking in the society (credit facilities, for example, or technical institutes).

Projects will contribute to development and to performance if they help existing institutions to operate better. This includes the more effective establishment of institutional goals, the better tapping of information channels, improved efficiency (properly defined), orientations of action that are in tune with social goals, and, above all, more sensitive adjustment to each other. The more individual institutions improve internally, the more sensitive they are in their reactions to each other, the greater their contribution to the total position will be.

If these conditions are internalized, there will, on technical definitional grounds, be an improvement in development from the point of view of the independence, maturity, and functioning of the society in question. From the point of view of world society, however, there may be an optimum, beyond which restrictive and autarchical nationalism may emerge to the detriment of the world condition. If the internalization of skills means that the users of them are no longer dependent on continuous stimulus from outside, but can make their own contributions, this will be positive. But if it means the creation of new barriers, it will fail to maximize a continuous dynamic.

CHAPTER 14

Working Close to the Community

THERE are those policy makers and administrators who produce their plans from offices, assisted by data banks, statisticians, and calculations. There are those who, by contrast, work directly in interaction with the people whose lives are affected by the policy. Again, I must be illustrative and selective. Those who are working in the field in different contexts from those I have chosen—for example, whose field of action is trade union organization, or agricultural extension in Europe, or remedial action in American ghettos—will not recognize themselves in the following pages. Yet in a certain sense, they are there.

All action agents who are working with communities must wrestle with three crucial variables. These are (a) variation along the axis social distance/social intimacy, (b) choices in the style and meaning of influence and power, and (c) the sectoral implications of the knowledge and the mandate that the action agent brings to his work. In addition, where an action agent is part of an administrative hierarchy, he is responsible not only to the people with whom he is working, but also to the organization of which he is a part. This creates special dilemmas, common it is true to all organizations, which I shall call the African-chief syndrome.

The consideration of action in a former colonial setting has now become so befogged with simplistic ideological views, which have affected even sophisticated anthropological argument, that it will be difficult to bring observation and analysis back to objectivity. Nevertheless, since I began my personal involvement with mature action in such a setting, I shall start my discussion there. The first point to note is that colonialism, unless defined *a priori*, has considerable differences in theoretical and empirical content in different times and places, even within the same colonial regime. In some the regime is direct, brutal, and exploitative. In others it is aimed at providing a return to interests in the country exercising political power. In some alien settlers occupy the best land and acquire the most significant resources; in others there are no alien settlers, or the alienation of land is

224

forbidden in law and practice. In very few preindependence colonies were the costs of government covered by revenue; where private enterprise exported profits, metropolitan governments subsidized colonial adminis- trations. The attitude of many colonial regimes to private enterprise was rather like that of the State or city that attempts to attract external investment by offering tax concessions, in the hope that in the long run it will be possible to remove the concessions and use the established enterprise as a source of revenue. In many instances the level of alien private enterprise in colonies, though large by comparison with indigenous cash-oriented commerce, was infinitesimal by comparison with develop- ment needs, any notion of systematic "exploitation," or subsequent postindependence alien investment.

In some instances, colonies were protective devices, frankly and unashamedly paternalistic, in which the act of colonizing—that is, the act of establishing government—was composed of two parts: introduction of internal peace, and protection of the population from external aggression, including slavery and kidnapping. Those who condemn colonialism in all its forms, or who reduce the phenomenon to simplistic ideological terms, might note the influence and work of the Society for the Protection of Aborigines, the anti-slavery groups, and the missionaries who endeavored to arouse public opinion to a consciousness of the horrors that in the 19th century were being blatantly perpetrated in all corners of the globe. Of course, these movements were wrapped up in Protestant ideology, views about the civilizing influence of labor, and a belief that commerce could bring enlightenment. This was part of the intellectual baggage of the time.

When I was a young man, I spent three years as a colonial administrator in the field; what I experienced and saw was rather different. I was "recruited" by a senior field official (now a Professor of Pacific History), who had the reputation of being sensitive, knowledgeable, and analytic, whose political opinions were to the left of Fabian socialism, and who was known to have turned down considerable promotional opportunities in favor of staying close to the field. I asked him how I could reconcile colonial administration with my own left-wing political opinions. He told me and convinced me.

My first field experience was a shock and seemed to confirm all the worst caricatures I had seen drawn. I was assigned to an experienced District Officer, whose idea of action was to sail from village to village, disembark at each one, salute an honor guard of police, stalk around the village and excoriate the people, and embark with a sigh of relief. The gentleman concerned went home, and never again did I see such behavior. My colleagues were a human mixture of bureaucratic conservatism, snobbism, eccentricity, idealism, and above all sensitive intelligence.

The goal was simple, and became clearer as time went on: to prepare the country for *viable* independence as quickly but as surely as possible. Such revenue-producing activity as had existed had been destroyed or abandoned during the War; there were almost no revenues. The budget came almost entirely from United Kingdom sources. Viable independence meant, then, creating political institutions, education, public services, and an economic base almost from scratch.

As a field officer, at the very beginning of this activity (the beginning because the goal was of post-War definition, and the War had created a severe and sharp break in the continuity) my concern was to feed to the center opinions, information, and above all practical proof that the objective could be accomplished given time. The central administration had to be persuaded, it seemed, to stay with its objective, and above all had to be helped to think in local terms. This meant, among other things, that returning enterprise should come on conditions and in forms that did not threaten emergent indigenous enterprise. It meant encouraging local enterprise through cooperatives, small industry such as boat-building, and plantation and fishing activity. Since the territory was geographically and economically marginal, and was dependent on expensive external shipping for its links to the world, this was a painful, slow, and insecure process.

The policy also meant providing the local people with experiences of handling administrative services themselves. An anthropologist had already called for the establishment of representative Councils (with British African Indirect Rule in mind); but implementation of such an idea had to depend on its perception by the people as having a valid function. That, in turn, depended upon having some revenue to spend, and something valuable to do with it. In my area the discussions were long, and we puzzled over the conceptualization of what to do in small meetings, mass meetings, discussions with elected headmen, meeting after meeting. Short-term prisoners, in for petty offenses (sometimes for homicide), came up from "gaol" and talked with me at night. Local people produced material for a newspaper that was laboriously typed in six copies by my clerk and myself and was sent circulating from village to village by policemen-messengers, smartly uniformed (until they were out of sight) but with no physical power whatsoever. The Councils formed themselves ahead of legislation, considered priorities and ways of getting local revenue. Meanwhile, central revenue was obtained for some of their projects. For example, they asked for dispensaries, chose the siting, built the building, considered and accepted the nominees for the position of "medical dresser," and made plans for schools and communication.

The British Solomon Islands Protectorate is still a colony, but in a few years time, a little later than its vast and resource-rich neighbor Papua and New Guinea, it will without doubt be independent. It now has a central legislature of elected representatives and district councils that, in form, are not quite like those in any other country. The legislature and its ministers have effective control over policy. At the same time, cargo-cult-style religious–political movements rose and passed. The leaders were arrested—and educated. They were shown public administration in action in other countries; men who had never seen the inside of a school became devotees of public education; men who had never seen a factory learned through their senses that imported goods came through technology, not ritual and supernatural intervention; they learned, too, that their own considerable organizing ability, evidenced in their skill in the cargo-cult movement, could be used for secular achievement. This is what the cynics call co-option. Does anyone seriously believe that if the colonial government had not co-opted, or if it had walked out and left the Solomon Islands to themselves, the people would now be on the verge of a viable State? Or does anyone believe, seriously, that indigenous administrators will not find themselves, as they try to serve both State and local authorities, in a position of principle very different from that of the alien administrators they are replacing?

This is what I call the African-chief syndrome. The dilemma of the man in the middle was first clearly analyzed by anthropologists belonging to the now-unfashionable functional school who exposed the difficulties faced by chiefs in the African system of "Indirect Rule"—and, by extension, numerous other kinds of leaders (traditional or representative) who occupied similar structural positions in other polities. The argument is quite simple, and the situation so common and well-nigh universal that it is surprising that it was not first considered by political scientists or sociologists.

People who occupy middle positions in hierarchies—whether they be in nation-states, colonial governments, or private organizations—face two ways. In the simplest situation they may be concerned only with the passage of information, up and down. But in most situations they are expected to take initiatives; that is, they amend the information, give it significance, and initiate proposals and action. On whose behalf do they do this? On behalf of their superiors or those they are "administering"?

The answer is usually a mix, and the "success" achieved, however measured, is the result of checks and balances influencing the individual who is in the middle role.

The African chief is the case in point. The theory of Indirect Rule included the proposition that traditional authority be left as far as practical in its traditional structure. This meant that tribal authority be left alone, and that those who emerged as authority figures would be recognized. But colonial conditions were not static. Colonial authority established certain kinds of new laws. Thus, as a minimum, the second term of the theory of Indirect Rule was that local manifestations of *overall* policy be put into effect by the traditional authority; otherwise a second parallel authority would be necessary, which would undermine tradition. So the African chief, caught in the middle, had to be the administrative agent of the central authority on the one hand and the spokesman for his people on the other. When he acted, how much of his action was a response to his people's wishes and needs and how much a response to central administrative requirements? Obviously, this was linked to personal qualities and to the powers of pressure in both directions. And, obviously, the balance changed as the needs become more modern-administrative, and as the chief was assisted, or replaced, by elected councils or other institutions.

But the replacement of a traditional chief by an elected group, or even by a public meeting, does not change the dilemma. A city council or a mayor in a Western society faces the same mixture of responsibilities.* The replacement of a colonial government by a national independent government can actually increase the severity of the dilemma. Until this issue (one of the most important affecting the creation of new nation-states) is resolved, the likelihood of regional conflict against centralized administration is more probable in nationally independent situations than under colonialism.

A colony is a territory for which final governmental and policy authority is located in another country, or (by extension, to fit the North American internal situation) in institutions whose interests are outside of, and not controlled by, the communities governed. Colonization is the operating process. Colonialism is the ideological orientation toward such action. As I mentioned earlier, colonization and colonialism take many different forms; the British Solomon Islands were not and are not New Guinea, West Irian, Algeria, Batista Cuba, Angola, or South-West Africa. Those who treat of

---

*The same sorts of issues bear upon the argument, eternally rife in academic circles, between those who advocate university department chairmen as against university department heads; people holding such positions have both university and departmental responsibility, which the semantics do not change one whit. See my *Towers Besieged: The Dilemma of the Creative University*, Toronto: McClelland and Stewart, 1974.

colonialism as one single movement with one single exploitative expression in vent the kind of classification that is misleading in at least half the
relevant cases and obfuscates the issues. The following quotation could not
possibly be applied in full to the Solomon Islands, or indeed to a large
number of other colonies where social and political processes are
relevant:*

> Whether or not the mother country is keen about acquiring a colony, the colony must
> yield enough gain not to be a burden, and preferably must be managed to the positive
> benefit of the mother country in providing tribute such as head taxes, raw materials,
> cheap labor, and opportunities for commercial exploitation by private interests to bolster
> the mother country's economy. It must also serve as a place to send settlers.
>
> The enlightened way to govern a colonial territory is by indirect rule . . . the native
> leaders' power is shored up and their cooperation assured either by giving them a financial
> stake in the colonial status quo or by convincing them of the superiority of the colonial
> power and that, as a cooperative and informed elite, they as leaders are in a position to
> help their less capable brethren. Systematic, psychological estrangement of leaders from
> the people is necessary to avoid contrary input of information that might enable the
> people to manage for themselves in the modern world.
>
> The leaders are answerable to the colonial power for the flow of tribute, and the mother
> country conveniently lets them bear the brunt of the people's discontent while making it
> difficult for the people to actually dispose of them.

Let the following merely be noted. I have never heard of head tax or
similar levies—not even in the special and famous Boston Tea Party
instance—on indigenous people coming anywhere near the costs of
administration. Except in extraordinary circumstances (such as bullion
theft and forced mining in the Americas or the systematic exploitation of an
area extremely rich in natural resources, with direct interests of the
colonial government—as with the former Belgian Congo), examples of
"tribute" being returned to the metropolis are extremely rare. The process
of private development, it is true, was usually oriented to metropolitan
commercial interests, but by much more subtle and roundabout methods.

Again, psychological estrangement of leaders from people occurs again
and again in times of political movement as well as political stagnation, and
in numerous contexts outside of colonialism; one could even argue, as
some contemporary political scientists are doing, that it may be a necessary
condition for change. It is at least necessary to the extent that leaders of
change are innovators and see things a little differently from those who
have gone before; occasionally they are able to do this without psychological estrangement or elitism, but that is extremely rare. The two phenomena
are present even in millenarian and mass revolutionary movements. And

*Nancy Oestreich Lurie, "Menominee Termination: From Reservation to Colony."
Extract reproduced by permission of The Society for Applied Anthropology from *Human
Organization*, Vol. 31, No. 3, Fall 1972.

while many colonial governments did indeed "hold on"—and some are still holding on—beyond the time for them to go, and while several in the 20th century even refused to consider the conceptual possibility of independence, a large number were fully involved in preparations *for* independence; the differences were of timing and method. Lastly, the formulation of the process of "co-option" is in terms which put in a cynical light any form of agreement between persons who have different social roles. This kind of analysis puts any cooperation, other than that based on complete identity of culture and personal status, in a destructive light by ignoring the benefits of social exchange transactions. No social system that respects ethnic difference, no dynamic social movement, and no policy transition to a better world can be established on such a premise.

But let us return to the activity of regional or local action agents. The schema is normally that localized action is the responsibility of an administrative agent, acting alone, or with an elected or appointed council, or replaced by a council. Whatever the precise mode of appointment, the function is normally regarded as *generalized*, embracing all legitimized fields of action.

But this schema is modified in several ways. In the first place, a centralized government, looking down, is always departmentalized. Even if there is a central coordinating mechanism, the responsibility for action tends to be along sectoral lines. Thus, there is a line of authority and influence for educational matters, another for agriculture, another for public health, another for public works, and so forth.

Again, perhaps because it showed up in all its simplicity, this reality created problems which were evident most clearly in colonial contexts, and which were taken further in newly independent States. In the post-War reformist drive, British and French colonial administrators began to point out that sectoral policies and administrative actions lacked the theoretical dynamic that could be expected from integrated policies and action, that technical sectoral interests tended to favor technocratic answers which overlooked community and cultural aspirations and values, and that indigenous drives and motivations were not being used as a foundation for policy creation.

The first positive approach to these issues, of a self-conscious kind, came out of immediate post-War "think-tank" conferences of British colonial officers working with university colleagues; these were known as "Devonshire Courses." It was here that the idea of "community development" was first broached as an ideological position around which to organize a holistic and community-based policy and administration as opposed to sectoral and centralized approaches, which, it was felt, should be a response to local drives. In this method, the influence of anthropology (with its holistic analyses and its position that development could move in a variety of directions) on colonial administrative analysis made itself felt, but the main impetus came from colonial officers themselves.*

Thus, the colonial administrator, who was himself a generalist rather than a specialist (but oriented toward the bureaucracy), began to be supplemented by community development officers and teams of cooperating technicians. Their task, to simplify, was to concentrate attention on particular communities, to work with local people and leaders to define "felt needs" (each movement needs its jargon; "wants" or "goals" did not carry mystic or psychological flavor), and to translate these into local action programs. The prime responsibility of the teams was to the local community and its objectives, and the specialists were primarily responsible to the project rather than to their departments. This, however, could never be absolute; and it reintroduced, in subtler forms, the African-chief syndrome.

The movement gained momentum. In French territories the profession of *animateur* became established, and was later applied to social problems in Europe. The word sets the scene very well, since it puts at the forefront of the objective the notion of stimulation, and sets the essential dilemma for every such "people-based" program. One's performance is judged, in time, by the bureaucracy in terms of degree of stimulation or animation achieved; if the people said they wanted it, and invited you, and then backed off, your career is left high and dry. You have not delivered the goods. There is, thus, an extremely fine line between stimulation and influence or pressure.

In the meantime, international organizations began to pick up the threads. FAO's Rural Welfare Division was influenced by the form of cooperatives in China (Rewi Alley and his groups), which led naturally to the overall concerns of community development and local self-help. Home economics in FAO became more concerned with rural institutions than diet or domestic activities alone. UNESCO invented the concept of "fundamental education," which was an attempt to get at the wider community

---

* The remarks on community development and related movements are in part an outgrowth of my unpublished paper "A Critical Analysis of Community Development as an Economic, Social and Administrative Process," commissioned for the United Nations Bureau of Social Affairs in 1961 and used in a meeting on the subject in 1962. My interest was in part stimulated by anthropological concerns, and also because my father created the Rural Welfare Division of the Food and Agricultural Organization, which made considerable use of the principles.

needs for education and to provide team-approach answers with intensive shock-attack methods—directed in the early days toward mobile mass literacy and artisan projects. WHO began to place health questions in a cultural and total-educational context, which linked it with community development movements. ILO made community development (particularly in the famous Andean project) the crux of its rural involvement. And, by the mid-1950s, community development had also become an urban instrument for change and organization. By the 1960s, community development movements and organizations had grown up in Europe and North America. Out of its genesis sprang approaches to social welfare and community problems in the United States, the growth and new directions of group dynamics as a social instrument, and even, to some extent, the concept of volunteer groups such as the Peace Corps, Canadian University Service Overseas, and the like.

These outgrowths were, however, the result of changes in conception and drive over time, and significant and rapid evolution. The initial goal of community development was for animation teams to be present for short periods, to do their work and demonstrate the possibilities of change, to create the organizational and material basis for change at the discretion of the people, and to retire—leaving a newly dynamic community behind them. This in fact rarely happened. Despite the considerable changes which took place as a result of community development, the world is littered with failed projects as well as dramatically successful ones.

Internationally, community development was an ideal field for competitive projects by aid agencies. Because the goals were on the whole not specified in technological terms beforehand, no one could really say that the presence of this or that technical agency was unjustified. However, the overlaps led to criticism of a very sensitive movement. Coordination was necessary, and gradually was assumed by the Bureau of Social Affairs of the United Nations, the specialized agencies tending to provide technical help for the generalists. Since each international team had specialists from several agencies, and sometimes provided by bilateral programs, demonstration teams tended to be very expensive, and too high-powered to be concentrated on small communities; hence the typical field of action was often at a higher level.

A number of newly independent countries, led by India, retained and increased the emphasis on community development, and gave it special status in the administrative system. The Indian community development process was based upon large "blocks" of communities divided into smaller units for project purposes. It differed from normal administration only in that it was development project-oriented; it had definite output and similar goals, which provided indices of achievement; and it was intended to pay special attention to local initiatives and drives. But the vast task confronting India turned community development into a huge bureaucracy, with mechanistic achievement goals, and penalties for officers who failed to produce them. It was not for many years that maturity and the partial relief of urgency made it possible for the movement to come closer to the original spirit.

The initial concept of community development was one in which technical competence was of equal importance to generalist analysis. But where were the community developers to come from? In those days (in the late 1940s and early 1950s) the social sciences were not yet competent in developmental analysis; anthropology was too slow and vague, although it had an initial powerful impact. As time went on, the social sciences moved in the direction of technical specialization instead of toward the holistic synthesis of analysis that was called for. The vast increase in the field, perhaps even greater in numerical terms than the parallel development of urban and regional planning, meant that officials had to be recruited on the spot and learn as they worked. The only difference between community development officers and normal administrators was that the former tended to come from a greater variety of backgrounds and to bring their sectoral specialist training with them (which was the reverse of the objective). However, as they worked with teams, they became generalist administrators, and initially the presence of sectoral technical knowledge was better than its absence.

Two significant streams of influence then emerged, as training programs began to be established and the initial pioneers were replaced by career community developers. One was from social work, influenced by the connections of the Bureau of Social Affairs, which in turn spread out to influence individual countries, containing the kinds of social science viewpoints characteristic of social work, modified by some development experience. To oversimplify vastly, the key to this approach was in human relations, the dignity of the individual, the significance of organization, and the concept of cooperative self-help. From the beginning, the cooperative movement, social welfare, and community development were very close together.

The other influence was from adult education, with a smattering of social science (hastily assembled packages of the more populist cultural anthropology, and above all concepts of leadership and group dynamics derived from psychology and educational theory).

Out of these two influences came a marriage—sometimes close, sometimes uneasy, and sometimes overwhelmed by external facts of life. The first element in the partnership was the decline in the technical developmental competence required of community development operations and ideology. This was justified by the almost complete lack of integrated development-oriented social science training programs (a lack which continues even today), the expectation of being able to call on specialists when needed, and the argument that community development was people-need oriented, that such needs should not and could not be determined in advance; hence, the nature of the technical specialties required could not always be foreseen.

The decline in the analytic seriousness of the movement opened the door for an emphasis on method rather than content. Community development training programs and manuals are full of references to such problems as: how to find the natural social leaders, how to identify the emergence of schism and overcome it when it does emerge, how to get enemies to talk to one another, how to persuade leaders to stop manipulating people in the leaders' own self-interest, how to get a committee meeting talking, how—in short—to stimulate an interest in good fellowship and personal relations. This is, as many readers will recognize, in tune with a great deal of current educational theory, which is more concerned with pleasant human relations than with intellectual rigor or hard-headed action.

The good will and dedication involved were immense. This was true not only of indigenous community developers who ultimately chose this as their form of career contribution to the growth of their country, but also of many people from developed countries who became the secular missionaries of humility, service, international commitment, and personal subordination to the needs of the poor and unfortunate. They offered opportunity and hope to many who had given it up or had never seen it.

Yet one cannot help wondering where the world might have been if such fervent exponents of humanity and progress had carried with them greater concrete knowledge. I write feelingly on this topic. As a colonial administrator, I too had little knowledge, except a modest sprinkling of not very useful economics. Knowledge had to be gained by trial and error and by close interactions with the people, always affected by authority and status. The community developer also has bureaucratic status, and a difference of background, but often has time and opportunity to get close to the people. The young volunteer worker can often get closer still, through his youth, unpretentiousness, and submission to indigenous authority.* However, I left the colonial service, not because it was bad—it wasn't; not because it was unconstructive—it wasn't; not because it was oppressive, unimaginative, or failed to obtain systematic information of high quality— its record in these areas, by comparison with national governments, was surprisingly good. I left because I felt that, *against the measure of the need*, it was ignorant.

And that, too, would be my reaction to a great deal of community development activity. Good will and bureaucratic support are no substitute for analysis. Sometimes, it is true, community development action is based upon research, and sometimes community development officials are intuitively or by preparation good social analysts. To these people I owe respect and the world owes recognition.

Let me give one example of analytic confusion—central, however, to much of the movement. This is the weight placed upon community self-help. The idea is that the community is a network of social exchange relationships that make it a natural unit for cooperation. It is also that poor communities lack certain kinds of resources, particularly cash or commodities which they can exchange for cash, and thereby obtain capital supplies, equipment, marketable services, and the like.

So the natural response is to use the social networks of the community and its traditional leadership patterns and institutions, where feasible, to mobilize local resources of labor, materials, and, where absolutely indispensable, money. Very considerable accomplishments have been credited to this system. Where a central government is short of educational funds, it may supply a teacher if the community, by its own labor, builds the school and supplies the land free. Where government is short of public works funds, it may lend a bulldozer for the construction of an urgently needed road by local villagers—who work cooperatively and without wages. Where village houses are unsanitary, local initiative may be mobilized to rebuild the village, house by house, with local materials. In an urban slum, the government may provide certain materials free or at cost, provided the cooperative labor and self-help spirit is forthcoming.

* I except the Peace Corps from this generalization. Although some Peace Corps volunteers, much more often than is realized, do achieve close contact, the Peace Corps lost a major advantage when in many countries it created its own administration, encouraged the action of volunteers in self-contained groups, and thus failed to place them firmly under the authority of local officials. It is further hampered in some countries by political and strategic foreign policy considerations. By contrast, Canadian University Service Overseas, though far less well trained and less technically well prepared (for example, in languages), is more successful in placing its people in conditions where they act as instruments of *local* policy.

All this is to the good—at least in the sense that something gets done that, presumably, improves the well-being and sometimes the infrastructure, and at a saving to the internal taxpayer and external aid donor. It also gives the aid donor the satisfaction of knowing that his money is going to a country where initiative abounds.

But think of the cost—the real cost. Money which would have circulated in wages (if the government had risked some slight inflationary pressure) is not circulating. Thus, one of the prime movers for profit-taking, capital formation, the early economists' idea of "taking in each others' washing" and thus *creating* a continuous basis for wealth improvement—all this has been abandoned, if not destroyed. Certainly houses are built; but the community is reinforced as a self-contained minor autarchy. Each family or group within it does exactly, or almost exactly, what every other family or group does. They help each other build the houses, which perhaps is good for the spirit, and they run a community truck, at a loss, just like the community next door. Once again, a development dynamic—if people want it—has been denied them by misplaced analysis and, perhaps, sentimentality. For a key to development is *not* everybody doing exactly what everybody else is doing. It is precisely in specialized differentiation— once known as division of labor. This applies to organizations as well as to individuals; the appropriate kind of self-help (which is by no means missing from the effervescent development scene) is that which creates specialist organization—specialist construction industry, specialist public works contractors, specialist transport organizations, specialist agricultural marketers. There is no reason at all why some of these should not be run by public utilities, by communities, by lineages, or by families.

But this does mean other differences: in wealth, occupation, outlook, status, managerial role, skill. Isn't this what we mean by development?

Let me summarize by returning to some of the issues raised at the beginning of the chapter. I shall do so by setting out a number of propositions.

All action agents external to the community itself, or gaining legitimacy by being members of organizations external to the community, exhibit some degree of social distance from it. This means that there is not a precise cultural correspondence between the agent's values and those of the people with whom he is dealing, and also that there are differences of interests and objectives. This further means that *no* external action agent is in a position to predict reactions to proposals or opportunities, or directions of initiatives, with certainty. An action agent, if he is to act at all, must have some sense of commitment, some direction to his thoughts. To this extent he is a professional rather than a researcher or enquirer. While he may personally have an open mind and be ready to learn and experiment, his commitments place limits on that openness.

There are situations in which close identification with the community, as distinct from wider policy organs and issues, can result in a disservice to the community itself. In the first place, as we have seen, the community may be wrongly identified as a set of bounded networks, and the stranger who moves within it may not see the external linkages for what they are. More seriously, the espousal of community goals *can* mean acceptance of their limitations; too great a cultural identification can mean ignoring alternatives and failing to make these known to the people; it can mean a failure to appreciate and understand the possibilities and limitations of the wider system of which the community is but a part.* We shall see (Chapter 17) that the issue of social distance is also crucial to research understanding and research models.

This means that action agents must have differing views of the legitimacy of power and influence from those of their "clients." There is something of a myth developing in anthropology now to the effect that if clients pay you, you are somehow washed clean: payment is evidence that they want you (yes); if they want you, you are in a better position to help them (no). A paid adviser or action agent is little different in this respect from the agent of another organization. He is still a stranger and he must still come to grips with the dialectic between local and wider views. He is still a professional and, as such, is wedded to a series of assumptions.

An action agent, whether paid by the people or not, whether working in close cooperation with them or not, must still decide where in the political order of things his conceptions, his influence, and his authority fit. If he is governed by an overriding missionary zeal, or has an enthusiastic commitment to the goals of the organization for which he works, he will use every possibility he knows to persuade, influence, or direct (if he has that power) the people to react accordingly. No public health doctor will stand by and see contagious diseases spread if avoidance measures can be taken. The greatest difficulty with some young volunteers is to persuade them that their own analysis of "obvious" solutions might be wrong or unacceptable, that bureaucratic inaction is not necessarily bad or inept in the long view, and that humility and patience are in truth often virtues.

I shall argue that an "adviser" as a particular form of action agent has the responsibility of placing *alternatives* before the groups he is advising, and

* This point is well illustrated by Nancie L. Gonzalez, "The Sociology of a Dam," *Human Organization*, Vol. 31, No. 4, Winter 1972, pp. 353–360.

238 The Sorcerer's Apprentice

of allowing them to make their choices. Before this can be effective, the people must have sufficient political strength to resist the blandishments of the organization he represents, and the administrative power to work out yet further alternatives and to follow them up, if necessary, by tapping external sources of support.

Finally, there can be little doubt that any action is multisectoral. Too much stress on this point may mean the reduction in the technical competence of action agents. Where circumstances make it possible, it would be better to have a multisectoral analytic process undertaken prior to action, and to monitor results, stressing the sectoral technical strengths of those who make themselves available for the action itself. Quite often, however, this is done the other way about, primarily because professional analysts are trained in universities to have sectoral loyalties above all else, rather than to see their work in relation to that of others. In this respect, anthropology, with its holistic frame, could have an advantage.

CHAPTER 15

Of Politics and Conflict

A SOCIAL system in dynamic equilibrium is one in which there is some general acceptance of values and objectives so that creative energies are diverted primarily to technological devices. Of course, this is not the common condition of life.

Social systems that seek a dynamic equilibrium are faced with the problem of maintaining the dynamic in the political and administrative hierarchy, either to provide leadership and focus for the social effort or to respond to changes in the popular will.

This is not easy, and contemporary nation-states have not found enduring answers. I hope my colleagues in political science will forgive me if I trespass on their territory for a while in this chapter to relate some issues to my main theme.

The idealized British system of government provides for an alternation of Government and Opposition. As each Opposition becomes Government, it finds itself facing conditions left to it by the previous Government, and it makes use of the same information flow from the permanent apolitical civil service. Only after a long passage of time in opposition, or in special circumstances, are Opposition and Government sufficiently far apart that accommodation between them is impossible. A new Government can therefore normally adjust its official policy to what it now perceives to be the realities, as it opens the ministerial files, and it begins to act very much like the previous Government. There are, to be sure, differences of style, emphasis, and philosophy; but unrealistic promises are amended or tucked away out of sight as the unreality becomes apparent. There is no direct control of government by the public during the course of office; the government is elected on trust. But should that trust fail, the pressures and mechanisms are there to secure recall through parliamentary defeat.

This is a system which both moves and is stable, although there are signs of disillusion with the apparent lack of difference, when in office, of the major parties. In the countries that have adopted the British system in an integral manner such disillusion can express itself only in altering the mood and balance within each political party, giving a radical swing to one of the existing parties, or, much more difficult, creating an appeal for the upgrading of a minority party to represent the disillusion. The last solution, in our technocratic society, is difficult because it encounters the skepticism of the voter who has not seen the minority party in office, and who has doubts about its administrative capability to run the civil service machine. It is instructive to note that, as also with the United States, the major national disagreements are usually to be found *in each of* the political parties in a traditionally two-party system. Such a system is not geared to major swings, changes, or revolutions.

Most of the world is not run on a two-party system. It is run on a one-party system, of which there are numerous varieties. The simplest and most adaptable appears to be that which has been chosen by many African States, some Asian ones such as, until recently, Thailand, and by some of the Latin American *juntas*, as in Peru. It is, of course, always difficult for an outsider to be sure of the facts that relate to such systems.

Nevertheless, the more enduring of them have a balance between continuity and dynamics that runs somewhat as follows. In the first place, the "one party" or the "government enshrined in the constitution" is not in fact monolithic. It consists of numerous forces, which (if unrestrained and unleashed) would move in quite different directions. The art of government, just as in Britain or the United States, but using quite different forms, is to maintain a balance between these opposing forces, to give each of them its appropriate outlet and to allow them (within limits) to vie for influence and power within the system. Usually the press for power and influence results in compromise or consensus; in some instances, this is achieved only at the cost of outlawing those whose opinions or activities are judged to be too far away from the possibility of consensus.

Clearly, in any consensus or outcome, some element must be predominant, although numerous examples indicate a remarkable ability to retain quite different strains of thought and action within the unity. This can be expressed as rivalry between ministries and departments and differences in conception tolerated at different levels of government. It is sometimes said that such systems can only maintain themselves through reliance on military support; this is, however, a variable, and it is more than likely that the differences in position are represented in both the police and the military, or between them. Change in the balance, if it must be visibly effected at the top, can frequently only be achieved through some such technique as the military coup, a movement in and out of military and civilian government, or cancellations and reinstitutions of a succession of constitutions, with power being used to hold the balance, to make visible the point at which a change in balance is necessary, and to ensure that it comes about.

More sophisticated variants of this can be identified in Switzerland and France. In Switzerland, the parties reaching representation are incorporated simultaneously into the administration of government as a total national coalition, and reach consensus on policies within it. While the parties themselves are as "political" as in any other country, the technocratic role in which they appear when they reach responsibility in joint government invites other groups, and ad hoc organizations, to formulate alternatives. This is also encouraged by the system of referendum and private initiative for policy directives to government. It is interesting to note that although initiators and opponents of proposals show considerable enthusiasm and ability to mobilize interest (which is the envy of populism in other countries) the frequency of referenda and of the voting that is entailed results in very low voting turnout.

At first sight, France seems very different. The multiplicity of parties and the individualism of party opinion and leadership is remarkable by any standards. Yet the 1973 elections seemed to indicate quite strongly that French political power can only conceive of continuous operation in terms of a set of balances masterminded from the center of power in response to continuities and changes in the public mood.

When this continuity was threatened by the relative success of the union of the left, two events dominated the outcome. One was the intervention of the President of the Republic who, in spite of the real danger of popular backlash, made it quite clear that the constitution would be interpreted and manipulated to treat the left, not as a parliamentary opposition which could expect power in time, but as political pariahs who would never attain power. This brought back memories of Gaullist constitutional cancellations and referenda, and introduced an interpretation of Presidential powers that has not been completely spelled out but remains as a possible threat, all of which is quite typical of one-party systems.

The second event was the movement of the Reformateurs from a state of opposition to official Gaullism to one of cooperation at almost all costs to keep the left at a distance. In other words the multiplicity of the official parties hid their essential unity of interest—to maintain continuity through negotiated balance and to interpret the opposition not merely as a threat to their policies but to the very system of government itself. However, in France, the unified system is not fully enshrined, and a capture of the seat of power by those who are in real opposition is both possible and likely, if it occurs, to have much more upsetting effects on political operations than is the case with many one-party militarily supported regimes.

Most variants of the above systems do allow for change in style, personality, and policy. It has been noted that totalitarian dictatorships cannot make such a transition, and that technocratic oligarchies of the communist form have great difficulty, not in providing for succession but in linking changes in office to changes in policy and attitude. Many commentators have observed the conservatism of aging communist leaders, and reflected upon the outmoded styles of many of the upper administrative echelons. The remarkable thing is not that this should be so, but that, despite it, changes in mood and policy are effected, not always with the prodding of troops and tanks. Mao's Cultural Revolution was in part a recognition of the dangers of stasis for a bureaucratic regime, but it became apparent that, apart from the organizational disorder which resulted, the open-ended, almost revivalist, group-dynamics methods led to a dangerous lack of intellectual rigor when it came to the handling of practical problems. The Chinese apparently stepped back just in time; the intellectual destructiveness of a dependence on slogans instead of critical thought can be a useful political tool to those in charge, but pragmatic leaders also know that slogans do not provide technical solutions to issues.

In all the above systems, the emphasis is upon a certain stability. The system can be learned; when learned, it can be used to bring about limited change. So-called revolutions within such systems are often merely changes in policy, and sometimes not even that. More radical change is a very different kettle of fish.

The kinds of revolutionary attempts most commonly studied in anthropology (as distinct from history or political science) are social millenarian movements with religious messianic leadership. Such movements have usually taken place within contexts of established political power. I cannot recall instances in which they have succeeded in subverting or overthrowing that power and replacing it with their own enduring government. (Historically, Muslim expansion in its heyday might be an exception, but this seems more akin to religiously supported imperialism, as with some of the Crusades.) Occasionally, they have carved out territories of control, but in time these have collapsed through internal secularization and isolation under siege, or they have been repressed—often tragically.

Nevertheless, the movements have significance. They tend to emerge in situations of frustration, in which the leadership points the road to hope, and the frustration is not so extreme that initiative and activity are completely destroyed. There appears to be a correlation between the reality of the hope, as perceived, and the secularization of the movement. That is, the less the perceptions correspond to an accurate analysis of the system in which the movement finds itself, the more it must depend on religious charisma to give it direction and dynamic. In some instances, such as Melanesia and Africa, the religious messianism exists side by side with secular solutions to problems, the differences being largely in the world of conceptualization and perception.

For this reason, the movements have sometimes been characterized as "nonrational." It now seems generally agreed, however, that this is a poor label to use. The departure from objective analysis is not based upon "poor thinking" but upon the limited experience and selected information that the people concerned have at their disposal. When Melanesian cargo-cult leaders held that manufactured goods were made by God and that they were distributed in response to effective ritual, the leaders were not being "irrational" in a psychological sense. Their speculative conclusions followed quite logically from their premises, which in turn were not contradicted by their experience and were indeed reinforced by limited observation. But the action content of the movements, leading to the hope of reversals in social relations and the flow of wealth, was the expression of hope and frustration.

In addition, the movements were given force through two organizational elements. The first and most obvious was the development of charisma in the religious leader, who (consciously or unconsciously) knew how to tap the conceptions and perceptions of his people, using innovative creativity to provide an ideology and a justification for action, which appeared to offer a miraculous road toward the relief of frustration. But this in itself was not sufficient. The movements vary a great deal in their population spread, their drive, their cohesion, and their durability in the face of pressure. Such variation can be traced to the social and political context in which they find themselves, and to their internal organization. If the charismatic leader is also an administrative executive of talent, or if he is supported by a group of such people, the chances of the movement maintaining itself to the point of a climactic challenge by the political power are so much greater.

This, of course, is also the case with political movements where charisma has emerged or is necessary for a symbolic drive to overcome lethargy, lack of personal interest, or division in the ranks. Revolutionary leadership of a secular order, aiming at the overthrow of entrenched governments or the establishment of new nations, must provide clearcut (if vaguely formulated) ideology—best expressed in the person of the charismatic leader. At some point, the charisma must be backed by administrative delivery, and the tension between those whose role it is to preach and those whose role it is to solve problems must be resolved.

I have said that millenarian movements are not necessarily irrational. However, some 20th-century political–social movements, with at least 19th-century origins, are irrational in the strict sense of the word. Nazism contained a direct appeal to the emotions as a legitimate dominant force for the organization of the individual and of society. It contained a deliberate denial of the primacy of logic and evidence, particularly where this conflicted with ideology. It used symbolism and slogans to replace argument and persuasion in its only too successful task of controlling the minds of the masses. In particular it was successful in attracting university students—at the age when idealism and emotion combine to make simple and symbolic solutions particularly appealing—and some academics—who felt that by succumbing to this posture they were, to use present jargon, moving from the ivory tower to the world of relevancy.

The lessons of Nazism have been largely forgotten, and similar viewpoints and techniques have been emerging more recently as widespread political phenomena.

Marcuse is merely one of the ideological spokesmen, but his message is typical of a great many of them. Logic, runs the argument, with its special language and its demand for the scarce resources of information and data, becomes a loaded weapon that favors those in power and the technocratic capitalist establishment. The vices, wrongs, and injustices of the world are laid at the door of the powerful establishment, hence at the technocracy that supports them, hence at the ideology of logic that supports the technocracy. The solution is to invent a new mode of communication based upon emotion and nonlogical language.

This has indeed been done. The primacy of emotion *over* thought, as distinct from thought harnessed to emotion, is now firmly embedded in a host of institutions—from teacher training colleges and schools to student movements, Western Maoist agitation, and urban guerrilla action. The most disturbing and vicious feature of the retreat from reason is its manipulation by some university students and its blind acceptance by a number of intellectuals who fail to draw the totalitarian parallel.*

Nowhere has the retreat from reason produced working political answers to man's problems; indeed, in one anarchist form, it specifically denies that problems can be solved by *a priori* thought, but can only be approached by the release of innate human movement after the structural restraints on humanity (which happen to include, but this is obfuscated, the social exchange element in relations with others) have been entirely removed. Naturally, since empirical evidence for such a view is lacking, the validity of empirical evidence must be denied.

We have also seen the reemergence of an old phenomenon in new terms. Political assassination and the violence of terrorism are very old, and one may argue that in the modern world they are one of the results of an inability to use political opposition as a form of leverage and of the limitation of war as an instrument of political goals. There are, of course, other responses to such a state of frustration, and its existence is insufficient as an explanation of the recourse to terror and violence.

Sociologists and anthropologists from Max Weber and A. R. Radcliffe-Brown deeply influenced the theory of political institutions by holding that, in the final analysis, political systems and the rule of law on behalf of organized society were dependent on sanctions that could be brought to bear against transgressors. The main sanction was the use, or threat, of physical force. Indeed, the existence of such a sanction, applied on behalf of a social group, came to be the index of the existence of political organization.

Nevertheless, both as definition and as explanation, this is clearly inadequate. Political organizations also *administer*, on behalf of a collectivity. The act of policy making and administration is at the heart of much of the approach of political science, which, curiously, anthropology has almost ignored. This requires power, but of an entrepreneurial kind— much more akin to the management of an enterprise; it requires the ability to call forth and command resources, including the organized endeavors of members of the collectivity.

Law, whether written or not, remains dormant until there is a dispute between members of a society or between individuals on the one hand and the guardian-administrators of society on the other. It is out of the

* See my *Towers Besieged*, op. cit.

mechanisms and judgments brought into play as a result of disputes that one can determine the principles that authority uses to maintain the operation of the social system.

Several anthropologists, although on the whole missing the administrative function of politics, began to enter caveats against the operative notion of physical force. Many societies do not have a central authority to use force; blood feuding, murder as recompense, ceremonial payment or exchange to stop the consequences of murder or to bring overt hostilities to an end—these kinds of phenomena were not imposed by an authority, but emerged out of the thoughts, expectations, and conventions of self-interest of involved parties, sometimes using intermediaries. Max Gluckman, in a long series of analyses of judicial acts in more formal court-like contexts in tribal groups, has shown that even where such institutions exist one dominant principle is the recognition that an act is in breach of the expected and approved mode of operation of the social system, coupled with restitutive or adjustment acts designed to make the social system work again. E. A. Hoebel applied a theory of law to anthropological materials, in tune with sociologically oriented jurisprudence, which held that, whatever might be the phraseology of stated law, it dealt with social relations and defined them. One may describe property law in terms of X's linkages to particular items of property through defined rights; this, however, implies that X, when concerned with the property in question, has expectations about the way A, B, and C should interact with him (e.g., by keeping out of the picture, by accepting an exchange, by cooperating in exploiting, by receiving rent, by elbowing him out of the way).

It is but a short step from such bases to a fully-fledged social exchange description of political and legal interactions, used ethnographically in the work of Edmund Leach and Fredrik Barth, developed in terms of abstract sociological models by Peter Blau, and adopted by an exchange theory school of political science.*

In such an approach, as we have seen, society is thought of as a web of social relations, of interactions between self-interested parties who work with conventional and limited perceptions of goals, and who adopt strategies to get what they can out of the conditions confronting them. Law becomes the set of myths or principles to which they refer when they find themselves in conflict, in order to justify their actions. Juridical or

---

* See F. G. Bailey, *Strategems and Spoils*, Oxford: Basil Blackwell, 1970, for the application of exchange interaction analysis in a context that moves from peasant conditions to the behavior of political parties.

legal institutions are the devices to which they refer their conflicts if they are beyond their own resolution or when elements in society insist that they do so.*

Power then becomes that aspect of social relations which has the effect of constraining or directing the behavior of another.** Power is thus present to some degree from near zero up to very high orders in all social interaction. Any interacting social group in which the theme of power may be traced can be abstracted into a political model, just as it can, through the theme of interacting choice, be abstracted into an economic model. To dramatize the point, a family is a political system, not because someone is thought to have authority but because the exchanges and interactions that take place in the family have the effect of influencing, constraining, and giving direction to the behavior of its individual members. If there happens to be an "authority figure" in the family, his behavior is nevertheless influenced, constrained, and directed by those over whom he has authority—to varying degrees.

It will become immediately apparent that a modern commune, a syndicalist organization, an anarchist action group, or a public meeting type of democracy does not remove power (that is, influence, constraint, and direction). It merely changes one form of power structure for another, and the individual is still but one element in that structure. The appeals of Maoists to destroy the "structure" so that men and women may live without one is so much nonsense, at least while men and women need each other, live in company, and exchange services, emotions, and ideas. The plea to destroy or revolutionize a structure of power is more rationally based when it attempts to demonstrate that a new structure or organization will result in a new pattern of social exchange in which power and influence affect human behavior so that it works in more satisfying ways. This is what most positive political reform or, on occasion, revolution is about; but, on the whole, it lacks the inventive sociological base to link a change in the quality of social interaction, a change in the type of outcome that can be guaranteed, and a change in structure and organization, all together.

---

* The apparent paradox is well exemplified by the titles of two papers written by Georg Simmel, recently republished in one volume, *Conflict and the Web of Group Affiliations*, New York: The Free Press of Glencoe, 1955.

** This is my definition. A more standard definition, with Radcliffe-Brownian and Weberian ancestry, would relate power to those conditions in which sanctions may be invoked. See, for example, Peter M. Blau, *Exchange and Power in Social Life*, New York: John Wiley, 1964. In my view, this fails to take into account the phenomenon that the differences between influence, persuasion, reward, and sanctions are of degree as well as kind, and schematically may be represented on a continuum.

I moved into this theoretical digression in order to avoid having to tackle the issue of violence in the political order head-on. Too often the attempt is made to consider the question of violence in absolute terms. Like justice, it is always good because it is always the outcome of frustration and conflict which must be resolved; or it is always bad because it hurts people in ways which, considered abstractly, the majority of civilized people regard as barbarous and unworthy of 20th-century idealism. Violence hurts the more because it does look as if the world is on the verge of keeping major international conflict between the super-powers at arm's length, it does seem as though world opinion recognizes that violent repression by government is normally improper, and it even begins to appear that the world is fumbling its way to the restriction of limited armed conflict between small nation-states. Just when these achievements seem to be within reach, terrorist violence returns to the scene on a scale, and with an efficiency (despite incredible political naïveté) and, to the ordinary person, an unpredictability in its timing and targets that increases fear and insecurity. As is intended by some of the adherents of violence, it undermines faith in the ability of social systems to deliver the conditions of peaceful creative living.

The current mixture of criminal and political small-scale violence is a much greater threat to the growth of civilized, creative, and tolerant values than is the outbreak of world war. The one could, of course, lead to the other; this, after all, was one of the deliberate tactics of earlier revolutionary movements, which, in the case of the USSR, in fact paid off. Nuclear power makes such a payoff unthinkable though not less possible today.

There is little point in attempting a taxonomy of violence to determine which kinds are justifiable and which are not. Violence is frequently a response to intolerable conditions for which there is absolutely no other way out. Those who are violent are desperate—sometimes to the point of madness, often to the point of suicide, and occasionally because in fact the violence *does* pay off according to the definitions of cost and benefit that the action agents have set themselves. Whether the payoff, the cost in terror, maiming, and innocent lives,* is worth it is the same kind of

---

*The Costa Gavras film on the Tupamaros of Uruguay (*L'Etat de Siège, Confession*), unlike his other films, becomes one-sided political propaganda instead of dramatic analysis because it focuses entirely on the misuse of governmental power and the resort to innocent-looking covers for US influence in the direction of repression and torture, but directs the camera away from those who suffer innocently; this must have been deliberate choice. It is quite different in this respect from his more powerful film, *La Bataille d'Alger*, on a similar theme.

political judgment that is entered into when governments decide to go to war or to use other means of conflict settlement. The decision—the judgment—depends on what one sees from one's position in the world, and it is not a bit of use moralizing. The people who kill have family values, believe in loyalty and correct behavior, read, argue, and debate, and, without cynicism, are quite capable of showing their wives and children on TV as suffering because they, suspected killers, have had their movements circumscribed with the effect of separating them from their families.*

Though incompletely known, there are certain features of the current condition of political violence that are necessary to its understanding, and certainly to any attempts at judgment or control.

In the 19th century, anarchist terrorism and assassination were based on sophisticated philosophy—so sophisticated it often inhibited action—and the pessimism of personal martyrdom. The political action was directed at a mixture of symbolic revenge and the destruction of tyrants which would possibly distill crisis and the possibility of revolution. The successful revolutionaries, however, would countenance such action only if based upon the foundation of a thorough organization and plan ready to move, and if the combination of symbolic violence and revolutionary organization had some hope of triggering the support and welcome of the masses. However much violence might escalate into armed conflict, revolution had some hope of succeeding if there were organization and mass support, since the technology of combat was within the possibility of revolutionary tactics and means. Assassination, and terrorism itself, was based on simple technology—the anarchist bomb of caricature, the pistol.

Present-day terrorism is based on a much more elaborate technology. The weapons used are the most up-to-date portable dealers of death available, including automatic guns and rifles with telescopic sights. Timed bombs of great destructive power are indiscriminate in their damage. Miniaturization makes possible the letter bomb. Such is the complexity· and availability of the technology that as each technique results in protective measures, however incomplete, the tactics change. Without doubt, new technological weaponry will appear.

Tactics are highly organized and internationally communicated between otherwise separate movements. This is carried out in part in

---

* After the Munich Olympic Games killings, despite the upsurge of horror and the apparent determination to take preventive action, I saw such films on Swiss television, without any analysis of why this was an almost inevitable consequence of terrorism.

training schools, sometimes tolerated, sometimes actively encouraged, by host nation-states. At one time Algeria was such a host, but it appears that some of the welcomed movements became rather too arrogant and dangerous; in neither Algeria nor Cuba does political refuge mean license to engage automatically in propaganda or terrorist organization any more. It does, however, appear that North Korea, perhaps China, and certainly Lebanon are countries where terrorist tactics and instruction are readily available to those who show cause. (Although some known terrorists visited China, it is probable that the type of instruction given there is oriented more toward revolutionary insurgency than to terrorism as such.)

This presumes a network of communication, however episodic, between groups which are widely separated geographically and in objective. It does not presume coordination of tactics between them or anything approaching a world political movement at this stage.

In the operations themselves, plans must be laid with great detail, which implies local intelligence. (The individual assassin, not operating directly to a political plan, can probably get away with opportunism; but organized terrorism aims at objectives beyond the act of terrorism itself, and cannot afford to bungle once the operation comes into the open.) There is, thus, a network of prior communication before the operation begins.

During the operation itself, communication is necessary between the political masters and the operatives, unless the latter have been cut loose or the operating team has a senior political figure with it. As the experience with team terrorism grows, the possibilities of distant control are seen to be more important, if there is to be long-term continuity. Whereas some terrorist groups, such as Latin American urban guerrillas, operated over relatively short time spans, Black September and related Palestinian movements have to think in the long term and hence develop their procedures on the basis of experience. It seems that communication is one area where learning and change are taking place.

Whereas the simpler movements use trick devices to get their messages and communiqués to the media, Palestinians can be more direct. Press reports indicate that communiqués in the Khartoum Embassy incident, and directives from the political masters to the operatives, came in the form of a mixture of coded and open messages from radio transmitters in Libya, Lebanon, and probably Iraq. Some Arab transmitters are readily received throughout Europe on ordinary radios, and it is known that coded messages are used; however, it is also known that the transmissions are monitored by security services, so that considerable ingenuity is required for this method of communication to continue. The impossibility of using it in the case of the Bangkok Embassy incident possibly accounts in part for the collapse of that attempt. There is little doubt, again, that the techniques of radio communication will change since they are at present far short of the ultimate possibilities.

Neither terrorism nor revolution can be maintained without resources. In the case of revolutionary guerrilla movements in Africa, the sources of support are sympathetic governments. The cause of recent popular revolt against Portuguese control and the guerrilla movement against White control in Rhodesia are so generally (though not universally) approved that the only need for caution in admitting support is to avoid being drawn in too far or too directly. In these movements, the combatants and lines of combat are clearly drawn, and innocent bystanders do not get hurt unless they get in the way.

I do not know where the Ulster combatants get their material support and how they finance it; if weapons were not available, a great deal of the activity would freeze, although it does not take much money to create devastating bombs and Molotov cocktails. Black September and its parent organization Al Fatah obtain very substantial sums from Arab oil states—Libya alone is said to have provided $30 million to Black September, and until at least the Khartoum affair, Saudi Arabia was also a financial supporter. The weapons used in Khartoum were smuggled in through the Libyan diplomatic pouch, just as another Arab State smuggled weapons into Pakistan, it is reported, to create trouble in Pakistan–Iran border areas which cut through ethnic minority divisions.*

Hence we reach our first conclusion. Terrorism on the present-day scale would not be possible if it were not actively supported by governments, through the provision of funds and facilities. The United Nations, taking each case individually, runs immediately into vested interests and has its resolutions destroyed by biased voting. Nation-states which are involved in weapons trading if not as manufacturers (the minor problem), then as financiers and suppliers (the major problem), and who are political supporters, are in sufficient number to prevent the United Nations from adopting a *generalized* policy of effective sanctions against those States whose arms are found to be in terrorist hands. No one to my knowledge

---

* Sources include *The Economist* and *The Sunday Times* of London. It is ironical to note that the World Council of Churches, which, in my opinion, correctly urges the cessation of investments in South Africa as a symbolic protest against apartheid, has so far failed to draw attention to the fact that the motorist who uses oil from some Arab States is quite directly subsidizing Black September!

has ever asked in the United Nations that States should account for their behavior in subsidizing violence or explain their abuse of diplomatic privileges or how it is that arms which they have supplied or manufactured are found in the hands of individuals committing crimes in third-party countries.*

Nationalism, and the fear of internationally effective control, get in the way once more.

And, of course, there is the other side of the question. People who engage in aggression are regarded as victims of their circumstances. Political groups internal to countries, and disturbed individuals who kill dramatically, are indeed victims of circumstances. And society is deficient in not having found answers or in putting into effect the answers that it knows are applicable. But solutions are not easy, they will not be arrived at overnight, and when applied they will be found to create yet other circumstances which create disturbed individuals and angry groups. This is no argument whatsoever for society to tolerate armed aggression that makes the innocent pay. I find the argument that individuals must have the right to hold arms, for self-protection and *for sport*, nothing short of sick.** No symptom is more indicative—not even environmental issues—of the inadequacy of outlook of contemporary national government.

International terrorism and aggression is more difficult. It is indeed true that it is symptomatic of grave ills and that in most instances these can be pinpointed. The people without a home who created Israel did so with the

---

* It is interesting to note that the United Kingdom and France, after the April 1973 Israeli raid on Beirut, endeavored to introduce a resolution in the Security Council condemning Israel and carefully making a distinction between raids officially operated by governments and raids that are of a nongovernmental nature. The speeches indicated that the former could be controlled and were hence more reprehensible than nongovernmental terror, which could not be controlled. The opportunity was not taken to ask governments why they could not control terror or to make them responsible.

The cynic could point out that (after the United States and the USSR) Britain and France are by far the largest arms exporters in the world. A cutback on raids by Israel is not going to reduce Israel's demand for arms. A cutback on raids by Palestinians, on the other hand, would reduce armament demand in the Middle East both directly and through a lowering of tension.

This curious posture by Britain and France came at a point at which, for the first time in history, French Protestant and Catholic church leaders at the highest level joined together in a common political move—namely, to condemn French arms exports. At the same time, French Catholic bishops formally recognized the right of Israel to undisturbed political identity, a position which the Vatican itself has not yet formally endorsed.

** My own solution to this issue is straightforward, but obviously unacceptable—round up arms of every kind, make their individual possession illegal, and take care of the "sporting" urge (if necessary) by having arms held by sporting clubs under license and very strict control.

mythology of a religiously unified State, even though the society on which they were imposing their presence was probably the most religiously heterogeneous in the world. Part of the cost was the creation of *another* lost and wandering people. One would have expected the Israelis, above all, to have understood this, sympathized with it, and refused to let it happen. But the messianic fervor with which they acted obscured the issue to them, and now, for demographic and for bitter political reasons, it may be too late.

In the meantime, the Arab brothers of the Palestinians rejected them socially. Using the excuse of Israeli aggression, they confined (not completely) their help to charity in the form of refugee camps (primarily supported by American funding) and took advantage of Palestinian helplessness to encourage their belief in the return of their homeland as a political tool which could be turned against Israel. The millions of Arab dollars which flowed to the Palestinians were used to forge a weapon of war, not to provide means for settlement, income earning, and integration into a new way of life. The Palestinian ghettos are as much an Arab creation as an Israeli one. It is Arabs who have created social and economic ostracism and who have made it harder for Palestinians to change toward integration or political independence on the Arab side of the border. No wonder the Palestinians, in desperation, have on occasion turned toward Arab targets.

But if their actions are explicable, they are not tolerable. And time is running out. I say this not because of the dangers of armed conflict. On the contrary, there is a further danger of a different order and I have not seen it referred to in political circles.

We are too accustomed to thinking in terms of power and economy, and not enough in terms of religion. Religious messianic movements that have occurred in recent decades have been small scale, usually remote, and (when they have happened in wealthy countries) may offend morals but seldom affect the public order. They therefore pass as exotic.

But the conditions of the Palestinians are of the precise kind that are fertile ground for original messianism. Up to the present, Arab and Palestinian leadership has been divisive; Nasser's charisma was limited and was not of the kind that initiated aggression. There is now no generally accepted charismatic leader in the Arab world. But the chances are very great that at some point, if Palestinian frustration and desperation continue, a charismatic religious–political leader will emerge for them, and that his influence will be dynamically aggressive, appealing to frustrated Arab peoples of other backgrounds. The gap between ability and possibility on the one hand, and the conditions of action on the other, is of precisely the right order to make messianic political control a distinct chance. If that does come about, never will the world have experienced such a movement supported on such a scale by resources and modern technology.

It is not to be taken lightly.

CHAPTER 16

Politician as Sorcerer; Social Scientist as Apprentice

THERE is a battle going on for the minds of the peasants, the rural peoples, the urban workers, and even the well-to-do committed to a consumer society. It is no longer true (if it ever was) that those who have become the folk heroes and literate spokesmen of the path of revolt—the Che Guevaras and the Franz Fanons—know what it is to be a working peasant; their task is taken up with battle, not with understanding. The Viet-Cong and similar agents who have infiltrated villages spotted from Indonesia and Malaysia to Thailand and Vietnam were usually strangers to the village, or were trained by strangers, although they placed tremendous and powerful weight on participation; they are the anthropologists of politics. The tactics that govern opposition and political movement seldom grow out of the limited experience, resources, and power to organize of the rural people themselves. Thus, although revolutionaries always speak in the name of the people, their claim to do so is not automatically valid, and its acceptance or rejection is an act of political analysis, choice, or judgment. This applies whether you are a peasant facing the ideas and pressures of revolutionaries on the one hand and established authority on the other, whether you are a political observer, or whether you are an anthropologist attempting to make sense out of the sociopolitical scene.

In the real world, the politicians of all kinds call the shots. The anthropologist, if he does his work of research properly, feels he knows the situation and the people better. On the whole, he doesn't. He knows some aspects better, and his analysis reveals forces that others would miss. But he is often blind to the wider political realities, misjudges them because they are further away from his perception, and makes political choices which are just as naïve, emotive, and one-sided as those of any other citizen.

The information acquired by anthropologists, and indeed by other social scientists, contains political dynamite. The economist, political scientist, psychologist, and sociologist, working in a foreign country (whether privately or in a technical assistance capacity), obtain important systematic information about its operation, sometimes in the most sensitive governmental organs. This tends to be achieved quietly, without fanfare, and seldom leads the observer into regions where he is forced to question basic political assumptions. Some anthropologists are fortunate enough to work in contexts where life is quiet, the changes and disturbances are politically "normal," and the deeper ethical implications of change can all but be ignored.

But all this is changing. The village anthropologist, more than any other social scientist (because he commits himself to participant observation, because he goes to areas that are far removed from central government, because he finds himself in situations where rural political battles—unknown to the world's press—are in progress), can find himself in the midst of drama. These are some of the kinds of things he sees in the middle 1970s.

He sees people forcibly removed from lands in tribal occupation and placed in reserves to make way for plantation settlement; he sees them shot when they resist. He finds evidence that individuals have been forcibly removed from their villages and provided to employers as forced labor, probably with cash compensation to the officials who effected the move. He sees mining operations start with minimal compensation to the land-owners and debatable arrangements for royalty payments, if any. He sees people demoralized by alcohol, and now drugs. He sees differential police treatment which involves brutality. He hears of torture inflicted by revolutionary agents seeking revenge or discipline, and he sometimes sees the results. He sees villages bombed, deliberately or mistakenly, because guerrillas have converted them into fortresses or because they have received hospitality there. He hears of plans to carve great new highways out of jungle and to establish industry and agriculture under urban control almost overnight, with minimal concern for the culture, the property, or the well-being of nomadic or stone-age inhabitants. He sees tribal peoples turn on one another from motivations of political control and power, creating carnage, repression, and flight. He sees ethnic minorities persecuted because they know more or are better off than the majority.

Because he sees these things at first hand, or hears about them from those who have suffered, the anthropologist's first reaction is nearly always in human terms; he becomes angry, alarmed, and frustrated because there seems little that he can do. His accounts can only occasionally be backed by the kind of evidence that a court would accept; in many instances national law does not make the events illegal. In any event he lacks the personal resources to take legal action or initiate processes. In some instances, despite the overwhelming sensory impression, the larger question of who is right and who is wrong is not nearly as clear-cut as the observation would indicate. As he becomes involved, he is inevitably drawn into a political position.

If he takes up the case publicly, he is likely to be preaching to the already converted. The opposition can usually discredit the accounts by reference to the political opinions of the advocate or weaknesses in the evidence, or by appeal to such overriding considerations as national independence and development. Further, the chances are high that his colleagues in the country concerned are politically vulnerable, fearful, and without influence, and that if he himself speaks out he may be deported and refused reentry. Under such circumstances, anthropologists are neither welcome nor influential.

The anthropologist, if he is not to live forever as a perpetual witness and complicit observer of brutality, repression, and the violation of the most elementary human rights, can opt out by choosing less difficult areas in which to work; or else he must make some political decisions and find ways of exercising influence. One such potentiality is to develop the international connections of the social sciences—a topic I shall explore in Chapter 18. The other is to ally himself directly or implicitly with one or other of the political forces, in an attempt to influence it in humane directions. If he chooses this course, he had better know what he is doing.

Many anthropologists and other social scientists talk revolution; very few engage in it. The circumstances in which revolution is likely to improve the life of the people are few and far between. Anthropologists, whether they like it or not, are working in a context of power and have little chance of improving man's lot except through influencing directly or through the force of ideas the uses to which power is put. The option for this kind of solution leads to the probability that power will corrupt and that social science will be drawn into the corruption. Yet, unless social scientists take that risk and prepare themselves for the consequences, they will lose the right, the privilege, and the chance of being relevant.

While other social scientists are sitting on the sidelines (with partial exceptions in sociology and political science), anthropologists have been drawn into fierce and destructive debates on these issues, which have at times threatened the professional aspects of the discipline. Other disciplines (particularly developmental economics and geography) should perhaps take note and learn from the crisis of the anthropological conscience before it is too late, for time is also catching up with them.

A minority of anthropologists have had a long history of honorable involvement with government. I do not believe that the work of F. E. Williams, Government Anthropologist to a rather crude colonial regime in Papua, had repressive results. It aided not only scientific but human understanding, and it helped humanize the bureaucracy. I do not believe that the work of Harry Hawthorn and myself on Indian administration and social movement in British Columbia in the 1950s, and later work of Harry Hawthorn and his colleagues on the Indian condition in Canada, was at all damaging as a consequence of its sponsorship by the Federal Government. That work, in fact, opened up debates on a series of issues which would not otherwise have been aired, and has been used as a point of reference and a foil for argument by Indian leaders such as Harold Cardinal, as well as in government circles.

Nevertheless, the judgment even in these instances is not straightforward. It has been argued that F. E. Williams and the Canadian Indian reports played into the hands of government authority; by acting within the terms of such authority, the modern jargon goes, you are "co-opted" and you fail to commit yourself to revolutionary resistance. That is a matter of political judgment and realism, and I agree with the critics that such a choice is implied and has to be made. But I affirm that anthropologists, and other social scientists, in making such judgments must do so in the light of knowledge and personal convictions and must take the individual responsibility for them. They will not make the judgment better or more knowingly by responding to codes of ethics or rules of conduct imposed by a profession, which in effect replace thought by automatic propositions—that is, slogans. This has become probably the most serious *professional* issue of the social sciences.

The issue, as with many others, has been most fully explored in the United States, with a great deal of self-conscious searching for guilt. While there are anthropologists in that country who have accepted applied assignments, not even all the members of the Society for Applied Anthropology have seen the inside of government or know what it is like to have to take administrative actions and live with the responsibility. The alienation of large numbers of scholars from the United States Government (exacerbated by attacks on academic liberty in the 1950s, by moral positions taken in relation to the Vietnam war, and by internal poverty and violence) and the culminating politicization of student life and to some degree academic professional bodies are almost unbelievable to those who have not been involved. While other countries face similar moral dilemmas and controversies, anti-government sentiments have not often been elevated into absolute action principles, almost uniting both left and right, as in the United States.

The situation, for scholars, is sharpened by the existence of well-organized scholarly associations, and the interest of the membership in using them as instruments of professionalization (which implies ethical commitments). The American Anthropological Association has had the most severe challenges to deal with, but the issues are also present in critical form in other bodies, not only in the social sciences; and they are also being debated now in countries other than the United States. Indeed, some of the sharpest questions have been raised in Africa, Asia, and Latin America. I have to limit the field of my discussion, and shall do so by showing some of the significance of relevant events which impinged upon the American Anthropological Association.

In 1964 and 1965 the Office of Research and Development, US Department of the Army, began the famous Project Camelot.* In the words of Senator Fulbright, this was conceived as a "basic social science project on preconditions of internal conflict, and on effects of indigenous governmental actions—easing, exacerbating or resolving—on these pre-conditions." The project was immense, funded to over six million dollars; it was to include social scientists from a variety of disciplines—including sociology, political science, economics, psychology, and anthropology; and it was oriented toward studies of Latin America.

The project was contracted to the Special Operations Research Office of the American University, which conducted research on behalf of the Army. This connection was not concealed, and anyone knowing of the connection between specific research and SORO sponsorship should have known of the ultimate sponsor.

It does not automatically follow that those who knew should have withdrawn their association. The irony is that social scientists have for years drawn attention to the link between establishment government and "exploiting" interests in some Latin American countries, to the role of the Army in affecting political and social outcomes, and to the ways in which American military and political advice have had the effect of bolstering such regimes and hence inhibiting both reform and popular revolution.

* Sources and discussions include Gideon Sjoberg, ed., *Ethics, Politics and Social Research*, Cambridge, Mass.: Schenkman, 1967; I. L. Horowitz, *The Rise and Fall of Project Camelot*, Boston: MIT Press, 1967; Ralph L. Beals, *Politics of Social Research*, Chicago: Aldine, 1969.

One would have thought that it would have been rather important that an increased understanding of such linkages be developed so that such gross errors could be avoided and so that scholars themselves would be better informed and hence in a better position to buttress liberalizing argument with hard data. It would be naïve to assume that the mere existence of a foundation of understanding would bring about such a result; many other social science actions and many other conditions inside and outside the United States would have their impact. But it is equally evident that without some such understanding one could not expect United States policy to change, and that the only weapon of social science in such matters is to bring understanding home where the decisions count, and to communicate more widely to the general public, which in turn can influence government. These are weak weapons, but they are better than none. It is not at all surprising that highly respected social scientists seized what seemed to be an opportunity.

But the project as conceived had naïve flaws. First, six million dollars, though tempting, was neither necessary nor productively usable. A great deal of knowledge already exists, and much can be gleaned from an ordinary reading of newspapers. The existence of such a fund meant that inexperienced and ill-prepared people were prepared to embark on not very essential projects. Second, those who had lower contractual status apparently did not always know the source of support or the potential uses; they were thus not given the basic information upon which to make their moral judgments. Third, there was of course no guarantee about the direction or weight of use within the United States Government, and many critics were able to argue that such information would be used to repress justifiable protest and, conversely, that such information would be used to encourage protest and revolution against legitimate government. Fourth, although social scientists of Latin American origin were involved, it was from a US base and there was no *international* partnership in what was an international piece of research. Fifth, when attempts were made to recruit cooperating social scientists in Latin American countries themselves, through the lavish use of money, the approach was botched and blown up as a result of initial secrecy and lack of candor, so that it had the appearance of interference in the internal affairs of other countries (which it was) and of a CIA-type intelligence network (which it probably wasn't).

Nevertheless, the accusation of CIA-type intelligence was not unfounded, since the project did not have the quality of partnership and sharing of information between nations. Further, it was known that US intelligence sources were always interested in the products of social scientists and had approached social scientists to work for them* and that they often used a social science role as "cover" for persons who were simply and plainly intelligence agents.

Hence, it is not surprising that when the operation was "blown" in Chile every possible Macchiavellian interpretation could be and was placed upon it. After a furor in Latin America and in United States academic and political circles the project was cancelled in 1965.

This was merely the climax of an era of suspicion between social science and government; but the case was, in a sense, so classic and so much came to be known about it that it became the model of reference when other events revealed themselves.

Within the American Anthropological Association, the reaction was immediate and sharp. Resolutions were passed condemning "clandestine" research and research dealing with "counterinsurgency." A committee on professional ethics was created, which produced a report which became the policy of the Association.** Thus the stage was set for the next big "scandal."

At the same time, other events were taking place which created localized controversy and which did not become major Association issues in the same sense. (They did affect some of the attitudes of members, and they did have a bearing upon the wording of later Association documents.) For example, some African governments, scholars, politicians, and newspapers began to question the operations of foreign social scientists in their countries. The basis of this questioning was not only the issue of possible intelligence secrecy and political mastery, which I think was more of a rhetorical tool than a reality, but came to be called (with some justification) "intellectual imperialism." That is, only a minority of

---

* This kind of thing has existed since the first days of social science. During World War II, most of the social science leaders beyond fighting age were involved one way or another in intelligence activities, some in the field. When the German spy-master Gehlen directed his attention to the communist countries on behalf of the Allies, he used at least one social science research institute as a source of direct information and as a cover. Openly and freely published social science monographs are basic intelligence information, however innocent their purposes and sponsorship. So is journalism. When certain of our colleagues demand that information should not be provided in forms that can be used for political purposes with which they disagree, the logical conclusion is that *no* information *ever* be published. Further, those who argue in this way are putting themselves in the position of judging political right and wrong for others.

** Known as the Beals Report. It is printed in the *American Anthropological Association Fellow Newsletter*, Vol. 8, No. 1, January 1967, and has been used as the base for the more extended discussion of R. L. Beals, *Politics of Social Research*, Chicago: Aldine, 1969, which of course is a personal contribution not attributed to the Association.

social scientists were concerned with *subordinating* their intellectual strategies to the views and priorities of their colleagues in the countries concerned. They tended to ignore these views. Their contact with local colleagues was often of the most perfunctory kind, without intellectual meat, and they often brushed off the growing originality of the ideas being produced in the country concerned. Only a small minority used their research resources to assist local scholars or cooperate with them; very few helped to train researchers. Their reports and books were often unavailable or too expensive for local use. Add to this the frustration of local social scientists, often without the time or means to carry out research (let alone publish), ignored in fundamental respects by the international scholarly community, lacking funds and time to participate in scholarly international meetings, ignored, distrusted, and even perse-cuted by their own governments if they said the "wrong" things. This atmosphere, while by no means universal (and usually overcome by direct personal contact and the attraction of intellectual concerns), was very sharp in anthropology, which lives on cross-cultural observation and activity. Asian and Latin American countries shared similar views.

About this time, the late Oscar Lewis published his best-selling "raw data" books on the lives of Mexican urban working-class families and on Puerto Ricans. These books told a truth, though that truth (as Lewis was very careful to point out) was limited to the families observed. Despite the limitation, it was sufficient for Lewis to develop his ideas about the culture of poverty. I personally have considerable reservations about the methods used and the legitimacy of the deductions, but it cannot be denied that the material was dramatic and the force of the idea was powerful.

If Lewis had kept the reports to learned journals, or if he had treated his research as "confidential," which is a variant of the forbidden "clandestine," many people would not have felt themselves hurt. As it was, the Mexican public, to whom the book was made available in a Spanish edition in accordance with the canons of free communication, became, at least for a while, upset at what seemed to be a slur on their national culture, and Mexican scholars joined the debate. I do not know whether the Mexican, Puerto Rican, or New York governments have taken any notice of Lewis' work, nor do I know what interpretations, if any, have been drawn from it as an influence upon policy, either directly or through public opinion. But I am reasonably certain that there has been *some* effect. No one can approach the reality of life among the poor in those jurisdictions without thinking of Lewis' data; indeed, no one can think of poverty anywhere in the world without in some form or other wrestling with Lewis' point of view—even in rejecting or modifying it. Would Lewis have been a better scholar or a more relevant scientist if he had avoided the risk of hurting feelings?

Meanwhile, University of California scholars began what appeared to be an exciting scientific program on the unevenly known peoples of Himalayan Border areas (described in the project title as "countries," but I have not seen a precise definition).* This was an ambitious, interdisciplinary program, partially funded by the US Department of Defense. Camelot again. This time questions were raised in the Indian Parliament, and the attitudes were influenced by previous disclosures that the Asia Foundation, which had operated in India, had received CIA money. The project was closed, and tighter supervision of foreign research was instituted in India. Despite Camelot, it took an Indian outcry to warn US scholars of their international moral obligations.

Since these incidents, and because of other problems (such as the sheer numbers and demands of researchers seeking the same data, the same officials, and the same informants), many countries have created licensing arrangements for foreign research, some with considerable intellectual and international understanding, some with very little. Conditions of intellectual cooperation are now usually required, including, for example, the filing of data reports or linkage with local scholars.

One country which has been operating such a system, with considerable skill, since the late 1960s has been Thailand. Regulation is carried out by the National Research Council of Thailand, formed in the early 1960s, which has a social sciences division. Since World War II, Thailand has made considerable use of foreign technical advisers from a wide range of multilateral and bilateral institutions. To some extent, it has also followed the Japanese example of encouraging professional study abroad, particularly in the United States and Europe. The social sciences are relatively low in national priorities, with few social or cultural anthropologists. There are some private social research institutes and a number of professional social science associations, and societies which bring together Thai, foreign, natural, and social scientists. There is in fact a *structure* of social and natural science activity, and a framework for

---

* My information on this episode is slender, and is derived mainly from Gerald D. Berreman, "Not so Innocent Abroad," *The Nation*, November 10, 1969. It is, however, an important incident in the development of attitudes.

discussion and policy representation, which, whatever its weaknesses, can be activated should the need arise. Indeed, it is said that it was a major influence behind the recent liberal coup.

Thailand, being a close neighbor of Laos and Cambodia, and involved in Vietnam (even to the extent of having a substantial population of Vietnamese refugees), is far from being an unaffected bystander of regional military activity. It is concerned about the possibility of a repetition of history, and draws a parallel between the effects of foreign-trained communist agents and infiltrators in its Northeast and Northwest border Provinces (as well as elsewhere). In the Northeast—a relatively poor peasant society—there has been a buildup of American military bases, and there are populations that have considerable affinity with ethnic groups across the border. There are also major (and therefore somewhat disturbing) development and resettlement schemes connected with Upper Mekong power and irrigation programs.

In the North and North-West—in mountainous country bordering Burma, China, and Laos—there are vast territories which have until recently been left alone except in the loosest sense. Approximately seventy years ago, the shifting agriculture techniques of the so-called Hill Tribes of the general region followed migratory patterns which brought a substantial movement of population into the Thai political territory. The Hill Tribes were connected to the outside world by patterns of trade in which Chinese held some of the key roles; even today the remains of substantial Chinese Nationalist armies are in nearby Burma, and the network of communication is substantial. The main commercial crop grown and traded in substantial parts of this international region was, and is, *the opium poppy.*

The Thai Government did not intervene; indeed, critics accused influential persons of benefiting from the traffic. But international pressure, emanating particularly from the United Nations, insisted that control be effected. The Thai Government, and international experts who came in the late 1950s and early 1960s to survey the scene, realized that a cessation of the traffic could not be imposed by fiat. If it were, whole populations would have been disaffected by the loss of cash income and the lack of alternative sources. It was also realized that, as a result of years of *laissez faire*, the Thai Government did not have at its disposal the information necessary upon which to base an alternative social and economic policy.

Thus, in the early to mid-1960s, a large number of reports were written, mainly by international advisers working with both multilateral and bilateral development aid programs. Aerial surveys of Hill Tribe and border territories were undertaken, and the first reasonably accurate calculations of land use and cropping were made possible. Teams of Thai government officials entered Hill Tribe areas, often for the first time, establishing contact and making plans for medical services, schooling, and agricultural and forestry analysis.

At this point, anthropologists began to be associated with the studies and with the analyses. I have read reports from Austrian, Singhalese, Australian, German, Indian, and Soviet, as well as American, anthropologists and related social scientists. I know of only one Thai anthropologist who was available at the time, although Thai counterparts were usually attached to the various research teams in other social science capacities, and some began to learn anthropological techniques.

A social science and medical university was established in Chiengmai, the northern town which can be considered the "take-off" point for the northern border areas. As a result of the work of the Australian anthropologist, W. R. Geddes (who had had the unique experience of observing closely related ethnic groups under communist administration in the People's Republic of China), a Hill Tribes Research Centre was established. It produced probably the first locally trained professional Thai anthropologists. This Centre, an academic and research activity, is not to be confused with the Hill Tribes Institute, set up as an official data archive and data bank, mainly for government purposes, collating material from all the various projects and reports that have been undertaken.

It is difficult, at a distance, to summarize the precise "policy" of the Thai Government. In its usual pragmatic way, it was evolving a policy, based on reports and studies, and the interpenetrating claims and rivalries of administrative departments. At least three threads of policy pressure could be discerned.

One, supported by some of the forces concerned with national defense, urged what might be termed a simplistic and counterproductive "solution"—namely, the settlement of tribal peoples on lower lands and their conversion to fixed agriculture. This solution was supported by hitherto liberal and well-informed advisers within the US bilateral assistance mission, out of a sense of desperation that otherwise no solution would be found, heroin would continue to flow, the tribes would become further disaffected, and there would be some kind of repetition of Vietnam. That solution ignored the actual lessons of Vietnam, and particularly the interpretation that forced resettlement, for administrative and economic policy purposes, of Hill Tribesmen in South Vietnam, dating back to French days, had created the foundation for disaffection which had made the Viet-Cong task possible.

Another was for a continuation of direct rule in the hands of the Border Police, whose first task was the security of the region. The Border Police were originally the only effective administration representing the national interest, and great efforts were directed toward giving them the training, the reorientation, and the public image that would be consistent with liberal administration. But their operative myth was that of security, and any measures that should be undertaken had to be justified in the name of security if they were to be the agents. Thus, advisers who were linked with the policies on the assumption that the agency would be the Border Police couched their language in terms which would have an effect by appealing to the established mythology. In report after report the Border Police were urged to establish councils and rapport with village figures, to modify their behavior to reflect local democratically expressed opinion, to establish policies at the rural level that met the needs and expectations of the village communities, and to create a sense of national loyalty and participation through a commitment to the things the Thai Government was attempting to do—rather than as an imposed symbol. This was to occur in an administrative vacuum even greater than that facing the post-War Australian administration of New Guinea.

But police can only turn themselves into civilian administrators if they have time to learn the new ways, and if their primary security duties permit this. They were not given that time. The intensification of military border problems and the appearance of political infiltration meant that they could never truly appear in a continuously democratic role. There was always the possibility that something could go wrong, that technical advice would mislead, that disappointment would turn to political disaffection, that political disaffection—real or imagined—would turn to shooting, or that bombs would be dropped and rifles fired and the innocent would be hurt, sometimes through deliberate political misinformation.

The third stream, which had to operate within the above climate, was that of multitechnical teams designed to learn, to communicate in two directions, to establish political linkages, and to create, in partnership with the people, viable policy alternatives and a viable supply of appropriate services. This proposal, as initially formulated, included a National Tribal Welfare Committee, working through fourteen local Tribal committees, under the general direction of the Minister of the Interior with the Director-General of Public Welfare as his agent. On each of these committees there were representatives of each technical division of government at the appropriate level. The proposal included the training of tribesmen for participation in mobile development teams, which were a kind of community development and fundamental education device, and the creation of representative rural institutions.

In practice it also retained the idea of resettlement, and the Border Police were represented, as they would have to be, on the committees. While the Director-General of Public Welfare was precisely what his title implies, the Minister of the Interior also had security obligations. Hence the policy battle between direct action and security preoccupations on the one hand, and long-term liberal development on the other, was ever present.

In such a context, external advice is there to be generated and used by forces within the government of Thailand, in the same way as internal advice.

This is the setting for the next stage in my theme. We had seen that anthropological opinion in the United States had been affected by a series of incidents, particularly the Camelot affair.

On April 2, 1970, the Student Mobilization Committee to End the War in Vietnam published its newspaper *The Student Mobilizer* (Vol. 3, No. 4), devoted almost entirely to what it analyzed as the involvement of American scholars in counterinsurgency-motivated research in Southeast Asia, particularly in Thailand, with special reference to the Hill Tribes. Primarily on the basis of documents stolen from the files of an anthropologist at the University of California at Los Angeles, photocopied, and then returned to the files, it revealed the following:

1. The University of California had a contract with the United States Agency for International Development which committed the university to activity making knowledge available to AID, including that produced at other institutions, bearing upon "developmental and counter-insurgency activities in Thailand."

2. The US AID taps academic advice through a series of committees connected in a complex organization. *The Student Mobilizer* approached this first by quoting extensively and selectively from the minutes of one of these committees—the Academic Advisory Committee for Thailand, chaired in 1969 by an anthropologist at Cornell, and including political scientists, historians, educators, geographers, and others. The quotations concentrated on the minutes of a meeting in 1968 and made clear, by underlinings and comment, that the discussion was preoccupied by AID's concern for village security. At a meeting on rural local authority in

Thailand, organized in 1969, the AID representative is quoted as identifying priorities as "(1) Strengthening civil security at the village level, principally through aid to the Thai national police department; (2) accelerated rural development" and (3) coordination of work in the Northeast. The quotations chosen frequently link such issues as local authority and education to the problem of security, in the most general terms.

3. *The Student Mobilizer* then traces some movements and communications relating to Thailand of persons known to have attended AACT meetings, including some activities specifically on behalf of AACT. One person, on behalf of AACT, is described as having visited Bangkok and having there met with forty-three listed individuals. Included among Thai and foreign officials and academics was "an adviser to the Border Patrol Police in the American consulate in Chiengmai," two members of AACT who, to use the writer's snide comment, "just happened to be in Thailand at the same time," and "four members (one of them a general) of the Thai National Research Council." Plans were laid for a conference on national integration and regional economics, with emphasis on the North. Letters are quoted about the organization of this conference, presumably by a non-AACT member, but those who were approached to participate and who were linked with AACT or SEADAG (see later) are carefully identified. The scholar who organized this conference also organized another on "shifting cultivation and economic development in Northern Thailand." The editorial comment does not indicate that AACT was concerned with this conference, but makes remarks about the sponsors, the Ford Foundation, and the Thai Government, supporting a topic of interest to AACT.

4. Lengthy quotations are made from a record (not minutes) of a 1967 meeting (we are going backward in time) of the Institute of Defense Analysis linked to what is known as Project Jason. This was a three-week seminar attended by natural scientists, military personnel, and social scientists. Clearly any quotations from semi-verbatim notes of a three-week seminar, and probably the original record itself, are necessarily highly selective. The quotations placed on record by *The Student Mobilizer* point to a *Realpolitik* analysis and commentary by the military and by militarily oriented representatives of *nonacademic* "research" organizations, such as one notorious group known as the "Advanced Research Project Agency." The social science academic representatives, judging by the quotations, were clearly on the defensive, trying to make known that social sciences were not oriented to the simplicities of *Realpolitik* and that the wrong kind of use was corrupting. There were discussions of the

effects of classification of data and similar worrying problems. There is no evidence that any of the social scientists accepted the *Realpolitik* analysis or committed themselves in any way to its assumptions. The quotations do make brutal reading, particularly in the simplified form in which they are recorded.

5. The discussion then turns to quotations dealing with the activities of an independent research group called "The American Institutes for Research." This group submitted a Thai project to the Advanced Projects Research Agency which is widely quoted but is otherwise not overtly connected with the other incidents. It is said, however, that one member of AACT took part in an advisory panel organized in Bangkok in 1969 (apparently a joint US–Thai Government meeting), and other persons are linked through having participated in AACT-linked meetings.

6. By this time, *The Student Mobilizer* had established a highly charged account intensified by "guilt by association" techniques applied not only to individuals but to organizations. An AACT meeting identified a problem, and an individual who was a major US figure in connection with that problem, and who would be a natural choice to organize a meeting or research. Such a meeting in fact takes place, therefore AACT is likely to be behind it. At this meeting, *X* and *Y* are present. Whenever they turn up elsewhere, *X* and *Y*'s presence is construed as implying AACT involvement, or their use as agents or tools of AACT.

The evidence that AACT itself is concerned primarily with counterinsurgency and security is based on rather abstract discussions at one meeting, plus the fact that AACT is an agency of AID, which in turn is a bilateral aid institution frankly serving (and bound by law to serve) United States policy, which has at various times been notoriously concerned with security and defense in extraordinarily naïve ways.

7. *The Student Mobilizer* then goes on to talk of SEADAG (the Southeast Asia Development Advisory Group), which is "a subdivision" of AID. The treatment of SEADAG in this sequence is a deliberate propaganda move; as the writer points out, "As such [that is, as a subdivision of AID] it will already be suspect to the reader of the preceding pages." A caveat is entered, but with a sting:

We wish to emphasise the fact that for professors listed below whose names appear in this story for the first time [but not for the others] there is no concrete evidence that they are involved in counter-insurgency research. But the number of academicians who are involved in both SEADAG and organizations like AACT, the representation of groups like the Ford Foundation and Rockefeller Foundation, and the ties to AID, certainly justify a demand that these professors make known the nature of their work for SEADAG.

The names then follow; it reads like a who's who of major scholarship in the United States.

There are indeed serious issues raised by these connections, and by their treatment in *The Student Mobilizer.*

1. If all the connections are taken at face value, there is a *conspiracy* at work in the United States—in which academics are involved—to support the Thai Government.

2. The incidents at which academics were present revealed utterly barbaric naïveté on the part of US government agents, including high officials in the Department of Defense and to a certain extent in AID. They do not imply that the academics held similar views or cooperated in actions designed to create policy furthering those views. For 99 percent of the social science participants, the reverse was the case.

3. If the presence of a Thai military man or police representative in a meeting is to imply that the meeting is specifically concerned with counterinsurgency repression in the normal sense of the phrase, then the whole of Thai society and government is concerned with counterinsurgency and repression, for military positions were common in government, and many roles that in US society are nongovernmental are, in Thai society, governmental. Such an interpretation would be nonsense, yet it underlies many of the ethnocentric and propagandistic innuendos of the *Mobilizer.*

4. An underlying assumption is that a concern with security and counterinsurgency is in itself improper, and that it is improper for a social scientist to be engaged in work directly or indirectly related to such a concern. That is in itself a dangerously silly or deliberately undermining position. Furthermore, it means that all social science should go out of business, since any social science data can be used *for or against* security, counterinsurgency, and the like.

Further, at certain points in Thai history, and in certain Thai governmental quarters, *any* positive or reform measure bearing upon the quality of life in the border areas was seen to be connected with security and was so described and politically justified in order to obtain funds and administrative support. The label is part of a mythology that social scientists who are up to scratch see through and place in proper perspective. Only symbolic propaganda does otherwise.

5. None of the documents quoted was secret or confidential.

6. The attempt of some social scientists to influence US government policy toward Thailand was probably highly ineffective and naïve. That

cannot be judged from the documents since it would require follow-up observation. But if it had been successful, even in part, in producing a libertarian, humanitarian bias, it would have had value. The attempt may have been a waste of time, but it was not necessarily evil for that.

7. Any government working in an international world seeks advice about the countries with which it is dealing, and much of this advice must come from internal sources. This is not a process from which social scientists should automatically remove themselves, though they need to exercise care, judgment, and wisdom in making their choices about cooperation. Some of this was lacking. It is unlikely to appear until social scientists develop a little more corporate wisdom, cumulative experience, and the power to choose their terms of work more positively.

8. Because of the nature of their task, social scientists should be more concerned than most other professionals about the equality and validity of international cooperation. Many of the activities referred to in the documents were activities in which the cooperation of *Thai* scholars themselves should have been key. Some social scientists recognize this, and have played a part both in training Thai scholars and in cooperating with those who exist. That aspect of work was not indicated in the selection of documentary material. It is indeed unfortunate that a very high proportion of consultation performed by US social scientists in Thailand has not been based on cooperation with Thai scholars.

9. Nevertheless, the documents do show a high involvement *in Thailand* (but not in the United States) of Thai officials of all persuasions and fields. Indeed, given the nature of Thai government at that time, and the skill that the Thai have shown in controlling their own destiny and *making use of* foreign advisers and assistants, this could not but be so.

10. There is no evidence whatsoever that *The Student Mobilizer* consulted Thai opinion or Thai social scientists about the desirability of the activities described, or their interpretation of them. In this respect the *Mobilizer* is as ethnocentric and colonialist as the US military personnel it quotes, and more ethnocentric than many of the aid officials and social scientists.

I have discussed this issue at length for a number of reasons. Unlike Project Camelot, although it has been commonly discussed in anthropological circles, the incident involving American anthropology in Thailand has not been put on record in the analytic literature, and its lessons for the professional behavior of anthropologists in action have only partially been drawn. The discussion of the "scandal" revealed by

The Student Mobilizer spread like wild-fire throughout a number of scholarly associations (not only in the United States), increased foreign suspicion of anthropology, and created a crisis of conscience in the American Anthropological Association.

The background I have related up to this point indicates that the action stance of any anthropologist working in Thailand was bound to be affected by a highly complex political situation involving diverse elements in Thai society and government, and international influences not only from the United States but from a considerable number of other governments and agencies. It was relatively easy to draw from this complexity points that could be used for propaganda purposes, and this is exactly what *The Student Mobilizer*, primarily interested in Vietnam, accomplished.

But the short-term ramifications, again stimulated by the atmosphere of crisis and excitement about Vietnam and similar issues in the United States, influenced the position of the American Anthropological Association on the ethical conduct of its members.* That Association had previously established a Committee on Ethics, charged with examining concrete instances in order to arrive at principles and procedures that should govern professional behavior. Copies of documents relating to *The Student Mobilizer* story were made available to a number of anthropologists, including the Chairman and a member of the Ethics Committee.

It would have been quite within the terms of reference of that committee to have enquired systematically into the issues, and to have related the results of that enquiry to its report on principles. Ideally, such an enquiry might have taken into consideration the complexities of the Thai social and political scene and, even more fundamentally, it might have incorporated the view of Thai social scientists on the various questions raised. Unfortunately, for whatever reasons, events did not develop this way.

The Chairman of the Committee, Eric Wolf, used the following crucial phrase in acknowledging receipt of the documents: "Since these documents contradict in spirit and in letter the resolutions of the American Anthropological Association concerning clandestine and secret research . . . ." In opening an enquiry, a letter he wrote to four anthropologists

---

*For this and following developments, written sources include Eric Wolf and Joseph Jorgensen, "Anthropology on the Warpath in Thailand," *New York Review of Books*, Vol. XV, No. 9, November 19, 1970; the issue of the same journal dated April 8, 1971, containing a long letter from George Foster, President of the Association, and others; and issues of the *Newsletter* of the American Anthropological Association in 1970 and 1971.

whose names appeared in the documents included the following phrases:

> ... You will be aware that your name appears in these documents. It is the announced purpose of the Ethics Committee to deal with cases on as anonymous a basis as possible, in an effort to develop an approach to cases without penalizing individuals; and we shall honour this commitment as much as practicable. However, I should like to invite you to make any statement to the Committee that you wish, especially in view of the past resolutions of our Association on the subject of clandestine research and restricted, non-public publication of research results.

The letter appended the document containing the statement quoted at the beginning of this paragraph.

It is not surprising that there was widespread interpretation that this position constituted the statement of charges of possible misconduct. To some degree, the guilt of the anthropologists concerned had been declared on the basis of an acceptance of the documents at face value. The Association was almost immediately polarized, with those who believed the documents and the charges on one side and those who wanted calmer enquiry or who disbelieved the documents and the charges on the other. There followed resignations from the Ethics Committee, the taking of the case to the membership through the medium of the public press, vigorous discussion on the floor of the annual meeting, the creation of a committee of enquiry under the Chairmanship of Margaret Mead, the presentation of a moderate and reasoned report from that committee, and its rejection by the membership.*

The mood of the Association at that time was to take formal responsibility for the professional conduct of its members. This is in itself a laudable objective, and it was further argued that it was necessary if the profession were to survive in an increasingly critical world. But also there lay, behind the passion, the determination to make that responsibility effective through the disciplining of colleagues who were thought to have behaved improperly. This view was not overtly shared by many, but the force of the actions adopted led in that direction.

But the Association had not given sufficient thought to the issues, and

---

* I should not conceal my own role in this debate. As a member of the Executive Board at the time, I was urging that the matter be handled in a way that would seek understanding through a conference on the issues in which Thai colleagues would play a major role. The Executive Board moved in this direction, but the proposal was overwhelmingly defeated at the Annual Meeting. I then felt that the Association was committed to an approach in which judgments were being made about the conduct of social research in Thailand in a manner that was, on all sides, offensive to Thai colleagues. Since I could not contemplate similar behavior vis-à-vis Canada, and hence any other country, I resigned from the Executive Board. At the same meeting, Canadians were granted the status of "Foreign Fellows" in the Association.

the impatience of the moment prevented it from doing so. There was a tendency to react to the symbols ("counterinsurgency," "clandestine research") as absolutes, and to interpret what was happening in Thailand as a reflection of Vietnam, Camelot, and the policies of the Defense Department. These were all relevant issues, and it was important to know whether some anthropologists were being made fools of. But the possibility of such an enquiry was destroyed by hasty accusation and the use of the tactic of "guilt by association."

There are even deeper issues. No attempt was made, at least until the Mead Committee, to subordinate American judgment to that of Thai social science colleagues—indeed one eminent anthropologist even stated that there were no competent and independent social scientists in Thailand (not long afterwards Thai social scientists were instrumental in stimulating the coup that removed the military from the government). Little attention was given to the possibility that the Thai *might* have welcomed a liberalizing influence of American social science upon American policy agents. Still less attention was given to the right of social scientists to have differing political views among themselves and to act upon them. Very few deprecated the reasoning by innuendo and false association, which was the basis of the attack in *The Student Mobilizer*, or questioned the authenticity or completeness of the documents.

It is not easy to judge one's colleagues by reference to emotionally established absolutes; one is usually in the realm of value differences with political implications. The judgment depends in part upon one's political position. The anthropologist who gives advice, who consults, who engages in applied research is moving in a world in which he does not and should not make the decisions. He takes personal responsibility for this position and the way in which he handles the accumulation and presentation of knowledge. As colleagues, we cannot make such judgments for him; he is alone, and must have sufficient courage to do what he thinks right. We can discuss, analyze, and reveal relationships that may surprise and enlighten him; in short, we can hope to educate the profession to its limited powers and its immense responsibilities.

The questions remain. Is it then possible to have *an* ethics of social research? Is it possible to have *a* politics of social research? A discipline such as anthropology must be especially concerned with complexity and variety. Yet there are movements afoot to establish codes of conduct, a new orthodoxy. Is this the way to master the art of judgment?

CHAPTER 17

On the Mastery of Judgment

SOCIAL scientists will always be apprentices. Their craft is seldom a firm technique; when it is, it tends to be banal. If social sciences are unified in the future, it will not be the result of an Einsteinian equation but because concepts, methods, and language are mutually understood. For as long as we can foresee, there will be a rich variety of methods, of kinds of problems, and of individuals who make their contribution. They will continue to write for different publics; indeed, they will probably learn to address themselves more widely than they do now.

Social scientists are trained *not* to know everything. They assign themselves to disciplines which practice the art of exclusion—of shutting one's eyes to inconvenient truths and complications in order to concentrate the better on the matter at hand. Even if this were not so, a social scientist could seldom control, by means of data, theory, and his own genius, all the factors that impinge upon a policy or applied problem. His approach to prescription, then, has to be "perhaps" or "it looks as if" or "why don't you try it this way and see what happens?"

The social scientist, then, should be reasonably modest in his claims; he should not go as far as many of my colleagues who say, for example, that since we don't know everything perhaps we know nothing, and that we should not use our knowledge as the basis for advice, since it is bound to be incomplete. Our responsibility, if we decide to enter this world, is to use our knowledge, give our advice, generate ideas, but never pretend that they have the kind of authority that can be provided in certain circumstances, in other fields, by physicists or engineers.

If this is admitted, then the intensity of a certain kind of issue is slightly reduced. Social scientists neither control policy nor influence its outcomes in ways that should make them take *themselves* too seriously. This does not mean to say that they should not take their *role of adviser* seriously, or should not try to work out ways of establishing the consequences of their actions and advice, or should not be prepared to answer for their conduct if, as a result of their advice, persons suffer. But no one can yet claim that the ills of the world are the result of the influence of mistaken or wicked social scientists. That day may come, and we must beware of it.

The social scientist is an individual, operating with individual responsibilities and expectations. He is *not* part of an organized profession in the normal sense of the word (unless he is a technical psychologist)—a very important point to which we shall return. At this stage of the development of the discipline, he is not normally subject to a licensing and controlling professional organization, and it is by no means certain that he should be.

However, because of this, he is more than usually dependent upon his own personal values—political, ethical, and scientific. He does not refer them to an outside body for approval or judgment, except insofar as he is directly employed. If there is a commonality in the value assumptions in any given group of social scientists, it is to be traced to common backgrounds of training, of social and cultural origin, of political goals, and of scientific philosophy, rather than organized professionalism.

I cannot speak for other social sciences clearly, except to record that economists seem least self-conscious in their questioning of their own behavior, psychologists the most professional, and political scientists, sociologists, and anthropologists in a nice state of muddle. But it certainly comes as a shock to read the proposition seriously advanced by two colleagues (and unanimously supported by commentators) that self-consciousness in ethnography has recently emerged as a phenomenon, and that anthropologists as never before are looking more carefully at their own characteristics and impact on the field situation they are studying.* The argument is advanced by citing large numbers of instances in which contemporary writers refer in detail to their field problems and interactions, and examine, sometimes *ad nauseam*, their own personalities and characteristics as part of the interactional scene.

The first point to note is that this is little more than a numerical increase related to the increase in the numbers of anthropologists who are in fact writing. Of course, one would expect the frequency of such accounts to increase, just as there is an increase in the number of accounts that do *not* do this!

The second, more important point is that of *déjà vu*. Anthropologists

* See Dennison Nash and Ronald Wintrob, "The Emergence of Self-consciousness in Ethnography," *Current Anthropology*, Vol. 13, No. 5, December 1972, pp. 527–543, including comments.

have almost always been self-conscious. They have changed their modes of expression; some are more public today, to the point at which some discussions have the character of group therapy for purposes of self-healing and exorcism of guilt rather than that of controlled analysis. There is a slightly strident tone of hysteria and of personal upset in the political and emotional accounting that makes one wonder whether the persons concerned should ever have entered such an emotionally demanding field.

But setting that aside, the discussion of one's interactions and role in the field, the impact of one's views and personality, the nature of the technology one brought, the type of recording used, the conscious or unconscious incorporation of ideology and biases in one's conversation, one's emotive reaction to the people and theirs to you, the whole phenomenon that (with the Peace Corps) came to be dubbed "culture shock"—these were standard items of consideration, writing, and training, and the subject of endless discussion in and out of graduate seminars and research reports from the days of Malinowski, Boas, and Kroeber.

Indeed, a little later, as psychiatry and psychology entered anthropology with more formal impact, arguments were made and debates raged on the subject of psychoanalysis as a prerequisite to being allowed to enter the field. It was never, so far as I am aware, imposed as a condition of fieldwork, but I do know that the influence of such scholars as Bateson and Gorer was in this direction, and that with the approval and even encouragement of their supervisors a high proportion of the current generation of senior anthropologists (trained just after the War) went off to be analyzed.

Nor is it necessarily a "good thing" to be self-conscious in the field. Obviously, one must be aware of one's impact, and the way interactions are affecting all parties concerned. Obviously, one must try to be sensitive and to see one's actions to some extent through the eyes and perceptions of others. And one must try to be aware of ways in which one's personal structure affects and biases the data and the interpretations one obtains and presents. Even W. H. R. Rivers and C. G. Seligmann knew that, as did others working at the turn of the century.

They also knew (and by modern standards overemphasized the point) that too much intimacy and self-consciousness could be counterproductive. In the present age of participant observation it appears that they themselves made the wrong judgments, as do a very high proportion of contemporary anthropologists, by depending upon formal interviews with minimal emotional content. Yet the person (fabled in denigrating myth, but very rare in fact) who goes to the other extreme by entering family life to the extent of establishing customary sexual relations for himself or herself is unlikely to gain much more significant knowledge, is likely to have a great deal deliberately hidden from him or her, and may end up wrecking himself or herself and traumatizing the community.

One must be self-conscious to the extent of knowing these things and seeing them in their various guises when they impinge on one's experience. But to spend one's life in the community—over the long period of twelve, eighteen, or twenty-four months of fieldwork (which are typical periods), continuously asking oneself "is this reaction going to be helpful or harmful?"—is to turn oneself into a kind of artificial puppet.

One's role depends on one's personality, which one must live with as naturally as possible. If there are limitations, both in one's personality and in the nature of the people with whom one is working, one must be sufficiently aware to allow them to govern the choice of subject matter and of society studied. I do not have the right kind of subtlety to open up deep questions of philosophy or religion; there are certain questions closed to me by limitations in linguistic and mathematical ability; I have an old-fashioned approach to opening up questions of sex in communities where I am still a stranger, however long my residence. Hence, I make no pretensions to deal with these kinds of issues in fieldwork terms. And I choose communities where my interests in economic, political, and transactional systems can be followed up with profit, particularly in a modern context. Other people choose differently. But if I chose a topic or a community where I felt I had to alter my "natural" behavior except in clear, overt, symbolic ways, I would rightly consider myself to be misplaced.

Thus, for me as an anthropologist, and for many other social scientists, there are choices as to field and topic, in which my knowledge of myself and prior knowledge of the nature of the community or organization in which I will be working play an enormous part. And, as present-day radicals were by no means the first to observe, my views on ethics and on political and other values are intertwined with these considerations.

In choosing my field, and to an even greater extent in choosing my topic, I must decide who my sponsors and my "clients" are going to be, and I must develop, as I become engaged with the research material, a conception as to how and to whom I am going to communicate the results.

If I am working in a foreign country, or in an area where colleagues are already established, I must consider ways in which it is possible for me to consult with colleagues and amend my plans so that they can complement and contribute to their goals as well as my own. I do not want to be accused of scientific "imperialism," of raiding and mining data, or of using my connections to provide tactical advantages in a competitive scholarly situation.

It is necessary for me to know the interests and backgrounds of my sponsors, and to determine whether they are compatible with my own; whether there are any "hidden" elements in the understandings, such as debriefings or conversations with third parties, or a need to maintain good relations with officials, which will affect my conduct. Who in fact are my "clients"? Am I writing under contract to the sponsors, so that in case of conflict their interests must predominate? Are we both committed to the scientific community, to the communication of dispassionate knowledge, to the statement of truth *whatever the social consequences might or might not be*? Am I free to withhold communication, if it, in my judgment, results in "bad" consequences—if, for example, a detached analysis shows that conditions are inflationary, but that the publication of that analysis would in fact contribute to increased inflation, or if the revelation of information would result in punitive action against my informants? Does this mean that I cannot investigate criminal groups, since I would be in possession of information of value to the police and since I could not ever fully guarantee complete security of documentation (particularly in the light of the fairly widespread practice of justifying the theft and copying of documents by moral purposes)? As a scientist, how "scientific" am I if I withhold key information of a generalized character because readers would interpret that information as indicating a social situation that required "correction" or cast people in a less than perfect light—for example, if I withhold information about the presence of prostitution, the former existence of head-hunting or cannibalism, the recourse to violence or vendetta, the practice of falsifying tax returns?

It is by no means an answer to discharge the responsibility by saying that I, as scientist, should not make such decisions; they should be made by the people I study. In some circumstances, this is practicable and possible. There is a difference in both my moral and my scientific position if I say to a parent, I have a tape-recorder in my pocket which I am using to record your interactions with your children, or, alternatively, if I use the recorder but fail to inform the parent. This is not a black and white matter, and the judgments depend on a host of circumstances. As I write, there is a scandal in Italy because of the publication of material drawn from tape recordings of confessionals treating sexual matters. If this material is genuine, it is probably data which have never before been objectively recorded, despite the obvious political motivation of the "investigators." Where does scientific and political justification begin and end? If the Italian investigators had been American anthropologists, would they not have been breaking the code of ethics? Yet, if they considered that this was the only way of getting at data that revealed a scandal, was it not justifiable? And if the material is obtained, do we as scientists then ignore it because of its provenance? We certainly bear its provenance in mind in interpreting its significance.

Field anthropologists are as different in their approaches as they are as individuals. In sensitive areas, a little knowledge, combined with confidence, opens up a lot more; the key is sometimes to obtain the first element of knowledge, which then opens the door to further enquiry and additional confidences. Several anthropologists—S. F. Nadel and Gerald Berreman, to name only two—have indicated techniques (bullying in the first instance, pretense in the second) which most colleagues avoid or frown upon. In the school of anthropology in which I was trained, it was accepted that notebooks and similar devices be frankly shown, never hidden, until over a period of time they came to be expected, taken naturally, treated almost as an article of clothing or an additional limb, so that activity goes on almost as if they were not there. Yet there are times when this is not appropriate. The anthropologist either abjures the enquiry or trusts to his memory and later recording; but is this not a kind of pretense? I once sat for days on end with people ready to participate in a religious revival ceremony; because they knew that I would be recording the events, they politely postponed the event from day to day until I gave up. If I had not had recorders, they still knew what I was doing and were able to adjust their behavior accordingly.

And when one reacts in situations of knowledge and intimacy, the line between passive enquiry (waiting for events to happen) and manipulation (making them happen) gets pretty thin. The use of informants—beloved by American anthropology, particularly when paid for—is manipulation. The frankness of the interaction is admirable, but it is also artificial and liable to abuse just because of the frankness. Yet passivity may not lead to results, and the distortion of time and chance observation is very possible. Sometimes the temptation to test one's hypothesis is strong. Once, in Fiji, I needed a small bridge for the use of my vehicle. I paid for it by "Western"-style colonial contract—it was badly built and collapsed. The next time I made use of my hypotheses. I called upon lineage feeling and the links of interaction, and made traditional ceremonial prestations. The bridge was rebuilt, solidly. If I had said, I'm doing things this way because I *think* this is the way your system works and I'm curious to see if I'm establishing the right stimulus, I would have destroyed the "experiment," and I don't think I would have been a more "ethical" anthropologist.

When I consider the great variety of types of research, of kinds of political and field situations that one faces, of varieties of persons with whom one is interacting, I find that codes based upon negative statements have a quality of absolutism (even where qualifications are entered) that render them quite unsuitable as mature professional guides. When such codes are linked to the possibility of punitive professional sanctions, they become positively dangerous.

The proposal of the Committee on Ethics of the American Anthropological Association, as published in the *Newsletter* of November 1970, is indicative of the problems. It was the result of long reflection and discussion and is couched in quite careful language. As a document to be used as the basis of discussion, for educative and developmental purposes, it is unexceptionable; one must begin somewhere, and any statement that leads to further clarification, and that can be used as a foil for argument, is worthwhile.

Unfortunately, the authors also had professional sanctions in mind, and made proposals for investigative procedures of individual cases, not for the purposes of further understanding but in order to lead to the possibility of discipline. As the report states: "Any sanctioning mechanisms which might be recommended would have to emerge from the experience of applying this procedure and with the approval of the membership. For example, they might range from simple publication of the ad hoc committee's findings, to a recommendation for expulsion from the Association. It is now premature to recommend such mechanisms." It is indeed.

But the linkage of the "Principles of Professional Responsibility" to such mechanisms even as a potentiality puts the statement in a totally different light, no longer as an educative mechanism but as a code—a quasi-legal one. Such a code should be clear, unambiguous, precise. Yet even the most innocent-looking proposals, which can be accepted at a superficial level, are inappropriate when interpreted absolutely.

Let us take one of the most innocent-looking provisions. "There should be no exploitation of individual informants for personal gain." The word "exploitation," while having a denigratory overtone, is now used in certain political circles in contexts where any commercial relationship is involved that results in profits or returns being made. If I combine factors of production of any kind, I exploit them. The intention of the prohibition is presumably to cover extreme cases in which, for example, an anthropologist obtains the life history of an individual and publishes it for royalties that accrue to him, the anthropologist, or collections of mythology that have been recounted almost as works of art. But the language does not distinguish these situations from others, where the issues are not clear-cut.

Every anthropologist is aware that when he enters the field and talks to people of the possibility of writing scientific papers and books, he arouses the image of royalty fortune making. The idea that scientific monographs do not on the whole produce meaningful income is rather subtle to explain, and when explained is frequently treated with frank disbelief. If this is so, why do it? Further, some of our more fortunate or skilled colleagues do in fact make an income from the publication of materials which, while usually at an analytic level, are sometimes very close to the field data. The work of Oscar Lewis, which was commercially successful, is a case in point. Was this not the use of material gained from informants and did it not result in an element of private gain?

More indirectly, one uses the fruits of one's experience for more general statements of wider appeal. The only book I have published that can be said to have made significant financial returns (and then by no means compensatory for the sum total of effort that produced it) drew heavily on my own field studies as well as on those of others. The book I am now presenting also does so. There is thus a considerable element in them that is derived from ideas and information of individual informants. To go one step further, one's progression in the academic hierarchy is based in part on research; this surely is personal gain, and one owes it in part to the people with whom one has talked.

Such a proscription rapidly becomes meaningless. One would have more sympathy with a formulation couched in positive terms, to the effect, perhaps, that one has an obligation to explain as best one can the sponsorship and personal interests that one has in the research to the people with whom one is working. Even that can seldom be done in the initial stages, at least with real accuracy. Most of us have had experience of letters of accreditation, of meeting with Band Councillors, of explaining to families and to village assemblies what it is we are up to. The initial conceptions, despite the fullest efforts, are often very superficial or off the mark. But as one makes personal contact and talks in a relaxed manner about one's own background and one's own society, an understanding has a chance of taking hold.

And then, at some point, if explanations are made, the people can indicate objections. I was recently involved at a distance in the possibility of making arrangements for Claude Levi-Strauss to be filmed in an Indian community. It was reported that previous films had been made in the community by academic groups, by documentary television companies, and the like, and that the people were fed up. We decided to hold off rather than risk rebuff. But I knew that the people concerned were fundamentally hospitable and generous, and that they knew what Professor Levi-Strauss's interest meant for the recognition and indeed the dissemination of their culture. As they came to know him as a person they in fact *wanted* the film to be made. In anthropology, one must take time, one must not rush things, and the results are based on interactions, not on rules.

The document of the American Anthropological Association goes on to say:

> In accordance with the Association's general position on clandestine and secret research, no reports should be provided to sponsors that are not also available to the general public and, where practicable, to the population studied

and

> [The anthropologist] should not communicate his findings secretly to some and withhold them from others

and

> [The anthropologist] should undertake no secret research or any research whose results cannot be freely derived and publicly reported.

In principle, and with glosses, there is good reason to consider these issues to be important and serious. But the formulators do not appear to realize the force of exceptions to the rules, and the many occasions in which it would be nonsense to apply them literally. The key to the complication lies in the consideration of the implications of further statements made in the same document:

> Every effort should be exerted to cooperate with members of the host society in the planning and execution of research projects

and

> All of the above points should be acted upon in full recognition of the social and cultural pluralism of host societies and the consequent plurality of values, interests and demands in those societies. This diversity complicates choice-making in research, but ignoring it leads to irresponsible decisions.

Indeed. Here are illustrations of some of the complications linked to the last two quotations that make nonsense of a literal interpretation of the first three proscriptions.

In the early 1950s, in the Territory of Papua, an Englishman and a Papuan woman announced their intention to marry. Both were influential, engaged in innovative and significant socioeconomic activities, often of a politically controversial nature. The notion of such a marriage was at the time almost unheard of, and the Administration was under attack (from Papuans as well as Australians) to try to prevent it happening, perhaps even to expel the Englishman. I was present in the Territory at the time as an independent anthropologist, and was approached by the Administrator of the day to make a quiet enquiry into the opinions and state of feeling of the village people with whom the couple were in closest contact, particularly since allegations had been made that violence might ensue. I agreed to do this, and presented a *confidential* report. The Administrator was able to use that report to reinforce his position, and to call the bluff of the critics; but he did it quietly and without raging public controversy. The couple married and remained in the Territory to its benefit. No purpose would have been served, and much damage would have been done to the two individuals, whose private lives were at stake, by the publication of the details of my research. If any professional body had then informed me that by doing this I was *unprofessionally* engaging in clandestine research of a confidential nature and keeping the results secret, I would have told them to mind their own business.*

On another occasion, I was asked by the British Columbia Credit Union League to examine internal interactions between constituent organizations, and the ideology and rationale which lay behind an internal struggle for power which was threatening to destroy the League through schism. I accepted, in part because I felt that this would provide me with an interesting insight into the workings and stresses of a federated organization. While the eventual report became public, it was cast in a generalized

---

* An opposite incident occurred about the same time. I gave a talk to a scientific society in Port Moresby, explaining my research methods and how I arrived at figures showing malnutrition and below-minimum income for urban villagers. Unknown to me there was a reporter present, who splashed the story sensationally across the front page of the local paper. No harm was done, except to the self-esteem of the Department of Territories in Canberra, which formally protested to the Australian National University, then employing me. The Head of my Department rapped me over the knuckles and placed complete restraints on any public statements I might make and on any consultation with government! I refused to comply and told him that the material would appear in my research report anyway, and that in this kind of instance it did no harm for both government and public to know the truth.

form that raised issues for the League to tackle, with suggestions as to how to go about it. But the report would have been much more trenchant, and more useful, if I had *not* insisted on its public nature as part of my contract. For, as the enquiry progressed, it became quite clear that a major element in the problem was a determined attempt to gain control of the League by an *American* organization concerned with profit making and objectives quite contradictory to those of the credit union movement in Canada. This was by no means the only concern, and it was referred to in general. But by insisting on publication, I removed the possibility of providing key factual and concrete evidence; in my concern for neutrality, I failed to put weapons in the hands of my clients. If I had made this choice as the result of the application of a professional code, I would have been even less responsible and the profession itself would have been guilty of irresponsibility. Yet if I were to take the "principles" of the American Anthropological Association literally, this in fact would be the result.

On one occasion I accepted a mission from the United Nations to work on a project which raised important issues with regard to technical assistance, and was destined to have a significant impact on the evolution of that process. As is normal in such cases, my curriculum vitae was supplied to the government for approval and clearance of my appointment. The vita was full and frank, but the United Nations correspondence described me as a sociologist, not as an anthropologist. The public mythology of the time, insofar as this government was concerned, was that anthropologists were concerned with the archaic past, and to admit them to study in the country implied that the country was primitive. No one was in fact deceived by the deception, but deception it nevertheless was in principle. Had it not taken place, the appointment would not have been made. I decided that this was not the time or the place to make an issue on behalf of the prestige and importance of anthropology, and consider now that my judgment was correct, and that the results of the activity amply justified the judgment.

Further, when one is working under such circumstances, it is with a team of persons from different nationalities. The country in which one works is quite likely to have had the experience of obnoxious, mischievous, and patently erroneous reports presented to it in the past. Given the current force of the principle of nationalism, it is not going to agree in advance to an international team publishing a report without at least preliminary review and possibly clearance. Insistence on the right to publish *a priori* means in most instances that the national government considers that you, the foreign worker, are insisting on an imperial kind of superiority to its authority, and the work will simply not get done. In most instances, the publication depends on negotiation, upon mutual confidence, and upon the right of the government to make its reservations known. In the case of the study that Harry Hawthorn, Stuart Jamieson, and I carried out on the position and administration of the Indians of British Columbia in the late 1950s, the sponsoring agent (the Government of Canada) did agree *a priori* to publication, but they saw the text first and had ample opportunity to raise points of fact or disagreement. Nevertheless, we as authors held final responsibility.

Any study of the social, economic, and political condition of a people in the contemporary world implies placing their condition in a wider setting. The moment you enter a village or urban district and begin an enquiry, you establish social relations and place yourself in a political context, committed or neutral, allied or opposed. There is no escaping this, though its effects may be substantially modified. This is what is meant by the American Anthropological Association's phrase "social and cultural pluralism of host societies." If you do as is called for—namely, "cooperate with members of the host society"—you must choose which members. If you look at questions of political power and authority, you are led to study, for example, such diverse mechanisms as the police and courts, political parties standing for very different things, individuals exercising patronage, families in feud and vendetta, banks and foreign businessmen, even agents of multinational corporations or guerrilla movements. Are you obliged by this fact to *represent* them all in your reports? If you are obliged to respect the "rights, interests and sensitivities" of those you study in all cases, then you rule out criticism; you rule out reporting facts that have significant political repercussions; you cannot tell the Colombian Government that its actions are destroying peoples to the point of near-genocide, for you will have studied that government and must respect its sensitivities; the fact that it has allowed you into the country to do your work implies that it has trusted you.

No. As an anthropologist you must make political and ethical judgments at every step of your procedures, just as you make intellectual, methodological, even aesthetic judgments. Research and learning are judgmental operations; you judge significance, you judge the validity and quality of the work of your colleagues and students, you judge the world in which you live, you judge the "relevance" of the phenomena you observe. No professional code and no professional society can stand between the individual anthropologist and the situation he faces in the field, or as he writes. The beginnings of a trend in this direction must be stopped, and stopped firmly. Anthropologists must insist—vis-à-vis their colleagues and, above all, vis-à-vis governments—on their right and responsibility to pursue their activities in the light of their individual judgment. The role of professional associations should be to help, not hinder, them in this task.

This does not imply anarchic nonresponsibility. The ultimate sanction is the reputation of the anthropologist among the people with whom he works and among his colleagues as time renders the judgment mature. An anthropologist cannot, in this day of manifold views, be equally judged by all parties; if he is, he has probably made a very minor or insignificant contribution. The "neutral" anthropologist is judged by his intellectual attainments and contributions, but may be denigrated by men and women who search for immediate reform. The "applied" anthropologist is bound to be in the midst of debate and controversy. The moment the two are fused by professional demands, the moment a code is put into effect that unjustifiably rules out legitimate value stances in the name of majority morality, at those moments anthropology, and its contribution to human knowledge, understanding, and welfare, are in serious jeopardy.

CHAPTER 18

The Social Sciences Organized

SOCIAL sciences primarily oriented to research and understanding in the academic world are not professions in the normal sense. The profession that most social scientists adopt is that of university teacher, with research as well as teaching functions. It is here that he has specific duties and obligations to others that must be stated, and he has power and influence with students which, despite the theory of academic freedom, imply *organized* constraints, in the name of responsibility, upon his behavior.

There are also social scientists in other roles. It can be argued that social scientists who work as civil servants not only link to the profession of civil servant—with its attendant expectations, duties, obligations, and rights—but within that category have *special* obligations attached to their mode of analysis and the way it is used by the remainder of the civil service and by government. Social scientists in this role, it can be argued, have *different* professional obligations from those who teach in universities.

I make these points because the concept of a profession, while it may have subbranches, is built around a relative unity of social role, implying that the variety of objectives and experiences of its members is bounded. This makes it possible to attach professional expectations of behavior, usually embodied in a code or set of principles, to its members, who accept the code on joining the profession. There is a certain sense in which every organized profession sets limits upon its activity through the enshrinement of a mythological charter; indeed, this deliberate and necessary characteristic of professional organization frequently puts it in inherent conflict with university values, since these are based on the consideration that *any* fact, theory, or moral principle is open to enquiry and free examination. The entry of professional control into university professional schools is nearly always to the detriment of free enquiry at the professional moral level.

Within the social sciences, but not yet very much within anthropology, it is possible to find groupings which are sufficiently large and united in mode of operation to constitute small professions. Clinical psychology, educational psychology, economics in government, and economics in industry are possible examples in which action demands a professional stance, the rights and wrongs of which could be linked to the symbolic unity of a statement of professional principles.

But for the social sciences and individual disciplines writ large, the variety of experience and objective in action is so great as to make professionalization in this sense unwise, damaging, and unduly restrictive of the freedom to act in terms of the dictates of one's sense of responsibility. It is likely that, as the social sciences extend their applications, elements in them will attain the kind of unity and coherence and the need for corporate protection that is implied in professionalization. For these subgroups, ethical and professional codes may become essential. But every step in this direction implies a constraint, and ultimately a sacred area in which questions are seldom debated and answers are a matter of professional faith. The character of the social sciences implies that if they are to retain their sense of questioning in all social matters, those matters must include their own character and role. Hence, it is essential that a significant proportion of social science should lie *outside* those professional elements that adhere to professional doctrine.

This does not mean to say that social science associations do not have professional roles of a kind. They do, but I am arguing that they stop short of *full* professional characteristics.

There is indeed a considerable need for social scientists, at the national level, to be able to act together for special purposes. This is most evident in the discipline associations that are channels for the organization of scholarly and research-oriented interaction. Social scientists also have an interest in the conditions that affect their own work and the ways in which external authorities and organizations approach the questions that fall within their field of competence.

With regard to the former, in some countries (perhaps especially the United States, Britain, and France) social scientists, acting within the institutional arrangements open to them, have been extraordinarily successful in ensuring that certain *kinds* of support are available, when needed, for research. In other countries this has not been so. For example, in Canada *no* organization exists anywhere to which a social scientist can turn as a matter of course to apply for material equipment of substantial size (such as computer retrieval devices or social laboratory construction) unless he is in a field such as psychology, which can be defined as a biological discipline. Again, an essential element in the training of students in modern social research is to be able to handle teams of data gatherers who can obtain the raw information or make use of photographic or recording equipment. In many countries such resources are available for fully qualified researchers, but are excluded from supply to the research students who are supposed to be learning how to undertake complex enquiry. Where such conditions occur social scientists have failed to persuade financing authority of their needs and must clearly learn to act corporately with more effective influence.

Again, the use of social science outside the standard academic sphere is often pathetically weak. This is partly because in-house social science advice to government about the scientific viability of projects is often low in quality, or good advice is swept aside by the political need for haste, so that the terms of reference are unrealistic. This means that many of the best social scientists refuse to cooperate or find excuses not to, and the level of work is directed at inappropriate questions and is poorly carried out.

This, in turn, can sometimes be traced to two sets of conditions. The first is that many social scientists in key fields such as sociology, anthropology, and political science have been trained in an atmosphere that is not directed toward applied considerations, but where the rewards lie in esoteric theoretical constructions. In Britain this has at times gone so far in some disciplines that (for example, in sociology) the applied elements have almost constituted a separate discipline with only the most tenuous links with "standard" fundamental studies. This is not necessarily "bad." The later fusing of these two trends in Britain is at present leading to a conception of sociology rather different from that in other countries and with a more penetrating and "relevant" empirical base.

The other condition is that the institutional apparatus for social science research is defective. In France, through the organization of the Centre National de Recherche Scientifique, a more or less permanent network of specialized research institutions exists that is devoted systematically to the *long-term* study of social science questions (at least, in theory). This organization is by no means ideal, since in its detailed application it contains many professional tensions and conflicts of interest with universities, and there is a considerable difference between the theory and the practice. Yet, in principle it contrasts with the situation in most other countries.

In these, although there are examples of specialized research institutions working in the long term, by far the bulk of social science research is carried out in universities. Universities, however creative their objectives, have fields of study to cover through teaching; this means that there is an inherent interest in spreading, rather than in concentrating, competences. You do not employ two people in a field where one will do. Universities overcome this limitation from time to time by grafting research positions onto the structure over and above the basic teaching requirement. But this is usually financed by grants or contracts, and the institutes or teams so formed are notoriously dependent on "soft money" with the possibility of termination at any time. If the field of research becomes unfashionable to donors, or if there is a general cutback in financing, such work is the first to suffer, and it sometimes takes a courageous, unusually independent, or desperate man to accept such a "career."

What is needed is a recognition that applied social research as well as fundamental studies require patient, detailed work, with the fitting together of many analytic parts and elements of data over long periods of time. Answers to complex issues (such as, for example, the genesis of social violence) will not be found by the coordination of interdisciplinary research teams, or reflective think-tanks, operating on a one-, two-, or five-year contract. They will be found through numerous research enterprises addressed to different aspects of the problem over decades. This is understood in medical research. It is time it was understood in social research.

Further, social research results in changes in the phenomena themselves, even in the abstract principles and theoretical generalizations used to interpret the phenomena. Even if this were not so, social conditions are continually changing, much faster, for example, than biological or geological conditions (except where influenced by man), so that monitoring of changes in data and consequent reinterpretations are necessary. In the natural sciences there are complex monitoring devices to keep track of meteorological conditions, the population of biological species, conditions affecting the formation of water, vibrations in the planet, and a host of other matters. In the social sciences, statistical services provide some monitoring activity, but the range is limited, the global distribution so crude as to be quite misleading, and the link with scientific thought in some instances primitive. Private or university monitoring organizations are extremely rare.

These conditions suggest that, at a time when many of the richer countries are complaining of an oversupply and underemployment of social scientists, the institutional basis for their constructive use is inadequate. It can even be said that there is a danger that it directs social scientific activity in uncreative directions. The situation and need are so complex that no government or academic group acting alone is likely to produce a social science policy for a nation that is capable of forging adequate new institutions with appropriate mixes of continuity and flexibility, from fundamental theory to routine monitoring, capable of providing both short-term answers and long-term attacks overnight.

In these kinds of issues, dialogue between scholars and financing authority is obviously essential, and the professional discipline associations provide an important element of analysis and representation of the academic analysis. Where (as in Canada and Switzerland) the individual discipline associations have an organization that provides the possibility of intercommunication and contact,* the growth of the dialogue is even more likely to be fruitful. There are, however, two limitations. One is the entrenched university orientation of academic social scientists, unwilling to see the possibility of important research outside the university context, contrasted with the sense of haste in government. The other is that despite the possibility of some concentration of existing effort, the true establishment of monitoring and long-term research institutions is likely to involve an increase in social science manpower and expenditure of considerable dimensions if it is to be effective.

An additional issue, which cannot be handled entirely by isolated national effort, is the maldistribution of social science skills among disciplines, between applied and fundamental research, and even more between countries. A very high proportion of the world's social scientists lives and works in the United States; if you put the United States and Europe together, they might well account for 90 percent of employed social scientists. Many of the social scientists working in other countries have been trained to see perspectives and to use methods that inhibit them from developing original viewpoints appropriate to the real problems that face them. This is sometimes obscured, as in some forms of economics, by the apparent similarity of statistical data and the mechanistic nature of the methodology. It is also often reinforced, and counterten-

---

* The Social Science Research Council of Canada is a formal federation of individual social science discipline associations. The Société Suisse des Sciences Humaines (changed in 1974 to an Academy) does not have quite the same authority as its Canadian counterpart, but also groups discipline contacts. It is interesting to note that in 1973 the Swiss Federal Constitution was amended by referendum to make it a formal responsibility of the Federation to support scientific research.

dencies are obscured, by the strength of orthodox publication devices and the fac* that international social science journals are frequently dominated by the viewpoints and criteria of their main readership, established in the richer countries. There are signs of changes, as unorthodox social scientists (rightly or wrongly) challenge establishment assumptions, and as publications media become stronger in non-Western countries. Nevertheless, as a broad generalization, the standing and distribution of social science in a large part of the world, including some of the richer countries, are extraordinarily weak by comparison with the better established countries and even more by comparison with the jobs that need to be done.

In the natural sciences there is a considerable amount of international cooperation. Governments at all levels have supplied moral and financial support for scientific development. This has to be built on a basis of training, so that educational institutions everywhere now have at least the elements of instruction in fundamental science and mathematics. While the higher organs of research in some countries may be limited to apparently applied problems, many of these cannot be tackled without some rearrangement of fundamental knowledge, so that the existence of an applied issue in the natural sciences has the merit of demanding some kind of link with fundamental work.

This seems easier to escape in some social science sectors; commentary or intelligent observation can take place without a knowledge of the literature, and it does not take much to put this in a form that asserts "science." This is in itself often valuable and not to be denigrated. The point is, however, that it does not *necessarily* call forth fundamental science, and may indeed bypass it, so that fundamental social scientists, where they exist in many countries, find their knowledge and skills ignored by the politically oriented commentators.

Social science communities in many countries, then, need help for them to establish their own role, their own strength, and their own power base; while they must resist the old forms of intellectual imperialism, they need to participate in world scientific life and to draw support and strength from it. This, after all, has not been unusual. Russian social science is weakest where it is most inward-looking, strongest where it has learned from and argued with others. The United States has drawn great strength from foreign inputs, and is showing signs of a hardness of the arteries since they have become less recognized. Canada is likely to gain great vitality from the fact that about 60 percent of her social scientists are non-Canadian in origin. Britain has continuously drawn inspiration from abroad into its milieu, though it has perhaps been slow in using it; and France seems to be beginning to realize that its intellectual autarchy is not good enough to last forever.

Support for international cooperation in social science comes in three ways. National funding agencies will, occasionally, support work abroad in the interests of their own national scholarship. If this is well conceived, it can sometimes have a component of financing and design that provides for cooperation with scholars in the host country; foundations can occasionally make this specific. But, on the whole, funding agencies are becoming even more nationalistic, often require special arguments to justify work abroad, restrict their financing to their own scholars, and fail to insist on equality in cooperative projects with foreign scholars. By far the greatest proportion of overseas scholarship still fails to be cast in a cooperative mold, except in the most symbolic and inoperative of senses, and the number of overseas scholars funded from national sources from the richer countries is infinitesimal, unless they have migrated to the funding country in question.

The second type of support comes within the rubric of bilateral cultural agreements, which provide for exchanges of scholarly and scientific personnel among other things. While some such agreements (for example, that between France and Canada) have fairly ambitious statements leading to the idea of long-term cooperation between institutions, in practice administrative devices limit the application to the short-term and the small-scale. Such arrangements are invaluable for increasing understanding based upon the movement of professors and students. But they do not go far beyond the provision of one-year visits for professors (often much shorter) or opportunities for postgraduate students to obtain research degrees. Worse, they are almost entirely limited to arrangements between the richer countries, and have little application to countries outside this circle.

This leaves the variety of arrangements that can be brought together under the heading of technical assistance, although sometimes they fall outside of that rubric. UNESCO Fellowships, for example, are available for short-term visits, particularly involving several countries, and such rich countries as the Soviet Union have used them for visits of scholars to Canada. This is hardly technical assistance in the narrow sense of the word. But the same mechanism is available for scholars in developing countries to improve their applied knowledge and basic training through almost all the multilateral international agencies. Further, projects under the aegis of the United Nations Development Programme, and numerous bilateral assistance arrangements, are available for assistance for the improvement of social science infrastructure. Nearly all of this work, where it can be identified, is limited either (a) to the welding of a social science component onto an applied project concerned with some other objective—let us say agricultural extension or the resettlement of a population as a result of dam construction, or (b) to creating a training institute (say, for planners or criminologists) or a university department.

Such assistance does have the effect of improving infrastructure and of producing identifiable research. It is not, however, directed toward the needs of the social sciences themselves, except occasionally in a university or similar context. I do not know of any systematic program in any international agency (including UNESCO) or any bilateral aid arrangement that is specifically oriented to the priority of establishing a self-sufficient, well-balanced social science infrastructure in any country, linked to a conscious social science policy. The accordance of status to social scientists that would enable them to advise governments responsibly and freely and handle relations with foreign social scientists on the basis of equality and strength is rare. Despite the great hullabaloo and rhetoric that holds that the next great priority in man's welfare lies in the ordering of the social realm and the orientation of action to cultural and "life" values, the work of the social scientist and the cultural scholar and artist is still at the bottom of development priorities. And this as much as anything is a result of the technocratic influence of the developed countries, which have in some instances given such programs low priorities themselves, and which tend to define these areas out of the realm of development aid. (Their representatives will tell you that the developing countries do not ask for this kind of assistance; this is in part true, but we have analyzed the reasons for the vicious circle in Chapter 13.)

The situation will not change until national governments themselves translate platitudes about social objectives into realities for the support of social science infrastructure and of the intellectual base that makes research and well-founded advice possible. In the meantime, social scientists themselves, linked in various associations with their colleagues in other countries, have a great deal to do to put their own international house in order. They need a framework to exercise influence on governments and on international organizations, particularly in the United Nations setting, on matters of professional concern to them; and they need it for their own international action and coordination. Here are some of the more concrete things that must be done.

First, there is a need to improve the state of comparative and cooperative research. We have already seen how this tends to be done nowadays. In a very few instances, the concept of the way in which such cooperation can come about has evolved to the suggestion of projects in which mixed teams from countries A and B—possessing complementary characteristics of viewpoint, training and methodology—conduct projects in country A, supplemented by similarly mixed teams working on replicative or comparative projects in country B. If any scholar reading this stops to consider the administrative difficulties involved in handling such a series of projects through existing funding arrangements, he will see that very few, if any, government funding agencies have the slightest idea of what such research involves by way of techniques of support. Hence it does not happen.

Allied to this concept is the desirability of encouraging research conducted by scholars from countries that tend to be thought of as developing, or recipients of aid, *in the richer countries* themselves, not for training purposes, but to obtain comparative knowledge through their *own* examination of data, and not merely through the eyes of scholars in the richer countries. It is also to make a contribution to general knowledge by looking at, let us say, American or European institutions and phenomena through the perspective of non-American and non-European values. Some of this kind of thought is in fact being applied in Canada, though on a modest scale, through the immigration of social scientists from elsewhere and their observations of Canadian society. This, however, is so far very low key, and is not quite the same thing as, for example, Japanese or Indian or African social scientists visiting Canada or the United States to conduct research there on a basis of reciprocity and operational equality.

We have also noted that many political, economic, and cultural phenomena of great importance have international cross-cultural repercussions, even organization. Despite the archaism of nationalism and the occasional strengthening of autarchic ideas the significance of both multiethnicity within national boundaries and the crisscross of international phenomena is bound to grow. If there is any truth in this, it suggests that a similar phenomenon is likely to occur in social science viewpoints and organization. We can see the possibility of social scientists of different persuasions, differing methods and premises, organizing and acting across national boundaries with colleagues of like mind.

In all of this there is the need for a certain kind of peacekeeping mission among social scientists. It is regrettable that social scientists from different countries (just as members of other disciplines and professions) have reason to resent the presence and behavior of foreign colleagues. This is particularly true where the foreign colleague thinks he has observed all protocol and is highly cooperative but in fact has merely tipped his hat to his fellow scientists and then gone off to monopolize the research field, with a team of students and with minimal further interaction. It is true where the foreign colleague works with political values that the resident colleague dislikes. It is true where the foreign colleague has considerable funds (or, more frequently, seems to have them), which he unconsciously uses to establish his dominance, sharing, if at all, on the basis of patronage rather than in design and control. It is true where the foreign colleague is more or less guaranteed a publication outlet and hence international recognition. It is true where the foreign colleague is accorded respect by the host government, and a freedom to express himself, which is denied to the scientist of the country or is dangerous for him. It is doubly true when the foreign colleague comes from a country that would itself resist, formally or by convention, the entry of foreign social science research into its territory.

I use the term peacekeeping only to indicate that at a modest level such differences make their own contribution to international tension and misunderstanding. Sometimes these may blow up into incidents, in which it could be necessary or desirable, for example, for an objective, international social science association to use its good offices to resolve or modify disagreements or misunderstandings between, let us say, the social scientists of the United States and India, of Australia and Fiji, of Russia and Yugoslavia. It is more important in the long run that such associations address themselves to the basic issues and find ways and means of exercising influence to modify them. Such issues include political linkages of social scientists, the status accorded indigenous social science in its own country, its ability to finance cooperation and representation in international social science circles, the infrastructure and resources with which it can operate, and its general intellectual recognition. If the world distribution and status of social scientists could be rectified, many of these issues would fall into place and solve themselves.*

There is another, even more tricky, concern involved in international social science relations. The world hears a great deal of the persecution of artists and writers by authoritarian governments. Not so well known, but

*The International Social Science Council is establishing a project along these lines.

just as vicious, is the persecution of social scientists and the nonrecognition of certain fields as a whole. Social and cultural anthropology are completely absent in certain countries as a result of decisions about social science policy based upon ideological considerations. It is well known that it would be impossible for Western scholars, and even local scholars, to conduct field studies on sensitive topics in most of the Soviet bloc and in China, even though communist social science has broadened its base substantially in recent years. While particular instances of persecution (for example, in Spain, Greece, and Brazil) have been made the subject of international social science protest—largely by groups of colleagues acting privately—I know of no organization that is internationally active to protect freedoms of enquiry to justifiable limits or that is prepared to say bluntly, formally, and with pressure that given countries are restricting social science intellectual freedom and persecuting those who try to exercise it.

The United Nations Assembly, justifiably, gangs up on South Africa and Rhodesia to attack apartheid (after which many countries, in their private national interest, avoid the logical consequences). I do not see either UNESCO or the United Nations Commission on Human Rights prepared to come to grips with the less "popular" issue of the protection of intellectual freedoms in the fields covered by the social sciences. Social scientists will themselves be hypocritical and powerless unless they can find ways and means of persuading them to do so.*

Not unconnected with this is the problem to which I have referred elsewhere in passing: the dilemma of the social scientist who finds himself in possession of "evidence" of severe unethical or criminal conduct, particularly when perpetrated by or with the connivance or encouragement of governments. The social scientist who is in this position, and whose conscience drives him to the point of action, needs advice, help, and support. If he attempts to move alone, he is normally in trouble and can do more harm than good. He may place his colleagues in jeopardy as social scientists, his naïveté with regard to political and legal processes may lead to his own persecution and punishment, and he may drive the offending parties to use more subtle ways of covering their behavior.

In some instances, he may be able to secure aid from more specialized

---

*The great weight of UNESCO's concern with universities, for example, has been with administrative and technical matters, general coordination, and studies of higher education's linkage with such processes as development. I see very little reference to, let alone examination or defense of, intellectual freedom and the bases of creativity in the university context.

groups, such as Amnesty International. He does not on the whole have effective access to United Nations organs, where these are able and willing to be committed, since to move them to action requires complex international government pressure—by its nature difficult to achieve in such cases. He may find that the issues he is protesting about are defined outside the conventions of international law and agreement and are regarded as the internal affairs of the country concerned.

The road to action and pressure varies according to the circumstances, and the identification of the correct method is in itself a matter of skill and knowledge. Social scientists in this position remind me very much of the 19th-century missionaries who were often in a unique position to observe slavery and brutality, but who in almost all instances failed to bring successful court cases because their knowledge of legal process and of the legal opportunities which were open to them was limited. Further, in most instances, their knowledge of the rules of evidence acceptable to courts of law having jurisdiction was incredibly naïve; case after case was lost in Australia, for example, because the missionary litigants depended upon evidence that could be branded as hearsay.

At the moment, it is almost impossible for social scientists to handle these issues effectively and systematically. The International Union of Anthropological and Ethnological Sciences has established a commission to begin work in this field, but the experiment is only now being organized. There are a number of active public-information-style groups in various countries, some of which are unfortunately undermined by a political reputation. The most successful, in its modest activity and political objectivity, is the group based in Copenhagen called the "International Work Group on Indigenous Affairs," which, however, has the funds only to produce a series of documentary descriptions and papers.*

As long as such efforts lack the support of legal and international advice, they will not get very far. There is, however, evidence that elements in Brazilian policy, for example, have responded as a result of widespread international pressure. It may well be that the information effort will result in an increasing public awareness and the creation of instruments which social scientists can use to make their observations and opinions more seriously felt.

---

*The papers have so far dealt with such topics as genocide, cultural attacks, and interference with property possession, for example, in Australia, Eritrea, the Bihar Province of India, the Amazon, Colombia, the forest areas of Peru and Paraguay. Each is based on anthropological experience. The papers and a newsletter are published by the Group from its address at Frederiksholms Kanal 4A, DK-1220 Copenhagen K, Denmark.

To sum up, there seems to be a need for social science international organization to address itself to the following kinds of tasks:

(a) considerations of the nature of social science policy from the point of view of the healthy growth of basic social science, including the principles that govern support;
(b) considerations of the modes of applying social science to applied problems, national and international, and the modes of interaction between government and other authority and social scientists;
(c) the direct undertaking of suitable coordination of research effort and communication on particular themes;
(d) the consideration of the infrastructure and mechanisms for improving the nature and scale of international social science cooperation on scholarly projects;
(e) acting as an agent for good offices where tensions exist between social scientists in different countries;
(f) defending the freedom of research and the liberty of expression;
(g) assisting social scientists to find or create instruments for the defense of cultures and the protection of human rights where they observe these to be in danger; and
(h) influencing governments and taking direct action to improve the position of colleagues in other countries, and to secure a more equitable distribution of social science roles and expertise throughout the world.

The main formal instruments that social scientists can use for these purposes are the international discipline scholarly associations, usually bringing scholars together in large World Scientific Congresses held every four or five years. Such associations include the International Economics Association, the International Sociological Association, and the International Union for Anthropological and Ethnological Sciences. A minority of such associations has been effective in maintaining cooperative research committees with special programs between Congresses, for which they obtain special funding. On the whole, they lack the administrative structure and the finances to back up the activity of lobbying government and official institutions, let alone of undertaking direct action programs themselves. There are also regional associations beginning to become operative in Africa, Asia, and Latin America—each with its own characteristics.

A major problem is the representation and participation of scholars from all but the richer countries. This is a constant criticism, but very difficult to overcome given financial limitations and the fact that in some disciplines in many countries there are no representative groups which can choose delegates and participants.

The international discipline associations are now (since September 1972) federated into the newly reconstituted International Social Science Council, but it is too soon, at this time of writing, to foresee the extent to which the new arrangements will result in an updated role, increased resources and financing, and an expansion of administrative structure to enable these most complex tasks to be pursued effectively. The International Social Science Council is also developing lines of contact and coordination with national Social Science Research Councils or their equivalents, but it is symptomatic that these vary from private nonfunding associations to government funding and policy institutions, and that they exist in only a handful of countries. Most countries lack any institution at all which can speak for social science, or in some instances any discipline within social science, let alone influence the formation of national social science policy.

The complexity of the handling of matters on an international scale is very great indeed, so that it is no wonder that many social scientists give up. The following hypothetical illustration, though of an extreme case, is indicative.*

Let us assume that the Social Science Research Council of Canada, which is a nongovernment organization federating the national discipline associations, through its Standing Committee on International Scholarly Relations, decides among other things to focus on three objectives: (a) to influence UNESCO to place a greater proportion of its total effort in the support of fundamental social science, on the grounds that applied social science cannot be built on inadequate foundations; (b) to create a framework that makes long-term social science cooperation possible between Canada and India; (c) to bring about an active program of technical assistance with the objective of improving the possibilities of Third World participation in international social scientific organizations and programs.

For goal (a), since the Council and its Committees federally represent the disciplines, it may be assumed that the Canadian associations representing each discipline are in agreement or are prepared to cooperate where they have the ability. Contact is therefore made through each

*While the illustration is not intended to be historical, it grows out of a related experience. The facts are, however, somewhat "invented" in order to illustrate relationships that were not used as systematically in the historical event.

national discipline association to the Canadian representatives to each *international* discipline association. Where the international discipline association has consultative status with UNESCO as a nongovernmental organization, it can make direct representations to the UNESCO secretariat. Further, it is now possible for each international association to make representations to the International Social Science Council, which in its turn can make equivalent representations to the UNESCO secretariat. All this is on the assumption that in each discipline the Canadian initiative is well handled by the Canadian delegates who must convince their colleagues from other nations.

In addition, since the proposal will not be without effect on the total distribution of the UNESCO budget, and possibly its total size (and, hence, the proposal must be seen within the overall scheme of UNESCO priorities involving other interests), the pressure must deal with these. The social science secretariat in UNESCO is unlikely to be able to change such priorities itself; the overwhelming trend is to maintain existing proportionate relationships in emphasis. The Canadian Social Science Research Council must therefore persuade first of all the Canadian Government and official representation of the validity of its argument.

This in itself is not enough, since the pressure must be timed to fit the formation of UNESCO program outlines and budgetary priorities, and one government is insufficient to make major changes. It is essential, therefore, that the Canadian Research Council put forward its proposals at the right time and with good basic information, for which it is dependent on its relations with the National UNESCO Commission. It must also seek international support and complementary pressures. It therefore asks the Canadian delegations to the international disciplinary associations to draw the tactic to the attention of their colleagues in other countries, asking each of them to communicate with their national UNESCO Commissions and if necessary directly with the officials who are responsible for their country's policy vis-à-vis UNESCO. If this worked in each member country there would be eight or ten voices representing different disciplines, each urging much the same policy.

In addition, the Canadian Commission for UNESCO, acting in approval of the suggestion, is theoretically in a position to contact each of the other National Commissions directly and urge them to support the proposal and to ask their national representatives to support it and help initiate it. If Canadians have taken such a concerted line of initiative, it is probable that there will be a reflection of the pressure in the secretariat's proposals to the General Conference, and that contacts of Canadian delegates with members of other delegations will ensure that there is little difficulty in its passage.

Of course, such systematic contact and agreement are never achievable. But even half that achievement is likely to constitute a major initiative. To do it requires an awareness of the part they are playing by all the Canadian social scientists involved in international representation—in itself not easy to achieve—and their success in mobilizing the interests of their colleagues from other countries. This takes coordination, time, energy, and indeed money. It also takes the initiative to formulate agreed and practical proposals.

The second goal, the creation of long-term research coordination between, let us say, India and Canada, has different complications. In each country there are Social Science Research Councils, which (though their statutes and functions differ—the one being governmental, the other voluntary) at least partially simplify the issues. It is possible for discipline associations interested in such cooperation to coordinate approaches through the discipline associations themselves or through the Councils. When the principle of cooperation has been agreed upon as an objective, with the possibility foreseen of joint teams working on allied themes in each other's countries, the proposal is still a long way from implementation. It is likely that, apart from the interest of one or two initiators, neither group really knows the extent to which there is an interest in coordination, nor what the range of concrete topics is likely to be, except in an illustrative theoretical context. Hence, each national group is immediately confronted with a major task of communication with colleagues to survey the degree to which an interest exists, and what the scientific objectives are likely to be. If there is little interest, the matter will presumably be closed. If there is interest, the examination then proceeds to the consideration of ways and means, for it will be certain that existing forms of funding will be operating with inadequate rules, based upon nationalistic concepts. It is therefore a major task for the initiating institutions in each country to influence funding agencies to amend or bend the rules to make long-term package cooperation, involving scholars of differing seniority and skills and nationality, to participate in joint enquiry, in each other's countries, upon explicitly stated agreed research themes.

The third goal is perhaps in some ways the most difficult of all. Technical assistance agencies have, I think, been defeated by unimaginative, sometimes incompetent, sometimes politically disturbing, and considerably outdated approaches to social science growth. There is an atmosphere on all sides of unwillingness to face the significance and importance of social science freedom, training, and infrastructure, and the long-term subtle arrangements that are necessary to encourage a climate of creativity in which questions can be posed and answers arrived at and discussed.

A Canadian initiative in this field requires new approaches to overcome the hurdle. The first would be to make use of the private connections of Canadian scholars to identify countries and subject areas in which their colleagues in other countries established need—that is, through the Canadian Social Science Research Council to initiate communication and knowledge and an input from other countries.

If and when such need were identified, overseas scholars might be in a position to persuade their own governments to include aid requests for specific purposes in their technical assistance agenda. That, however, is not likely to happen unless the countries concerned *believe* that Canada or United Nations agencies are likely to supply such aid if requested. It is therefore necessary for the Canadian Social Science Research Council, armed with specific information, to collaborate with their overseas colleagues and to put pressure on the relevant aid-giving agencies to recognize the potentiality of assisting on a more adequate scale with the improvement of particular capacities that are required. The Canadian International Development Agency needs to have its bluff called, and to be shown that it is not making known, through Canadian Embassies and other means, the potentiality for providing social science support—in part because it has only limited knowledge of Canadian social science capacities.

On the other hand, the Agency has a unique department that is available for the support of *private* aid initiatives, so that the technique is available for the Social Science Research Council of Canada to put a case to the Agency for its own direct involvement with nongovernmental aid-requesting groups overseas, with Agency backing. This is a potentiality that the Council has not faced up to, primarily because it has not yet established working day-to-day relationships with institutions in appropriate countries, a formula that requires considerable secretarial backstopping. Similarly, such an objective would require that the Council be in a position to make its capacity and interest directly known to the numerous multilateral agencies of the United Nations family, which, one way or another, contain highly significant applied social science components, often with insufficient social science back-stopping in technical assistance-receiving countries. Such a program requires a great deal more knowledge of Canadian social science capacity, institutions, experience, and manpower in relevant fields than is currently visible. And it almost certainly requires the appointment of a Commissioner—armed with such knowledge, available to discuss the potentialities in the multilateral agencies and with social scientists in the countries concerned.*

In the three examples, I have drawn upon Canadian conditions and the Canadian institutional setting. This, of course, is a result of familiarity with that setting. But I know enough of conditions in other countries to be able to say that in none of them, not even in the United States or France, have these problems of representation, action, and communication been solved. Although the details required for solution are likely to be different in each national case, the complexity and challenges are very similar. If social scientists are to play a part in the construction of a better world, they will have to learn not only to continue to produce good research, but to communicate it to the public and to organize to increase the sharpness of its focus and the validity of its influence.

The social scientist as enquirer is central to teaching, education, publicity, politics, and public affairs. Too much of his energy is wasted by his fear of organization and his use of it for restrictive rather than creative purposes.

* Since the above was written the Canadian SSRC has in fact worked with CIDA and the ISSC to build the first steps in this direction.

PART V

Values and Options

CHAPTER 19

Values, Choice, and the Problem of Science

THE anthropologist, as social scientist, works in a profession in which objective knowledge is valued for its own sake and as a foundation for human understanding and social action. He is immersed in a complex of values as an analyst and as a participant. He knows that social science is imperfect, because crucial knowledge is not, and to some degree never will be, obtained, but he strives to improve its extent and quality. He knows too that value choices and the consideration of alternatives among possibilities of policy action, however much overladen with emotive and subjective significance, will be defective in the absence of reason and evidence. He thus confronts a world in which the rational and the nonrational come together, and in which an understanding of the scope and limits of science is important for its effective use.

Because rationality is imperfect, because values are contained in scientific activity, because emotive perceptions are important and valued in themselves, because there are costs and evils linked to superficially rational action, there is a serious move to challenge the validity of rationality as a guide to social thought. Because liberal tolerance exists in a world of exploitation and injustice, because no social system permits the completely free flowering of the individual spirit, and because wrongs should be attacked, there is also a serious move to reject the tolerance of variety in human life and replace it with politico-moral control of a group or absolutist character. Such positions have always existed in the modern intellectual world. They were dramatic in university life during the tense period of the late 1960s. But they have by no means disappeared. They are a continuous force which anthropology, with its central interest in values in intellectual method and in alternatives of living, must face directly. There is a challenge to the classical liberalism of anthropology which is crucial to its intellectual foundations and which will affect fundamentally its public policy role.

One choice to be faced in deciding upon or influencing policy is the degree of rationality and objective knowledge which should be used. There is a school of thought which argues that rationality and knowledge contain hidden premises which operate to maintain the system in which they are contained and to inhibit individual and social movement toward newer and juster forms of social interaction.* The *critical* part of such arguments contains a considerable degree of truth, which students of the interaction between language and culture, and language, symbol systems, and logic would recognize. Nevertheless, it can be argued that improvement, if it is to be achieved, can be approached through the clarification of the premises and issues and of the hidden value elements in the symbol systems and logic rather than through the overturn of rationality and logic itself. This view gains weight when it is seen that *no alternative* proposed in theory or in practice, on a large or a small scale, removes the ambiguity in symbol systems used in communication or creates a line of thought or conclusion-reaching that avoids bias, value stances, or simplistic assumptions.

Logic and reason and respect for evidence, with the use of emotion to load our values, choices, and experiential judgments, remain the most productive instruments of thought and of shared communication for constructive purposes. The retreat from reason can perhaps have psychic value for group therapy and for the individual discovery of experience that can result in creativity and artistic communication, and in similar special contexts that at some point or other affect us all. This is likely to be more creative when it is expressed not as a retreat from reason but as a discovery of the emotional self, and when it is then *allied to* the arts of communication and reasoning. Herbert Marcuse leads in this direction, but also argues for the *supplanting* of reason by emotively based thought. It is this element which has been picked up by numerous political and social commentators.

The senses, and the emotional interpretation of what they discover, are an essential element in human perception—to be nurtured and enjoyed. It would be incongruous to think of man as a mathematical calculator or machine for the manipulation of symbolic logic, and no political or social theorist does so; nor do political philosophers or practical policy makers base their ideas on any such assumption. The evidence of the senses (objectively controlled or subjectively experienced), linked to what we have learned from the past and from our fellows, filtered by psychological

---

*Cf. Herbert Marcuse, *One-dimensional Man*, Boston: Beacon Press, 1964; and the less well-founded tracts of Ivan Illich.

and emotive reactions, judgments, and memories, becomes emotively loaded and translated into action patterns, preferences, goals, desires, and cost balances—in short, choices. We *use* logic and rationality (to the extent of our training, knowledge, and capacity) to bring order and power to the implications of our experience and to help us derive conclusions that influence our action. If we are not careful, we can *misuse* logic and rationality also, through defective applications, because of inherent biases in the system we adopt, through imperfect mixes of rational and emotional input, and in a host of other ways. The claim and the attempt to use reason are different from its achievement.

All this must be accepted. Since no person among us has the power of perfect rational judgment, or some perfect mix of value assumptions upon which to base rationality, we have on the whole learned to accept the ability of our fellows to make judgments and rational calculations with values and conclusions which differ from our own. The imperfection of the practice of rationality is admitted and is built into our political and institutional systems.

A certain style of political rhetoric justifies its form as a rejection of rational logic and a use of poetry in its place. The contemporary manifestations of this style derive from the philosophy of Marcuse, although it has many forms, including the fascism of the 1930s, justified by other writers. The style has significance here because it represents a deliberate and consciously designed replacement for the use of science or critical thought in public affairs. It has no room for the kind of anthropology of public policy I have been advocating. The images of poetry juxtapose statements of experience in *unusual* ways, striking the reader or listener with the novelty of the thought, stimulating him to see a connection (which can usually be expressed in logical form) between two or more otherwise quite differentiated phenomena. If the images of poetry are repeated, they lose their effect and become banal clichés.

Occasionally, contemporary political rhetoric can be poetic. But the deliberate anti-rational mode depends for its effect on making a symbolic statement of connection, surrounded with emotive meaning, and using this repeatedly like the rhythm of percussion. Those of us having less power who agree with, cooperate with, or temporarily ally ourselves with those having more power are "co-opted." End of statement, end of argument. But the phrase is used to imply a distasteful state of having been bribed into a situation that we would otherwise have rejected, and of becoming the willing but tarnished tools of others who use us for their ends rather than ours. The cliché when repeated for political purposes carries with it its own judgment; it avoids the necessity for examining the underpinnings objectively; it is used selectively in those power relationship situations that the user is attacking, but it is avoided in others; its continuous repetition creates acceptance; it arouses emotional reactions which, in the light of the anti-rational attack, are quite sufficient as the basis of political or policy judgment.

But *all of us*, including anti-rationalist spokesmen, find ourselves from time to time cooperating with or in agreement with persons who according to any objective evidence have more "power" than we have. All of us are in fact "co-opted;" there is no society in which this is not true. No society has yet been devised in which there is not a distribution of power of some sort—that is, any member of any society is, by virtue of his membership in that society, "co-opted." By using this idea as a simplistic term of abuse, the anti-rationalists show up the banality and poverty of their analysis—*if we stop to think about it*. But if we accept the premise that emotional reaction should replace evidential and rational attempts at judgment, *we will not stop to think about it*.

In a more general way, the defense of anti-rationalism as a way of life (that is, as a set of principles that would govern policy, or nonpolicy, if you will) has been clearly set out in the best-selling paperback of Charles Reich, *The Greening of America*.* He calls the state of mind Consciousness III, and shows that it is based on the importance of self-fulfillment rather than social duty or service, and upon a sense of community (but fails to indicate that these have been traditional dominant forces in America, influencing both the left and right, both conservatives and reformers). It rejects analytic thought, and aims at complete sensory self-awareness—the full living of every moment. Reich writes:

> One last aspect of trying to escape imposed consciousness is concerned with so-called rational thought. Consciousness III is deeply suspicious of logic, rationality, analysis, and of principles. . . . Consciousness III has been exposed to some rather bad examples of reason, including the intellectual justifications of the Cold War and the Vietnam War. . . . It believes that "reason" tends to leave out too many factors and values—especially those which cannot readily be put into words and categories. It believes that undue faith is put on "principle" when there are always other principles that have been neglected. . . . It believes that thought can be "non-linear," spontaneous, disconnected. It thinks rational conversation has been overdone as a means of communication between people, and it has invented a new term, "rapping," for communication when it does take the form of words. Above all, it wants new dimensions. (p. 278.)

* *The Greening of America*, New York: Random House, Inc. © 1970 by Charles A. Reich, Bantam Books, 1971. See also Philip Nobile, ed., *The Con III Controversy*, New York: Pocket Books, 1971.

It works, says Reich, as a *secret code* (p. 234)—that's why it is misunderstood. Above all "no one judges anyone else" and "it rejects the whole concept of excellence and comparative merit" (p. 243). It rejects the use of clothing as hierarchical identification, but stresses its use as identifying the lifestyle of the wearer. It uses music and drugs to communicate and to develop "new" dimensions of experience.

I am not attacking Consciousness III as a way of life for those who wish to live that way and know what they are doing. Unfortunately, many of those who opt in this direction are young and do *not* know the alternatives; in this they are little different from other young people who have been socialized in a different way. But one result is that some of those who opt for Consciousness III *also* have social consciences and want to do something about the world. They then use the assumptions of Consciousness III as a basis for trying to rearrange the world, mixed with a desire and a need to succeed in their actions.

Yet mankind cannot live and solve its problems, except in specially arranged and nurtured communities, on the basis of secret codes. Even the new dimensions so beloved of Consciousness III—the manufactured LSD, the highly complex electronic instruments, the lights and the scent machines—are dependent on a technology which itself is dependent on rational problem solving.

We have seen that extra-rational approaches to thought can and do have creative aesthetic and intellectual power when properly used, and, it may be said, when undistorted by drugs and psychedelic phenomena. The danger and paradox come when extreme advocates transform extra-rationality into anti-rationality. Of recent years, not for the first or last time, we have seen advocates of important moral positions attack scientific activity with the techniques of nonrational politics. In so doing they have threatened the values and, in some instances, the existence of intellectual freedom, have sought to place limits on the questions to which science can address itself, have demeaned the integrity of the intellectual experience, and have introduced orthodoxy as a replacement of skepticism. This unfortunately has been manifest in anthropology as in other social science disciplines. When this happens, social science becomes a tool for politically oriented moralists, and is no longer free to determine facts, elucidate relationships, or add to our understanding. The rule book replaces debate.

From 1969 to 1973, primary targets of attack in universities were scholars who reopened questions about the biological basis of man's "intelligence," as defined in psychology. The attacks mounted at that time have since broadened, so that, in Germany, we have had professors driven from their posts by politically organized students and faculty, while in England in 1974 the National Union of Students affirmed its policy of preventing university appearances of blacklisted speakers. In 1974 the University of Toronto, following an incident in which an outside speaker with views unacceptable to the Students for a Democratic Society was forcibly denied the opportunity to address a class, was forced to set out a procedure whereby freedom of speech would be protected when violence and disruption threatened.

The pressure on the proponents of certain psychological theories has received most press and most analysis, and illustrates the manner in which unpopular, and probably invalid, scientific positions can become targets of the anti-rational attack, undermining the whole process of scientific debate and discovery. The controversy was about Intelligence Quotients.

In 1969, Professor Arthur R. Jensen of the Institute of Human Learning at the University of California, Berkeley, published an article in the *Harvard Educational Review* addressed to the problem of "boosting" IQ and scholastic achievement.* In this article he summarized, among other things, controlled research which indicated that there was a genetic factor contributing to IQ, and put the cat among the pigeons by indicating that this was one significant part of the explanation of IQ differences between Black and White children in the United States.

To simplify, there are two major emphases in the explanation of "fundamental" elements in personal characteristics. One tends to stress the impact of physical, cultural, and socioeconomic environment on the responses and behavior pattern of individuals, the other tends to stress genetic heredity. Most scholars in most fields accept a mixture of explanations, but the policy implications tend to be related to the cultural rather than the genetic because cultural processes are subject to policy influence and a genetic explanation seems to imply that there is little you can do to remedy any social injustices which may occur. Further, it *seems* to be the case that in most relevant processes the cultural (broadly defined) elements are strongly dominant, hide the genetic, and even perhaps counterbalance them.

* Some of the sources on this matter are: A. R. Jensen, "How Much Can We Boost IQ and Scholastic Achievement?" *Harvard Educational Review*, No. 39, 1969, pp. 1–123; A. R. Jensen, *Genetics and Education*, London: Methuen, 1972; H. J. Eysenck, "The New Zealots," *Encounter*, December 1972, pp. 79–90; Peggy R. Sanday, "On the Causes of IQ Differences between Groups and Implications for Social Policy," *Human Organization*, Vol. 31, No. 4, Winter 1972, pp. 411–424. These works refer to a wide range of other publications on both sides of the controversy.

Extreme postures in this matter are rare; the argument is about weight, relative force, and balance. There is some evidence that of recent years, after a very considerable decline in fashion, genetic explanations are coming more to the fore. One only has to think of the considerable popularity of such works as those of Robert Ardrey, Lionel Tiger, Robin Fox, and Konrad Lorenz, which have popularized as never before the theme of continuity between animal and human behavior, and have drawn heavily upon studies of ethology in so doing. In social science circles these works are treated with considerable caution, since many of the claims seem overdrawn and the evidential gaps in the argument are huge. Nevertheless, when such authors suggest that there is a *biological* base for such phenomena as aggression, territoriality, or male social bonding, nobody as yet suggests that the proponents of this thesis be drummed out of the scientific world or that they are racist. It is generally recognized that there are theses here to be examined, and that the knowledge attained through such challenges to our ways of thought will ultimately have implications for social policy.

Biology itself has awakened to many social science issues, and is, as it were, using its methods to attack some favorite predispositions so that the cultural explanations will find themselves more and more on the defensive. I happen to believe that biology can oversimplify issues of human conduct. But I do not deny the intellectual significance of the dialectic sponsored by the disagreement and its importance for human understanding. I find also that many of my anthropological colleagues are more disposed to consider ideas from biology than I am. This should not be surprising considering the weight attached to evolutionary and ecological explanations in present-day North American and European anthropology.

Given this background, one might have thought that Jensen's propositions would have been regarded as legitimate to examine, important to study further and to resolve, and to warrant further research. There is, after all, little schematic difference between saying that aggression and population movement and territoriality relate to biological components in our make-up *as well as* cultural and environmental influences, and saying that results attained in handling IQ tests also do so.

The curious feature is that even if a biological, and therefore genetic, feature is at work, a very large number of questions still remain to be answered before one can put that conclusion in perspective. For example, can the genetic feature be overlaid by cultural forces? Is it possible to have a culture-free IQ test—I don't think it is—and if not, how does one then interpret the interplay?* Perhaps IQ tests are little more than special kinds of aptitude test, and hence their whole significance for educational theory may be open to question, particularly when differing components in a population are distinguished. I do not think that these problems and others similar to them have been overcome by Jensen in his work or by other psychologists who have stressed IQs. Nevertheless, this in a way should have *reduced* the controversy by making the issue of less current practical significance; instead, it added fuel to the flames.

The Harvard Educational Review found that it had a political issue on its hands, and that scholars of different persuasions, in their commentaries, were suggesting that Jensen was not only wrong (a legitimate argument) but was governed by racist attitudes. Instead of tackling the issue head-on by means of rational argument, the editors of the *Review* began to deny responsibility, falsely stated that they had not suggested to Jensen that he treat the topics he did, and used most peculiar techniques to deny Jensen copies of his own material and comments made upon it.

In order to defeat Jensen's arguments, students, reputable scholars, and the public (influenced by accounts of the dispute), instead of engaging in objective studies to determine crucial facts, made *ad hominem* political attacks, in symbolic language of demagogic and emotive appeal, used crowd behavior to drown Jensen out at a public meeting, put pressure on the conduct of his academic classes, and secured the cancellation in midstream of a complex research enterprise that had begun before the publication of the original article.

Jensen had made it clear in his accounts and interpretations of his work that IQs were individual phenomena, and that the discovery of genetic factors did not in any way indicate that a group as a whole, used for identification and statistical purposes, should be considered inferior or superior because of differences in IQ distribution, or that membership in such a group meant that the individual concerned should be accorded treatment as an inferior or superior, particularly since group differences were by no means so great as to prevent very high numbers of individuals in any social group having very high IQs. In other words, Jensen's

---

*My own broad summary would be: all intelligence tests involve skill; all skills have variable significance according to cultural selection; this applies even to such matters as numeracy, literacy, physical manipulation to solve problems identified by the senses, and the speed with which tasks are accomplished; hence all tests are culturally weighted. Nevertheless, within weights that are culturally influenced, skill varies from individual to individual. While skill may be linked to motivation, practice, and so forth, some element of it relates also to differences in biological, mental, motor, and sensory processes. At this level, there *must* be some genetic factor, and it is most unlikely that it is the same for all persons. The questions are: What is it? To what extent does culture overlay it?

argument was the reverse of racist, for racism implies that characteristics are attributed to all members of a race or to an overwhelming proportion of them, in an automatic manner, and carrying immediate consequences of prejudice, intolerance, and persecution in the extreme, "justified" by reference to such universal group characteristics. This was the opposite of Jensen's position, and that of some others who also came to be persecuted.

The SDS at Berkeley nevertheless gave the "White Supremacist Award of the Year" to Jensen, and described the justification for it as follows:

> Professor Jensen has earned this award by his unswerving devotion to the rulers of this country and its racist "educational" system:
>
> 1) He has worked to give new respectability to discredited theories of racial inferiority. When he speaks of "dysgenic trends" among the black population, he is talking about inferiority. The threat of genocide is clear.
>
> 2) He has actively promoted segregated schools, for example in Bakersfield where he was paid to justify inferior schools for Chicano students.
>
> 3) He is travelling to Australia on his sabbatical where he hopes to apply his theories of "innate inferiority" to the aboriginal population.
>
> (Quoted from an SDS broadsheet posted on the Berkeley campus, calling for a "ceremony" to take place at Jensen's class.)

The use of non sequiturs and loaded language (genocide) is typical of Consciousness III when it moves from the nonjudgmental (as described by Reich) to the *ad hominem* judgmental.

The effects of such missionary zeal were widespread, perhaps culminating for sheer irrelevancy in two resolutions of the American Anthropological Association in 1970. These resolutions had the decency to say that *ad hominem* responses to scholarly papers were regrettable, but then specifically stated that the data assembled in Jensen's article were inadequate for the conclusions drawn. At this point, the judgment is, if you like, reasonable. After the point had been written into the resolution, it was placed before the membership for a vote. Now, since *The Harvard Educational Review* had withdrawn the article from further distribution, how could it be expected that the membership would acquaint itself with the article directly and make individual judgments about its scholarly nature, including whether Jensen was putting forward conclusions or hypotheses to be tested—a very different matter?

Further, the sponsors of the resolutions coupled the assertion about what Jensen had said to a previous resolution of the Association, which stated that "there is no scientifically established evidence to justify the exclusion of any race from the rights guaranteed by the Constitution of the United States." This coupling left the distinct impression that Jensen

318   The Sorcerer's Apprentice

was asserting that there was such evidence and that exclusion of races was justified; he was not. And then the main resolution ruled out of consideration the main bone of contention, dismissing it from further examination: "we specifically repudiate any suggestion that the failure of an education program could be attributed to genetic differences between large populations."

Jensen *did* say that Operation Headstart and similar programs were doomed to failure if they did not reflect accurate knowledge of the mix of genetic and nongenetic factors, and use that knowledge positively. In this he entered highly debatable and controversial territory. But in doing so, he called for further research, knowledge, and understanding. Whatever one's judgment is about Jensen's thesis (at this time), it is quite clear that we do *not* know enough to pronounce upon it with dogmatic certitude. The American Anthropological Association, in the terms of this resolution, stampeded by the need to show itself to be relevant and anti-racist and to say something of meaning to the public, performed a distinct disservice to the cause of understanding by saying, in effect, *there is a question that must not be put.* Science is not *allowed* to examine it, because existing knowledge, as represented by the current opinions of five scientists "competent in the relevant disciplines," has provided an answer not consistent with Jensen's argument.*

The attacks of the SDS and other similar groups on unpopular scholars and enquirers could not have force if they were not supported by more moderate persons of liberal sentiment and gently leftish views. Yet the link between a "scientific" position and a policy issue is seldom direct and

---

*R. W. Rader summarized the more general intellectual–political issue with admirable lucidity and thrust in a statement published in *The Daily Californian,* May 6, 1969, as follows:

> The point is, of course, that Jensen did not need to be so resplendently right to be justified and that his attackers are not so simply reprehensible as they seem. The attackers were moved by humane ideals to what they conceived to be moral action. They forgot that morality without knowledge based on critical enquiry is not a virtue but a vice. "Be not righteous overmuch" was a saying popular in the eighteenth century, the century of reason; and it remains the perpetually valuable counsel of reason. (Not the villainous but the righteous, Mill points out, put Socrates and Christ to death.) Because we need the counsel of reason and because we cannot know what it is until it has stood the test of free debate from all quarters (and even then not certainly), we do not persecute for opinion even those who appear as harmfully wrong as Professor Jensen was made to seem; more plainly—to repeat the truth which will always need repeating—we do not persecute for opinion at all.

The 1972 Annual Meeting of the American Anthropological Association passed an additional resolution removing the very concept of hereditary reasoning from the analysis of racial questions. This, in other contexts, is known as thought control.

is usually far from clear. The horror expressed at the genetic thesis is in part motivated by the possibility that its acceptance might lead to policies accepting or reinforcing social difference—the reverse of Jensen's apparent intention. But another psychologist at Oxford used the genetic argument to challenge the motivational base of a policy of income differential—a left-wing position if there ever was one. Jeffrey Gray published an article in the London *Times*, September 8, 1972, headed "Why should society reward intelligence?" The inference of the article is that if there is a genetic factor in intelligence and aptitude, a policy of equality of opportunity is bound to create class and income differences. If this is so, the use of differences in income to provide incentives that are really the natural outcome of differences in personal drives will reinforce inequities. The author concludes:

> Thus the evidence for genetic control of IQ cannot justify the fact that upper and lower classes are paid differently for the jobs they do. On the contrary, it suggests that this policy is a wasteful use of resources in the guise of "incentives" which either tempt people to do what is beyond their powers or reward them for what they would do anyway. If we are ever to frame a rational incomes policy, this might not be a bad place to begin.

Gray is not putting forward a firm dogmatic conclusion. He is putting forward a provocative hypothesis. It is sufficiently serious to warrant examination, first of the "causative" and "descriptive" facts (our knowledge of which is in an elementary and challengeable state) and second of the implications of those facts and interpretations which can be supported.

Such understanding, coupled with other important changes which are occurring in our world, is bound to challenge many of our basic "principles" and "judgments." To this extent, *the critical element* in Consciousness III and its parallels and derivatives has much to be said for it, but it is also present, more effectively, in the rational world. But Consciousness III, providing for the submersion of the senses and mind of the individual, in the name of "self-awareness," into the *olla podrida* of group dominance, provides no basis for the *creative* use of questions. In its impure political dimension it becomes totalitarian and repressive. The fact that I have taken an "unpopular" intellectual position as my example should prove my point.

Gray, in the quotation made above, has of course put his finger on a serious basic issue of great importance for the shape and interpretation of democracy and society. In one important sense, the genetic-environmental argument does not affect the outcome. If we reject the genetic argument, we are still left with the interesting position that "equality of opportunity" only has meaning in the most meaningless sense. It is not, and never can be, an absolute. If it were, it would imply nothing less than that at the moment of birth all children be taken from variable influences, from home and society and family, from self-controlled interaction with the world, and placed in a completely monitored and controlled physical and social environment which was the same for each little test-tube being until at least the main formative years had passed. And even then, later opportunity, and later experiences, would differ. Clearly, equality of opportunity is judged in practice in terms of opportunity costs, and of alternative competing values.

Since individuals are *not* equal, and since we are surrounded as part of our environment by unequal individuals with differing traits and characteristics, our experiences vary and the principle of difference, though not its form, is perpetuated. In part Consciousness III is struggling against this. Difference is seen as negative. Most of us see it as positive. If we were all the same, we would have no need of democracy; for democracy is a range of devices to enable very different people to make decisions that respect their differences.* The realization of this poses major policy choices: What value should be placed on the perpetuation of the richness of variety? Can it be overdone? Can costs in terms of misunderstanding and tension be minimized? Does such minimization remove functional stimulus? And what should be the relationship, if any, between differences in characteristics and the differential command over resources through income?

Such questions are not merely "philosophical" and abstract. The overt variety of special interest groups emerging around given issues appears to be growing with kaleidoscopic confusion. Powers of coercion have dramatically moved to small groups willing to hold others to ransom, with attempts to force (however inadequately) solutions to policy issues. We have noted the manner in which group linkages refuse the confines of national boundaries.

The dilemmas posed are numerous: competition between understanding and social evolution on the one hand, and dogma and autocratic action on the other; the search for general principles that will unite humanity while encouraging social and cultural variation; the establishment of governmental systems that will overcome the defects of nationalism and

---

*It is true that some democracies, writ large or in micro-environments such as some university departments or some industrial organization democracies, operate to repress minority difference. These I regard as pathological, though real, forms.

bureaucracy; the invention of techniques to give individuals and groups the ability to express themselves creatively and politically with effective results that respect the positions of others, without resort to violence or improper pressure.

Even if knowledge and understanding were available to a much greater degree than at present, the operations and articulation of the political system clearly leave much to be desired, and far too little thought is being given to innovation in the world political structure. Reactions against the current forms of exercising power obtain their most critical strength from revolutionary movements, but these tend to be removed from reality, insofar as prescriptions are concerned, by their linkage to broad philosophical ideologies which are held to with mystical devotion unmodified by realistic criticism. The resistance of revolutionary reform to data and knowledge is as great as that of orthodox government, and ideas drawn from both sources modify and blind the observations and appraisals of much social science. In this world the anthropologists, political scientists, and their colleagues stand weakly on the sidelines when it comes to institutional innovation.

Government is responsive to the way information and values are fed to it, and those who are skilled in this, through bureaucratic position, political parties, personal connection, and lobbying will normally have the upper hand in determining policy values. In the Western democratic world we still tend to think of one-man-one-vote providing the pressure of linkage ensuring that persons sensitive to the "electorate" exercise power. This does indeed happen, but even in electorates there are differences between those who habitually make their views known and those who don't.

When we move out of electorates, we are still befuddled by outdated and I believe downright erroneous notions of the political interests of socioeconomic classes.* But groups having specific political interests and values, that wish to express themselves effectively to bring about policy choices, are *not* class representative in the Marxian sense. Their variety is legion. There are indeed occupational and regional interests, which have strong links to the structure of the economy. There is now organized activity based on age-perceptions of the world and how to deal with it. Ethnic and minority enclaves want action. Activists organize around

* I am not alone in this heresy. Note the letter of Peter Cadogan to the *Times Literary Supplement* of November 20, 1970, under the heading "Where Marx Went Wrong" in which he justifies the view that "there is not now and never has been any such thing, politically or economically, as a working class."

specific concerns, such as environmental protection, women's liberation, medico-legal reform. The electorate and the traditional forms of capitalist lobbying are simply not sufficient instruments (even where they are as refined as they are in Switzerland) to keep the pulse on public opinion and the active communication of views in ways that ensure that opinions are heard, heeded, and acted upon.

Unless we can find ways and means of improving this political element in the selection of policy choices, we can expect group lobbying to grow, each group seeing its own issues and values in dangerous isolation from the rest of public policy, forced to take this position because unless it does public policy will ignore or downplay its significance in favor of the viewpoint of those who have the decision-making ear. This can only lead to conflict and frustration, perhaps with escalation of tension and resort to violent pressure.

I do not have a blueprint. But I offer the following as a basis for thought. The Swiss example of frequent referenda on policy issues is important and useful, provided the mandatory elements are carefully defined; so is the resort to referendum on the basis of petition. It should be stressed that, unlike American initiatives, such referenda apply to the most basic and technical considerations of national federal policy as well as to local concerns. Modern electronic devices, though expensive, can ease the process in larger countries and make some form of automatic referendum technically feasible.

But this as an instrument breaks down if it becomes conservative, as it tends to do, if the issues are too frequent or too banal so that voting proportions drop, or if there is a lack of trust in the legislature or executive to see the matter through. What seems to be needed is a much more formal, automatic, and accessible system for the hearing and airing of lobby-type views in public, *coupled with* a system that (a) arrives at a decision by normal methods where urgency is involved, and (b) creates objective research for the less time-urgent questions, assembles existing knowledge objectively for the time-urgent questions, and creates further research that can be seen to amend policy even where immediate decisions have been taken. No government at present has the research organization to do this on sociopolitical questions. Further, it would be absolutely essential, if the aims of restoring group-public confidence and of creating participatory communication were to be achieved, that the research be openly publicized, that its value premises and implications be clearly stated, and that the interest groups be associated with it without dominating it. If such possibilities were to be developed, they would require very sensitive handling, particularly in the formative years, and the evolution of a political attitude moving some considerable distance toward enquiry and the open balancing of alternatives, rather than upon *a priori* public platforms.

We have already seen that some quite abstruse scientific questions and results can be linked, albeit in uncertain ways, to the analysis of policies affecting the distribution of wealth and opportunity, which remains one of the major world politicoethical issues. There is growing evidence that analysis is still unduly weighted by outmoded 19th-century preoccupations, although these are being questioned. In the questioning it may be that anthropology will find a role, derived in part from its interest in distribution and transactions.

A major part of both Western capitalist and communist ideology alike is that wealth is built on labor. Both ideologies also create a vision of a future in which man's toil will be reduced, if not eliminated. Yet in practice, both systems are trapped by distributing wealth primarily as a reward for labor performed. In developing countries, needed growth is linked to increase in employment in the cash sector, and "underemployment" is identified as a source for increasing energy and the place where misery occurs.

This view has been seriously questioned, but the questioning has had only beginning effects on public policy. The Weberian type of view that links growth to the Protestant value of work and labor is now a matter of argument, with the introduction of historical perspectives which show that while workers had to work, entrepreneurs were, and are, often motivated by the possibility of using wealth for sybaritic purposes. Sir Arthur Lewis, in his approach to growth, has built upon the statistical comparisons of Colin Clark and others to indicate that fastest growth occurs where human labor is saved by the use of machinery, and people are moved from back-breaking inefficient labor into productive arenas where physical labor becomes a much smaller component in the factors of production. Anthropologists such as Leslie White have talked of evolution in energy terms, an approach which is compatible with the notion that growth and development are functions of supplanting labor with other forms of energy as a proportion of the energy going into any given unit of production. Other anthropologists (and philosophers) have raised questions about the satisfactions to be gained from work in employment as against other types of time-use, questions which raise issues about how we define per capita income.

There is some evidence that, particularly in boring, repetitive industries with high wage income and security, striking is welcomed by the ordinary worker as a day off rather than a bludgeon for increased pay, and that frequent absenteeism should be seen in the same light. Journals of commentary are now carrying articles that question the concern with unemployment, though they are still regarded as somewhat daring.* Sebastian de Grazia, in a most thorough and illuminating examination,** has shown that on the whole machines have not been used to improve leisure, either because of employment decision or by employee action to use "freed" time for other kinds of work or activity controlled outside himself—for example, in household obligation. Much of the time freed from employment occupations has been taken up by other "duties."

At the same time, industrial countries have been puzzling over such phenomena as stagflation, the threat of runaway inflation, and heavy, if not increasing, unemployment in times of major industrial growth. The Society for International Development, in its 1971 meeting in Ottawa, was thoroughly preoccupied with the problem of increasing unemployment in developing countries, regarded with the utmost seriousness by the major economic and political figures who were present. There is no doubt that both inflation and unemployment, given existing institutional arrangements, are damaging. In most advanced countries institutions have changed since the Great Depression, so that with the tools at our disposal, they need not be the unmitigated and unparalleled misery creators that they were in the 1920s and 1930s. Inflation raises issues of monetary management that are beyond my technical competence, but it may be said that one of the reasons for its classification as something to be combated is that our mechanisms for distributing wealth through income are unevenly flexible so that in times of moderate inflation some persons can protect themselves and some cannot.

Unemployment raises even stronger issues of distribution, linked to public morality and to cultural preparation for long-term leisure or self-directed creativity. Provided income is there, unemployment (that is, the state of not having one's activity directed by others, or by the need to maintain income) is in fact a pejorative name for a state we all in theory aim for. While institutions and public morality still make unemployment a state of defeat for many, the pejorative connotation is justified, but it is by no means necessary.

* For example, Peter Swerdloff, "Learning to Love Unemployment," *Esquire*, December 1971; J. R. L. Anderson, "Has Unemployment a Future?" *Encounter*, November 1972.
** Sebastian de Grazia, *Of Time, Work, and Leisure*, New York: Twentieth Century Fund, 1962, Anchor Books, 1964.

Already it is clear that some individuals have learned to use unemployment well, and to gain satisfaction from it, even using it for creative purposes. It is also clear that the movement toward Guaranteed Minimal Incomes will make unemployment a little less unattractive. Even without such devices, many of those who opt for pure Consciousness III are opting also for a removal from the state of employment (this is not to say that work does not take place or is unnecessary, but it is directed to immediate life goals rather than other-directed production). Early retirement and shorter and shorter working weeks are other ways of modifying the employment pattern. Given this general but confused set of alterations, the insistence of some rural communities in otherwise rapidly developing countries on retaining their relatively simple material base is no longer necessarily to be thought of as an anomaly, and even "underemployment" in rural communities is not necessarily something to be combated.

The problem of unemployment is still thought of in terms of job creation. Show me a single government that does not make that response! Yet job creation is not the only way of dealing with the evils of unemployment. Another thrust, destined to have great weight in public values, is to accept unemployment as a fair choice for individuals to make, and to treat unemployment not as a moral evil but perhaps even as a moral and social good. To do this successfully means a considerable move in policy priorities.

For example, it is questionable whether, even today, jobs should be created *in order to* remove unemployment. Such a dynamic priority leads potentially to the creation of industry with little social need, to the vaunting of consumerism to keep the system going, and an urgency which removes the chance of thinking about socially needed production priorities. A different way of approaching policy influence on production incentives, aid to industry, and so forth, is to remove employment from the goal, and analyze instead the areas of production that are socially required but that normal profit incentives do not bring into being adequately.

This then leaves employment to be taken care of through distribution mechanisms, which in turn affect policy decisions. You cannot distribute an adequate income to unemployed persons without moral judgment unless there is a sufficient total income to provide for the distribution. Just the same, while unemployment is thought of in terms of direct job creation, adequate attention is not being given to the moral climate and the possibility of alternative distribution mechanisms. Except, almost by accident, within the European Community, and then still tied to the ethos of job creation, the international implications of wealth distribution are also not getting very imaginative attention. Migration of labor and of persons with skills, and the funneling of aid into job-creating institutions, represent almost the limit of thought.

But it could be argued, for example, that aid would have more humane effects if it were sent in the form of international income redistribution; just as the unemployed in advanced countries are coming to be taken care of by a proportion of the national income, so a proportion of the national income could be distributed for consumption purposes to the unfortunate of other countries. There is no objective need for this to be thought of as charity, since we are well on the way to removing the odium of charity from unemployment and welfare payments. Further, the provision of aid in the form of increased consumption power enables the recipients to make their own choices of consumption emphases, and pumps industry creation stimulus with a greater weight attached to consumer choice.

To go even further, the opening of frontiers to increased migration would enable richer countries to use their income redistributively either by making immigrants eligible for participation in the guaranteed income (obviously with numerical controls) or the labor force. Something like this is bound to come in the long run, if for no other reason than being a price exacted by high population growth countries for responding to international pressure to control growth.

We are thus led directly to a further controversy, that which is raging between, to simplify, advocates of the priority of ecological balance in as natural a form as possible and advocates of the priority of human goal attainment in other forms, of which preservation of the natural environment is only one to be judged among others.* It is not my intention to summarize the increasingly complex data and hypotheses which the debate is usefully creating, which would require a book in itself, but only

---

*The useful references here are: Barbara Ward and René Dubos, *Only One Earth, The Care and Maintenance of a Small Planet*, Harmondsworth: Penguin Books, 1972; Donella H. Meadows *et al.*, *The Limits to Growth*, London: Potomac Associates, Earth Island Limited, 1972 (for the Club of Rome); and Alfred Sauvy, *Croissance Zero?*, Paris: Calmann-Levy, 1973. The original world model was set out by Jay W. Forrester in *World Dynamics*, Cambridge: Wright-Allen Press, 1971. By far the most useful and competent critique, which subjects the data, methods, and ideas to detailed review, and which in my view supplants the conclusions of the Meadows team, is prepared by the Science Policy Research Unit of Sussex University, and published by H. S. D. Cole *et al.* in *Thinking About the Future: A Critique of the Limits to Growth*, London: Chatto and Windus, 1973. My own discussion was formulated prior to the appearance of the Sussex report and raises different and less technical issues.

to record once again some of the fundamental issues and questions that the debate has raised and that require resolution. The debate has an additional value in that it opens up, rather directly, questions about the competence of scientific method to provide future-oriented data.

The most dramatic statement of the interweaving of the issues is the world simulation model sponsored by the Club of Rome and developed by Potomac Associates based at MIT, as presented in their joint report *The Limits of Growth*. The model takes eight major variables—population, industrial output per capita (in dollar terms), food (kilogram-grain equivalent) per capita, pollution as a multiple of the 1970 level, the fraction of the 1900 reserves of nonrenewable resources remaining, the crude birth rate, the crude death rate, and the services available per capita. The model provides for effects on each of the variables by elements in the others, and hence the projections change according to which assumptions about movement are used, and what the significance of the factors may be. The generators of the model use a number of different possibilities.

They first use a "standard" world model run based simply on historical projection of known data. In this set of conditions, they show that "finally" within the next century (they are deliberately and sensibly imprecise about dates, but the model ends at 2100, so that all predictions are prior to this date) population growth is "halted by a rise in the death rate due to decreased food and medical services" (presumably per capita). In another model they double the assumption of 1900 resource reserves, thus providing the effect that industry grows to a higher level, but the effect of this is that pollution also increases, causing an increase in the death rate and decline in food production. Rising pollution also stops growth if the standard model is changed by providing unlimited nuclear power, which doubles the exploitable resource reserve and makes possible "extensive programs of recycling and substitution." In another variant, pollution control is assumed so that, per unit of production, pollution is one-quarter of the 1970 level, and resource policies are based on nuclear power. Here growth is possible until the limit of arable land is reached. The next set of assumptions is that agricultural productivity increases with a wide industrial resource base and improved pollution controls per production unit. But although pollution controls are less per unit, the vastly increased production increases total pollution, with eventual effects on population and food supply. In the next model, an increase in food production is *replaced by* perfect birth control effectiveness, the latter, however, being governed by individual values rather than public policy, so that population grows, but at a slower rate. This merely postpones the food crisis "by a decade or two." Finally, a model is presented on the assumption of "unlimited" resources (in fact the model limits them), pollution control to one-quarter of the 1970 level, doubling of land yields, and effective birth-control methods. In this model a constant population with world average income nearly that of the present US level is achieved temporarily, but comes up against pollution increase, with declining food production as a result, and an eventual decline in industrial production and increase in death rates through resource depletion.

The proponents of the policy implications of the report hold, therefore, that if current policies are allowed to proceed in any of the named sectors, the conditions in that sector will become so critical before the year 2100, and in most instances well before, that there will be a world crisis with devastating effects on the human population brought about through misery. These words are not used, but are clearly implied.

The authors therefore seek to avoid such a crisis and suggest that the following conditions represent the possibility of global equilibrium: (a) Bringing capital plant and population to a constant size. (b) "All input and output rates—births, deaths, investment and depreciation—are kept to a minimum." (c) "The levels of capital and population and the ratio of the two are set in accordance with the values of the society. They may be deliberately revised and slowly adjusted as the advance of technology creates new options" (p. 174). The third point is designed not to permit a breakdown of the constant, but to permit redistributive adjustments within it.

I do not see how the conditions postulated for global equilibrium use the model to provide a solution. A policy based on those conditions is, to say the least, highly complicated, and could not under any circumstances be built upon national government. The setting of the ratios in accordance with "the values of the society" immediately raises a redistributive hornets' nest, as has been indicated by the topics previously considered in this chapter. This will without doubt lead to the demand for some growth, as well as redistribution, prior to the achievement of a constant, which will then put some of the variables of the model into motion. Further, despite the word "unlimited" to describe resources in some tabular headings, the authors of the report in fact consider resources to be limited. In their models of "stable" policies, introduced at various times, resources are *always* shown as declining. You can for yourself project the decline, which, since the model has been stabilized, is at a predictable angle, to the point at which resources hit the baseline (it is not clear whether the baseline used is zero or some quantity), that is, have long passed the permissible limits. At the most optimistic projection, this is some three times the time period of 200 years used in the model (1900–2100), so that under the most optimistic stability assumptions we would have passed the point of decline in performance and acceptable levels of living well before the year A.D. 2500. The report does not mention this outlook, nor does it deal with it.

No wonder that many commentators, looking not only at the world model but at immediate national and local issues, lose hope and speak in terms of ecodoom. But if the facts and assumptions of the Club of Rome are correct, *there is nothing we can do about it*, except delay it, unless it be through controlled population reduction *pari passu* with resource depletion and pollution increase to the point of *zero population*.

That is really what the report indicates: not zero population growth and/or zero economic growth, but zero population and zero economy.

The exercise of the Potomac Associates, like the national futurology projections of the Kahn group, is useful. Its support by the weighty influence of the Club of Rome and other thinking groups is by no means a bad thing. The criticisms that it has provoked and will engender show up the limits of our knowledge and our methods, and stimulate us to do better. In the practical policy sense it helps to dramatize the need for action and for better thought, and it puts the proponents of alternatives on the defensive, with the need to justify them more carefully and rationally than before. But there is also evidence that many thinking people, who have positive and creative ideas to contribute to the world, are so depressed by ecodoom that they feel action is useless, and retire into pessimism, defeatism, or Consciousness III (which certainly won't help us or our great-grandchildren). Where this result occurs, the errors and the false dramatics of the report and similar statements require combat.

The first element to be discussed is the nature of statistics and fundamental data. World statistics are simply not reliable enough for even approximate support for many of the key trends. In many countries of the world, even approximate statistics have not been kept longer than fifteen or twenty years, yet the Potomac Report uses a 1900 baseline. In countries where some kinds of relevant statistics did exist at the baseline, subsequent growth is in some degree an artifact of continuous improvement in figure-gathering and movement of activity from nonquantified areas to quantified areas (e.g., production from subsistence to cash). It is extremely difficult to project backwards objectively; such projections are inevitably influenced by current data and knowledge. Ten to fifteen years of *relatively* accurate social statistics, with huge areas of uncertainty, are simply not good enough for us to make dogmatic assertions about the past, necessary for projection-trend statements.

It can in fact be argued that there might have been a fairly sharp decline in world population in the mid-19th century, which only began to correct itself in the early 20th. If this were to be correct it would change the shape, implications, and inevitability of questions of trend. It is only forty years since the alarmist opinion of students of population was that world population was about to take a tumble, and family allowances were designed to correct this trend. While there is some evidence for the belief that family size is variably related to income (the variables including estimates of future income, beliefs about the way family size affects level of living, cultural variants affecting the pleasure obtained from having children in one's household, and the career implications of women's liberation), the propositions and data conclusions in this field relate to *hypotheses*. Any feedback relationships affecting population growth built into the Potomac predictions are no more than that: intelligent guesses. Such guesses should be used, but the results should be described in hypothetical, not in predictive, terms. Further, other models can be built using alternative, equally valid assumptions; and a model closer to reality ought to include calculations for different population principles operating in different parts of the world. There is no such thing as a world population policy, and no such thing as universal reactions to the same stimuli. A change in the effects and directions of population policy in China and India alone would have a considerable influence on world population trends, and it is not beyond the powers of the government of China and India to put into action specific chosen policies. (This does not mean to say that they would work as predicted, but only that there would be effects.) But if governments do not change their policies, and world trends are left to themselves, no one is really in a position to say what the results of changes in living conditions and values will or will not bring about. Most demographers in the world are Americans, who know their own country and its culture well; I do not believe that many of them were in a position in 1945 to predict changes in the net reproduction rate in the United States that occurred between 1945 and 1973.

This is not to say that trends in this connection, as described in the Potomac Report, are not possible; they are, and in that sense should be, *one* of the conditions we are prepared for.

Similar arguments apply to the concept of resources. Resources are not what are given in the world in nature, but what are seen to be utilizable.

What is utilizable depends on values and costs as well as technology; it is, therefore, the result of a complex interplay between knowledge of nature, knowledge and costs of techniques of production, values about the desirability of particular kinds of production, and even the willingness of labor to handle it.

If you define a resource as a physical entity that comes from the earth or air, most of it, except for the biological, is nonrenewable. (I say most of it, because air and water under certain conditions are renewable.) But if you change your definition and say "a resource is that which is required to fulfill a particular production or consumption purpose," resources are both renewable and ever-changing in nature. They are in fact cultural artifacts influenced by economic reality. It is this difference in implied definition and approach that separates the analysts who lean on the givens of natural and engineering science and those who lean on social science arguments about culture and economy. Engineering science both grows out of and depends for its application on economic and cultural conditions.

Coal has been out of favor, relative to the 19th century, as a source of energy and chemicals; there are signs that changes in technique, demand, and cost structures of competitive sources may bring it back into favor. A new metal was invented in 1972 for use in the Swiss watch industry; a new plastic in the same year for use in the Swiss optical industry; an electronic air-monitoring device was installed in the same year in a region dominated by three major chemical firms near Basle in which a computer controls production methods to the point of shutting off production when the composition of the air requires it.

The concept that energy is a part of resources, as indicated in the Potomac Report, indicates still further reservations. Differences of opinion about energy sources are as great as, if not greater than, differences of opinion about social data.

The 1973–4 energy crisis was not caused by a physical shortage of resources, but by politically influenced alterations in supply and cost structure and by delays in moving the world production and distribution economy to alternative sources. The world food shortage has not been and is not a shortage of the physical things, including land, required to produce more food, but is a cumulative result of wrong production decisions coupled to an accidental and artificial increase in demand for key cereals as a result of Soviet purchasing on the world market, which set in motion a chain reaction of high world prices. The wrong production decisions were in part based upon an extrapolation of short-run trends interpreted as long-run trends, leading to the abandonment of the policy of stocking key grains. Whereas five years ago stocking of grains was thought to be wasteful, it is now recognized to be an essential tool to cushion the world from wild seasonal fluctuations. But that realization may have come too late to stop inflationary results; it is doubtful if national governments are willing to use the tool, or international organization is capable of honing it. Similar major readjustments are taking place for many other commodities, and it is likely that we are witnessing alterations in the economic and power balance between industrialized countries and hitherto poorer commodity suppliers rather than the appearance of absolute physical shortage.

The Sussex Science Policy Research Unit assembled data at least as authoritative as those used in the Meadows Report, but indicating a vastly greater reservoir of energy even if cautious assumptions are used. Reaction to the Meadows Report in the European Economic Commission brought about the same difference of opinion. Raymond Barre, the energy economist, objected to political statements in favor of the report by pointing out that proven fossil fuels would satisfy the needs of a population of ten milliards with a consumption level double that of the United States at present, that in itself being seven times the present mean world level. He also held that nuclear reactors could permit the same results, not for forty years, but for a million.* Of course, such global statements do not rule out the appearance of shortages during periods of technical and price-cost adjustment, or in particular parts of the world that do not have access to them or the means to pay for them.

Alfred Sauvy goes on to talk of tidal energy, at present limited by cost and technology, and we know of experiments being undertaken with solar energy. Possibly one of the most useful and fruitful extensions of the American–Soviet space program is not its use to explore outer space but its very "down-to-earth" potentiality, ultimately, for energy tapping and for certain forms of chemical industry.

Whether or not these *particular* changes in technology bear fruit, the Potomac Report has ignored what is known about their implications. (This is strange, since an important member of the Club of Rome is a Director of a Battelle Institute, which is concerned in part with advanced technological innovation.) It did not include in its parameters what is known about the movement of knowledge—that until the recent brake upon scientific activity in the United States, followed by Europe and other countries, growth curves for scientific activity and applied technical

*A. Sauvy, *op. cit.*, pp. 178–179.

knowledge *are also exponential.* In fact, if such activity were given its head and allowed to include a greater component of social science, and with a higher proportion of coordinated mission-oriented activity to particular issues, it would lead to an improvement in education at high levels in developing countries, the greater spread of research institutes, and new types of scientific infrastructure.

Such a policy could have the outcome of increasing scientific, social scientific, and technical knowledge not only at an exponential rate but at a rate faster than population growth itself. It is not inconceivable that when applied with concentrated effect, even on nondemographic issues, it could have an indirect effect on the rate of population movement itself. It is also possible that technical innovation could proceed at a rate beyond the capacity of human institutions to put into effect, which raises yet other problems.*

From the vantage point of 1974, it would appear that *none* of the projections used in the Potomac Report are likely to be very correct; the two closest probabilities are population growth and, with some serious modifications, food supply, but not even these need be correct. A Swiss-style exploitation of British Columbia, for example, could maintain several times the present population; and the present population of New Zealand is nearly twice what was calculated in the 1930s to be a maximum beyond which the level of living would have to fall. Any projections used at this time are bound to be incorrect; our bases of knowledge are insufficient, and human beings do not behave predictably for more than short periods.

One of the reasons the Potomac Report will be incorrect is its own existence. I have already mentioned that social science differs from natural science by influencing the events it observes, sometimes by

---

*Economists think of many of these issues under the heading of "elasticities of substitution," and some have roundly criticized the Club of Rome and the Potomac Report for ignoring what is known about such matters. Sauvy quotes calculations that show that if the Potomac Report had been written with a baseline in the early 19th century, we would all be dead in 1973, and that part of the reason for this not happening was precisely technical substitution. The London *Economist* in an amusing article some years ago showed that if the same projection techniques were used on factors affecting life in London, again with the technological knowledge and baseline of the early 19th century, the city would have been polluted out of existence by horse dung. More seriously, economists such as Wilfred Beckerman, a member of the Royal Commission on Environmental Pollution in England, has seriously challenged the methods used in the Report, particularly on substitutability, and on failing to follow through the possibility of changes in all the limiting factors simultaneously (see *The Economist*, June 3, 1972, pp. 78–79, and *The Sunday Telegraph*, September 24, 1972. Note also the view of Everett Hagen, "Limits to Growth Reconsidered," *International Development Review*, Vol. XIV, No. 2, 1972, pp. 10 ff., an article that was the subject of correspondence in later issues.)

creating self-fulfilling prophecies. In this instance, the direction of influence is the reverse. The Potomac Report would not have existed had it not been for a preconditioning moral and social climate; each of the theses brought together in the model was based upon points of view already existing in the public and scholarly community, and the study was financed because influential people believed that these issues were of overriding importance. The Report added to this view by the force of its presentation; although it is open to criticism, as any attempt to bring these matters together would be, it has helped inch the world a little nearer toward corrective actions.

The Club of Rome has announced that further studies are to be made, following criticism of the Report and indications of lacunae. In particular, more attention there and elsewhere is to be given to socioeconomic considerations and matters of political decision making. The Battelle Institute of Geneva has announced a study of important economic and social phenomena as seen by top-level political decision makers and persons holding similar influential roles. This will be an interesting study in itself.

But I hope I have shown that the decision-making apparatus of the world is itself in sorry shape. Many of the most important questions for the future of mankind are concerned with distribution—of knowledge, of income, of resources, of power to make decisions. The environment as we know it is not a natural given; it is in very large measure a man-made artifact. What it looks like and the operation of its ecosystems are man-influenced; whether we like it or dislike it, it is a result of man's aesthetic, moral, and intellectual judgment. It is continually evolving; this is by no means the only era in which species have been destroyed and others have adapted themselves to new conditions. This is not the only era in which large areas of the earth have been threatened with physical destruction—the earth bears scars of earlier damage—or populations have grown beyond environmental capacity. But it is the only era in which man has clearly understood that his own values affect not only the units of decision, be they households or nation-states, but everyone else as well. On the negative side, this means that to prevent self-destruction, major reforms of decision structure are indicated; the nation is simply not adequate in its present form.

On the positive side, let me still argue that ugliness and beauty, content and discontent, the achievement (and failure) of high social and cultural performance in terms of human values—all these are not to be laid down *a priori*. They come from the interaction of ideas, from the ability of men and women to influence decisions, from the creation of ways of life in which resources are interwoven with aesthetic principle, and from the ability of governmɔnts to foresee.

This means planned decisions in the light of knowledge and belief. But the decisions that are needed affect the very structure of decision making itself and the potentiality of the international world community to rise above its petty bickering to constitute government in the world interest. Ecodoom, if not social doom, could certainly come about if the major advances based on technology and improved knowledge, with environmental and energy protection, were to be exploited in the interests of a limited number of nations holding the monopoly of knowledge, and if the crises that have been predicted were allowed to develop in other parts of the world through lack of resources. David Lilienthal, in a speech in Geneva in October 1972, said that the most obvious pollution was not that of air and rivers but that of poverty and unemployment. These are primarily value and distribution problems, and problems of political will; if those questions are resolved, the economic solutions will accompany them.

We talk of a knowledge explosion. The fact is, we need much more, and we need the will to allow it to overcome prejudice, exaggerated self-interest, and political dogma.

We then return to our original question: can anthropology, as a social science, help? The affirmation of this book has been, most definitely, yes. But anthropology, by exercises in unwisdom and by narrowness of professional perspective, can also hinder. Constructive anthropology, applied to public policy, will help rather than hinder if its practitioners are thoughtful about their methods and responsibilities. My argument has tried to lead in this direction.

I have tried to emphasize that applications, and policy, should be based on firm knowledge wherever it is forthcoming and that our values should be consistent with that knowledge. But knowledge is never certain, and can never be taken as completely definitive. It is always open to question, and an anthropology that limits questioning and that abandons skepticism for dogma is no longer useful. I therefore inject a plea for professional humility, but urge that this not be based upon false modesty. We can apply our ideas and methods to a rich world of institutions and experience far beyond the mythical confines of the conventional discipline. Indeed, if we do not move beyond our conventional fields, we will be denying the advantages of the potential impact that comes from applying old ideas to new issues. I have at times written as an amateur, without the authority of original research. But I hope the mistakes and questions will indeed yield research, and that the arguments and errors may suggest new answers.

Index

342   *Index*